"*The Prophets and the Apostolic Witness* is a real treat of a book. It wrestles in healthy dialogue with the content and relevance of Isaiah, Jeremiah, and Ezekiel. It examines questions about how they work canonically as well. The book shows we should not ignore these prophetic voices, and it makes us think carefully about how to do that well."

Darrell Bock, senior research professor of New Testament studies
at Dallas Theological Seminary

"*The Prophets and the Apostolic Witness* is an outstanding book and is extremely helpful for Christians seeking to interpret and apply the Old Testament Prophets. The editors have assembled many of the top scholars in this field (most of whom preach this material as well), each bringing expertise and insight into the issue of Christian interpretation of the Prophets and engaging not only with the prophetic text but also with the use of the Prophets in the New Testament and in the early church. This is a great book and I recommend it wholeheartedly."

J. Daniel Hays, Ouachita Baptist University and Southwestern Baptist
Theological Seminary

"This volume provides a delightful overview of ways Old Testament and New Testament scholars engage the issue of how to interpret the Major Prophets, especially in light of how the apostles handled those texts. Each author writes with clarity and fairly interacts with their conversation partners. In this one volume, readers can enjoy exposure to different views on key interpretive questions."

Michael A. Grisanti, distinguished research professor of Old Testament
at The Master's Seminary

"These essays offer a range of answers to a foundational question of biblical hermeneutics: How are the apostles reading their Bible, and ought we to follow suit? Here readers have the privilege of listening in as thoughtful exegetes formulate their answer to this timeless question in conversation with others who disagree. The result is both enlightening and useful. Readers will gain not only an understanding of the complexity of the hermeneutical question but also a greater appreciation for the fundamental theological truths that draw the volume's contributors together."

Michelle Knight, associate professor of Old Testament and Semitic languages
at Trinity Evangelical Divinity School

The PROPHETS and the APOSTOLIC WITNESS

Reading Isaiah, Jeremiah, and Ezekiel as Christian Scripture

EDITED BY
ANDREW T. ABERNETHY,
WILLIAM R. OSBORNE, AND
PAUL D. WEGNER

An imprint of InterVarsity Press
Downers Grove, Illinois

InterVarsity Press
P.O. Box 1400 | Downers Grove, IL 60515-1426
ivpress.com | email@ivpress.com

©2023 by Andrew Thomas Abernethy, William Russell Osborne, and Paul D. Wegner

All rights reserved. No part of this book may be reproduced in any form without written permission from InterVarsity Press.

InterVarsity Press® is the publishing division of InterVarsity Christian Fellowship/USA®. For more information, visit intervarsity.org.

Scripture quotations, unless otherwise noted, are from The Holy Bible, English Standard Version, copyright © 2001 by Crossway Bibles, a division of Good News Publishers. Used by permission. All rights reserved.

Figure 2.1 from *Tyndale Old Testament Commentaries: Isaiah* by Paul D. Wegner. Copyright © 2021 by Paul D. Wegner. Used by permission of InterVarsity Press, P.O. Box 1400, Downers Grove, IL 60515, USA. www.ivpress.com.

The publisher cannot verify the accuracy or functionality of website URLs used in this book beyond the date of publication.

Cover design: David Fassett
Interior design: Jeanna Wiggins

ISBN 978-1-5140-0058-8 (print) | ISBN 978-1-5140-0059-5 (digital)

Printed in the United States of America ∞

Library of Congress Cataloging-in-Publication Data
A catalog record for this book is available from the Library of Congress.

29 28 27 26 25 24 23 | 13 12 11 10 9 8 7 6 5 4 3 2 1

CONTENTS

Introduction		1
	Andrew T. Abernethy	
Abbreviations		7
1	How the Apostles Read Isaiah as Christian Scripture *Nicholas G. Piotrowski*	9
2	We Are Not Apostles: Another Way of Reading Isaiah *Paul D. Wegner*	29
3	Emulating the Apostles: Reading Isaiah as Christian Scripture in the Footsteps of the Apostles *Andrew T. Abernethy*	51
4	The History of Interpreting Isaiah as Christian Scripture: A Selection *Mark S. Gignilliat*	70
5	Preaching Isaiah as Christian Scripture *John N. Oswalt*	85
6	How the Apostles Read Jeremiah as Christian Scripture *Dana M. Harris*	103
7	We Are Not Apostles: Limits on Reading Jeremiah Like the Apostles *Gary E. Yates*	122
8	Emulating the Apostles: Reading Jeremiah as Christian Scripture in the Footsteps of the Apostles *Lissa M. Wray Beal*	143

9	The History of Interpreting Jeremiah as Christian Scripture: Patristic Interpretation and Its Modern Legacy *Andrew G. Shead*	163
10	Preaching Jeremiah as Christian Scripture *Philip Graham Ryken*	186
11	How the Apostles Read Ezekiel as Christian Scripture *Alicia R. Jackson*	208
12	We Are Not Apostles: Limits on Reading Ezekiel as Christian Scripture *John W. Hilber*	229
13	Emulating the Apostles: Reading Ezekiel as Christian Scripture in the Footsteps of the Apostles *William R. Osborne*	249
14	The History of Interpreting Ezekiel as Christian Scripture *Iain M. Duguid*	270
15	Preaching Ezekiel as Christian Scripture with Focus on Ezekiel 37:1-14 *Daniel I. Block*	290

CONCLUSION — 311
William R. Osborne

SELECT BIBLIOGRAPHY — 321

CONTRIBUTORS — 329

NAME INDEX — 333

SCRIPTURE INDEX — 335

INTRODUCTION

Andrew T. Abernethy

How should Christians read prophetic literature? This is the central question of the book in your hands (or on your screen). In answering this, many additional questions arise. The range of issues one might wrestle with is vast. For instance, one might ask:

- Can prophecies written to Israel address the church today?
- How do we avoid supersessionism, erasing any notion of national Israel, when reading the prophets in and for the church?
- How did the apostles read the prophets, and can Christians today emulate the apostolic hermeneutic, or was this confined to the apostolic office?
- How has the church throughout history read the prophets?
- What might the modern, grammatical-historical approach contribute to the interpretation of the prophets?
- How should preachers and teachers in the church proclaim ancient prophetic passages today?

Any Christian reading of the prophets needs a multilayered, multitextured approach. With a focus on the Major Prophets—Isaiah, Jeremiah, and Ezekiel—our volume draws readers into a multilayered approach to interpreting the prophets as Christian Scripture.

A Template

We need a robust template for how to read the prophets. Within educational settings, training in how to read the prophets often revolves around helping students and future pastors develop skills in original-context exegesis. It takes time and tremendous effort for students to decipher ancient languages and genres, to become familiar with preexilic, exilic, and postexilic contexts in Israel and Judah, and to get accustomed to the messages of each prophet in its original context. As a result, less attention is given to the interpretive question most pressing for preachers and those in the pews regarding how to read these prophetic books as God's Word today, in the age of the church. Without dismissing the value of original-context exegesis, we must devote more attention in this volume to what is unique about a Christian reading of these prophets.

The template adopted in this volume presents the opportunity to engage the question "How should Christians read the Major Prophets?" from a range of essential vantage points. For each prophetic book, there are five essays addressing the same set of topics across each of the books:

1. How the apostles read [prophet] as Christian Scripture
2. We are not apostles: limits on reading [prophet] as Christian Scripture
3. Emulating the apostles: reading [prophet] as Christian Scripture in the footsteps of the apostles
4. The history of interpreting [prophet] as Christian Scripture
5. Preaching [prophet] as Christian Scripture

The opening essay for each Major Prophet will sketch how the apostles interpreted the given book. The next essay will identify hesitations in terms of Christians applying the apostolic hermeneutic when reading the prophets. The third essay will be more favorable toward reading the prophet like the apostles. The following essay will invite readers into the history of the church as it pertains to the interpretation of the designated prophetic book. The final essay in each set will examine how to preach these Scriptures. No individual essay exhausts one's interpretive approach, but by keeping each essay in a given lane readers can become better alert to the contours within interpretation.

Since all of the Major Prophets are massive in scope, we have selected a common passage from each prophetic book to bring focus to the discussion and cohesion across the essays. For Isaiah, it is the Servant Song in Isaiah 42:1-4. For Jeremiah, it is the New Covenant passage in Jeremiah 31:31-34. For Ezekiel, it is the valley of dry bones in Ezekiel 37:1-14. Other parts of these books will receive attention, but an extended focus on these texts creates the opportunity for the hermeneutical underpinnings of each essay to become clearer in comparison to the other essays.

Our Contributors

The topic before us cannot be adequately addressed by a single author. We have assembled a range of scholars and practitioners whose voices contribute to the conversation as only they can. Experts in the interpretation of the prophets by the apostles are at the table in this volume. Nicholas Piotrowski, with expertise in Matthew's use of the Old Testament and the apostolic hermeneutic more broadly, tackles the question of how the apostles interpreted Isaiah. Dana Harris, with expertise in Hebrews and innerbiblical interpretation, explores how the apostles read Jeremiah. Alicia Jackson, whose dissertation is on the use of Ezekiel in Revelation, examines the impact of Ezekiel on the New Testament authors.

From the field of Old Testament, experts contribute uniquely from within their disciplinary approaches. Several important voices in the historical study of the prophets raise important hesitations when it comes to interpreting the prophets in a way that leaves behind historical elements, particularly in relation to Israel. On Isaiah, Paul Wegner draws on his decades of study, which recently culminated in the publication of a commentary on Isaiah. On Jeremiah, Gary Yates speaks with the voice of a bivocational professor and pastor who has published several books and articles that promote the faithful reading of the prophets, including Jeremiah. On Ezekiel, John Hilber writes from a lifetime of experience in wrestling with the ancient Near Eastern background to the prophets, including contributions on Ezekiel. These three scholars, although not entirely opposed to the apostolic approach, pump the brakes to identify areas of caution and clarification.

Other Old Testament scholars present a more favorable case for emulating the apostles. On Isaiah, Andrew Abernethy writes out of his own work in reading Isaiah with theological interests at the foreground. On Jeremiah, Lissa Wray Beal draws on her vast experience as a commentator, having recently completed a commentary on Jeremiah. On Ezekiel, William "Rusty" Osborne branches out from his work on tree imagery in Ezekiel and other prophets to explore continuity between ancient context and apostolic interpretation when it comes to resurrection.

As for tracing the reception of the prophets as Christian Scripture within the church, three other Old Testament scholars offer their voices. On Isaiah, Mark Gignilliat has made his mark on the field of Isaiah in the areas of reception and theology. He speaks as part of the lineage of Brevard Childs, who had great interest in reading Isaiah in conversation with church history. On Jeremiah, Andrew Shead moves beyond his expertise on the LXX reception of Jeremiah and a biblical theology on Jeremiah to sketch how the church read Jeremiah. On Ezekiel, Iain

Duguid is a commentator on Ezekiel whose ecclesial outlook and theological interests contribute to a delightful sketch of Ezekiel's reception across church history.

Finally, a strong assembly of preachers offer their vantage points on preaching from these books. Any who are familiar with John Oswalt know he is fundamentally a preacher who is also an excellent scholar on Isaiah. His ability to speak to the heart and with the tenor of the prophet is apparent from the pulpit, the lectern, and even a podium at conferences. This comes through in his impressive commentary on Isaiah in the New International Commentary on the Old Testament series. On Jeremiah, Philip Graham Ryken perhaps has more experience preaching from Jeremiah than any living person today, having preached through the entirety of this book during his time as a pastor in Philadelphia. On Ezekiel, Daniel Block reflects the same characteristics as John Oswalt. With the verve and tenor of a prophet, he has written a tremendous commentary on Ezekiel in the New International Commentary on the Old Testament series and has affected many in the classroom over four decades. He recently finished preaching through the book of Ezekiel, so he offers a contribution that breathes with freshness.

Conclusion

Our volume will conclude with one of the editors, William "Rusty" Osborne, tying some threads together from across the book. Over the past four years, we have had exciting and rich discussions around these essays between panelists and audiences at annual meetings. Such engagement has allowed for transforming papers into essays that we hope will serve you, our reader, well. We trust and pray that these essays will propel you forward in your quest to read and minister from the Major Prophets as Christian Scripture.

ABBREVIATIONS

GENERAL ABBREVIATIONS

HB	Hebrew Bible
LXX	Septuagint
NT	New Testament
OT	Old Testament

SCRIPTURE VERSIONS

ESV	English Standard Version
KJV	King James Version
LEB	Lexham English Bible
NA^{28}	*Novum Testamentum Graece*, Nestle-Aland, 28th ed.
NASB	New American Standard Bible
NIV	New International Version
NRSV	New Revised Standard Version

PRIMARY SOURCES

Comm. Jer.	Jerome, *Commentariorum in Jeremiam libri VI*
Hom. Jer.	Origen, *Homiliae in Jeremiam (Homilies on Jeremiah)*

Secondary Sources

AB	Anchor Bible
ANET	*Ancient Near Eastern Texts Relating to the Old Testament*
BBR	*Bulletin for Biblical Review*
BST	The Bible Speaks Today
BZ	*Biblische Zeitschrift*
CC	Continental Commentary
CTJ	*Calvin Theological Journal*
ICC	International Critical Commentary
JBL	*Journal of Biblical Literature*
JETS	*Journal of the Evangelical Theological Society*
JSNTSup	Journal for New Testament Studies Supplement Series
LHBOTS	Library of Hebrew Bible/Old Testament Studies
LW	*Luther's Works* [= "American Edition"]. 82 vols. planned. St. Louis: Concordia; Philadelphia: Fortress, 1955–1986; 2009–
NAC	New American Commentary
NICOT	New International Commentary on the Old Testament
NIVAC	New International Version Application Commentary
NovTSup	Supplements to Novum Testamentum
NSBT	New Studies in Biblical Theology
OTL	Old Testament Library
TOTC	Tyndale Old Testament Commentary
VT	*Vetus Testamentum*
VTSup	Supplements to Vetus Testamentum
WBC	Word Biblical Commentary
WUNT	Wissenschaftliche Untersuchungen zum Neuen Testament

1

HOW THE APOSTLES READ ISAIAH AS CHRISTIAN SCRIPTURE

Nicholas G. Piotrowski

We are those "upon whom the ends of the ages have come," Paul tells the Corinthians to exhort them with the example (*typikōs*) of Israel (1 Cor 10:11).¹ Why should Israel's behavior in the wilderness serve to warn Christians millennia later? The answer is in this phrase, "the ends of the ages." Surely Paul sees some kind of temporal change but also a bringing of the prior ages to their purposeful end—the intended goal of the ages, indeed the telos (*ta telē*) of the ages.² To Paul, the resurrection of Jesus Christ marked not only the turning point of history but the dawning of a new era to which all previous eras had

---

¹Unless otherwise noted, all translations in this chapter are the author's own.
²Geerhardus Vos, *The Pauline Eschatology* (Phillipsburg, NJ: P&R, 1994), 26; Richard B. Hays, *Echoes of Scripture in the Letters of Paul* (New Haven, CT: Yale University Press, 1989), 168-69.

been surging.³ The church in Corinth, "together with all those everywhere who call on the name of our Lord Jesus Christ" (1 Cor 1:2), comprises the eschatological substance of history's types and shadows.

Such an opening theological reflection is helpful for us because to ask how someone reads Isaiah *as* Christian Scripture requires first considering what would make a hermeneutic particularly Christian. The apostles' involvement with the earthly ministry, death, and resurrection of Jesus of Nazareth, as well as the reception and influence of the Holy Spirit, was an entirely reorienting experience. How could it not be? These events brought the subsequent New Testament authors to read the sacred texts of the Hebrew canon as a story that at long last had reached its conclusion.⁴ In describing the death and resurrection of Christ, the coming of the Spirit, and the creation of the church, Peter cites Moses (Acts 3:22-23) and then declares, "And all the prophets who have spoken, from Samuel and those that came after him, also proclaimed these days" (Acts 3:24). They proclaimed *these days*, the days of the Spirit and worldwide heralding of the gospel.

We begin our particular focus, therefore, with the observation that the apostles did not read Isaiah in the abstract but as a significant piece of a story starting in Genesis and extending through the prophets and poets. For their part, it is clear that the New Testament authors understood their own writings as continuing that story line in the consummative eon.⁵ In the following we will see such Christian convictions at play in various patterns of how Isaiah was read and applied by the

---

³As Gordon D. Fee dynamically renders 1 Cor 10:11, "toward whom all history has had its goal." See Fee, *The First Epistle to the Corinthians*, New International Commentary on the New Testament (Grand Rapids, MI: Eerdmans, 1987), 459.

⁴See, e.g., N. T. Wright, "Yet the Sun Will Rise Again: Reflections on the Exile and Restoration in Second Temple Judaism, Jesus, Paul, and the Church Today," in *Exile: A Conversation with N. T. Wright*, ed. James M. Scott (Downers Grove, IL: IVP Academic, 2017), 45-72; Chris Bruno, Jared Compton, and Kevin McFaddon, *Biblical Theology According to the Apostles: How the Earliest Christians Told the Story of Israel*, NSBT 52 (Downers Grove, IL: IVP Academic, 2020).

⁵G. K. Beale, *A New Testament Biblical Theology: The Unfolding of the Old Testament in the New* (Grand Rapids, MI: Baker Academic, 2011), 1-25, 129-60.

apostles. Along the way we will consider the blessed tie that binds these patterns together. We will conclude by looking particularly at Matthew's reading of Isaiah 42. In all, we will see that the apostles read Isaiah as a redemptive-historical depot through which historical and literary types are funneled into a future that the church now inhabits through Jesus Christ.[6]

PATTERN ONE: ISAIAH AS A MAN OF HIS TIME

Before we get too far ahead of ourselves with all the ways the apostles' experience with Jesus provided a new frame for understanding Isaiah, it will be helpful to recognize that the old frames were not destroyed in the process. The apostles still read Isaiah as a historic document that attests to another time and another place with another audience.[7]

No better text to start with than the first quotation in the New Testament, Matthew 1:23, where the evangelist says that "the sign" of Isaiah 7:14, "the virgin shall conceive and bear a son," is fulfilled. This may seem like an odd choice because Matthew is commonly indicted for ahistorical exegesis, with this verse as exhibit A.[8] But the prosecution has not proven its case. Matthew 1 is insatiably concerned with the house of David: after Jesus, David is the first person mentioned (Mt 1:1); the genealogy clearly revolves around David (Mt 1:17); Joseph

---

[6]There are a lot of issues that bear on how the NT authors used the OT. The first is the kind of use: direct quotations are common, but so are echoes and allusions. See Nicholas G. Piotrowski, *In All the Scriptures: The Three Contexts of Biblical Hermeneutics* (Downers Grove, IL: IVP Academic, 2021), 169-77. This essay, however, is less concerned with such nomenclature and instead focused on what evidence we can see for how NT authors *read* the OT, specifically Isaiah. This essay will also not have much to say about text forms. It is clear that a variety were used, HB and various LXX versions. For such questions see G. K. Beale and D. A. Carson, eds., *Commentary on the New Testament Use of the Old Testament* (Grand Rapids, MI: Baker Academic, 2007). Summaries of various hermeneutical warrants that explain NT authors' uses of the OT also abound. For a short summary see Andrew David Naselli, *From Typology to Doxology: Paul's Use of Isaiah and Job in Romans 11:34-35* (Eugene, OR: Pickwick, 2012), 118-28.

[7]Joseph A. Fitzmyer observes such historical awareness too. See Fitzmyer, "Use of Explicit Old Testament Quotations in Qumran Literature and in the New Testament," *New Testament Studies* 7 (1961): 297-333. What he calls "accommodated texts," however, seem to be the result of underappreciating what I call "typology" below.

[8]See, e.g., John D. W. Watts, *Isaiah*, WBC 24 (Waco, TX: Word, 1985–1987), 1:103.

is a "son of David" (Mt 1:20); and of course Jesus is born in Bethlehem (Mt 2:1-6), a fulfillment of Davidic prophecy (Mic 5:1-3; see also 1 Sam 16:1; 2 Sam 7:8). It is quite significant to observe, therefore, that "*all this occurred* to fulfill the words by the prophet" (Mt 1:22). It is not just Mary's virginity that fulfills Isaiah 7:14, but "*all this*" specifically concerning David. When we look at Isaiah 7:14 in its original literary and historical contexts, we see that the very reason Isaiah gave the sign to Ahaz is that he was the then-current embodiment of the house of David. This is emphasized in Isaiah 7:2, 13. Jerusalem was under threat by two larger armies, but the Lord reassured Ahaz that they would not succeed in their plans because of his zeal for the house of David.[9] So the son born in Isaiah 8:3 sufficiently fulfilled the sign for Ahaz's sake because he needed assurance there and then in that historical situation.[10] That Matthew uses Isaiah 7:14 in his own thickly Davidic prologue shows that he read Isaiah 7–8 for what it is: a text historically concerned with the house of David. Of course, Matthew does not stop there, and so we will return to this reading of Isaiah 7–8 in just a moment. It suffices for now to see that Matthew did not just grab a verse that might exonerate Mary but sees in Isaiah's wider historical context something more meaningful that is fulfilled by "*all this*" in Matthew 1.[11]

In Acts 7 Stephen concludes his review of Israel's history with a quotation of Isaiah. While Solomon had built a grand temple (Acts 7:47; see 1 Kings 8), the sinfulness of subsequent Davidic kings led to its demise (2 Kings 23:26-27; 25:8-17). Israel's story, therefore, is primarily a story of the presence of God (a consistent point of Stephen's speech; note all the locations in Acts 7:2, 4, 9, 29-30, 34, 36, 43-44).[12] How

---

[9]Nicholas G. Piotrowski, *Matthew's New David at the End of Exile: A Socio-rhetorical Study of Scriptural Quotations*, NovTSup 170 (Leiden: Brill, 2016), 42-53.

[10]Norman K. Gottwald, "Immanuel as the Prophet's Son," *VT* 8 (1958): 36-47; J. Alec Motyer, *The Prophecy of Isaiah: An Introduction and Commentary* (Downers Grove, IL: IVP Academic, 1993), 86, 90-101.

[11]Piotrowski, *Matthew's New David*, 33-59.

[12]David G. Peterson, *The Acts of the Apostles*, Pillar New Testament Commentary (Grand Rapids, MI: Eerdmans, 2009), 261-62.

fitting that Stephen's final point races through the history of the temple (Acts 7:44-47) and ends with the question of Isaiah 66:1, "Where is the house that you would build for me?" (Acts 7:49). That was exactly the question on Isaiah's audience's mind leading up to and during the exile. Thus, in his critique of the current leadership (Acts 6:12; 7:51), Stephen concludes his soliloquy with a quote from a historical context analogous to his own: while the goodness of the temple may be in doubt (e.g., Is 63:10, 15, 18) God will someday rebuild a holy sanctuary for himself and brings Gentiles to it (Is 66:20-21).[13]

That Isaiah was originally written to a particular people at a particular time and in a particular situation is not lost on Matthew or Luke. Yet, they fluidly move beyond original-context exegesis, to which we next give our attention. I have little doubt that other New Testament authors had a historical conscientiousness as well; however, that is not the hermeneutical hand most commonly played.

Pattern Two: Isaiah as a Man for All Seasons

The New Testament authors are not interested in merely surveying the past. They are interested in what that past has to say about their own time. They find in Isaiah adumbrations of a future day, when Jesus and his church bring the prophet's words to completion. To see this, let us return to the early chapters of Matthew. I mentioned above that Matthew is drawn to Isaiah's historical setting, not just the convenience of pinning Isaiah 7:14 to Mary. But more than that, Matthew sees a fulfillment (Mt 1:22) of that historical situation. How is it a fulfillment? Not in the sense of fulfilling a pledge or keeping a promise or completing a prophecy. Isaiah 7:14 is no pledge, promise, or prophecy in the strictest senses. It is a *sign* to Ahaz that God favors the house of David and will continue his purposes in Israel through the house of David.[14]

---

[13]Bruno, Compton, and McFaddon, *Biblical Theology*, 63.
[14]Piotrowski, *Matthew's New David*, 42-53.

This is where it gets interesting for Matthew: if God saved the house of David once before, in Ahaz's day, he can do it again in this day of eschatological culmination. The house of David was spared from near death then; it is resurrected from the grave of exile *now*.[15] There is a thematic outline in the history and sacred texts of Israel that only the messianic age can fill out. Fulfillment should therefore not be understood in terms of prediction and accomplishment but as bringing an original idea or event to its full meaning.[16] As R. T. France summarizes, fulfillment in Matthew is concerned with "how God's previously announced purpose has reached its due conclusion in Jesus."[17]

Let us compare this to Luke–Acts. When Jesus is asked the meaning of his parable of the sower, he replies, "To you all it has been *granted* to know the mysteries of the Kingdom of God, but to the rest [it is given] in parables" (Lk 8:9-10), and then he quotes Isaiah 6:9, "so that seeing they would not *see* and hearing they would not *hear*." Jesus goes on to explain the parable to his disciples (to them it has been granted to know the meaning) and tells them to *see* to it how they *hear* so that knowledge of more mysteries can be *granted* (Lk 8:18). This is a strange use of Isaiah 6 because it was originally spoken to Israel as a rebuke of their idolatry at the dawn of exile (Is 6:9-13).[18] How does it apply over six hundred years later? Again, Israel's historic rejection is read as a pattern of eschatological realities.[19] Indeed, Isaiah 6:9-10 comes up again at the end of Acts. There Paul is "persuading [Jewish leaders; see Acts 28:17] about Jesus from the law of Moses and the prophets" (Acts 28:23).

---

[15]Piotrowski, *Matthew's New David*, 53-56.
[16]Paul D. Wegner, "How Many Virgin Births Are in the Bible? [Isaiah 7:14]: A Prophetic Pattern Approach," *JETS* 54 (2011): 481-83. See J. R. Daniel Kirk for a survey of more understandings of fulfillment in Matthew in "Conceptualising Fulfilment in Matthew," *Tyndale Bulletin* 59 (2008): 77-98.
[17]R. T. France, *Matthew: Evangelist and Teacher*, New Testament Profiles (Downers Grove, IL: InterVarsity Press, 1989), 172.
[18]G. K. Beale, "Isaiah vi 9-13: A Retributive Taunt Against Idolatry," *VT* 41 (1991): 257-78.
[19]David W. Pao and Eckhard J. Schnabel, "Luke," in Beale and Carson, *Commentary on the New Testament Use*, 308.

Some believe and some do not (Acts 28:24), to whom Paul applies Isaiah 6:9-10. Thus the situation of Israel's historic exile has been eschatologized. Those who listen to the preaching and believe that Jesus sums up Moses and the prophets are those who *hear* and *see*. But those who do not are those who are still in the throes of idolatry (though, of course, never irredeemably so).[20] The writer's use of Isaiah evinces both an understanding of the historical milieu of the prophet and a new eschatological reality.

We can briefly survey a couple more passages in this regard. In the parable of the vineyard (Mk 12:1-11), the language of Isaiah 5 is applied to Jesus' generation. That which once spoke a word of judgment against Solomon's temple (Is 5) now speaks against Herod's (Mk 12).[21] In John 2:10 Jesus turns water into "good wine" (*kalon oinon*) at a wedding celebration. There could be multiple Old Testament backgrounds to this (e.g., Jer 31:12-14; Hos 14:7; Joel 3:18; Amos 9:11-15), but Isaiah 25:6 describes the new age as a time of feasting with "well-aged wine" (*šəmārîm məzuqqāqîm*; LXX *oinon*).[22] That is likely where John gets the images, at least in part, seen in the language of resurrection in both Isaiah 25:8 and John 2:20-21.

Paul also reads Isaiah eschatologically in defending why more Israelites do not believe his gospel when he says, "It is not as though the word of God has failed" (Rom 9:6). Rather, Paul contends, through a litany of Old Testament citations, that God's working in the present day is congruous with his plan for Israel from the beginning. For our study, it is intriguing that Paul draws from Isaianic passages that pertain specifically to the state of Israel in exile.[23] He uses Isaiah 10:22 and Isaiah 1:9

---

[20]David W. Pao, *Acts and the Isaianic New Exodus*, Biblical Studies Library (Grand Rapids, MI: Baker Academic, 2002), 105-9, 181-212.
[21]Craig A. Evans, "On the Vineyard Parables of Isaiah 5 and Mark 12," *BZ* 28 (1984): 82-86.
[22]Herman Ridderbos, *The Gospel of John: A Theological Commentary*, trans. John Vriend (Grand Rapids, MI: Eerdmans, 1997), 108-10.
[23]James M. Scott, "'And Then All Israel Will Be Saved' (Rom 11:26)," in *Restoration: Old Testament, Jewish, and Christian Perspectives*, ed. James M. Scott (Leiden: Brill, 2001), 489-527.

in Romans 9:27-29 to describe the state of gospel progress and why more Jews do not believe (see Rom 9:6). Thus, Paul sees Isaiah's description of Israel at that time still applying to his own.

All this makes sense to Paul because Isaiah 52:7 announces the "good news" that Israel's God will again reign, and so Paul understands this pertaining to "the preaching of Christ" in Romans 10:15-17. But, in the same context, Israel's indictment for not obeying the gospel in Isaiah 65:1-2, while Gentiles do, is part of Paul's explanation of how the gospel has progressed in his day (Rom 10:20-21). Isaiah 52:15, concerning the sprinkling of many nations at the end of the exile, applies to the "offering" and "obedience of the Gentiles" through Paul's missionary work (Rom 15:14-21).

Equally, Paul uses Isaiah 29:14 to speak of the power of "the word of the cross" in 1 Corinthians 1:18-19, causing Roy Ciampa and Brian Rosner to state, "God's eschatological judgment and salvation are taking place in the midst of the Corinthians."[24] Isaiah 49:8 celebrates God's promise of salvation to Israel; Paul sees that his day is the day of that salvation in 2 Corinthians 6:2, indeed, the day of the new creation (2 Cor 5:17-20).[25]

First Peter and Hebrews show the same eschatological reading of Isaiah 40:6-8 as a bold statement of the effectiveness of God's word to recall the exiles. First Peter 1:23-25 uses it to speak of the life-giving word of God that was preached in his time. Specifically, he calls that word of God the "good news." Isaiah 26, an encouragement to Israel "to remain faithful in the midst of oppression and to trust God to vindicate his faithful people and avenge for them," is used in Hebrews 10:37 to elicit fear of God's vengeance and confidence in God's eschatological reward for the church.[26]

---

[24]Roy E. Ciampa and Brian S. Rosner, "1 Corinthians," in Beale and Carson, *Commentary on the New Testament Use*, 698.

[25]Mason Lee, "'Now Is the Acceptable Time; Now Is the Day of Salvation': Reading 2 Corinthians 5:11–6:2 in Light of Its Narrative Substructure," *Restoration Quarterly* 56 (2014): 1-13.

[26]Chee-Chiew Lee, "The Use of Scriptures and the Rhetoric of Fear In Hebrews," *BBR* 31 (2021): 191-210; quote from 201.

Each of these uses has this in common: they are all applications of Old Testament texts to the cross and resurrection of Jesus and/or the effects on the other side thereof. The apostles read Isaiah, therefore, as a "prophetic script" of which the life of Jesus and the early church became the "dramatic enactment" on the stage of history.[27]

Pattern Three: The Book of Isaiah as a Unified Literary Work

We also see that the apostles read Isaiah as a complete literary piece with sustained focus over large contexts.[28] This is particularly observable in the way Isaiah 40–55 is used in the New Testament. A clear example of this is in Luke–Acts. David Pao convincingly shows how the use of Isaiah 40:3-5 in Luke 3:4-6 "presupposes the knowledge of the wider context of Isaiah 40–55."[29] This can be seen as Luke constantly returns to Isaiah 40–55 at key moments in his two-part narrative of Jesus and the early church.

Table 1.1. Isaianic Quotes at Key Structural Moments in Luke–Acts

Is 40:3-5	in Lk 3:4-6
Is 42:7; 52:7; 58:6; 61:1-2	in Lk 4:17-19
Is 42:1; 43:9-12; 49:6 (and Is 44:3, 8-9; 45:22; 48:20)	in Lk 24:47; Acts 1:8
Is 53:7-8	in Acts 8:28-33
Is 55:3; 49:6	in Acts 13:34, 46-47

It seems Luke did not simply read these verses in the abstract to drop into his Jesus story wherever convenient. He saw that entire Isaianic discourse as a literary unit, which he used as scaffolding for his own work.[30] The effect is to shape the entirety of Luke–Acts as a fulfillment

---

[27]Max Botner uses these terms specifically for Mark, but they are just as apt for the rest of the NT. See Botner, "Prophetic Script and Dramatic Enactment in Mark's Prologue," *BBR* 26 (2016): 369-80.
[28]For the classic articulation of this see C. H. Dodd, *According to the Scriptures: The Sub-structure of New Testament Theology* (London: Nisbet, 1952), chaps. 2–3.
[29]Pao, *Acts and the Isaianic New Exodus*, 37.
[30]Pao, *Acts and the Isaianic New Exodus*, 70-110.

of Isaiah's vision of the eschatological new exodus. Acts particularly funnels Isaiah 40–55 into a polemic against idolatry, and an identity claim by the first Christians when they call themselves "the Way" (Acts 9:2; 19:23; 24:14 et passim). They are the international people of God responding to the Lord's own sovereign word (cf. esp. Is 40:3-11; 45:22-24; 46:11-13; 55:10-11).

Matthew also shows a focus on literary contexts larger than just the cited verse. As mentioned above, the First Evangelist quotes Isaiah 7:14 in Matthew 1:23, but then also quotes Isaiah 9:1-2 (HB 8:23–9:1) in Matthew 4:15-16. Further, Matthew quotes Isaiah 8:8, 10 in Matthew 1:23. By repeatedly drawing on Isaiah 7–9 at the beginning and the end of his prologue, Matthew demonstrates a contextual awareness of the entire Isaianic narrative that spans those several chapters.[31] Add to this the likelihood that Matthew has Isaiah 11:1 in view in Matthew 2:23, and this pattern of reading is seen all the more clearly.[32] Matthew's repeated use of various verses from Isaiah 53 shows the same (compare Is 53:7-12 with Mt 8:17; 20:28; 26:28; 27:12, 57).[33]

A similar focus on large contexts can also be found in Mark, where Isaiah 40:3 is quoted right at the beginning, in Mark 1:3. Throughout the rest of the Gospel the language of Isaiah 40–55 is evoked time and again.[34]

---

[31] See Wim Weren, "Quotations from Isaiah and Mathew's Christology (Mt 1,23 and 4,15–16)," in *Studies in the Book of Isaiah: Festschrift Willem A. M. Beuken*, ed. J. van Ruiten and M. Vervenne, Bibliotheca Ephemeridum Theologicarum Lovaniensium 132 (Leuven: Leuven University Press, 1997), 450-53; Warren Carter, "Evoking Isaiah: Matthean Soteriology and an Intertextual Reading of Isaiah 7–9 and Matthew 1:23 and 4:15-16," *JBL* 119 (2000): 508-18.

[32] Nicholas G. Piotrowski, "Nazarene," in *Dictionary of Jesus and the Gospels*, 2nd ed., ed. Joel B. Green, Jeannine K. Brown, and Nicholas Perrin (Downers Grove, IL: IVP Academic, 2013), 624-25.

[33] For the use of Is 52:1-2 and its context in Mt 27:51-53, see Timothy Wardle, "Resurrection and the Holy City: Matthew's Use of Isaiah in 27:51-53," *Catholic Biblical Quarterly* 78 (2016): 666-81.

[34] See esp. Joel Marcus, *Mark: A New Translation with Introduction and Commentary*, 2 vols., AB 27 (New York: Doubleday, 2000–2009).

Table 1.2. Isaianic Echoes in Mark

Isaianic Language	Echoes in Mark
Is 40:9-10; 52:7 "herald of good news [LXX: *euangelizō*]"	Mk 1:1, 14-15; 13:10 "The beginning of the gospel [*euangelion*]"
Is 52:14 "many were astonished [LXX: *existēmi*] at you"	Mk 2:12; 5:42; 6:51 (Mk 1:22; 16:8) "they were immediately overcome with amazement [*existēmi*]"
Is 42:6-7 "I will take you by the hand . . . to open the eyes that are blind"	Mk 1:31; 8:22-23 "he took the blind man by the hand"
Is 43:25; 44:22 "I am he who blots out your transgressions . . . and I will not remember your sins"	Mk 2:5-7 "'Son, your sins are forgiven'. . . Who can forgive sins but God alone?"
Is 49:24-25 "the captives of the mighty [LXX: *hischyontos*] shall be taken/saved"	Mk 3:27 "plunder his goods . . . first bind the strong man [*hischyros*]"
Is 50:4-6; 52:13, 15 "the Lord has given me . . . that I may know"	Mk 4:11 "To you has been given the secret"
Is 49:8-10 "they shall feed along the ways; on all bare heights"	Mk 6:32-44 "a desolate place . . . they all ate"
Is 43:16 "the Lord who makes a way in the sea"	Mk 6:48-49 "he came to them walking on the sea"
Is 41:4; 43:10-11, 25 "I am he [LXX: *egō eimi*]"	Mk 6:50 "it is I [*egō eimi*]"
Is 40:3 "prepare the way of the Lord"	Mk 8:27; 9:33-34; 10:32, 46, 52 "on the way"
Is 51:17, 22 "O Jerusalem, you who have drunk . . . the cup of his wrath"	Mk 10:32, 38 "going up to Jerusalem . . . Jesus said to them . . . 'Are you able to drink the cup . . . ?'"
Is 52:13, 15; 53:11-12 "my servant . . . bore the sin of many"	Mk 10:43, 45 "to serve and to give his life as a ransom for many."
Is 52:15; 53:12 "he shall sprinkle many nations"	Mk 14:24 "my blood of the covenant which is poured out for many"
Is 53:7 "so he opened not his mouth"	Mk 15:4-5 "'Do you say nothing?' . . . But Jesus still answered nothing"
Is 52:15 "many nations will marvel [LXX: *thaumazō*] at him; kings will shut their mouths"	Mk 15:5 "Pilate was amazed [*thaumazō*]"

Because Mark has used the opening of the literary block Isaiah 40–55 at the beginning of his Gospel and then echoes various Isaianic themes throughout the rest of the narrative, we can see how Mark had the entire literary discourse in view.[35]

It is also evident that Paul read with an eye toward contexts, not just individual verses. Paul returns to Isaiah 52–53 four times in Romans (Rom 2:24; 10:15, 16; 15:21). He also combines Isaiah 45:23 and Isaiah 49:18 in Romans 14:11. Paul also references Isaiah 28:22 and Isaiah 28:16 in Romans 9:28, 33. Such revisiting different parts of both narrower and wider sections of Isaiah shows Paul had an understanding of the scope of the whole of the book, or at least unified sections thereof.[36] This can be seen not only in repeated uses of whole contexts but also in the logic of Paul's arguments that mirror (and sometimes depend on) the context of an Old Testament citation.[37] Isaiah 40:12-31, for example, is about how God is superior to idols because no one gives him advice, specifically for the task of restoring his people. Paul cites Isaiah 40:13 in Romans 11:34 to conclude his argument for how God is working to restore his people.[38]

A clear example of contextual reading is found in the way 1 Peter uses several lines from Isaiah 53 in quick sequence. In 1 Peter 2:20-23 Peter references Isaiah 53:4, 6-7, 9. Again, understanding Isaiah 40–55 as a complete literary unit, we can also note the use of Isaiah 43:20-21 in 1 Peter 2:9. I mentioned above that 1 Peter 1:23-25 uses Isaiah 40:6-8 to emphasize the life-giving gospel. Yet that term *gospel* comes from

---

[35]Regarding John's contextual reading of Isaiah, see Jonathan Lett, "The Divine Identity of Jesus as the Reason for Israel's Unbelief in John 12:36-43," *JBL* 135 (2016): 159-73; Andreas J. Köstenberger, "John's Appropriation of Isaiah's Signs Theology: Implications for the Structure of John's Gospel," *Themelios* 43 (2018): 376-86.

[36]See also Jonathan M. Lunde and John Anthony Dunne, "Paul's Creative and Contextual Use of Isaiah in Ephesians 5:14," *JETS* 55 (2012): 87-110.

[37]See esp. J. Ross Wagner, *Heralds of the Good News: Isaiah and Paul "In Concert" in the Letter to the Romans*, NovTSup 101 (Leiden: Brill, 2002); J. Edward Walters, "How Beautiful Are My Feet: The Structure and Function of Second Isaiah References in Paul's Letter to the Romans," *Restoration Quarterly* 52 (2010): 29-39.

[38]Naselli, *From Typology to Doxology*, 51-61.

Isaiah 40:9. Thus, Peter had at least some of the wider context in view than just the verses from Isaiah he actually quotes.[39]

The apostles seem to have read and applied portions of Isaiah, not just isolated verses, seen in the way they return to the same Isaianic contexts for their arguments and in the thematic coherence between the Isaianic contexts and their own discourses.

Pattern Four: Isaiah as a Typological Visionary

In several ways, this last pattern is a synthesizing of the previous three. It is the one that makes sense of how Isaiah can be read in such diverse ways. For how can something be historical (pattern one) and pertain to the future age (pattern two)? How can something have meaning in a particular literary context (pattern three) and then be employed in a new literary setting? The answer is found in particular theological convictions about the nature of both history and texts. The apostles read with the conviction that the sovereign Lord sketched within Israel's history a basic eschatological design.[40] Biblical texts were crafted in a way to create objective correspondences between Israel's history and that eschaton.[41] Together these twin convictions create a typological way of reading, where images and themes across Scripture resonate with Christ and his people. We can call typology, therefore, *"a hermeneutical conviction that God has sovereignly organized history and revelation such that Old Testament people, events, and institutions prefigure the person and work of Christ in concert with literary genre and history."*[42] Such Old Testament people, events, and institutions are the

---

[39]D. A. Carson, "I Peter," in Beale and Carson, *Commentary on the New Testament Use*, 1019-22.
[40]Francis Foulkes, "The Acts of God: A Study of the Basis of Typology in the Old Testament," in *The Right Doctrine from the Wrong Text? Essays on the Use of the Old Testament in the New*, ed. G. K. Beale (Grand Rapids, MI: Baker, 1994), 365-66.
[41]Such correspondences are, therefore, not contrived by the reader but found *in* the literary details of texts. See Frances Young, "Typology," in *Crossing the Boundaries: Essays in Biblical Interpretation in Honour of Michael D. Goulder*, ed. Stanley E. Porter, Paul Joyce, and David E. Orton, Biblical Interpretation Series 8 (Leiden: Brill, 1994), 34-45.
[42]Piotrowski, *In All the Scriptures*, 71.

types in history to which Jesus becomes the antitype, the full expression of what the types intimate.[43] This is the kind of reading the apostles were particularly adept at, and it created the hermeneutical space to read Isaiah in any combination of the previous three patterns.

We saw this already in Matthew with his strong Davidic emphasis (Mt 1:1, 17, 20; 2:6). The passages of Isaiah that Matthew turns to commonly have a Davidic subtext (Is 7:14 in Mt 1:23, as mentioned above; likely Is 11:1 in Mt 2:23; Is 11:2 in Mt 3:16; Is 9:1 in Mt 4:16; Is 11:10 in Mt 12:21). Matthew sees in Isaiah, therefore, a means by which to access the larger biblical-theological images and expectations surrounding the house of David. The Lord's handling of the house of David in places such as Isaiah 7, or the dawning of the light of restoration in Isaiah 9:1 (HB 8:23), are typological of Jesus' birth in Matthew 1 and his preaching in Matthew 4:13-17.

Consider again the quote of Isaiah 40:3 in Mark 1:3, where the Evangelist does not *merely* quote Isaiah but draws together Malachi 3:1 and Exodus 23:20 as well.[44] Yet, Mark 1:2 simply says, "As it is written in Isaiah the prophet." What Mark identifies as Isaiah is actually drawing together other Old Testament material. The common bond between these Old Testament passages is the language of the exodus and the Lord meeting with his people in his designated place.[45] Mark's subsequent use of exodus themes (e.g., Mk 2:10-12 and Ex 9:14; Mk 3:13-14 and Ex 24:4; Mk 5:13 and Ex 15:4-5; Mk 6:48 and Ex 14:24; Mk 10:45 and Ex 6:6; Mk 14:24 and Ex 24:8) and focus on the temple (Mk 11–16) are the antitype of Isaiah 40–55.[46] Thus, for Mark, Isaiah is a kind of depot for ideas gathered up from other prophetic sources.

---

[43] For seeing such dynamics in the Old Testament itself, not just retrospectively, see Foulkes, "Acts of God," 342-71.

[44] For much more on the significance Mark's mashup citation, see Rikki E. Watts, *Isaiah's New Exodus in Mark*, Biblical Studies Library (Grand Rapids, MI: Baker Academic, 2000).

[45] Nicholas G. Piotrowski, "'Whatever You Ask' for the Missionary Purposes of the Eschatological Temple: Quotation and Typology in Mark 11–12," *Southern Baptist Journal of Theology* 21 (2017): 97-98, 101.

[46] Piotrowski, "'Whatever You Ask,'" 97-121. On Mark's exodus themes, see, e.g., Bryan D. Estelle, *Echoes of Exodus: Tracing a Biblical Motif* (Downers Grove, IL: IVP Academic, 2018), 208-25.

We can see this as well in Luke when he quotes Isaiah 61:1-2 in Luke 4:18-19, which is itself a development of the theology of Leviticus 25 (see esp. Lev 25:10).[47] Isaiah is predicting a future restoration in terms of the Levitical Jubilee. He has gathered up the theology of the Jubilee and projected it into the future—that future Luke now sees. The preaching of Jesus and the life of the church amount to the antitype of Isaiah's Jubilee vision.

Paul also reads the new exodus language of places such as Isaiah 43:18-19, and the new creation language of Isaiah 65:17, to apply to believers' reconciliation with God. The gospel is the "new thing" shaped like the old, and wherever "anyone is in Christ" the new creation has dawned (2 Cor 5:17). As Tom Holland puts it, Paul was "immersed in [the] Old Testament stream of expectations," most of which "are found in embryonic form in the book of Isaiah."[48]

Such typology is also evident in the way references to Israel are applied to Jesus and subsequently to the church. Isaiah 49 is about the redemption and future missionary fruitfulness of one whom the Lord calls "my servant, Israel" (Is 49:3). Yet, this servant has a ministry to "the tribes of Jacob" (Is 49:5-6) and is equally "a light to the nations, that [the Lord's] salvation may reach to the ends of the earth" (Is 49:6; LXX: *heōs eschatou tēs gēs*). Luke 2:32 calls Jesus "a light of revelation to the Gentiles, and [the] glory of your people Israel." In turn, in Acts 13:47 Paul and Barnabas call themselves "a light for the Gentiles, [bringing] salvation to the ends of the earth" (*heōs eschatou tēs gēs*; see also Acts 1:8). Typology is the basic hermeneutical principal at work whereby words spoken to Israel are applied to Jesus and then to his people.[49]

---

[47]Walther Zimmerli, "Das 'Gnadenjahr des Herrn,'" in *Archäologie und Altes Testament*, ed. A. Kuschke and E. Kutsch (Tübingen: Mohr Siebeck, 1970), 330-32; Christopher R. Bruno, "'Jesus Is Our Jubilee' . . . But How? The OT Background and Lukan Fulfillment of the Ethics of Jubilee," *JETS* 53 (2010): 85-86, 93.

[48]Tom Holland, *Contours of Pauline Theology: A Radical New Survey of the Influences of Paul's Biblical Writings* (Ross-shire, UK: Mentor, 2004), 31.

[49]Michael A. Lyons contends that such individual/corporate dynamic (servant-Jesus-apostles) originates out of Is 40–55 itself. See Lyons, "Paul and the Servants[s]: Isaiah 49,6 in Acts 13,47," *Ephemerides Theologicae Lovanienses* 89 (2013): 345-59, strengthening the contextual reading observations above.

The same hermeneutical understanding is at play in Luke 1:79 and Acts 26:18. In the former Isaiah 42:7 is used to speak of Jesus' ministry; in the latter the same is applied to Paul's evangelistic preaching. Equally, the Isaianic language of "the Way" is taken up and applied to the church in Acts 9:2; 19:9, 23; 22:4; 24:14, 22.[50]

Let us consider also Paul's use of Isaiah 25:8 in 1 Corinthians 15:54. Isaiah 25 is a text of national restoration where swallowing up death forever is a promise made to Israel. Paul applies it to the resurrection of Jesus and of believers (1 Cor 15:51-57). Thus, the eschatological hope of the nation is applied to Jesus and his international people. The warrant for this is the solidarity between Israel and Jesus, and in turn between Jesus and the church.[51] In this way, Israel is typological of the combined Jewish and Gentile worshiping community.[52]

The same typological dynamic is at work in Paul's reading of Isaiah 52:11. There Israel is called to come out of exile. In 2 Corinthians 6:17 Paul uses that verse to call the church out of the pagan culture.[53]

We noted above that Isaiah 40:6-8, which is about the recalling of the exiles, is used in 1 Peter 1:23-25 to celebrate the new life provided by the gospel. Again, there are words spoken to Israel being applied to the church, which makes sense if Israel and the situation of exile are typologically related to the church.

In sum, that which Isaiah applies to Israel, the New Testament writers apply to Jesus. That which applies to Jesus is then also applied to the church. If Jesus, therefore, is the antitype to the Old Testament's types, the church is "a gathering place of supratypes."[54]

---

[50]See Pao, *Acts and the Isaianic New Exodus*, 51-69.
[51]E. Earle Ellis, *Prophecy and Hermeneutic in Early Christianity* (Grand Rapids, MI: Eerdmans, 1978), 170-71.
[52]Richard B. Hays also points out how dependent Paul's argument is on the original Isaianic context. See Hays, *First Corinthians*, Interpretation (Louisville, KY: Westminster John Knox, 1997), 275-76.
[53]It is worth noting that typology is not the same as allegory, the latter of which "is not one of Paul's primary hermeneutical strategies" (Hays, *Echoes of Scripture*, 166). On the difference between the two, see Piotrowski, *In All the Scriptures*, 21-28, 68-71.
[54]David Schrock, "From Beelines to Plotlines: Typology That Follows the Covenantal Topography of Scripture," *Southern Baptist Journal of Theology* 21 (2017): 44-46.

It is essential to recognize that hermeneutics is not just a mechanical how-to process, like the way I assemble IKEA furniture. Rather, hermeneutics is intensely *theological* and, therefore, employs interpretive frames.[55] For the apostles, that interpretive frame was created by the conviction that history was real, purposeful, and under the Lord's providential guidance (pattern one) to bring about the fullness of time (pattern two) as types give way to their eschatological fulfillment (pattern four). This is all to be expected because God himself has spoken it and transmitted it to successive generations by way of literary conventions (pattern three). It is these convictions that the apostles brought to bear on their reading of Isaiah. They can show up in any one or combination of the above four patterns.

Matthew's Reading of Isaiah 42:1-4: A Confluence of Patterns

Each contributor in this section will comment on the use of Isaiah 42:1-4 in Matthew 12:17-21. For our purposes here, what do we learn about how Matthew reads Isaiah from this use? It seems three of the four patterns can be observed.

To begin, we can observe pattern two at work: Isaiah as a man for all seasons. Note that Matthew sees Jesus' healing ministry as a fulfillment of Isaiah 42:1-4. As mentioned above, fulfillment in Matthew should be understood as bringing an original idea or event to its full meaning. Thus, the evangelist sees Jesus' ministry as the landing pad of God's prior announcements, the finish line to which his purposes had always been traveling. In this way, Isaiah is read eschatologically.

Next we observe that Matthew has more than just Isaiah 42 in view, thus reading according to pattern three: Isaiah as a unified literary work. While the main quote is that of Isaiah 42:1-3, Matthew splices

---

[55]Especially helpful is G. K. Beale, "Did Jesus and His Followers Preach the Right Doctrine from the Wrong Texts? An Examination of the Presuppositions of Jesus' and the Apostles' Exegetical Method," in Beale, *Right Doctrine from the Wrong Text?*, 387-404.

in Isaiah 11:10 for specific language that serves his theological purposes more directly. Thus, he has an eye toward the wider theology of Isaiah.[56]

What are those specific theological purposes Matthew saw in Isaiah 11:10 to draw it into the larger quote? Here we observe pattern four: Isaiah as a typological visionary. We have already seen how Matthew is thoroughly focused on Jesus' role as the eschatological heir of David's house. Turning to LXX Isaiah 11:10 in Matthew 12:21 brings with it that Davidic theme. The entire Isaianic verse reads, "And it will come to pass in that day—the root of Jesse, who rises to rule the nations—of him shall the nations hope, and his resting place will be glorious." The "root of Jesse" is a reference to the house of David. This is clearly Matthew's intent, as seen in the question only two verses later, "Can this be the Son of David?" (Mt 12:23). Matthew 12:15-21 also dovetails with four other healing episodes in the Gospel where Jesus is again called the "the Son of David" (Mt 9:27; 15:22; 20:30-31; 21:14-15).[57] That tradition of the eschatological Davidide as a *healer* comes from Ezekiel 34:2-4, 22-25.[58] Matthew has found in Isaiah, therefore, a chance to redouble his Davidic emphasis and splice in the eschatological hopes of Ezekiel 34.

Conclusion

What caused the apostles to read Isaiah, or anything else, as *Christian* Scripture? The answer is the reorienting experience of the Christ event. Isaiah was written in another time, under different circumstances from the New Testament. But because sacred history is under the Lord's control, and that history has reached its intended goal in the gospel and

---

[56] See Jeannine K. Brown, "Jesus Messiah as Isaiah's Servant of the Lord: New Testament Explorations," *JETS* 62 (2020): 51-69.

[57] See H. Daniel Zacharias, *Matthew's Presentation of the Son of David: Davidic Tradition and Typology in the Gospel of Matthew*, T&T Clark Biblical Studies (New York: Bloomsbury T&T Clark, 2017), 79-103.

[58] Young S. Chae, *Jesus as the Eschatological Davidic Shepherd: Studies in the Old Testament, Second Temple Judaism, and in the Gospel of Matthew*, WUNT 2/216 (Tübingen: Mohr Siebeck, 2006).

the church; the texts that record such history can never be read the same way again. Richard Hays says it this way: "Because God has acted in Jesus Christ to initiate the turn of the ages, everything past must be read with new eyes."[59]

The new hermeneutical frame shows up in observable patterns in how the apostles read Isaiah. They read Isaiah as a historic text (pattern one) that nonetheless spoke to their unique moment in time (pattern two), while giving attention to large textual discourses (pattern three). Together, these patterns evince a *typological* reading of the Isaiah wherein it is specifically the death and resurrection of Jesus, together with his creation of the church, that brings the full meaning of history and sacred texts to their climax (pattern four).

It is critical to note that the apostles are not simply updating the significance of the Old Testament to jive with their unique audience, like a twenty-first-century preacher will make so-called relevant application. No! To live on the precipice of history is quite different from living downstream. Instead, they understood that the Old Testament was intentionally written for their moment. First Peter 1:10-12 comments:

> Concerning this salvation, the prophets who prophesied about the grace that was to be yours searched and inquired carefully, inquiring what person or time the Spirit of Christ in them was indicating when he predicted the sufferings of Christ and the subsequent glories. It was revealed to them that they were serving not themselves but you, in the things that have now been announced to you through those who preached the good news to you by the Holy Spirit sent from heaven, things into which angels long to look. (ESV)

The heaviest objects in the universe exert a gravitational force on other objects because they press down on the fabric of space-time and create a slope toward themselves. In so doing, they gather objects

---

[59]Hays, *Echoes of Scripture*, 168.

around themselves. The New Testament authors understood Jesus' person and work as such a theological lodestar, sloping the terrain of redemptive-historical toward itself, wherein all biblical themes and types rush along to finally revolve around the gospel "at the ends of the ages."[60]

---

[60]Special thanks to Jonathan Zavodney for his help with resources and editing.

2

WE ARE NOT APOSTLES

Another Way of Reading Isaiah

Paul D. Wegner

This book explores one of the most complicated and important issues in interpreting Scripture: how the New Testament authors applied Old Testament Scriptures to their own historical context. Dr. Piotrowski provides an interesting and thought-provoking method for how he believes the New Testament authors completed the meaning of Old Testament passages. While I agree with much of what he says in the previous chapter, I will comment on a few areas where my view of what the New Testament authors are doing differs.

Even as a seminary student at Trinity Evangelical Divinity School, I remember sometimes wondering how the New Testament authors arrived at the meaning they did when quoting the Old Testament. How could Matthew, for example, say that Jesus fulfilled Hosea 11:1, "from Egypt I called my son" (Mt 2:15), when the context of Hosea clearly says that it refers to Israel?[1] Or how could Herod's slaughter of babies in Bethlehem (Mt 2:18) fulfill Jeremiah 31:15, which refers to a different city (i.e., Ramah, not Bethlehem) and a different time period (i.e., the exile, not events surrounding Jesus' birth)? Even more difficult is Isaiah 7:14, in which a sign to King Ahaz is somehow said to be fulfilled by Jesus seven hundred years later.

There is no doubt that God guided the process and caused the Old Testament prophets to use specific words and phrases that would allow New Testament writers to develop these ideas or thoughts in new ways. There is also no doubt that once the New Testament came into existence, the fulfillment of Old Testament passages became much clearer and were even seen in new ways. Nevertheless, in some cases it can be quite difficult to reconcile the statements made by the New Testament authors with the Old Testament passage(s) they reference. William Klein, Craig Blomberg, and Robert Hubbard agree: "We are convinced, with most, that there are instances where NT authors attribute meaning or use an OT text in ways that the OT author did not intend."[2]

It is far too simplistic to argue, as some scholars do, that these fulfillment passages understand the passage from the perspective of God, who knew how they were going to work out, and the apostles were just following God's perspective. While there are elements of truth in this perspective, it is important when we are attempting to think God's thoughts after him that we also should attempt to do it in the way that he gave Scriptures to us—as a progressive revelation. Thus we aim for not just right conclusions but also the right process.

Reading Isaiah as Christian Scripture

Reading Isaiah as Christian Scripture demands that both the Old Testament and the New Testament be read as part of the same canon. It is

---

[1] Translations in this chapter are mine unless otherwise noted.
[2] William W. Klein, Craig L. Blomberg, and Robert L. Hubbard Jr., *Introduction to Biblical Interpretation* (Grand Rapids, MI: Zondervan, 2017), 250.

evident that the Old Testament served as the foundation for many concepts expressed by New Testament authors, especially the concept that God would send a deliverer to save his people. The Old Testament does indeed bear witness to this future deliverer, but this concept was only fully developed in the pages of New Testament revelation. Christians throughout church history have argued that the mystery of the gospel was concealed in the Old Testament but revealed in the New Testament (Col 1:26). The Bible itself lays out this story line as God progressively revealed himself and his truth across history—a concept commonly called "progressive revelation." Somewhat similar to a mystery book that gradually hints and foreshadows the truth until that truth is fully revealed, the New Testament ultimately provides the answer to the crucial question that runs throughout the Old Testament: How will God restore his people?

To read into Old Testament passages meanings that the author would not have been aware of essentially negates the progressive unfolding of God's plan by assigning meanings that were never intended to be fully disclosed until the New Testament. We can take an example from history to illustrate this principle. Before the twelfth century the word *cleave* had two opposite meanings: "to stick together" or "to split apart." Thus the KJV translates Genesis 2:24 as "Therefore shall a man leave his father and his mother, and shall *cleave* unto his wife: and they shall be one flesh," whereas today's usage has narrowed to "divide, separate, split" (e.g., a meat cleaver). It is easy to see that it would be incorrect to translate the word *cleave* with its meaning from today and read it back into the King James Version.[3] What seems an obvious error to avoid on the word level should be equally avoided on the concept level; that is, to force the New Testament's meaning into an Old Testament passage misses both the glorious mystery and the developing climax that finds its fulfillment in Christ. To argue that the biblical text is different

---

[3]D. A. Carson, *Exegetical Fallacies*, 2nd ed. (Grand Rapids, MI: Baker Academic, 1996), 33-34.

because it is a divinely inspired text and that God intended the Old Testament to be read in light of the New Testament seems to me to put the focus so much on the end of the story that the richness of the progressive revelation may be overlooked.

There is still a very important role for a canonical reading of Scripture, one in which the reader is finding new significance in an Old Testament text rather than new meaning, a distinction E. D. Hirsch points out in his classic work *Validity in Interpretation*. He argues that *meaning* refers to ideas that "the author meant by his use of a particular sign sequence," whereas *significance* is "the relationship between that meaning and a person, or a conception, or situation." The meaning of a text is set by the author and does not change, but there are any number of valid significances, as Hirsch notes: "Each generation must interpret texts afresh, the meanings of the texts do not change; instead only the perspectives of their interpreters shift."[4] It has become increasingly common to confuse the meaning of a specific passage with its multiple significances.

Over the past several decades scholars have called into question the definitions of the terms *meaning* and *significance*. It has been argued that (1) because we can never know the author's exact "thought processes," we can never be entirely certain of the author's meaning; and (2) true communication also depends on how well a reader or listener understands a text, correctly or incorrectly grasping its full significance.[5] These debates have helped to clarify just how complicated the communication process is; however, complete skepticism is unwarranted. Even though it is not possible to identify the original meaning of a passage with 100 percent certainty, as with any other text, we can analyze the words, grammar, genres, rhetorical cues, relevant cultural norms, and so on to arrive as closely as possible to the approximate

---

[4] E. D. Hirsch, *Validity in Interpretation* (New Haven, CT: Yale University Press, 1967), 6, 133.
[5] James D. Hernando, *Dictionary of Hermeneutics: A Concise Guide to Terms, Names, Methods, and Expressions* (Springfield, MO: Gospel, 2005), 26n24.

meaning the author intended to communicate.⁶ My understanding is that the divine authority of the biblical texts resides in the meaning that the human author intended by his words. If we give up on at least attempting to accomplish this goal, then we may as well abandon exegesis of biblical texts.

Ways the Apostles Use Scriptures

Before assessing whether we should use a similar hermeneutic as the apostles, we need to examine more carefully exactly how the apostles used Old Testament passages. Dr. Piotrowski and others in this book seem to suggest that the apostles used one consistent method when applying Old Testament passages. Most scholars, however, would agree that there are at least two basic methods of applying Old Testament passages: (1) direct fulfillments of prophecies and (2) some type of reapplication of an Old Testament passage to a new historical context. There are a variety of ways that the New Testament authors reapply an Old Testament passage, and a well-informed understanding of how the apostles used Old Testament passages will be helpful in determining whether we can use similar techniques when interpreting passages not quoted in the New Testament.

Direct fulfillments. Some of the easiest fulfillment passages to interpret are "direct fulfillments."⁷ These were not fulfilled during the time period of the Old Testament but at a future point (some eschatological passages are fulfilled in the very distant future). Because they each have a very clear direct fulfillment by events referenced in the New Testament (e.g., Is 9:1-2; 52:15–53:12; Mic 5:2-5), we can apply these Old Testament passages just as the apostles applied them. A good example is Philip's explanation to the Ethiopian eunuch in Acts 8:32-35 that

---

⁶Craig S. Keener, *Spirit Hermeneutics: Reading Scripture in Light of Pentecost* (Grand Rapids, MI: Eerdmans, 2016), 141.
⁷Because of space limitations, I will not address allusions or echoes. For a seminal treatment of allusions, see R. B. Hays, *Echoes of Scripture in the Letters of Paul* (New Haven, CT: Yale University Press, 1989).

Isaiah 53:7-8 refers to Jesus: "'About whom, I ask you, does the prophet [Isaiah] say this, about himself or about someone else?' Then Philip opened his mouth, and beginning with this Scripture he told him the good news about Jesus."

Highlighting the significance of a passage. New Testament authors also quote the Old Testament for the purpose of applying its principles or its significance to events during their lifetime, similar to what today's preachers might do in applying Old Testament passages to their congregations. C. S. Lewis calls this concept "second meanings" (although Hirsch is more correct to refer to it as "significance" in that the words' meaning remained unchanged, but this meaning took on new significance in light of later events). Lewis provides a good illustration of the concept from the Roman time period:

> One of the Roman historians tells us about a fire in a provincial town which was thought to have originated in the public baths. What gave some colour to the suspicion of deliberate incendiarism was the fact that, earlier that day, a gentleman had complained that the water in the hot bath was only lukewarm and had received from an attendant the reply, *it will soon be hot enough*. Now of course if there really had been a plot, and the slave was in it, and fool enough to risk discovery by his veiled threat, then the story would not concern us. But let us suppose the fire was an accident (i.e. was intended by nobody). In that case the slave would have said something truer, or more importantly true, than he himself supposed. . . . The slave's reply is fully explained by the customer's complaint; it is just what any bath attendant would say. The deeper significance which his words turned out to have during the next few hours was, as we should say, accidental.[8]

Hebrews 1:5 and Hebrews 5:5 appear to be examples of new significance for Psalm 2:7, a verse positioned right in the heart of an accession psalm. The context of Psalm 2:7, "You are my son; *today I have begotten*

---

[8]C. S. Lewis, *Reflections on the Psalms* (New York: Harcourt Brace, 1958; repr. San Francisco: Harper and Row, 2017), 86.

you," refers to the accession of a king, which took place long before Jesus' time (see Ps 2:6). Hebrews 1:5 and Hebrews 5:5 pick up this verse and highlight its significance to Jesus, even though the language is somewhat awkward when applied to him since he has always existed as God's Son.[9] Neither verse claims to be a fulfillment of Psalm 2:7, and yet the verse from Psalms is applied to Jesus, the true Son of God, in a way that is truer than its application to any human king, who was merely adopted by God at his coronation.

Prophetic patterns. The term *prophetic pattern* refers to the concept, person, event (or all three) that a New Testament author applies from the Old Testament. During my PhD studies, I observed that the Greek word *plēroō* ("to fill, fulfill") had more than one nuance: (1) It could mean "fulfill" in the sense that an Old Testament prophecy could foretell an event that would be realized in the future. Some Old Testament passages, such as Micah 5:2, are said to be fulfilled in this sense—even the chief priests and scribes understood this (Mt 2:5). (2) It could also mean "to fill up to capacity; to fill to the brim, to make full/complete" (see Mt 3:15; 13:48; etc.). Matthew sometimes uses the word *plēroō*, "to fulfill," in this latter sense of "filling up" an Old Testament passage with more meaning—not in the sense of completing it but to add to its meaning.

For example, the verse, "Behold, the virgin is pregnant and will give birth to a son and they will call his name Immanuel" (Mt 1:23, a quote from Is 7:14) contains several changes to arrive at this meaning in the book of Matthew: (1) The Hebrew word *'almâ*, "young maiden," does not necessarily mean "virgin"; even the Greek word *parthenos* most likely did not mean "virgin" originally (i.e., Dinah is called a *parthenos* even after she was raped, LXX Gen 34:3) but rather appears to have

---

[9]Wayne Grudem states, "The Nicene Creed in 325 affirmed that Christ was 'begotten, not made. . . . ' In addition, the phrase 'before all ages' was added after 'begotten of the Father,' to show that this 'begetting' was eternal." Grudem, *Systematic Theology* (Grand Rapids, MI: Zondervan, 1994), 244.

taken on this meaning later. (2) Rather than foretelling a future event, the adjective *hārâ*, "pregnant," suggests that the young woman is already pregnant. (3) The Hebrew text reads "she" (or possibly "you") "will call his name Immanuel," not "they will call." The New Testament author is actually modifying the text to achieve the meaning he desired. Thus in this passage the New Testament author goes beyond merely completing the Old Testament text; he actually modifies it. New Testament authors sometimes use the Old Testament in a way that requires an authority given by God, similar to authorship; since the biblical canon is closed, this technique should not be used by interpreters today. While this may appear to be a question of mere semantics, it has crucial ramifications for the progressive revelation of the Bible.

Typology. Biblical typology refers to a person, object, or event in the Old Testament that is said to prefigure or foreshadow a person or event in the New Testament. For example, Adam is said to be a type of Christ (Rom 5:14), and the earthly tabernacle is said to be a type (or pattern, model) that serves as a copy or shadow of the heavenly sanctuary.[10] Some scholars use this terminology in such a general sense that it can refer to almost any correspondence between two persons, objects, or events. For example, death and resurrection are said to be typified by (1) Moses, who was left in the water to die, then later was drawn out; (2) Joseph, who was thought to be dead but was later found alive; and (3) Jonah, who thought he was about to die but then was delivered by God.

For our purposes, I limit the usage of the terms *type* or *typology* to those correspondences identified by Scripture itself. Adam is said to be a type of Christ because through "one man" sin and death entered the world. Jesus is the "one man" who brought grace and the gift of righteousness (Rom 5:17). The New Testament thereby draws a strong correspondence between the two, one that is much more substantial

---

[10]See the classic work by Leonhard Goppelt, *Typos* (Grand Rapids, MI: Eerdmans, 1982).

than the experiences of Moses, Joseph, and Jonah that are said to typify death and resurrection. Jesus refers to the bronze serpent being lifted up (Num 21:8) as corresponding to his approaching death: "And as Moses lifted up the serpent in the wilderness, so must the Son of Man be lifted up" (Jn 3:14). Notice that John highlights the correspondence but does not call it a type; thus not all passages that correspond to each other constitute a type.

The Lordship of Jesus. Richard Bauckham argues that the New Testament authors believed so strongly that Jesus was the Lord that they sometimes applied passages referring to God (i.e., the Lord) in the Old Testament to Jesus in the New Testament.[11] An example of this analogical method is the classic passage in Philippians 2:6-11 regarding Jesus' *kenōsis* (from *kenoō*, "to empty"). In Philippians 2:10 Paul quotes from Isaiah 45:23, which states that everyone will bow down and swear allegiance to God, and applies it to Jesus. The clear implication is that because Jesus is equated with God (Phil 2:6), Isaiah 45:23 can therefore be applied to Jesus as well. In the same way, in Revelation 1:17 and Revelation 22:13 the names for God quoted from Isaiah 44:6 and Isaiah 48:12 (i.e., "the first and the last") are applied to Jesus (see also Joel 2:32 in Rom 10:13; Jer 9:23-24 in 1 Cor 1:31; Is 40:13 in 1 Cor 2:16; etc.).

Summary. It should not be surprising that the New Testament authors used a variety of methods when applying Old Testament passages in their writings. Matthew, in writing to a Jewish audience, focuses on Jesus as the long-awaited Messiah; in so doing, he uses the Greek word *plēroō* when showing how Jesus fills up certain Old Testament passages. But Matthew also points out direct fulfillments, introduced by the phrases "for so it is written by the prophet" (Mt 2:5) and "this is he of whom it is written" (Mt 11:10). There may also be a reference to a new significance in Matthew 3:3 when he introduces a

---

[11] Richard Bauckham, *God Crucified: Monotheism and Christology in the New Testament* (Grand Rapids, MI: Eerdmans, 1999).

quote from Isaiah 40:3 with the words "for this is he who was spoken of by the prophet Isaiah."

My concerns with attempting to imitate how the apostles apply Old Testament passages are threefold: First, as I pointed out above, the process of how the New Testament authors sometimes use Old Testament passages is complicated and difficult to ascertain. For example, (1) sometimes only specific parts of an Old Testament passage are applied in the New Testament, (2) at other times specific translations of an Old Testament passage are chosen, and (3) occasionally the author demonstrates an awareness of how words changed in meaning between the Old and New Testament time periods. Second, the progressive nature of God's revelation of himself can be lost. Third, when we attempt to apply the significance of an Old Testament passage, it does not carry the same authority as when an apostle points out a new significance of an Old Testament passage.

Should We Imitate the Apostles in Their Use of Old Testament Scripture?

Following both Nick's and my overview of how the apostles read Isaiah, we may naturally ask, "Should we imitate the apostles in our own reading of Isaiah?" In this chapter I will offer some reservations about such attempts, and in the next Andrew Abernethy will offer a more positive answer to this question.

As stated above, there are two legitimate ways we can follow the apostles in how they read Old Testament passages: (1) by taking note of the direct fulfillments that the apostles have identified, such as Micah 5:2; and (2) by highlighting a new significance of an Old Testament passage to a New Testament passage, similar to how the author of Hebrews 1:5 and Hebrews 5:5 applies new significance for Psalm 2:7, originally an accession psalm, and reapplies it to Jesus. Pastors today frequently and appropriately refer to Old Testament stories or principles to accurately illustrate New Testament concepts. However, it is inadvisable for us today to seek new meaning in an Old Testament passage by means of *plēroō, sensus plenior* (a deeper meaning intended by God, but not by the human author), typology, or pesher methods (*pesher* means "interpretation" and here it describes a Jewish method that attempts to give the clear meaning of the author's words). In this aspect I am in substantial agreement with Gordon Fee and Douglas Stuart, who favor a *sensus plenior* explanation of the apostolic hermeneutic yet limit its use to the New Testament authors, stating that it is a matter of inspiration, not illumination.[12] Richard Longenecker also states that, while we can appreciate the New Testament authors' exegetical methods and as Christians be committed to their conclusions, it does not necessarily follow that we can imitate their methods: "Apart from a revelatory stance on our part, I suggest that we cannot reproduce their *pesher* exegesis."[13]

First, let me sound a note of caution and offer a bit of perspective. Ever since the New Testament was written, people have sought to comprehend how New Testament authors used Old Testament passages. There has been little agreement in identifying their methods. Each method that has been identified, whether pesher, *sensus plenior*, typology, and so on, has had its heyday and then fallen into disfavor. The canonical-theological approach that is so popular at present is likely no different.[14] This should at least cause us to pause and reflect as to whether the apostles' methods can indeed be imitated.

---

[12] Gordon D. Fee and Douglas Stuart, *How to Read the Bible for All Its Worth*, 4th ed. (Grand Rapids, MI: Zondervan, 2014), 208-211.

[13] Richard N. Longenecker, *Studies in Hermeneutics, Christology and Discipleship*, New Testament Monographs (Sheffield: Sheffield Phoenix Press, 2006), 67.

[14] C. R. Seitz, *Word Without End: The Old Testament as Abiding Theological Witness* (Grand Rapids, MI: Eerdmans, 1998); Seitz, *Figured Out: Typology and Providence in Christian Scripture* (Louisville, KY: Westminster John Knox, 2001); Kevin J. Vanhoozer, "Toward a Theological Old Testament Theology? A Systematic Theologian's Take on Reading the Old Testament Theologically," in *Interpreting the Old Testament Theologically: Essays in Honor of Willem VanGemeren*, ed. Andrew T. Abernethy (Grand Rapids, MI: Zondervan, 2018), 293-317; C. A. Carter, *Interpreting Scripture with the Great Tradition: Recovering the Genius of Premodern Exegesis* (Grand Rapids, MI: Baker Academic, 2018).

Second, the ultimate conclusions of my friend Andrew Abernethy's theological-patterning view in the following chapter and my progressive-fulfillment view will in fact be quite similar, but our interpretations of Old Testament passages and how we come to our conclusions vary significantly. One statements of his with which I agree wholeheartedly is, "The apostles would have known what a passage meant in a more historical sense, yet their methodological uniqueness comes as they reappropriated these texts in light of Christ." However, the question still remains as to how and why they reappropriated these specific texts.

Third, while Abernethy's overall approach has the worthy goal of understanding the whole of the canon as Christian Scripture, he seems to imply that the canonical-theological approach is the primary way that the entire canon ought to be read as Christian Scripture. But as I have pointed out above, the mystery that the gospel was hidden in the Old Testament and revealed in the New Testament has been a common view throughout church history, and is in line with how the Bible itself presents its message (see Rom 16:25; Col 1:26-27).

Fourth, Abernethy argues that the Old Testament "bore witness" to Christ even before the New Testament was written and that "the Old Testament was seen in a completely different light after Christ had come." While I agree with both statements, it is doubtful that we would agree on how these statements are to be applied. Some scholars believe that Luke 24:27, 44-47 gives them license to find Christ virtually everywhere in the Old Testament. There is a maximalist approach to these verses (i.e., where Christ is referred to almost everywhere in the Old Testament) and a minimalist approach (i.e., a very limited number of specific verses, scattered across different parts of the OT, refer to the Christ). My guess is that the truth is somewhere in between these positions, whereas Abernethy clearly takes a maximalist approach: "The implication of this is that every passage in Isaiah—not simply those quoted in the New Testament—has the potential of speaking of the Son and as addressing the church."

Yet even the context of Luke 24:27, 44-47 seems to limit that to which Luke 24:27 refers. Luke 24:25 states that the disciples were "slow to believe *all that the prophets have spoken*"; then Luke 24:26 implies that their message was about the suffering of Messiah and his subsequent glory, similar to 1 Peter 1:10-11. But could the disciples have found that information from every passage in the Old Testament or even in Isaiah alone? I think not, although it is clearly an overarching message of the Old Testament.

Fifth, the canonical-theological method appears to border on a reader-response method. One of Abernethy's clearest statements concerning how an Old Testament passage is applied by the New Testament authors is, "In this process, the human author's intent is not discarded; instead, the human author's *intent is extended and clarified* as a fuller referent now comes into view and within a larger literary context." I fail to see how the events around Bethlehem during Jesus' birth are a fuller referent to those around Ramah during the exile, as recorded in Matthew 2:17-18. If this extended and clarified significance stopped at the New Testament's intended meaning, then I would not take issue with this view; but if one allows a reader to extend even further and clarify an Old Testament author's intent (i.e., meaning) beyond what the New Testament authors have noted, then this amounts to a reader-response method. Klein, Blomberg, and Hubbard face a similar dilemma:

> As we become aware of God's working and purposes, we may read texts in new lights and craft our plausible interpretations of the biblical texts we are studying, even though such interpretations were *not strictly intended by the biblical authors. The fresh interpretation must be consistent with the text's historical meaning . . . , but it need not be limited to the original perlocution.*[15]

Interestingly, most scholars (except Walter Kaiser) argue that the New Testament authors found further meaning in the text than the Old

---

[15]Klein, Blomberg, and Hubbard, *Introduction to Biblical Interpretation*, 279, emphasis added.

Testament authors intended.[16] Where we differ is in our explanation as to how the New Testament authors arrived at that further meaning. Lewis notes the problem with drawing on these general methods of typology to arrive at a second or hidden meaning (which he refers to as an "allegorical" sense) in the biblical texts:

> As we all know, almost anything can be read into any book if you are determined enough. This will be especially impressed on anyone who has written fantastic fiction. He will find reviewers, both favorable and hostile, reading into his stories all manner of allegorical meanings which he never intended. (Some of the allegories thus imposed on my own books have been so ingenious and interesting that I often wish I had thought of them myself.)[17]

Lewis's point is well taken—there are no limits to the connections that readers can draw that go beyond the original author's intended meaning. I think it is preferable to keep meaning within the bounds of the original author's intent and then allow for multiple significances that are not authoritative. Only the New Testament authors could take up an Old Testament passage, see the pattern created by the Old Testament author, and add further authoritative meaning to it.

Abernethy argues that a canonical reading of Isaiah demands that it would "need to be reread in view of God's subsequent acts in the drama and in view of the other books that bear witness to these acts."[18] I would argue, however, that the book of Isaiah does not need to be reread in light of God's subsequent events; rather, as the book itself suggests, it should

---

[16]Walter C. Kaiser Jr., "Single Meaning, Unified Referents," in *Three Views on the New Testament Use of the Old Testament*, ed. K. Berding and J. Lunde (Grand Rapids, MI: Zondervan, 2008), 45-89.

[17]Lewis, *Reflections*, 85.

[18]Kevin Vanhoozer argues for a *referens plenior*: "A *theological* Old Testament theology sets out the divine intention, manifest in what we could call the plain canonical sense, which makes it clear that the ultimate referent of the Old Testament prophets—*a function of what we might call the extended literal sense*—was the promise of redemption and its fulfillment in Jesus Christ" ("Toward a Theological Old Testament Theology?," 305). It is difficult, however, to see how Mt 2:18 is an "extended literal sense" of Jer 31:15.

be read from the stance of the prophet looking forward to these events and to their eventual fulfillment. He did not know who would ultimately fulfill the events envisioned or how long it would be before they were fulfilled. Yet he eagerly looked forward to them and their ultimate fulfillment, a perspective borne out in the apostle Peter's explanation in 1 Peter 1:10-12. With the arrival of Jesus many of the Old Testament passages would gain new significance. Their meaning did not change, but rather they gained a fuller significance. In her section on Jeremiah, Dana Harris correctly argues that the apostles operated out of a christological worldview; this perspective explains how New Testament authors could find new significance in some Old Testament passages.

Reading Isaiah 42:1-4

In considering the question whether we can use the apostolic hermeneutic, my primary concerns are that (1) there does not appear to be one overarching method that the apostles used; (2) we read into a passage something it did not mean in its historical context and undermine the progressive nature of the revelation as it was given to us; and (3) we miss the mystery, wonder, and even surprise of the gospel that Jesus came to fulfill.

Matthew seems to use the concept of filling up an Old Testament passage more than any other New Testament author. To illustrate this concept as a useful approach of reading the text in a way that is both historically rooted and fits into a larger story of progressive revelation, let us examine the original historical context of Isaiah 42:1-4 and then turn to Matthew 12:17, where the apostle says Jesus "filled up" (*plēroō*) these verses from Isaiah.

Reading Isaiah 42:1-4 in its context. Isaiah 42:1-4 is part of what is commonly called the first Servant Song (Is 42:1-9), which appears within the larger unit Isaiah 40–48. The primary theme of Isaiah 40–48 is that God would use Cyrus to deliver Israel from Babylon.

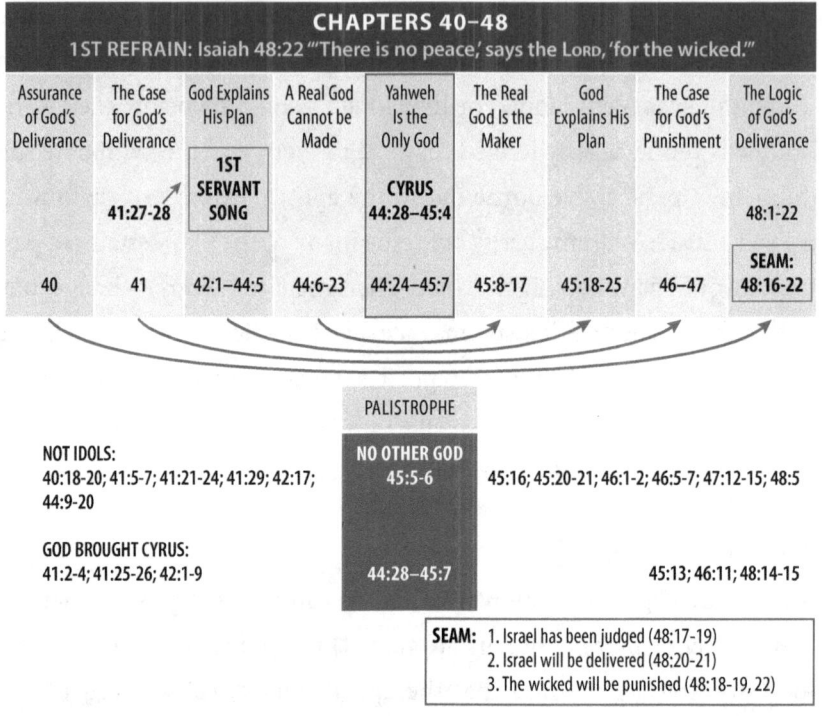

Figure 2.1. Isaiah 40–48 and God's deliverance of Israel

There are two main questions that God answers in Isaiah 40–48: Can God deliver Israel, and will he? The answer to both is a resounding yes. God states seven times that he will bring Cyrus, the pagan Persian emperor, to accomplish Israel's deliverance (i.e., Is 41:2-4, 25-26; 42:1-9; 44:24–45:7; 45:13; 46:11; 48:14-15), and thirteen times in Isaiah 40–48 that idols cannot do this (i.e., Is 40:18-20; 41:5-7, 21-24, 29; 42:17; 44:9-20; 45:5-6, 16, 20-21; 46:1-2, 5-7; 47:12-15; 48:5). Isaiah 44:28–45:7 and Isaiah 45:5-6 mark the middle points of the two series of verses and are also positioned in the middle section of a palistrophe (i.e., Is 44:24–45:7).[19] This middle section mentions Cyrus by name for the first time

---

[19]Sean E. McEvenue was the first to coin the term *palistrophe* in *The Narrative Style of the Priestly Writer* (Rome: Biblical Institute Press, 1971), 157-58. The turning point or key idea of a palistrophe usually appears in the middle section. See Gordon J. Wenham, "The Coherence of the Flood Narrative," *VT* 28 (1978): 336-48.

(see Is 44:28; 45:1). Since the key theme of Isaiah 40–48 is God's deliverance of his people by means of Cyrus, it makes sense that Cyrus be identified as the servant in the first Servant Song.

Abernethy notes in his chapter that Israel is said to be God's servant in Isaiah 41:8-9 and would therefore be the logical choice for the servant in Isaiah 42:1-9. However, this Servant Song, like the others in Isaiah (see Is 50:2; 51:18), is preceded by the introductory note that no Israelite was deemed fit to be the messenger of good news: "But I looked and there was no one from among these [i.e., Israel]—there was no counselor [among them], even no one to give answer when I asked them" (Is 41:28). Since no Israelite was deemed fit to serve as a messenger of good news, God would have to bring his own servant from outside of Israel, Cyrus, "to open the eyes that are blind, to bring out prisoners from the dungeon and from the prison those who sit in darkness" (Is 42:7). In the context of Isaiah 40–48 these images likely have a primary reference to the literal release of Israel from the Babylonian exile but may also have a secondary figurative reference to its release from spiritual blindness.

The phrase "Behold, my servant" at the beginning of the song draws attention to God's servant and his calling (Is 42:1). He is prepared to be God's servant because he is (1) supported by God, (2) chosen by God, (3) a delight to God's soul (i.e., he will accomplish God's good pleasure), and (4) endowed with God's Spirit (i.e., guided by God's Spirit). In Isaiah 44:28–45:2 similar distinctions are made regarding Cyrus, who (1) is God's shepherd, (2) will perform God's desire, (3) is God's anointed, (4) is held by the right hand by God (= protection), and (5) is preceded by God himself (= guidance).

Next, the servant's mission is described (Is 42:1-4): (1) "he will bring forth justice to the nations" (Is 42:1, literal translation). The syntax emphasizes *justice* to the nations, a concept that is repeated two more times in Isaiah 42:3-4. In contrast to Assyrian and Babylonian policies to deport the peoples of the nations they conquered, Persia allowed previously exiled peoples to return to their home countries and even serve their own gods. Persia had one of the most just legal systems in the ancient Near East.[20] Cyrus is also said to be "called . . . in righteousness" (a similar phrase in Is 41:2; 45:13), meaning that God called him to perform righteous acts (Is 42:6).

One of the most commonly mentioned details regarding Cyrus is that he will destroy other nations (Is 41:2, 25; 45:1-3), yet God uses him to deal gently with his own people (i.e., "he will not . . . lift up his voice . . . in the streets. . . . A bruised [*rāṣûṣ*] reed he will not break, and a faintly burning [*kēhâ*] wick he will not quench," Is 42:2-3). In this context the bruised reed and faintly burning wick most likely refer to Israel's languishing in the Babylonian exile. Far from destroying them, Cyrus allowed them to return, rebuild their temple, and serve their God.

Using similar terminology, Isaiah 42:4 states that the servant "will not grow faint [*kāhâ*] or be discouraged [*rāṣaṣ*] til he has established justice in the earth." The nations appear to have longed for the justice the Persian Empire would bring (i.e., punishment on Babylon for exiling them).

While the first Servant Song continues through Isaiah 42:9, only the first four verses are quoted in Matthew 12:18-21. The rest of the song goes on to confirm that God has indeed called the servant (i.e., "you," second-person masculine singular) and will support him until he accomplishes God's plan to bring out his captives from the metaphorical prison of exile and return home to rebuild his temple. This latter part of the song most likely was connected too closely to Israel's deliverance from the Babylonian exile, and thus the New Testament author does not include it.

Matthew's use of Isaiah 42:1-4. First, Isaiah 41:27-28 explains that God intends to deliver Israel but finds no Israelite qualified to fulfill the

---

[20]See "4e. Persian Empire," USHistory.org, www.ushistory.org/civ/4e.asp (accessed November 27, 2022).

role of deliverer; so God sends his own deliverer (namely, Cyrus) to rescue his nation. Matthew recognizes the prophetic pattern in Isaiah but chooses to follow the Hebrew text rather than his more common practice of following the LXX, which applies it to Israel. He "fills it up" (*plēroō*) with more meaning, not by developing a type-antitype relationship but by merely highlighting the correspondences between Cyrus and Jesus:

1. Just as the first servant was introduced in the Old Testament because of Israel's hardhearted reliance on idols instead of on God, so Matthew quotes Isaiah 42:1-4 in reference to the Pharisees' hardness of heart in seeking to destroy Jesus (Mt 12:1-32).

2. Just as God chose a special servant, Cyrus, to accomplish the specific task of delivering his people from the Babylonian exile, so he chose Jesus to provide a much broader deliverance, healing both physical and spiritual needs through him.

3. Just after describing how the Pharisees were counseling together on how to destroy Jesus (Mt 12:14), Matthew develops the peaceful and gentle nature of Jesus' ministry, similar to how Cyrus is portrayed (i.e., "He will not cry aloud or lift up his voice. . . . A bruised reed he will not break," Mt 12:19-20).

4. Just as God brought his own deliverer, Cyrus, because he could find no one in Israel to rescue the nation from exile (Is 41:27-29), so he will send Jesus to accomplish a deliverance that no one in Jesus' day can achieve.

5. Cyrus brought justice to the nations through his legal system and by allowing the exiles to return home; in an even greater way, Jesus will bring true justice to the nations.

6. Just as Cyrus did not break off a "bruised reed" (i.e., did not destroy the Israelites), so Jesus will not destroy his people but rather restore them.

7. The final phrase of Isaiah 42:4, "and the coastlands will wait expectantly for his law," is modified in Matthew 12:18 to read "and he will proclaim justice to the nations" (LXX), which better reflects Jesus' ministry. All of these points of correspondence come specifically from the context and the prophetic pattern that Matthew fills up with more meaning by applying it to events in Jesus' life.

Matthew is not simply completing the original meaning of Isaiah 42:1-4 but is adding new meaning and applying it to a different historical context. If typology merely highlights the correspondence between two events, statements, or persons, then in one sense this is what Matthew is doing; but if typology means that there is an integral connection between these two events, then I am not convinced that this is what Matthew is doing. Note that Matthew selectively shapes his quotation of the Old Testament passage:

8. He chooses to quote the MT and not the LXX (as he did in Mt 1:21-23) because it fits his purposes better.

9. In Matthew 12:20, he modifies the text ("until he brings justice to victory") and does not follow either the MT or LXX; it thereby fits Jesus' ministry better than that of Cyrus.

10. In Matthew 12:21 he follows the LXX and prefers the phrase "his name" (*onomati autou*) instead of "his law" ("and the coastlands wait for his law [*lətôrātô*]"), which originally referred to Cyrus's justice system.

11. He ends the quote at Isaiah 42:4 in order to issue a stern rebuke to the Pharisees who think they have no need of Jesus, in contrast to pagan Gentiles who put their hope in God's servant. The quote is also framed before and after by two incidents that illustrate the Pharisees' hardness of heart.

That Matthew shapes and switches between the MT and the LXX texts suggests that he is doing more than simply completing the Old Testament passage; he is modifying the text.

Conclusion

It is evident that the New Testament authors believed that the New Testament fulfilled or completed many prophecies initially found in the Old Testament. We can follow the apostles' example when the New Testament directly fulfills an Old Testament prophecy (for example, Jesus' fulfillment of Mic 5:2) or when pointing out a new significance of an Old Testament passage. By *significance* I am not suggesting that the Old Testament passage initially had this meaning or was completed by the New Testament person or event, but instead we can identify a new significance of an Old Testament passage in light of later events; for example, the accession psalm of Psalm 2:7 referring to a human king being adopted by God at his coronation can have new significance in light of Jesus being the Son of God (Heb 1:5; 5:5).

However, it would be incorrect for modern readers to attempt to follow the apostles' use of prophetic patterns, pesher, *sensus plenior*, or more detailed methods of typology. Even though the New Testament authors used a variety of methods when applying Old Testament passages to their New Testament contexts, they were purposeful in their selection of Old Testament quotes and deliberate in the meaning they assigned to them. Our example of a prophetic pattern from Matthew 12:17-21 highlights just how complicated the process is when Matthew shapes his quotation from Isaiah 42: (1) he quotes from both the MT and the LXX versions—depending which fits his intent better; (2) he changes certain words from his source texts (*name* vs. *law*); and (3) he quotes only Isaiah 42:1-4 of the Servant Song. Each of these features allows the Old Testament passage to better correspond to Jesus. Not only would it be unlikely that we as readers today could authentically imitate this process, but we have not been given divine authority to assign new, authoritative meaning to a text—only New Testament authors had divine authority to compose Scripture.

It is our job not only to better understand these methods but also to correctly apply the significance of these passages to our lives. Being able to follow how a New Testament writer found further meaning in an Old Testament passage, as well as understanding the progressive nature of God's revelation, can add depth to our preaching and ensure that the Old Testament does not become an ancient relic with no application to our contemporary lives. Grant Osborne expresses it well: "The hermeneutical process culminates not in the results of exegesis (centering on the original meaning of the text), but in the homiletical process (centering on the significance of the Word for the life of the Christian today)."[21] The chapters of this book help to provide a foundation for further research into the complex process of bringing out the Old Testament's relevance to today's audience.

---

[21]Grant R. Osborne, *The Hermeneutical Spiral* (Downers Grove, IL: IVP Academic, 1991), 343.

3

EMULATING THE APOSTLES

Reading Isaiah as Christian Scripture in the Footsteps of the Apostles

Andrew T. Abernethy

The recurring theme throughout my training in Old Testament was, "Don't read Christ into the Old Testament; focus on what the original author meant." When a student would ask, "What about the apostles? Didn't they do otherwise?" the answer was always, "Yes, but we are not apostles." Other essays in this volume by Paul Wegner (Isaiah), Gary Yates (Jeremiah), and John Hilber (Ezekiel) offer an important contribution through their adamancy that we must not leave the historical dimensions of the text behind. My perspective has changed over the years. After a few comments on methodology, I will argue that the church should read Isaiah in the footsteps of the apostles. A Christian reading of Isaiah asks how all of the book bears witness to the triune God's work in Christ, not simply those few texts quoted in the New Testament.

Should We Follow the Apostles?

Entire books have sought to justify an apostolic hermeneutic when reading the Old Testament, so my comments will by nature be limited.[1] The three principles I set forth below aim both to clarify what emulating the apostles entails and to legitimize this practice.

The incarnational principle. God spoke to real people at real moments in real places through the prophet Isaiah. Any reading of Isaiah that neglects this fact overlooks the fundamental theological conviction regarding God's incarnational character.[2] As a result, readers must use exegetical skills to understand not simply an individual word, or phrase, or a sentence, or part of a passage that is tweet-worthy, or an abstract principle, but rather the flow of thought across a given passage in view of what an author intends to accomplish through the utterance within a particular context.[3]

One may ask, however, whether the apostles even read the Old Testament at a literal, historical level. The answer is a qualified yes, as Nicholas Piotrowski showed in the opening chapter. For instance, Matthew's genealogy depends on a literal understanding of narratives about individuals, such as Abraham, Rahab, and David, and events, such as exile to Babylon. The author of Hebrews seems to grasp the flow of thought of Psalm 95. The apostles seem to grasp Isaiah's story line.[4]

---

[1] See, e.g., Christopher Seitz, *The Character of Christian Scripture: The Significance of a Two-Testament Bible*, Studies in Theological Interpretation (Grand Rapids, MI: Baker Academic, 2011). For a survey of apostolic interpretation, see Richard N. Longenecker, *Biblical Exegesis in the Apostolic Period* (Grand Rapids, MI: Eerdmans, 1999). Drawing an analogy to the "Teacher of Righteousness" at Qumran, he argues that the apostles were able to employ the hermeneutic they did because Jesus was the authoritative teacher who granted the apostles insight and authority in applying the OT to Christ. Today, since we are not apostles, he argues that we should not emulate this interpretive practice (pesher).

[2] Michael Gorman refers to this as the Chalcedonian principle in *Elements of Biblical Exegesis: A Basic Guide for Students and Ministers*, 2nd ed. (Grand Rapids, MI: Baker Academic, 2009), 149.

[3] For a tremendous introduction to discourse and speech-acts that involves more than grasping cognitive content, see Jeannine K. Brown, *Scripture as Communication: Introducing Biblical Hermeneutics* (Grand Rapids, MI: Baker Academic, 2007).

[4] See David W. Pao, *Acts and the Isaianic New Exodus*, WUNT 130 (Tübingen: Mohr Siebeck, 2000); J. Ross Wagner, *Heralds of the Good News: Isaiah and Paul "In Concert" in the Letter to the*

The apostles would have known what a passage meant in a more historical sense, but they would have reframed these in light of Christ.

Sensus plenior, *Christology, and worldview*. The apostles, in the fullness of time, saw, touched, and heard the very Son of God in the flesh and were witnesses to his resurrection. Since they viewed Jesus as the eschatological climax of the Old Testament and its themes, the apostles saw a fuller sense in Old Testament texts than the original authors knew.[5] In Isaiah 7:14, the "virgin"/"woman" of Ahaz's time conceives (through intercourse with a man) a human child whose theophoric name (Immanuel) points to the reality of "God with us" during the eighth century. Yet, the apostles recognized how this prepared for Mary's virginal conception and birth of a child whose name (Immanuel) describes the ontological identity of this child as Son of God. All the Gospel writers (Mt 3:3; Mk 1:3; Lk 3:4-6; Jn 1:23) read the expectation of Yahweh's return in Isaiah 40:3 as speaking about John preparing the way for Jesus, the divine Christ. John speaks of Isaiah seeing Jesus in his glory when the prophet saw Yahweh on the throne in Isaiah 6 (Jn 12:38-41).

Should we do what the apostles did when interpreting Isaiah? For some, such as Richard Longenecker, the answer is no. On the topic of emulating the apostles today he says,

> Where [apostolic] exegesis takes on a revelatory character, "No." Where, however, it treats the Old Testament in a more literal fashion, following

---

Romans, NovTSup 101 (Leiden: Brill, 2002); Rikki E. Watts, *Isaiah's New Exodus and Mark*, WUNT 88 (Tübingen: Mohr Siebeck, 1997).

[5]Although this *sensus plenior* is tethered to the literal/historical sense, it extends beyond it in light of the revelation made visible through Christ. Darrell Bock states, "This concept [sensus plenior] is not a bad one, provided it is clear what the human author said and whatever more God says through him are related in sense." Bock, "Use of the Old Testament in the New," in *Foundations for Biblical Interpretation*, ed. David S. Dockery, Kenneth A. Mathews, and Robert B. Sloan (Nashville: Broadman & Holman, 1994), 105. Richard Hays states, "Figural reading need not presume that the OT authors—or the characters they narrate—were conscious of predicting or anticipating Christ. Rather, the discernment of a figural correspondence is necessarily retrospective rather than prospective." Hays, *Reading Backwards: Figural Christology and the Fourfold Gospel Witness* (Waco, TX: Baylor University Press, 2014), 2.

the course of what we would speak of today as critical-historical-grammatical exegesis, "Yes." Our commitment as Christians is to the reproduction of the apostolic faith and doctrine, and only secondarily, if at all, to the apostolic exegetical conventions and practices.[6]

In other words, only in instances where the apostles followed the grammatical-historical approach may we emulate them, according to Longenecker.

A modernist worldview may be holding Longenecker and others captive here. The naturalistic worldview of modernity has backed Bible interpreters into a corner where human intent and divine intent are conflated and identical. For this reason, all one has to work with is the human authorial intention. What if God is able to communicate more through the words of human authors than they were aware of? This seems to be how the apostles viewed the world.[7] In fact, 1 Peter 1 describes the prophets as speaking about things they could not comprehend: "It was revealed to them that they were not serving themselves but you, when they spoke of the things that have now been told you by those who have preached the gospel to you by the Holy Spirit sent from heaven" (1 Pet 1:12). This brings us back to Longenecker's claim that we should "reproduc[e] the apostolic faith and doctrine" but not their hermeneutic. We must ask: Is it not the faith and doctrine of the apostles that led to their hermeneutic, to interpret the Old Testament in a way that led them to believe there was a fuller and christological sense?

Thus, although many evangelicals today, including colleagues and friends, often say, "The Bible wasn't written to us, but it was written for

---

[6]Richard Longenecker, *Studies in Hermeneutics, Christology, and Discipleship* (Sheffield: Sheffield Phoenix, 2006), 69. For Gordon Fee and Douglas Stuart, the answer is also no because "*Sensus plenior* (fuller meaning) is a function of inspiration, not illumination." Fee and Stuart, *How to Read the Bible for All Its Worth*, 4th ed. (Grand Rapids, MI: Zondervan), 209-10.

[7]Craig Carter makes a convincing case regarding the impact of worldview in *Interpreting Scripture with the Great Tradition: Recovering the Genius of Premodern Exegesis* (Grand Rapids, MI: Baker, 2018).

us," a biblical worldview suggests that the divine author was writing *to us*—we who would be living in the era of the New Covenant—all along!

The canon principle. Not only does a biblical worldview justify using an apostolic hermeneutic today, but the *canonical* status of Isaiah does as well. For one, the reason texts were preserved and shaped into a book stems from the conviction that God would continue to address future generations through these utterances.[8] Within Isaiah's vision, God acts and addresses audiences throughout the Assyrian, Babylonian, and Persian periods through to the new heaven and new earth (Is 65:17).[9] The book of Isaiah invites future audiences to read the words of God as God's self-revelation and address to his people until the end of the ages.

Moreover, Isaiah is part of a two-testament canon that bears witness to Jesus Christ. Isaiah's human author(s) did not know how the book would fit within a sixty-six-book, two-testament canon centered on Christ, but the divine author knew how this part, in all of its particularity, would figure into a larger whole and bear witness to a marvelous manifestation in God's work in Christ.[10] For this reason, Kevin Vanhoozer is right when he states that interpretation involves "grasping everything that God is doing in and with the various strata of biblical discourse."[11] Isaiah by necessity needs to be reread in view of God's

---

[8] Brevard Childs aptly states, "It is constitutive of the canon to seek to transmit the tradition in such a way as to prevent its being moored in the past." Childs, *Introduction to the Old Testament as Scripture* (Philadelphia: Fortress, 1979), 79.

[9] Andrew T. Abernethy, *The Book of Isaiah and God's Kingdom: A Thematic-Theological Approach*, NSBT 40 (Downers Grove, IL: IVP Academic, 2016), 9-10; Christopher R. Seitz, "Isaiah 1–66: Making Sense of the Whole," in *Reading and Preaching the Book of Isaiah*, ed. Christopher R. Seitz (Philadelphia: Fortress, 1988), 123; Odil Hannes Steck, *The Prophetic Books and Their Theological Witness*, trans. James D. Nogalski (St. Louis: Chalice, 2000), 20-65.

[10] Nicholas Wolterstorff, *Divine Discourse: Philosophical Reflections on the Claim That God Speaks* (Cambridge: Cambridge University Press, 1995), 202-5.

[11] Kevin Vanhoozer, "Imprisoned or Free? Text, Status, and Theological Interpretation in the Master/Slave Discourse of Philemon," in *Reading Scripture with the Church: Toward a Hermeneutic for Theological Interpretation* (Grand Rapids, MI: Baker, 2006), 71. The human author's intent is not discarded; instead, the human author's intent is extended and clarified as a fuller referent now comes into view. Vanhoozer helpfully introduces *referens plenior* as preferable to *sensus plenior*. Although the original sense remains, a passage's reference takes on a greater scope throughout the canon and in Christ. He explains, "A *theological* Old Testament theology sets out the divine intention, manifest in what we could call the plain canonical sense, which makes it

subsequent acts in the drama and in concert with the other books that bear witness to these acts.

The appeal to canon does not result in the New Testament imposing itself on the Old Testament because the New Testament is not required for the Old Testament to bear witness to Christ. How else could Paul command Timothy, before the formation of the New Testament, to continue in Israel's Scriptures, which "are able to make you wise for salvation through faith in Jesus Christ" (2 Tim 3:15)?[12] The Old Testament sounds forth, bearing its own discrete witness to Jesus, just as the New Testament bears its discrete witness. Now that we live in an era with the New Testament, the testaments mutually inform each other as they bear witness to a reality beyond the text, to a triune God involved throughout Israel's history and making all things new in Jesus Christ.

So, the canonical principle invites us to read Isaiah in view of its witness to God's ways in Christ and with the expectation that God will continue to speak through Isaiah to subsequent generations of God's people, Israel and the church.

Divine ontology and typology. A final reason for adopting an apostolic hermeneutic is the intersection between the nature of God (ontology) and typology. As Christopher Seitz argues, if the eternally existing, triune God makes himself known truly in Israel's life and Scriptures, then the Old Testament "served to preach Christ and show that his earthly life was in accordance with the purposes of God from all time, manifested in the literal and extended senses" of the Old Testament.[13] Continuity between God's revelations of himself in the life of Israel, in

---

clear that the ultimate referent of the Old Testament prophets—a function of what we might call the *extended* literal sense—was the promise of redemption and its fulfillment in Jesus Christ." Vanhoozer, "Toward a Theological Old Testament Theology? A Systematic Theologian's Take on Reading the Old Testament Theologically," in *Interpreting the Old Testament Theologically: Essays in Honor of Willem VanGemeren*, ed. Andrew T. Abernethy (Grand Rapids, MI: Zondervan, 2018), 305.

[12]This is central to Seitz's entire argument in *Character of Christian Scripture*.
[13]Seitz, *Character of Christian Scripture*, 18.

the manifestation of the Son in Jesus, and in the life of the church leads the church to receive the Old Testament as a genuine witness to the triune God, including the Son, ontologically and economically. Through God's providential involvement in Israel's history and the shaping of its Scriptures, God's "revelation given to Israel in concrete times and places says what it says meaningfully but also bespeaks realities subsequently to be disclosed. . . . This chiefly means accordances by type from the dispensations of Israel to the dispensation of the church."[14]

Due to my early training, I was allergic to the term *typology*. The human authors had no intention that the parting of the sea, the structure of the tabernacle, or Samson's role as deliverer would prefigure Christ, so how dare we abuse the text by viewing the exodus event, the tabernacle, or Samson as types of Christ and salvation? Gradually, I became more favorable toward typology, beginning with Michael Fishbane's *Biblical Interpretation in Ancient Israel*.[15] He displays how biblical writers drew on earlier traditions and reshaped them to speak about current and future realities. For instance, God's acts in creation serve as types by which Isaiah 65:17-25 expresses hope in a new creation. The exodus event becomes a type for conceptualizing a return from exile in Isaiah 11:16. This is not simply an "exegetical activity," according to Fishbane; instead, "it is . . . a religious activity of the first magnitude. . . . Typological exegesis is . . . a disclosure of the plentitude and mysterious workings of divine activity in history."[16] The foundation for typological exegesis is the correlation between God's past, present, and future actions.

At the heart of the apostolic hermeneutic is a recognition of correspondence between the God at work in Israel's life and spoken of in

---

[14]Christopher Seitz, *The Elder Testament: Canon, Theology, Trinity* (Waco, TX: Baylor University Press, 2018), 31.

[15]Michael Fishbane, *Biblical Interpretation in Ancient Israel* (Oxford: Clarendon, 1985). Along with Fishbane's work, Gerhard von Rad proved influential too. See von Rad, *Old Testament Theology*, trans. D. M. G. Stalker (Peabody, MA: Prince, 2005), 2:99-125.

[16]Fishbane, *Biblical Interpretation*, 352, 354-55.

Israel's Scriptures and the God at work in Jesus Christ and the church today. Whether we describe this interpretive strategy as typology, figural reading, or theological patterning, a Christian reading of Isaiah will read with an eye toward how what God reveals about himself through Isaiah providentially prefigures the triune God's work in Jesus and the church.

Summary. In our employment of the apostolic hermeneutic, grammatical-historical exegesis remains important but does not exhaust the interpretive process. If our worldview allows for a God to intend more than human authors knew, if Isaiah is part of a canon bearing witness to Christ, and if God's activity in Israel's life corresponds with and prefigures God's manifestation in Christ and his relationship with the church, then every passage in Isaiah—not simply those quoted in the New Testament—has the potential to speak of the Son and address the church. Jesus (Lk 24:27, 44-47) and Paul (Rom 15:4; 2 Tim 3:15-16) seem to agree.

READING ISAIAH 42:1-4

In order to clarify the differences in approaches across this volume, we have agreed to display our designated approach via reference to Isaiah 42:1-4 before moving on to other examples from Isaiah.

Isaiah 42:1-4 in its original context. The book of Isaiah presents exile in Babylon (Is 39:7; 43:14; 48:20) as the setting for interpreting Isaiah 42:1-4.[17] Israel is spread throughout Babylon, without a homeland, without a king, and without a temple. Israel wonders whether God's commitment to them has run its course (Is 40:27). Does Israel have a future with God? In Isaiah 41–42, God assures Israel of his unending commitment to them and offers a window into how he plans to use Israel among the nations. One of those plans is articulated in Isaiah 42:1-4:

---

[17]In a desire to affirm Isaiah's authorship, some attempt to interpret this part of the book in view of the Assyrian era. E.g., Gary V. Smith, *Isaiah 40–66*, NAC 15b (Nashville: Broadman & Holman, 2009).

> Behold my servant, whom I uphold,
>   My chosen, in whom my soul delights;
> I have put my Spirit upon him;
>   he will bring forth justice to the nations.
> He will not cry aloud or lift up his voice,
>   or make it heard in the street;
> a bruised reed he will not break,
>   and a faintly burning wick he will not quench;
>   he will faithfully bring forth justice.
> He will not grow faint or be discouraged
>   till he has established justice in the earth;
>   and the coastlands wait for his law.

In the first half of Isaiah 42:1, God speaks of his "servant." Prior to Isaiah 42:1-4, the term *servant* refers to Israel as a nation: "But you, Israel, my servant, Jacob, whom I have chosen.... you whom I took from the ends of the earth ... saying to you, 'You are my servant'" (Is 41:8-9). It is natural, then, to interpret the mention of God's servant in Isaiah 42:1 as the nation of Israel.[18] As in Isaiah 41, God reiterates how precious Israel, his servant, is to him here—the servant is his "chosen" (*bḥr*, root; Is 41:8; 42:1) and God "upholds" (*tmk*, Is 41:10; 42:1) him.

In the second half of Isaiah 42:1, the servant's mission comes into focus. As is the case with other agents in Isaiah, such as the future Davidic king (Is 11:2) and the anointed messenger (Is 61:1), God places his *Spirit* (*rûaḥ*) on his servant to empower him for a task. Like the Davidic king in Isaiah 9:6-7 and Isaiah 11:3-5, the primary task of the servant is to bring *justice* (*mišpāṭ*; Is 42:1, 3-4). Unlike the Davidic king, the servant will bring justice *to the nations*, not primarily to Israel.[19]

---

[18]Peter Wilcox and David Paton-Williams, "The Servant Songs in Deutero-Isaiah," *Journal for the Study of the Old Testament* 42 (1988): 86.

[19]This contrasts with Is 11:1-10, where the nations *come to* Jerusalem to receive justice from the king.

Isaiah 42:2-4 depicts the manner in which the servant will bring about *justice*. In Isaiah 42:2, the servant Israel will undertake the mission tenderly. Crying out (*ṣʿq*; see Deut 26:7; Ps 77:1; Jer 22:20), lifting up his voice (*nśʾ*; see Is 13:2; Jer 9:10), and making it heard (*šmʿ*; see Is 15:4) are expressions of conflict or grief, so this mission of justice will not be one where the servant is in dismay.[20] Instead of a time of terror, the servant's mission of justice will be gentle, as Isaiah 42:3 makes clear. The bruised reed and the faintly burning wick are metaphors for those among the nations who are suffering oppression. Isaiah 42:6-7 fleshes out how this servant will bring God's justice, reversing blindness and setting prisoners free, politically and spiritually.[21] The servant's justice—decreeing spiritual, physical, and political freedom—will be so gentle and tender that these wounded souls will not be crushed. The coastlands who await the servant's decrees of justice and instruction can rest assured that the servant will not grow weary in fulfilling this task (Is 42:4). Thus, Isaiah 42:1-4 aims to encourage disheartened, exiled Israel through a vision of how God intends to empower them to bring a gentle, redemptive justice to the nations.

As one continues reading in Isaiah, a problem surfaces with servant Israel.[22] God's servant is blind, unable to grasp God's ways (Is 42:18-25). How can a blind servant Israel (Is 42:18-19) restore sight to the blind (Is 42:7)? Since Israel is unable to undertake God's vision for servant Israel in Isaiah 42:1-4, a new conceptualization of God's servant develops in Isaiah 49–53. An individual servant will play a prophetic and priestly role in restoring corporate Israel and the nations to God through suffering (Is 49:1-7; 52:13–53:12). In so doing, the individual

---

[20]So John Goldingay and David Payne, *Isaiah 40–55*, ICC (London: T&T Clark, 2006), 1:216-17. Smith reads this as expressing that the servant will not be frustrated or exasperated (*Isaiah 40–66*, 162).

[21]On literal and spiritual interpretations of Is 42:6-7 and reflection on how Is 42:7 clarifies the nature of the servant's mission in Is 42:1-4, see Jan L. Koole, *Isaiah III*, vol. 1, *Isaiah 40–48*, Historical Commentary on the Old Testament (Kampen: Pharos, 1997), 233-35.

[22]For a more extensive treatment of the servant motif throughout Is 40–66, see Abernethy, *Book of Isaiah and God's Kingdom*, 141-60.

servant takes on the task of the corporate servant, Israel, and ultimately the suffering servant creates a community of servants (Is 54:17; 56:1-8; 65–66) who are empowered to fulfill God's mandate for corporate Israel in bringing justice to the world.

Matthew's use of Isaiah 42:1-4. Although Isaiah 42:1-4 can bear witness to Christ and God's ways with the church without recourse to the New Testament's usage, Matthew 12:15-21 offers an example of the apostolic use of this passage.

In Matthew 12, Jesus withdraws to a desolate area amid conflict with Pharisees over his willingness to heal and allow his disciples to pluck grain on the Sabbath. We are told that "many followed him, and he healed them all" (Mt 12:15). This leads Matthew to claim that Jesus fulfilled Isaiah 42:1-4. It seems most likely that Matthew had in mind the alignment between the manner of Jesus' mission and the servant when he quotes Isaiah 42; namely, the noncombative, gentle nature of Jesus' mission. By mentioning the healing ministry of Jesus, Matthew aligns with how Isaiah 42:1-4, when read in light of Isaiah 42:6-7, construes justice in terms of healing. What is more, even though Jesus is not healing "the nations" (Gentiles) in this immediate context, by quoting all of Isaiah 42:1-4 Matthew is drawing attention to a theme of Gentile inclusion that begins with the non-Israelite women in the genealogy and the magi and extends to the end of the book. Indeed, on another occasion when Jesus withdraws to the region of Sidon and Tyre, he brings healing to a Canaanite's daughter (Mt 15:21-28).[23] It is apparent, then, that Isaiah 42:1-4 aligns with Jesus' ministry in many ways—he is Spirit-empowered, has a humble manner of mission, and brings justice to the Gentiles. It would be a mistake, however, to

---

[23]For commentators who share a similar view, see David L. Turner, *Matthew*, Baker Exegetical Commentary on the New Testament (Grand Rapids, MI: Baker, 2008), 316-17; Craig Blomberg, *Matthew*, NAC 22 (Nashville: Broadman & Holman, 1992), 200-201; Craig A. Evans, *Matthew*, New Cambridge Bible Commentary (Cambridge: Cambridge University Press, 2012), 253-54; Craig Keener, *The Gospel of Matthew: A Socio-rhetorical Commentary* (Grand Rapids, MI: Eerdmans, 2009), 360.

suppose that Jesus' early ministry exhausts all of what Isaiah 42:1-4 expects; justice reaching a select few Gentiles is simply a precursor to an expectation of greater fulfillment. I will develop this shortly.

How does Matthew's application of Isaiah 42:1-4 to Jesus relate to an original understanding of the servant in Isaiah as corporate Israel? From the beginning of Matthew's Gospel, Jesus is portrayed in light of corporate Israel. Like God's son Israel, Jesus came up from Egypt (Mt 2:13-15). Like Israel, Jesus escapes the slaughter of firstborn children. Like Israel, Jesus experiences temptation in the wilderness (Mt 4:1-11). With Jesus' identity intertwined with Israel's, he embodies corporate Israel's task as God's servant in Isaiah 42:1-4 while also serving as the individual suffering servant later in the Gospel.

Thus, in Matthew's eyes, the servant's vocation of gently bringing justice to the hurting across the globe (Is 42:1-4) finds fulfillment in Jesus' life and ministry. Here in the flesh is a God who undertakes the servant's task of bringing justice gently in the form of healing (see Is 42:7).

More fulfillment of Isaiah 42:1-4 beyond Matthew's quotation. There are *many* other ways Isaiah 42:1-4 bears witness to Christ and God's ways with the church beyond Matthew 12. For instance, to what extent should Isaiah 42:1-4 serve as a corporate prophecy about the church too? Paul understood his own individual mission in light of another Servant Song (see Acts 13:47, quoting Is 49:6). Peter could apply the suffering servant passage as a vision for the life of the suffering church (1 Pet 2:20-23; quoting from Is 53:4, 6-7, 9).[24] Following this pattern, one could take Matthew 28:18-20 as a starting point for appropriating the vision of Isaiah 42:1-4. Jesus, the one who fulfills Isaiah 42:1-4, commissions his disciples to go to all nations through his empowered presence (Mt 28:18-20). As he is the servant-Lord who gently brought justice to the nations by the Spirit, the life and mission

---

[24]See John Goldingay, "Servant of Yahweh," in *Dictionary of the Old Testament Prophets*, ed. Mark J. Boda and J. Gordon McConville (Downers Grove, IL: IVP Academic, 2012), 702-6, for a discussion of how the servant passages apply to various groups (Israel, church, Christ) in the NT.

of Jesus is to live on in his disciples. In this way, just as the book of Isaiah anticipates a suffering servant taking on the mantle of corporate Israel and passing it along to a community of servants, so the church will take on the role of the servant in bringing gentle justice through the power of the Spirit across the globe. The church does not need the New Testament to verify that Isaiah 42:1-4 informs the mission of the church; instead, it bears witness to a God who aims to work through an individual servant and community of servants to bring his healing justice gently across the globe.

All of Isaiah as Christian Scripture

We should not limit how Isaiah bears witness to Jesus to occasions where we find quotations, allusions, or echoes in the New Testament. If, as I have argued above, there is correspondence between the God Isaiah bears witness to and the God the New Testament authors bear witness to, then we have a basis for allowing the Old Testament and the New Testament to mutually inform each other in deciphering their discrete witnesses to Christ and the life of the church. Below, my primary interest is to probe how texts in Isaiah—some cited in the New Testament and others not—might be read in the footsteps of the apostles in light of Christ and as a word for the church.

Messianic texts. There are four passages in Isaiah that speak of a future royal king (Is 9:1-7; 11:1-5; 16:5; 32:1). Within the context of Isaiah, these passages have in common the hope for a Davidic king who would promote justice and righteousness within society.[25] During a time when rulers within Judah were unjust, the hope for a just Davidic king was a radical reversal of Judah's experience. Additionally, in light of the placement of these passages in the book, the initial horizon of hope is that such a king would arise after Assyria—and later Babylon—brought destruction to Judah. This king would arise like a shoot from a stump

---

[25]See also Hugh G. M. Williamson, *Variations on a Theme: King, Messiah and Servant in the Book of Isaiah* (Carlisle: Paternoster, 1998); Abernethy, *Book of Isaiah and God's Kingdom*, 125-35.

(Is 11:1), a king emerging out of Israel's ashes. In what ways do these passages bear witness to Christ and God's ways with the church?

If we look to quotations of these passages in the New Testament for guidance, it is only Isaiah 9:1-2 that is quoted (Mt 4:15-16). Even if all of Isaiah 9:1-7 is meant to be activated in the mind of listeners through the quotation of these few verses in Matthew 4, its use in Matthew 4 does not exhaust all of what Isaiah 9:1-7 anticipates. By beginning his ministry in Galilee, Jesus certainly aligns with Isaiah 9:1-2's witness that God would bring light to a region often trampled and traversed by the Gentiles. Yet, Isaiah 9:3-5 goes on to speak of the ensuing joy that results from warfare being put to an end. In Matthew's Gospel, and the entire New Testament, for that matter, there is no fulfillment of this promise. Warfare, political and spiritual, continues even after the light of the kingdom of God comes through Jesus in the Galilee region. Furthermore, Isaiah 9:6-7 looks for a king who would bear the titles "Wonderful Counselor, Mighty God, Everlasting Father, Prince of Peace." Nowhere in the New Testament are these titles explicitly quoted in application to Jesus, nor do we see a fulfillment of what Isaiah 9:7 anticipates in physical terms—rule from a throne of justice and righteousness—yet, as I develop below, there is strong reason to see these verses as finding fulfillment in Jesus even if they are not quoted in the New Testament.

Even if much of Isaiah 9:3-7 finds neither quotation nor exhaustive fulfillment in the New Testament, Isaiah 9:3-7 does indeed teach a great deal about Jesus and God's ways with the church. As Jesus is a king from the line of David, we declare that Jesus is indeed the king hoped for in Isaiah 9:3-7. This passage points to a God who will bring an end to warfare and establish justice and righteousness. As we confess that Jesus will come again "to judge the living and the dead," Isaiah 9:3-7 wonderfully teaches us about the hope awaiting us when Jesus comes again. Even though it is not essential that the New Testament quote this or teach us this about Jesus, it should not be surprising that the New Testament's witness to Jesus correlates with this. Whether in his earthly life where he advocates for social justice (e.g., Mt 23:23), or when riding on his white horse judging in righteousness (Rev 19:11), or when sitting on the throne (Rev 20:12), Jesus will indeed end all war and establish righteousness across the globe. What may have initially been understood as a hope for a future Davidic king who would establish justice in an era of peace bears witness to a grander fulfillment to come in Jesus Christ's second coming.

Although Christ's second coming will involve the ultimate fulfillment of this, the era of the church is a time where the mission of the Son continues. Isaiah 9:1-7 serves as a word for the ethics of the church, expressing that our God and king desires to bring about political peace and establish justice in the world by his Spirit, even as we are awaiting its fulfillment. The church can join in this mission of bringing justice to the world through the power of the Spirit.

A Christian reading of Isaiah would interpret the other messianic passages (Is 11:1-5; 16:5; 32:1) in a similar manner to Isaiah 9:1-7, namely, aiming to recover what these passages are genuinely bearing witness to and pondering how this relates to the triune God evident in Christ's life, the life of the church, and the second coming.

Isaiah's gospel. In the book of Isaiah, the "good news" finds its clearest expression in Isaiah 40:9 and Isaiah 52:7. The herald declares to the cities of Judah, "Behold your God!" (Is 40:9). The blessed feet that bring the message of good news announce, "Your God reigns" (Is 52:7). The watchmen become full of joy when "they see the return of the Lord to Zion" (Is 52:8). During an era when it seems like God had abandoned Judah, the gospel of Isaiah is that God is coming to rule in Zion and work a remarkable salvation for Zion before the eyes of all nations.

Although these passages were originally read as a hope of God's return when Israel would return from exile, it becomes clear in Israel's life (as described in Ezra–Nehemiah, Haggai, and Zechariah) that the coming of God is further beyond the horizon than expected. The Gospels declare that God indeed has come in the person of Jesus and even quote Isaiah 40:3 in this respect (Mk 1:3). But nowhere do they quote from Isaiah 40:9 or the last part of Isaiah 52:7.[26] Even if these verses are called to mind in the Gospels or Romans 10 by quoting texts near them, the appropriation of these verses is not exhausted.[27] The church, often in shambles like Zion, is called in Isaiah 40:9 to muster up its courage and declare to the desolate the great news that God has come and will come again in Christ. The church can see in Isaiah 52:7 the great news that the kingdom of God has come in Christ—Your God reigns!—yet, this is an unfulfilled hope that God will return in an even more radical fashion, where the entire world will see the salvation of God. These texts bear witness to a God who will come for Zion, and this figurally bears witness to God coming in Christ, reigning in the life of the church, and coming again. This indeed is great news.

Transcendence and imminence. My favorite verse in Isaiah is Isaiah 57:15:

> For thus says the One who is high and lifted up,
>   Who inhabits eternity, whose name is Holy:
> "I dwell in the high and holy place,
>   And also with him who is of a contrite and lowly spirit,
> to revive the spirit of the lowly,
>   and to revive the heart of the contrite."

This passage addresses a context in the aftermath of God's judgment. Although God's anger has been the dominant tune in Israel's recent memory due to the Babylonian conquest, God plans to heal Israel of their backsliding and bring comfort to those who are mourning Zion's

---

[26] See Rom 10:15, where the first part is quoted.
[27] See Rikki E. Watts, "Mark," in *Commentary on the New Testament Use of the Old Testament*, ed. G. K. Beale and D. A. Carson (Grand Rapids, MI: Baker, 2007), 113-14.

demise (Is 57:16-18). There is no direct quotation or allusion to this passage throughout the New Testament. Does this mean that we have no business asking what this passage teaches us about Christ's life, the church, and the second coming? No. This passage speaks of the striking intersection between God's holy transcendence and his condescension to abide among the broken to bring them renewal. Here are just some of the directions a Christian reading might develop this passage: (1) the wonder of the incarnation, (2) Christ's life among the outcasts in his earthly life, (3) Christ's life among his lowly church today by the Spirit, and (4) Christ coming again as the dwelling place of God. These appropriations of the passage align with the original communicative intent, yet they also bear in mind what this verse is teaching about the eternally existing triune God and how this finds resonance with Christ's life, the church, and his second coming.

Oracles against the nations. In Luke's Gospel, Jesus says regarding those who would not embrace his message: "And you, Capernaum, will you be exalted to heaven? You shall be brought down to Hades" (Lk 10:15). This is a compiled quotation from Isaiah 14, where arrogant Babylon receives news of a forthcoming downfall (Is 14:13-15). Of course, Isaiah 13–14 is not predicting Capernaum's destiny, but Jesus draws a correspondence between God's ways with Babylon and how God would continue to act with subsequent proud entities. Can we do what Jesus did and appropriate oracles against the nations such as this toward those other than Babylon and Capernaum?

A feature of the book of Isaiah's strategy is to coordinate God's ways with Israel, the nations, and eschatological time. As others have observed, Israel (Is 2; 28), Babylon (Is 13–14), Tyre (Is 23), and an unnamed proud city (Is 26) will all experience judgment from God due to pride.[28] By decreeing judgment due to pride for different nations

---

[28]G. R. Hamborg, "Reasons for Judgment in the Oracles Against the Nations of the Prophet Isaiah," *VT* 31 (1981): 156; Christopher Seitz, *Isaiah 1–39*, Interpretation (Louisville, KY: John Knox, 1993), 116-19.

across many eras, the canonical form of the book of Isaiah invites a reader to appropriate its message to future times because God acts in similar ways throughout time. If this is correct, then the opportunity is open for Christian readers to ask how this corresponds with God's future activity in Christ and the church and the world today. Jesus is an antitype to Babylon and all that is proud; he descends to hell in order to exalt the lowly (see Is 25–26) in his first coming. Jesus warns those who are too proud to believe in him that a great judgment is coming—just as Babylon was warned. The church too can warn proud persons, nations, and institutions that their secure status will not last forever. God in Christ is overturning the powers of this world through a crucified king, and this will be fully realized when Christ comes again. I do not need the New Testament to quote from these specific passages from Isaiah to confidently consider how they bear witness to a God who counters the proud. There is continuity between the nature of the triune God from Old Testament times, in Christ's life, in the life of the church, and to the end, and the Scriptures were preparing in advance for the culmination of God's revelation in Christ.

These examples from messianic texts, hopes in the coming of God, declarations of transcendence and immanence, and the oracles against the nations do not exhaust the manifold ways that God by the Spirit can bear witness to Christ's comings and the life of the church. Instead, they aim to illustrate the sorts of ways one might read passages not cited in the New Testament as Christian Scripture.

Conclusion

By no means have I exhausted how one might read Isaiah in the footsteps of the apostles. Two characteristics are important in this endeavor: humility and openness. Humility recognizes that we are unable to satisfactorily answer how *all* of Isaiah will find fulfillment in God's mysterious outworking of his drama. Chief among these questions is how the future of Israel will intersect with God's continued faithfulness to the testimony of Scripture. For this reason, I cannot dismiss what Paul Wegner, Gary Yates, and John Hilber have to say in this volume. Openness reminds us that we must be open to God's freedom in fulfilling these promises.

While operating with humility and openness, this chapter argues that the church can and should read Isaiah as the apostles did. This involves two steps: (1) discerning what the passages intend to accomplish in their original context, including what they aim to testify about God and his ways in the world; and (2) pondering how the passage's witness to God corresponds with the triune God's work in Christ, the life of the church, and the second coming. At the heart of the apostolic hermeneutic is a recognition that God's witness to himself in the Old Testament corresponds with the manifestation of God in Jesus. Therefore, the Old Testament's witness can faithfully make us wise unto salvation through Jesus Christ. Far from being a dismissal of the Old Testament by imposing the New Testament on it, the apostolic approach can set the Old Testament free to bear its own discrete witness to Christ. *All* of Isaiah is indeed and should be read as Christian Scripture, as the apostles would have.

4

THE HISTORY OF INTERPRETING ISAIAH AS CHRISTIAN SCRIPTURE

A Selection

Mark S. Gignilliat

When Brevard Childs set out to write a commentary on Isaiah, his stated intentions were clear. "In my judgment, what is needed is a fresh interpretive model that does not get lost in methodological debates, and that proves to be illuminating in rendering a rich and coherent interpretation of the text as sacred scripture of both church and synagogue."[1] Commentaries of the historical-critical stripe were aplenty, and the value of a Hans Wildberger or John Oswalt commentary on Isaiah was not devalued in Childs's estimation. These

---

[1]Brevard S. Childs, *Isaiah*, OTL (Louisville, KY: Westminster John Knox, 2001), xi.

commentaries—along with others such as those of Willem Beuken, Jan Koole, and John Watts, and Hugh Williamson's recent International Critical Commentary work—are notable for their ability to engage the biblical text in light of various exegetical approaches and conclusions. They press for new or clearer ways to understand Isaiah's textual history, literary features, and historical background. What Childs believed might be lost in the trees of these exegetical and methodological explorations is the prophetic book itself and, perhaps most importantly for Childs, the proper social location for textual reception, namely, the synagogue and the church.

For Childs, the commitment to Isaiah's canonical form and shape coincides with his commitment to Scripture's nature, to a confession regarding Scripture's privileged role among believing communities as a canonical authority and living witness. Admittedly, Childs's confessional commitments and his critical training did not always sit comfortably next to each other in the exegetical boxcar. I think it is fair enough to say that tensions exist in Childs's work that may not have been tensions in his own mind but remain so for those who try to learn from him.

Nevertheless, Childs's formal commitment to a Reformation Scripture principle of some kind yielded a high valuation of the church's interpretive tradition for modern readers. Childs remained allergic to readings of the history of interpretation that tended to highlight the social or cultural forces of this history at the expense of recognizing, in his terms, "the effect of the coercion of the text itself in faithfully shaping the life of the church." This is not to say that social and cultural forces were not at work in this history of reception. But Childs believed if this social-historical bell rang more loudly than Scripture's canonical bell, then the focus would be on a history of misreading rather than one of faithful practice. Why would this be so? Because premodern interpreters engaged Scripture exegetically and theologically. Childs mentions John

Chrysostom, Augustine, Thomas Aquinas, Martin Luther, and John Calvin. These figures from the halls of the church's historical past "remain an enduring guide for truthfully hearing the evangelical witness of Isaiah in a manner seldom encountered since the Enlightenment."[2]

Writing a commentary is hard work, and seeking to hold together critical issues, scholarly opinion, the history of interpretation, and the text's theological witness in a single commentary is a challenging task and nigh impossible, especially when the stated exegetical goal is to keep the prophetic book intact before readers in the church and synagogue. Childs senses the commentary's shortcomings (necessary shortcomings, I should add, given the strictures of the Old Testament Library series) when he later admits: "After the commentary had been completed, I was painfully aware that many of the central theological and hermeneutical questions in which I was most interested had not been adequately addressed."[3] When all was said and done, Childs wrote a second volume titled *The Struggle to Understand Isaiah as Christian Scripture*. This volume appeared three years after the commentary and emerged as an effort to correct what he thought was still lacking in the final form of his commentary.

When speaking of the history of interpretation of Isaiah and of the Bible at large, Childs deploys two of his favorite terms to describe the phenomenon: *coercion* and *pressure*. Readers find these lexemes in the preface and introduction of his Isaiah commentary and throughout *The Struggle to Understand Isaiah as Christian Scripture*. *Coercion* and *pressure* are helpful because Childs believed that Scripture's nature and role—our doctrinal claims and descriptions of Scripture—were in "concord" with the Bible's "actual effects" on the church throughout its history.[4] Again, Childs relays his misgivings about reading the history

---

[2]Childs, *Isaiah*, 5.
[3]Brevard S. Childs, *The Struggle to Understand Isaiah as Christian Scripture* (Grand Rapids, MI: Eerdmans, 2004).
[4]Childs, *Struggle to Understand*, ix.

of interpretation as a "map of misreading": the kind of exercise where a hermeneutics course might hand out Origen's allegorical reading of the Noah narratives to show how silly his reading is, quickly dismissing the Alexandrian from the exegetical court. Childs believes such an approach is playing Mozart's "A Little Night Music" in minor key: something is familiar but not quite right.

Childs's chief concern with his history is to demonstrate what he calls a "family resemblance" in the Christian interpretive tradition. Childs borrows the term *family resemblance* from Hans Frei, who in turn borrowed the term from Ludwig Wittgenstein. The so-called family resemblance Childs speaks of is an effort to quantify the theological and interpretive instincts of the broad stream of Christian interpretation, taking into account the significant differences and divergences in exegetical outcome within this tradition. Faithful Christian practice demands the engagement of Scripture in each and every generation. It will not do as a faithful practice to regurgitate Luther or Calvin's reading of a biblical text without taking into account our moment in providential time and the particular challenges attendant to it. So, for Childs, the history of interpretation is not a project of atavistic retrieval but an effort to gain a bead on a broad set of interpretive instincts that create space for the real work of Christian theology and practice: the reading and hearing of Christian Scripture.

After Childs walks readers through a fascinating gallery of biblical reception and interpretation, beginning with the Septuagint and moving through figures such as Irenaeus, Justin Martyr, Aquinas, Luther, and Calvin through the modern period, he concludes with the following nodal points of this quest for an interpretive family resemblance.

1. Scripture's authority[5]
2. The organic relation between the literal and figural sense

---

[5] These seven points are my paraphrase of Childs's "Characteristic Features of the Christian Exegetical Tradition" in *Struggle to Understand,* 300-323.

3. The Christian Bible is composed of two testaments
4. Scriptural authorship is divine and human in origin
5. The whole of the Christian Bible has God's revelation in Christ as its subject matter
6. The dialectical nature of history
7. The final form's privilege when attending to Scripture's historical sense

All of these points are worth unpacking, but I mention them and offer this whole reflection on Childs's struggle to make sense of Isaiah in service of a simple point. The Christian interpretive tradition reads Scripture in accord with its canonical and privileged status, in accord with its sacred status as God's direct speech into Christ's church. Moreover, this privileged status as the direct speech of God for the sake of ordering the church's beliefs and prayers always shapes our attendance to the text's literal sense. If so, this understanding necessitates a definition of Scripture's literal sense that reaches beyond a limited historical account: for example, the literal sense is what it meant back then and there. However one defines Scripture's literal sense, this definition must include Scripture's nature and theological subject matter. Put precisely, Scripture's verbal character and its theological subject matter resist dissolution. As diverse as the church's actual exegetical conclusions may have been among its various and sundry constituents, Childs does well to remind us of this basic interpretive instinct or family resemblance.

Moving from the theoretical to the exegetical, I will briefly engage Isaiah 12 and Isaiah 42 and their history of interpretation. The examples on offer are nothing near a comprehensive view. That is not my intention, but these limited examples may provide a window into the way this family resemblance works itself out with two Isaianic texts. The current volume focuses on Isaiah 42, the first of the so-called Servant

Songs. I have added Isaiah 12 because it may prove helpful in terms of theological exegesis of a text not found in the New Testament. Isaiah 42 remains rich and fruitful as a Christian witness, yet its interpretive fruits hang a bit lower to the ground.

ISAIAH 12 AND ISAIAH 42: A BRIEF EXAMPLE FROM THE HISTORY OF INTERPRETATION

Isaianic studies for over a century now highlight the importance of the book's diachronic history for the sake of textual sense-making. Lurking in the shadows of these historicist instincts is the concern for authorial intentionality. For texts to make sense and refer to something, the reconstruction of the text's historical moment, immediate concerns, and original audience remains of signal interpretive importance. Moreover, Isaiah scholarship of the critical stripe has highly problematized the concern for authorial intentionality because books such as Isaiah are the product of an elongated coming to be that extends beyond the historical scope of the book's prophetic persona. These are seminary 101 kinds of questions, but they remain a challenge for faithful exegetical practices. Where, for example, do we place Isaiah 12 and Isaiah 42 in Israel's history? These questions betray simple answers.

Isaiah 12: In that day. Isaiah 12 is case in point of these interpretive challenges because this First Isaiah chapter shares too much in common with Second Isaiah's frame of reference, linguistic arsenal, and hopeful outlook. Wildberger's 1980 German commentary, translated into English in 1991, states with some confidence, "Scholars are almost unanimous in their assessment that chap. 12 does not come from Isaiah."[6] Now, as an interesting aside, J. J. Roberts's newish Hermeneia commentary on Isaiah 12 claims there is no reason to suppose Isaiah 12 could not stem from the eighth-century prophet, though he leans

---

[6]Hans Wildberger, *Isaiah 1–12: A Commentary*, trans. T. H. Trapp, CC (Minneapolis: Fortress, 1991), 502.

toward a later date. But all of this is somewhat beside the point, as interesting as the presenting issues are, because wherever one lands on the authorship question of Isaiah 12, the interpretive instinct remains clear: sorting out the historical location of Isaiah 12 is requisite on some level for coming to interpretive conclusions about its claims and intent, even if the historical location stems from a later redactional moment.

None of this comes as a surprise for anyone who has spent ten minutes in a modern Isaiah commentary. Yet it presses on Christian readers an exegetical approach whose governing instincts stem from later modernity's penchant for textual analysis as historical retrieval, with the search for intent shaped and to some degree determined by these concerns. I have to believe in some measure that these instincts, often left unexamined—Karl Barth's clarion call for the historical critic to be more critical comes to mind—make a commentary from the premodern era feel strange in our hands and leave us with some cognitive dissonance on what we are doing when we read Scripture, even as a scholarly exercise. The concern for intentionality is a feature of the premodern period, and a certain sensitivity to history is as well—more on this later—but both history and intentionality are shaped by the interpreter's commitment to divine agency as the primary author of Scripture's broad sweep. Thus, Aquinas can claim that Scripture is to be read in accord with the author's intention, quickly clarifying the identity of Scripture's author, namely, God. I will engage three premodern interpreters and their reading of Isaiah 12 in order to demonstrate the value of these premodern interpretive instincts. I will avoid ranging into the details of their reading and opt for a synthesis of their approach and conclusions.

Cyril of Alexandria attends to the *gramma* of the text and shows a concern for its *historia*. Cyril's knowledge of the historical events of the eighth to sixth century BC is limited. Nevertheless, the *historia* or *historikon* of Scripture relates to its spiritual interpretation. Yet, for

Cyril, the historical events of Scripture are simply the Scripture's narrative retold, the circumstances from which the prophetic material arose. These circumstances do not hem in the text's referential character. The ease with which Cyril reads Isaiah in christological terms is of signal interest because Cyril's reading of the *gramma* works within the constraints of Scripture's overarching subject matter. Almost without remainder, the mighty deeds of God expressed in judgment and redemption pertain to the gospel of Jesus Christ. Cyril reads figure and fulfillment within a single interpretive frame.

In his comments on Isaiah 12:1-2, for example, the context of praise and thanksgiving is the nations who "had been saved through faith in Christ and had come to knowledge of the truth." "Drawing water from the springs of salvation" is a phrase that deploys the metaphor of water as the source of salvation. Not surprisingly, Cyril reads the metaphor in light of its figural fulfillment: "So by *water* he refers to God's life-giving message, and by *springs* to the holy apostles and evangelists, to whom would be added as well the holy prophets themselves, and by *salvation* he refers to Christ." The inhabitants of Zion are those who do not let the Savior's glory go unnoticed before everyone. Their identity is the "members of churches who have a steady faith." Moreover, the Holy One of Israel dwelling in their midst is the incarnate Savior who has "become man," yet we know his nature by his deeds as one who "has been exalted in a manner befitting God."[7]

For Martin Luther (*Lectures 1527–28*), Isaiah 12 sits comfortably and necessarily in the context of the gospel of Jesus Christ. Isaiah 12 attests the centrality of the sacrifice of praise as that which in time would be the New Testament's singular sacrificial ritual: the Eucharist. He states, "The prophet foresaw this future preaching and confession of the Gospel, which did not take place in the Old Testament." Luther is sensitive to

---

[7]Cyril of Alexandria, *Commentary on Isaiah*, vol. 1, *Chapters 1-14*, trans. R. C. Hill (Brookline, MA: Holy Cross Orthodox Press, 2008), 274, 276, 278.

the temporal perspective of Isaiah's own plain sense, placing these promises of praise in a future moment: *in that day*. "To say" in Isaiah 12:1 is, for Luther, coterminous with "to confess." What is the substance of a Christian's future confession? He answers, "A Christian confesses that he was condemned and lost and that he has received from Christ everything that belongs to salvation and righteousness; all his own merits he considers nothing." In brief, the whole of Isaiah's salvation context within Luther's reading is the gospel of Jesus Christ. Postexilic restoration to the land could not be further from Luther's mind, and, according to Luther, from Isaiah's canonical mind either. To speak of God as one's strength and song, to identify God as "my savior," leads to one theological location for Luther: "I have no one to sing and chant about but Christ, in whom alone I have everything."[8]

Similarly to Cyril, Luther reads the metaphors of water and springs in light of John 7:38, linking the metaphor here in Isaiah with its association in John 7, the Holy Spirit. In an expected Reformational move, Luther links the Holy Spirit with the Word of God: "The comfort of the Holy Spirit through the Word of God is then most sweet."[9] Where Christ's Spirit is, so too goes his Word. The wells of salvation, for Luther, are the gospel, full stop.

John Calvin also reads Isaiah 12 as a word addressed directly to Christ's church whose current moment *is* Isaiah's promised future. Calvin's close reading of the Hebrew text, along with its verbal forms, never ceases to impress given his moment in time. The future-tense verbs of Isaiah 12:1, following the concessive *kî* clause, speak to the length of God's compassion despite the momentary infliction of his chastisement. The promises of God's mercy cast a long shadow, while his displeasure recedes quickly into the past. Like Luther, Calvin reads Isaiah 12 as a gospel word that comforts the afflicted and gives shape

---

[8] Martin Luther, "Lectures on Isaiah: Chapters 1–39," *LW* 16:128-29.
[9] Luther, "Lectures on Isaiah: Chapters 1–39," 130.

and substance to the assurance of the redeemed. Calvin explains, "When we have been relieved from distresses, let us call to remembrance that our punishment is ended, not because we have paid to the justice to God what we had deserved, but because through his fatherly love he spares our weaknesses."[10]

How and why can a believer "trust in him and not be afraid?" Calvin answers, "When we are fully convinced that salvation is laid up for us in God, this is a solid foundation of full confidence, and the best remedy for allaying fears."[11] Confidence rests on faith. Faith perceives that salvation is "laid up for us in God." Isaiah's ancient words, whose genesis is the historical moment of Israel's time before the advent of Jesus Christ, speak of and participate in realities not yet taking place in time.

Calvin attends closely to the metaphor of water within Isaiah 12's literal sense. Water is that which is necessary to life, and everything that is necessary to life flows from the fountain of God's mercy. That fountain, for Calvin, is Christ: "in whom all God's benefits are imparted to us." For Calvin, Isaiah 12 "is not limited to a short period, but, on the contrary, extends to the whole of Christ's reign."[12]

Isaiah 42: A meek and faithful servant. As mentioned in the introduction, Isaiah 42:1-4 offers its interpretive fruits more accessibly. Few Christians around the world whose weekly worship entails lectionary readings of some kind will fail to associate Isaiah 42 with Epiphany and the incarnation of our Lord Jesus Christ. This interpretive sensibility is manifest throughout the church's long and broad interpretive stream. Even a brief glance at Robert Wilken's editorial work in *The Church's Bible: Isaiah* attests to a basic, even simple, interpretive phenomenon.[13] Isaiah 42 speaks immediately about the nature of Jesus' humanity as

---

[10]John Calvin, *Commentary on the Book of the Prophet Isaiah: Calvin's Commentaries Volume VII*, trans. W. Pringle (Grand Rapids, MI: Baker, 2005), 398-99.
[11]Calvin, *Commentary on the Book*, 398.
[12]Calvin, *Commentary on the Book*, 402-3.
[13]Robert Louis Wilken, ed., *The Church's Bible: Isaiah Interpreted by Early Christians and Medieval Commentaries* (Grand Rapids, MI: Eerdmans, 2007).

God's agent of reconciliation. From the halls of interpretive history, Jerome, Eusebius of Caesarea, Cyril of Alexandria, Augustine of Hippo, Irenaeus of Lyon, Ambrose of Milan, Origen of Alexandria, Gregory of Nyssa, and Thomas Aquinas all concur, as would any premodern reader of Isaiah 42. Various shades of interpretive contrasts occur here or there, but the immediacy of the Isaianic referent in the person and work of Jesus Christ remains standard fare.

Luther's commentary follows in this tradition. In his own inimitable way, Luther presses into the language of Isaiah 42 in its relation to the person and work of Jesus Christ. Naturally, the servant refers to Jesus Christ, and the description of Jesus in these verses provides for Luther a strong footing for real knowledge. Over against the pope and the Enthusiasts who speak of Christ in ways untethered from Scripture, Luther presses the Scriptures themselves because they are "the most reliable voice." Isaiah's call to *behold* and its description of the servant as one upheld and the object of the Father's delight elicit in a Christian an overwhelming confidence and consolation in Jesus Christ. Luther argues, "Alongside Him all our wisdom and power and treasure are nothing in the sight of God. Not only does He say that He will provide a teacher of truth who will gather us, but He also says that He will grant the most delightful teaching."[14]

Luther, and Calvin with him, lays particular claim to the description of Jesus as "a bruised reed he will not break, and a smoldering wick he will not snuff out" (Is 42:3 NIV). For Luther, Isaiah paints a portrait of Christ in all his tenderness and mercy. Luther cites approvingly Gregory the Great's claim that "true righteousness" elicits "compassion," while "false" righteousness brings "condemnation." The falsely righteous "have a sour outlook on life, as if they were possessed. There is no serenity, there is a belch of smoke from hell, and they find favor with no one. But here in Christ you see the gentlest and most agreeable

---

[14]Martin Luther, "Lectures on Isaiah 40–66," *LW* 17:61-62.

appearance." Christ meets the believer, especially those tormented by Satan, with patience and sweetness.[15]

Likewise, Calvin reads Isaiah 42:1-4 in immediate relation to Jesus Christ. Describing Jesus as the servant highlights his assumption of flesh in the incarnation. This text speaks to the whole person of Jesus Christ, "yet it belongs to human nature."[16] Calvin reads Isaiah 42:1-4 in canonical association with Philippians 2:6. The incarnation is necessary in both texts, Isaiah and Philippians, for the eternal Son of God to learn obedience and reconcile a lost world. Isaiah speaks to the character of Christ's incarnation as a gentle servant.

Marilynne Robinson has done much to dispel some of the angular caricatures of Calvin and his Puritan heirs.[17] Far from lifeless killjoys, Calvin and his heirs embraced the joys of life and family. Still, as Bruce Gordon demonstrates in his biography, Calvin could be a difficult pill to swallow. His own austerity, however, offers no mirror in his portrayal of Jesus Christ as a gentle and caring shepherd. His comments on Isaiah 42 highlight the meekness of Christ's character. For those who struggle in their faith, "tottering" and "stumbling" along, Christ "does not at once cast them off as utterly useless, but bears long, till he makes them stronger and more steadfast."[18]

For Calvin, the gentle character of Jesus' ministry suggests a similar pattern of ministry for "ministers of the gospel." They are to "support the weak" and "gently lead them in the way, so as not to extinguish in them the feeblest sparks of piety, but, on the contrary, to kindle them with all their might." Yet, as the following phrase suggests, the servant brings forth justice. For "bruised reeds" and "smoking wicks" the Savior meets them in gentleness and compassion. For the obstinate and rebellious, they meet the servant in a different form. Calvin deploys the

---

[15]Luther, "Lectures on Isaiah 40–66," 62, 64-65.
[16]Calvin, *Commentary on the Book*, 284.
[17]Marilynne Robinson, "Puritans and Prigs," in *The Death of Adam: Essays on Modern Thought* (New York: Picador, 2005), 150-73.
[18]Bruce Gordon, *Calvin* (New Haven, CT: Yale University Press, 2009), 288.

metaphor of a hammer to describe the severity of Christ's judgment for the recalcitrant.[19]

The prophet describes the servant as one who will not "grow faint or be discouraged till he has established justice in the earth" (Is 42:4). Calvin draws this description into the overall frame of the servant's meekness. Meekness, for Calvin, does not turn aside to "excessive indulgence." In other words, the meek do not shy away from their calling, Calvin explains: "Many persons wish to profit by the name of gentleness, so as to gain the applause and esteem of the world, but at the same time betray truth in a base and shameful manner." Calvin extends this description of Christ's ministry to "the whole course of the gospel."[20] As Christ's gentleness addresses Christian ministers, so too does his fortitude speak to a Christian's call to persevere to the very end.

These selected readings of Isaiah 42:1-4 reveal the immediacy of the Old Testament text to describe the person and work of Jesus Christ. The readings are not fussy, marked by the interpretive white noise of jumping from the historical back there to the theological here and now. Rather, the prophetic text and its language witness to the person and work of Jesus Christ in its textual and linguistic givenness. Scripture's subject matter demands it, and the text's literal sense cannot be sequestered from its theological subject matter. Otherwise, readers are now reading something other than Holy Scripture. Christ's presence in the text as its subject and object demands that these words be read in association with him.[21]

Conclusion

I have a colleague who talks about the providence of walking the library stacks. Preparing for this chapter, I had such a moment, pulling off the

---

[19]Gordon, *Calvin*, 288-89.
[20]Gordon, *Calvin*, 290-91.
[21]For a robust, rigorous, and enlightening account of Scripture's figural/theological sense-making, see Ephraim Radner, *Time and the Word: Figural Reading of the Christian Scriptures* (Grand Rapids, MI: Eerdmans, 2016).

shelf of our biblical studies section a work titled *Isaiah Through the Ages*.[22] It is a clunky book in some ways, patristic comments on Isaiah followed by a Ronald Clements comment or some other such modern voice. Despite its unwieldy character, the volume offers a treasure trove of patristic comments on Isaiah from various sources in the tradition, even though the quotations appear inchoate.

The prologue by Georges Florovsky was worth the price of entry into this providential find. Listen to his comments.

> When I read the ancient classics of Christian theology, the Fathers of the Church, I find them more relevant to the troubles and problems of my own time than the production of modern theologians. The Fathers were wrestling with existential problems, with those revelations of the eternal issues which were described and recorded in Holy Scripture. I would risk a suggestion that St. Athanasius and St. Augustine are much more up to date than many of our theological contemporaries. The reason is very simple: they were dealing with things and not with the maps; they were concerned not so much with what man can believe as with what God had done for man.[23]

Florovsky continues, "The sacred character of the Bible is ascertained by faith. The Bible, as a book, was composed in the community and was meant primarily for its edification. The book and the Church cannot be separated." Moreover, the two testaments of Holy Scripture—Old and New—are distinguished from each other and not to be conflated in such a way as to lose their integrity. Yet, "Jesus the Christ belongs to both. . . . He is the very center of the Bible, just because He is the *arche* and the *telos*—the beginning and the end."[24]

What Florovsky claims is akin to Ephraim Radner's affirmation of what he calls *incarnational synecdoche*.[25] Namely, the event of Jesus

---

[22] J. Manley, ed., *Isaiah Through the Ages* (Menlo Park, CA: Monastery, 1995).
[23] Manley, *Isaiah Through the Ages*, ii.
[24] Manley, *Isaiah Through the Ages*, iii.
[25] Radner, *Time and the Word*, chap. 5.

Christ as a temporal moment, plotted on a forward-moving axis of time, transcends its temporality by giving meaning and scope to the whole of Israel's history and the world's history before and after this event. Robert Jenson speaks of the Christ event as the centerpoint around which the helix of time moves. With this metaphor, Jenson provides some metaphorical help in order to overcome time's reduction to linear or cyclical construals.[26] Or in the words of Paul, Christ is "before all things" (Col 1:17) in interpretive preeminence and temporal experience.

These instincts strike me most about the premodern interpreters with whom I briefly engage concerning Isaiah 12 and Isaiah 42. Their understanding of the character of the Christian canon as divine voice and divine interruption shaped their attendance to its verbal character. Scripture speaks, like Florovsky says, right into the concerns of modern humankind, wherever one's historical definition of *modern* might be. There is no interpretive clutter in Cyril's or Luther's or Calvin's reading between the literal sense of Scripture and its present proclamation to Christ's church. Isaiah just does it, and, for someone like Calvin, Isaiah's voice speaks without the loss of Isaiah's historical integrity as a prophet. Admittedly, some readings are more sophisticated than others. Calvin rarely disappoints in his ability to attend to the nuances of biblical language. But it is the instinct, or in Childs's terminology the family resemblance, of Christian reading where close attention to Scripture's verbal and literary details always sit comfortably within a larger Christian metaphysic. This is a metaphysic regarding the nature of God's being and his signal self-unveiling in his incarnate Son, whose revelation is upheld and furthered by the promise of the Holy Spirit.

---

[26]Robert Jenson, "Scriptures Authority in the Church," in *The Art of Reading Scripture*, ed. Ellen F. Davis and Richard B. Hays (Grand Rapids, MI: Eerdmans, 2003), 35.

5

PREACHING ISAIAH AS CHRISTIAN SCRIPTURE

John N. Oswalt

THERE ARE SEVERAL GOOD DISCUSSIONS available of preaching from the prophets in general and Isaiah in particular, and there is no reason to duplicate them here.[1] What I intend to do is to outline the assumptions that govern my preaching from the Old

---

[1] Elizabeth Achtemeier, *Preaching from the Old Testament* (Louisville, KY: Westminster John Knox, 1980), 110-35; Rein Bos, *We Have Heard That God Is with You: Preaching the Old Testament* (Grand Rapids, MI: Eerdmans, 2008), 324-33; Walter Brueggemann, *Preaching from the Old Testament* (Minneapolis: Fortress, 2019), 71-110; Foster R. McCurley Jr., *Proclaiming the Promise: Christian Preaching from the Old Testament* (Philadelphia: Fortress, 1974), 93-128; H. G. M. Williamson, "Preaching from Isaiah," in *Reclaiming the Old Testament for Christian Preaching*, ed. Greenville J. R. Kent, Paul J. Kissling, and Laurence A. Turner (Downers Grove, IL: IVP Academic, 2010), 141-56; Christopher J. H. Wright, *How to Preach and Teach the Old Testament for All Its Worth* (Grand Rapids, MI: Zondervan, 2016), 185-224. For further examples of my own approach, see John N. Oswalt, "Isaiah 24–27, Songs in the Night," *CTJ* 40, no. 1 (April 2005): 76-84; Oswalt, "Isaiah 52:1–53:12, Servant of All," *CTJ* 40, no. 1 (April 2005): 85-94; Oswalt, "Isaiah 60–62: The Glory of the Lord," *CTJ* 40, no. 1 (April 2005): 76-103; Oswalt, *The Holy One of Israel* (Seattle: Cascade, 2014).

Testament and then to use Isaiah 42:1-9 to illustrate the process of moving from text to sermon.

General Guidelines for Preaching God's Word

There are several assumptions about the Bible that guide all my Old Testament preaching, including preaching from Isaiah. The first of these is the theological unity of the Bible. The God and Father of our Lord Jesus Christ is Yahweh. Furthermore, the New Testament affirmation "Jesus is Lord" is saying that Jesus Christ is Yahweh. To suggest that there is theological discontinuity between the testaments, as I believe John Walton is doing in his recently published theology of the Old Testament, is to deny the witness of the church from its founder onward.[2]

A second assumption is that revelation is progressive. I do not mean by this what Harry Emerson Fosdick meant, namely that later revelation corrects inadequate and faulty earlier forms.[3] What I mean is that later revelation further develops or supplements concepts that were first presented in germ.

A third assumption is that the major themes of the Old Testament become minor themes in the New Testament and vice versa. One example will suffice here: In the Old Testament persons are saved and lost in community. Individuals clearly could have a saving relationship with God, as is evident in the Psalms, but individual salvation was not the major theme. In the New Testament the situation is reversed. The primary emphasis is that individuals can have a saving relationship with God. To be sure, that relationship is in the context of the

---

[2]John H. Walton, *Old Testament Theology for Christians* (Downers Grove, IL: IVP Academic, 2017). Although he says that the NT is an expansion of OT theology (23), his actual treatment of the various elements makes it appear that the NT has in fact imposed an alien system of thought on the OT (see, e.g., 141, 228). To Walton, the NT is answering questions that the OT is not asking.

[3]For a somewhat more recent expression of this understanding, see McCurley, *Proclaiming the Promise*, 28.

community, but the New Testament writers take it that the necessity of community has been amply demonstrated in the Old Testament and need not be emphasized in their writings. This feature is replicated in at least five or six other concepts, such as transcendence and immanence, justice and grace, wrath and love, and so on.

A fourth assumption is that the ultimate author of Scripture is the Holy Spirit. This means that whether a human author intended something or understood something is not the determining factor in the interpretation of a passage. Did the prophets understand the ultimate significance of everything they were inspired to say? It seems to me self-evident that they did not, nor should we expect them to have such understanding. To be sure, if they were simply speaking and writing out of their own capacities, then the meaning of what they said could not be legitimately extended beyond those human limits. But to say such a thing is to deny the very nature of the Bible. It is God-breathed. This means that to extend the meaning beyond what an Isaiah may have intended or understood, so long as that extension is constrained by his evident intent and by the larger bounds of biblical theology, is not something illegitimate or out of bounds but is arguably within the intention of God, its ultimate author.[4]

A fifth and final assumption for our purposes here is one that in some ways flows out of the previous ones. This is the idea that the good news of salvation does not have to be imported into the Old Testament. That is, it is not necessary to find Christ in every Old Testament paragraph. Precisely because Yahweh is the Father of the Lord Jesus, the cross is implicit in everything he says and does. This means that the Christian Old Testament preacher who preaches a text faithfully will be preaching the gospel in some aspect of that gospel.

These assumptions have significant bearing on how we preach a passage such as this one, which is explicitly quoted in the New

---

[4] See Wright, *How to Preach and Teach*, 19.

Testament, as opposed to another that may not be explicitly quoted. In my judgment, any Old Testament passage can and should be understood in the light of the New Testament. That is not to say that the first approach to an Old Testament text ought to be by way of the New Testament; the Old Testament passage should first be read for itself, as much as is possible for a Christian reader. In this way, we seek not to misread the passage or to make it say something that it manifestly does not say. But having determined what it does say, we must then read the passage in the light of its final context, the Bible.

But what about passages such as this one, passages that are quoted in some way in the New Testament? How does such a usage constrain our reading? If the Old Testament passage is presented in the New as referring specifically to what has taken place in New Testament times, then we must decide whether it is to be taken literally or analogically. So if one takes Isaiah 42:1-9 to be analogically related to Christ (as do other contributors to this volume), one will conclude that Isaiah is not referring to the Messiah in his description of the suffering servant, but what he says about that person and his ministry can be used effectively and faithfully to speak of the ministry of Christ. On the other hand, one can conclude, as I do, that Isaiah knew himself to be referring to the Messiah.

Preaching Isaiah 42:1-4

Determining the limits of the passage. We turn now to Isaiah. The first task in expository preaching is to determine the limits of the passage to be preached. The passage chosen for study (Is 42:1-4) in this book is in my judgment part of a larger poetic unit. That unit is Isaiah 42:1-9. The delimiting factors seem clear to me. The previous segment is Isaiah 41:21-29, which is the first presentation of Yahweh's case against the idols, of which there are several between Isaiah 41 and Isaiah 46. Then, Isaiah 42:10 begins a call to praise for Yahweh's promised deliverance. These factors suggest breaks between Isaiah 41:29 and Isaiah 42:1 and between Isaiah 42:9 and Isaiah 42:10. But is the material between these breaks united? Yes, it is. In Isaiah 42:5-9, just as in Isaiah 42:1-4, it is Yahweh speaking in relation to the servant. To be sure, in Isaiah 42:1-4 he is speaking about the servant, whereas in Isaiah 42:5-9 he is speaking to the servant, but that is hardly justification for dividing the unit.[5]

Understanding the larger context. The next issue that must be addressed is the situation of this passage in its surrounding context. It is generally agreed that Isaiah 40–55 constitutes a unit in two parts: Isaiah 40–48 and Isaiah 49–55. I would demur from this consensus only slightly, suggesting that Isaiah 40 functions as an introduction to Isaiah 41–48 and Isaiah 49–55.[6] Two questions are addressed in the two main segments. The first is, "Has Yahweh been defeated by the idols (Is 41–48)?" It is answered with a resounding no. The means by which the question is answered is a series of court cases against the idols by Yahweh. Central to these cases is the evidence that Israel, God's chosen servant, will present, namely that Yahweh has specifically foretold the exile and its related events, something the idols are absolutely unable to do. That God would call these people his chosen servants, although they are captive in Babylon because of their sin, condemned because of their blindness, deafness, and rebellion, and tormented by their fears, is nothing other than a sign of his unimaginable grace. The culminating statement of that grace appears in Isaiah 48 in Yahweh's announcement that since he alone is God and there is no other, he can and will deliver his people from Babylon.

But this pronouncement raises another question. How can a holy God use a people condemned in their sin as his servants? Will he

---

[5]Psalm 2 displays a similar formation: words about the Messiah coupled with address to him.
[6]Notice that the key word *naḥam*, conventionally translated "comfort," which appears at the beginning of Is 40, only recurs in Is 51:3. Note also that Yahweh's "arm" appears in Is 40:10 and not again in this sense until Is 51:5. But more significantly, both of the questions dealt with, the first in Is 41–48 and the second in Is 49–55, are introduced in Is 40.

simply pronounce by divine fiat that the consequences of their sin, the death that all sin entails, will be overlooked? He cannot do that in the cosmos that he has created, one that is predicated on truth, which means consistently operating cause and effect. If he were to violate his own system, indeed his own nature, surely reality itself would dissolve. So, yes, Yahweh has the power to take his people from the hand of Babylon and restore them to their land, but who will restore his people to himself? How can sinful people be the chosen servants of the Holy God?

That question is answered in Isaiah 49–55. The answer is the servant, the true Israel (Is 49:3), who will be for Israel and the world what Israel was never able to be in itself. In Isaiah 49–55 there are three passages describing that servant: Isaiah 49:1-12; 50:4-9; 52:13–53:12. Despite the insistence of modern Judaism that this servant is none other than Israel the nation, that can hardly be the case. A careful comparison of these passages with those that undoubtedly refer to the nation reveals striking contrasts. This servant is sensitive to God and obedient to his word; Israel is blind, deaf, and rebellious. The role of this servant is to bring God's *mišpāṭ* (conventionally translated "justice") into the world; the only role mentioned for Israel is witness. Israel receives rich benefits from God for its service; the servant receives no benefits at all, except that of being vindicated by God. The servant is confident in God in the midst of suffering; Israel is sure that God has forgotten it. But perhaps the most telling argument that Israel is not this servant is the plain statement of Isaiah 49:6: "It is too small a thing for you to be my servant to restore the tribes of Jacob and bring back those of Israel I have kept. I will also make you a light for the Gentiles, that my salvation may reach the ends of the earth" (NIV). Israel cannot even restore Israel; this servant is not Israel.

I have belabored this point this much because it has been very clear to commentators for a long time that the servant described in Isaiah 42:1-9 is identical to the one described in the three passages that occur in Isaiah 49–55. His role is to bring *mišpāṭ* to the nations; he is to be a covenant for the people (*ʿam* is almost certainly a reference to Israel); he will accomplish his task without faltering or becoming discouraged.

But if this servant is the same one described in Isaiah 49–55, why is he introduced at this point in the book, in Isaiah 41–48? Notice that every other reference to servant in Isaiah 41–48 is to the fearful, recalcitrant, disbelieving servant who is nevertheless by his very existence evidence that Yahweh alone is God.[7] I believe the reason for this early introduction is that Isaiah intends for us to read Isaiah 41–48 and Isaiah 49–55 together.[8] The restoration of the servants from Babylon back to the land is inseparable from their restoration to God made possible by the self-sacrificing work of the servant. I think it is unmistakable that Isaiah knew this servant was different from Israel and that his ministry was different from Israel's. This understanding must be prescriptive for the way in which the passage is preached.

It is also imperative that Isaiah 42:1-9 be preached in the full appreciation of the other three passages in Isaiah 49–55. We will not fully comprehend what is being said here unless we see it in that larger context. What they say will have a strong bearing on our understanding of the full meaning of this passage. It helps us to answer the question that has been hovering over us from the outset: Is this passage about Jesus Christ of Nazareth? I think the answer is an unequivocal yes. When we take into account the other three passages, and particularly the last, what other answer could we possibly give? But I hasten to say that I think it is probable that if you had asked Isaiah to give details of the Messiah's life and ministry apart from what had been revealed to him here, he might well have gotten those details quite wrong. That is, we know in retrospect who it was that the Holy Spirit guided Isaiah to

---

[7]The opposite is the case in Is 49–55, where only one reference is to the nation (Is 54:17).
[8]Which is what Is 40 is intending to signal in its introductory relationship to Is 41–55.

describe, whereas in prospect Isaiah himself might have come up with a very different picture.

So, would I unabashedly preach Jesus from this passage? Absolutely. Would that be an imposition on the human author's original intent? In no way. In the light of how God actually fulfilled this prediction, we can see more fully—but, I hasten to add, not other than—what Isaiah thought he was saying. I take this to be the point Peter is making in the 1 Peter 1 when he speaks of the prophets longing to "see into" what we now are privileged to see fully (1 Pet 1:10-12).

Examining the passage. It is now time to examine the passage itself, attempting to define the major elements of thought. They are four, in my judgment:

1. the calling of the servant (Is 42:1, 6)[1]

2. the character of the servant (Is 42:2-4a)

3. the role of the servant (Is 42:1, 3-4, 6-7)

4. the relationships between Yahweh and the servant (Is 42:1, 5, 8-9)

The way in which these elements are interwoven and interspersed throughout the poem suggests that the structure of the sermon should be synthetic rather than analytical, that is, that the structure of the passage should not be determinative of the structure of the sermon, which I think should be the default position in expository preaching.

Finally, we need to look at key terms in the passage. The one that stands out is the thrice-repeated *mišpāṭ*. The term is conventionally rendered "justice" or "judgment." This is certainly correct in the majority of cases. However, as we think of the concept of justice that is conveyed by the English term, is too sharply limited to legal equity: people being treated as they deserve, not being taken advantage of, and not being oppressed. But is that all the servant can offer to the world? Somehow, as a result of something he does, we will get what we deserve, or through him the legal requirements of justice will be served?

Much more is connoted by the term in this context than mere legal equity. We get a glimpse of this in the work of the so-called judges in Israel's early history. Did these figures—Gideon, Samson, and the rest—only restore legal equity in the nation after oppressors were dispatched? Surely they did more than that. They restored Israel in some measure, limited though it might have been, to that way of life their covenant Lord intended. When we look at *mišpāṭ* in its larger sense, this is exactly what we see. So the Danites found the people of Laish living according to the *mišpāṭ* of the Sidonians (Judg 18:7), and Solomon built the temple according to its *mišpāṭ* (1 Kings 6:38). In both cases we are talking about a pattern, in one case a pattern of behavior, in the other a pattern for a building.[9] So what is this servant going to do? He is going to play the part of the quintessential Judge. He is going to restore not only Israel but the entire world to that pattern of life that the world's Creator intended. Will that include legal equity? Absolutely! But it will include much more than that.[10]

Creating the Sermon

Introduction. The purpose of the sermon is to convince the hearer that the one to whom this passage looks forward, Jesus Christ, is able to bring God's divine order into the hearer's life.

The proposition is that this servant, called and empowered by the Creator, will make it possible for the divine order for life envisioned by

---

[9]In 2 Kings 17:26-27 the king of Assyria is told that lions are devouring the people who have been resettled in the new province of Samaria because they do not know the *mišpāṭ* of the god of that land. This is not the "law" of that god (as per ESV and NRSV) but his expectations, the pattern of behavior he expects. So KJV with "manner" or NASB with "custom" are more accurate renderings. For an example of this usage in Isaiah, see Is 28:26, where readers are told that farmers know how to carry out their tasks (in contrast to drunken priests and prophets!) because Yahweh has directed them according to *mišpāṭ*, that is, the right pattern or order for farming. Clearly, the priests and prophets are not leading according to *mišpāṭ*.

[10]For a very helpful discussion, see G. Liedke, "שפט *špṭ* to judge," *Theological Lexicon of the Old Testament*, ed. Ernst Jenni, with assistance from Claus Westermann, trans. Mark E. Biddle (Peabody, MA: Hendrickson, 1997) 3:1392-99. Note especially the comment that "*mišpāṭ* can no more be limited to the legal sphere than can *špṭ*" (1395). See also B. Johnson, "מִשְׁפָּט *mišpāṭ*," *Theological Dictionary of the New Testament*, ed. Gerhard Kittel and Gerhard Friedrich, trans. Geoffrey W. Bromiley (Grand Rapids, MI: Eerdmans, 1964–1976), 9:87-88, 96.

the Creator, to be restored on the earth. He will do so by releasing men and women from the prison of sin and enabling them through the Holy Spirit to live in covenant with their Creator and Redeemer.

Introduction. What is the greatest danger to human flourishing? We might suggest several answers, and the one I am going to suggest may surprise you. But if you will think for a moment, I believe you will agree with me. What prevents us from flourishing? It is disorder. Yes, disorder. Disorder in nature, disorder in politics, disorder in families, disorder in our spirits, disorder in our bodies. Life just does not work without order.

This is what the great myths of the ancient world were all about—how to prevent chaos, the chaos from which all order had so difficultly been wrested, from reasserting itself. In the same way, this is what every ancient king when first coming to his throne promised to bring about—order.

That idea of order is expressed in the Old Testament by the Hebrew word *mišpāṭ*. Like many Hebrew words, this one has a very large pool of connotations. The typical English translation of it is "justice" or "judgment."[1] Those terms are not incorrect, but they are too limiting. Legal equity is a central part of the divine order that Yahweh, the Creator, envisioned for his world, but it is only a part.

What was it that the Hebrew people were experiencing in captivity in Babylon in 550 BC, the time Isaiah was addressing? Were they experiencing injustice? Actually, no. They were experiencing the very just results of their inveterate covenant breaking over the past one thousand years. But were they experiencing an absence of *mišpāṭ*? Absolutely! God's intended order for their lives and that of their nation was in complete disarray. Why was this? It was for one reason and one reason alone. Not the overwhelming power of Babylon but the overwhelming power of sin.

Yahweh, the great I AM, sole Creator and sustainer of the universe, had made them and us to live in a love relationship with him in which we submit ourselves, our wants, our dreams to him and give ourselves to one another in love for his sake. But they and we refused. "It's my life, and I'll do what I want with it." The result? Just as jumping off a tall building results in physical chaos, so refusing to live our lives in a submissive relationship to God results in chaos, a chaos that affects every part of life as God designed it to be. The principles are identical. "There is a way that seems right to a man, but its end is the way to death" (Prov 14:12).

So, what to do? God could have just written off the entire human experiment as a tragic failure. But he did not; instead, he intends to restore his planned order in your life and mine and in the world through a servant, a servant whom Yahweh himself introduces to us in Isaiah 42:1-9. In this introduction he tells us about the servant's calling, about his character, and his commission.

The body of the sermon. 1. The first thing we see is the calling of this servant. At the very outset Yahweh asserts that he, Yahweh, has chosen the servant. And who is Yahweh? He is the Creator, the life-giver, the originator of this orderly system we call the cosmos. But more than that, he is I AM. He makes that plain when he specifies in Isaiah 42:8 that his name is Yahweh, which means something like "He is." This being alone can say this. Nothing else in all the cosmos is self-existent; everything else is dependent on something else for its existence. But not he. Repeatedly in this part of Isaiah Yahweh insists "I am" (Is 41:4; 43:10, 13, 25; 46:4; 48:12). In short, this servant's calling is from the originator of the cosmic order and no one else.

What does this mean? It means that the one who determined what the order for this cosmos and everything in it would be is determined to restore that order and has specifically called this person for that purpose. In a later description of the servant (Is 49:1), it is said that he was called from the womb. That is, this purpose was not something thought up later in the servant's life but from the very moment of his conception. Furthermore, Yahweh insists that calling this servant was the right thing to do (Is 42:6). What does that mean? One of the qualities of Yahweh's uniquely holy character is that he always does what is right— right for humanity and right for the cosmos. So, this choosing of the servant by the Creator of the cosmos was not simply a *good* idea; it was the *right* idea. The context of the statement is important. Look at Isaiah 42:5. Who is it who has done the right thing in calling this servant? It is the Creator and sustainer who brought the cosmos into existence and breathed his own life into the humans who were the apex of his creation purposes. So this is not plan B. Whatever the servant will do is exactly what is called for under the circumstances. It is the right thing!

2. But who is this servant? Notice two things that are said about him at the outset in Isaiah 42:1. They speak of a special relationship between him and Yahweh. He is not operating on his own but is supported, indeed, held securely, by Yahweh (see also Is 42:6), and as such is a personal delight to Yahweh. Furthermore, the dynamic of his life and ministry is God's Spirit. This reminds us of the Messiah as described in Isaiah 11, where he is said to have a completely different spirit from the one that animated the kings of that day—the Spirit of God. What can we say from these statements? We can say that this servant is manifesting the order that God has intended for human life: he is fully dependent on God, is motivated by him, and is a delight to him. Here is that relationship we spoke of a moment ago. This servant, whoever he is, is submissive to his divine calling, and he lives and functions in submissive love.

But could he not be simply the nation of Israel? Numerous times elsewhere in Isaiah 41–48 the nation of Israel is said to be called and chosen. Is this another reference to the nation? It is not. The character being described here is not the character of Israel. Whenever anything is said of the nation of Israel elsewhere in this section—and interestingly, not much *is* said—the description is not flattering. Israel is blind, deaf, and rebellious; they do not seem to be able to assimilate what God says to them about their condition. They are in captivity because God put them there as a result of their sin (Is 42:18-25). Yahweh chooses to use their testimony concerning his past predictions as evidence that he alone is God, but that has nothing to do with their character.

But what about this servant? He is a personal delight to God and is filled with the Spirit of God. Furthermore, he will not carry out his mission with bluster or self-assertion. In fact, unlike the redeemed nation, of which it is said will thresh the mountains and crush the hills (Is 41:15), this servant will not even break a bent reed or extinguish a guttering candle (Is 42:3). He will accomplish his task with divine power, not human power.

Finally, whereas the nation will be discouraged and fainting, the servant will not grow faint or weary but will quietly and steadily push forward until his task is accomplished. In the later descriptions of this servant, we learn where this persistence and endurance come from. They come from the servant's assurance that God will not forsake him but will persevere with him until he and his work are fully vindicated (Is 49:4; 50:7-8). Again, this is very unlike Israel, who is sure that God has forgotten them (Is 40:27; 49:14). In short, whoever this servant is, he is not the nation of Israel.

3. But what is this work that Yahweh will ensure will be accomplished through the servant? I have already alluded to it above. It is identified no less than three times in Isaiah 42:1-4. It is to bring Yahweh's *mišpāṭ* to the nations of the earth. That is, it is to restore God's divine order on the earth. It is to do what human kings boasted about doing but never did. It is to establish the kingdom of God in the earth, to bring about that beneficent order whereby life can flourish. He will *bring justice to the nations*. Let me say it again, however: we are not merely talking about establishing legal equity, making sure we all "get our rights." For so many of us, when we think of justice, that is exactly what we are thinking of: getting what we deserve. Dear God, no! What is it you and I deserve from the order maker, the judge, of the universe? It is eternal separation from him in that self-centered world we have made for ourselves. But what is God's just, ordered world? It is the one described in Isaiah 11:9, where "they will neither harm nor destroy on all my holy mountain, for the earth will be full of the knowledge of the LORD as the waters cover the sea" (NIV). This is God's plan, his *mišpāṭ* for us, that we should be so free of self-interest that we would not need to hurt each other in our scrabble to get "what I deserve."

This is the significance of the statement in Isaiah 42:4, that "the coastlands wait for [the servant's] teaching." The word here translated "teaching" is *tôrâ*. Throughout the history of English translations of the Bible, *tôrâ* has usually been translated "the law." But this puts a very unfortunate spin on the term, for in our culture we think of "the law" as only existing to put limits on our freedom. But the sense of the Hebrew word *tôrâ* is "the instructions," or, as here, "teaching." When God gave the Israelites and the world his covenant, his torah, at Sinai, he was not attempting to shut us in but rather to teach us how we were meant to live.

Unfortunately, many Old Testament believers saw the torah as only a guide to external behavior. But Jesus shows in his so-called Sermon on the Mount (Mt 5–7) that to take that position is to misunderstand the purpose of the covenant. It is intended to show us the need for a complete reorientation of our inner lives. So Jesus says that he has not come to do away with the Law and the Prophets but to fulfill them. He does that by showing that while the instructions certainly do forbid adultery, that prohibition was intended to deliver us from an adulterous way of thinking, and that if it had not achieved that purpose, it had failed. To live in the kingdom of God is to submit our wills to God in love and to allow him to remake us in his image so that love for others is our natural response. That is the justice the servant will not fail to produce in the world. That is the justice for which the nations pant in hope.

So how will he accomplish that task? First of all, we need to say that this is the first of four treatments of this servant, and the full answer is to be found in those later statements. However, we can see the outlines here, and those outlines are consistent with what we see in the later, fuller descriptions. Look at the statement in Isaiah 42:6, "I give you as a covenant to the people and a light to the nations" (my translation). What is the significance of that statement? What does it mean that the servant *is* a covenant? The prophet Malachi refers to "the messenger of the covenant," but that is different from *being* a covenant. We go further and notice that the servant will be a covenant and a light in order to "open the eyes that are blind, to bring out prisoners from the dungeon."

These are the same words that Jesus of Nazareth uses in announcing his messiahship, quoting Isaiah 61:1-2, as recorded in Luke 4:16-21.

I believe the answer to our questions, which may well be the questions the prophet was asking after being inspired to speak these words, are to be found in the gospel of Jesus Christ. Notice that the final words of Yahweh's introduction of the servant in Isaiah 42:9 point us in that very direction. He says that the former things, the things to which the Israelites were witnesses, have occurred or are about to occur. That is, the unthinkable has happened, and Israel left her land and went into exile. Now the pagan emperor Cyrus is about to deliver them from exile. But those are old hat, as it were. Yahweh is going to do something brand new. In this context, I believe this is a reference to the coming of this servant, in whose incarnation there will certainly be something brand new. There is yet a further intimation of Christ in Isaiah 42:8: Yahweh will not give his glory to any idol, made with human hands, made in the human image. To whom will he give his glory? His Son, who can declare, "So now, Father, glorify me in your own presence with the glory that I had in your presence before the world existed. . . . The glory that you have given me I have given them, so that they may be one as we are one" (Jn 17:5, 22, my translation).

Perhaps you are saying, "Oh, Oswalt, you are reading far too much into this Old Testament passage." Am I? This servant is not Israel. His character is demonstrative of the relationship with Yahweh that Yahweh planned for in his *mišpāṭ*, his plan for life. As for the task he has been given, restoring God's *mišpāṭ* to this broken world, bringing light to the nations of the world by giving instructions for life that the whole world is waiting for, that is no task any ordinary human could ever carry out. So, who is this if not the incarnate Son of God?

Driving it home. So, how has Christ made it possible for the divine order, the kingdom, to come in you and me, and someday in the whole world? He has delivered us from the prison house of sin. Just as the Judean people were held in the bondage of Babylon because of their sin, so you and I are in bondage to our desires because of our sin. That sin is much like that of the Hebrew people through all the years of their nation's existence. They continually insisted on making Yahweh in their own image in order to make it possible to manipulate him for their own ends. We have done the same. We have made God our servant, a device for delivering what our desires demand: pleasure, possessions, and power. Now we find ourselves in bondage to our desires, watching as chaos—familial, social, political, and religious—swirls higher and higher around us.

Against that background, God's covenant stands out like a rock in the swirling currents. Here are the instructions for life as God planned it, God's *mišpāṭ*. But its appearance is not at all comforting, for it is broken and cries out to the God of order for retribution. Perhaps you say, "But that is only for the Jews; there is no covenant with us Gentiles." Let me suggest that the teaching that is embodied in the covenant, although not legally binding on us as it was on them, is as fundamental to all of human life as it was to Jewish life. It is as true for me as it is the Jew that in the carrying out of these instructions, embodied in the "Ten Words" that we Gentiles call commands, there is life, and in the denial of them there is death. And we have denied them, starting at the first commandment, worshiping ourselves, the god of our own making.

So, what is to be done? The covenant cries out for blood. We can go no further. We can go no further, that is, until the servant who bears the same glory as the Creator becomes the satisfaction of the old covenant and in the same act becomes the ratification of a New Covenant, one that is written on the heart. But how is that to be done? If the submission of the Son to the Father delivers us from the consequences of our sin, what is to be done about the fact of sin, what the Bible calls iniquity? Here is where the very beginning of our passage comes into play. Why the assertion "I have put my Spirit on him"? And why in Isaiah 11 the repeated stress on the Spirit's work in the Messiah (as opposed to normal human power), and why in the ultimate declaration of the servant's work in Isaiah 61 does he begin by saying, "The Spirit of the Lord God is upon me"? It is for the same reason that when John protests at baptizing Jesus, Jesus says, "John, this is the right thing to do"? As the servant manifests God's *mišpāṭ*, so he also manifests the means by which that *mišpāṭ* can be realized in us. The ultimate work of the Messiah was to make Yahweh's Spirit available to all people to empower them to live the life of God. When Jesus tells the disciples to wait for "the promise of the Father," not one of them claims ignorance, as was so common at other times in Jesus' ministry whenever he makes a declarative statement. Has he finally said something they expected the Messiah to say? Yes, I think so. What they failed to realize was that in order for him, the Messiah, to make the promise of the Spirit available, he must first cleanse the human temple with his own blood.

Notice that Jesus closes his Sermon on the Mount with the assertion that God will not withhold "good things" if we are to ask him. What is he hinting at? He has described the *mišpāṭ*, the divine order for life that God intends, from what is now Matthew 5 onward. But anyone paying minimal attention to what he said would be despairing. "Who is adequate for these things?" they would ask. But Jesus says, "Now ask the Father for good things; he will not withhold anything from you." What is he saying? He is saying that if we ask God for the means to live the kind of life he has been commending, the Father will give those means. But what exactly are they, Jesus? Jesus does not tell us at this point. I think he, as a good teacher, was refraining from telling his students things for which they were not yet ready. But evidently later in his ministry he considered that they were ready, for in the Gospel of Luke we read the very same words that Jesus used in Matthew, except that here he does not say that the Father will give us good things when we ask, but rather that he will give us the Holy Spirit when we ask (Lk 11:43). That is, the kind of inner order, the *mišpāṭ*, that the Sermon on the Mount calls for is ours if we will avail ourselves of the full work of the servant of the Lord. That work, work that the cross accomplished, is the deliverance from the consequences of our sin, and empowerment through the Holy Spirit to live the life of God. This is what the servant has done for you and me; he has given us that order of life that our Creator intended for us, that order of life that makes true human flourishing possible.

Conclusion. So what about you? Is there chaos in your life? If there is, the servant has come to restore God's order in you. Oh, don't misunderstand me. He does not promise some easy path through this world, which is largely an enemy of him and his people. But he has come to restore his order in you, to enable you to love him with your whole self and to love your neighbor as yourself. Let him do his wonderful work. Are you in prison, a prison of sin? Let his blood unlock the prison doors. Are you in bondage, bondage to your desires? He wants to fill you with his Spirit to enable you for glad submission to God. Let him re-create in you his very own character, believing, persevering, loving, triumphant. He can do all this and more. That's why he came. But it's up to you.

6

HOW THE APOSTLES READ JEREMIAH AS CHRISTIAN SCRIPTURE

DANA M. HARRIS

AT FIRST GLANCE, the appropriation and influence of the prophet Jeremiah in the New Testament may not be as readily apparent as, for example, the prophet Isaiah.[1] Yet a closer reading reveals that Jeremiah plays a key role at many points in the New Testament. In addition to several shorter citations in the Gospels and Pauline Epistles, the longest Old Testament citation in the New Testament occurs in Hebrews 8:8-12, which cites Jeremiah 31:31-34. There are also numerous allusions to the text of Jeremiah in the New Testament, and the prophet likely had a significant influence on both Jesus' and Paul's self-understanding of

---

[1] I want to thank Andrew T. Abernethy for asking me to contribute to this project as well as William R. Osborne and Paul D. Wegner for their input. I am grateful to IVP Academic for publishing this volume.

their call and mission. This chapter will focus on this issue of self-understanding, along with a few key Jeremiah citations in the New Testament; footnotes reference additional citations, as well as some possible allusions.[2] But before we consider Jeremiah, a few comments about how New Testament writers viewed Scripture will be helpful.

How New Testament Writers (Appear to Have) Interacted with Scripture

It is somewhat speculative to claim that we can know what various New Testament writers thought about what they were doing when they were writing, but there are some general observations that are probably accurate. First, although New Testament writers may have had some sense that what they or other apostles were writing could be considered Scripture (e.g., 2 Pet 3:16), it is likely that they would not have drawn a sharp distinction between what we call the Old Testament and the writings that were emerging in the first century. Moreover, they would have viewed the canonical Old Testament as "Scripture" (*hē graphē*), the authoritative revelation of God. Other contemporary Jewish writings available during this time were not received with this same level of authority. This can be inferred from the citations and allusions found within the New Testament, which draw almost exclusively from what has become the canonical Old Testament.[3]

Second, even though scholars classify the various ways that Scripture is appropriated by New Testament writers (e.g., citation, allusion, typology), it is improbable that New Testament writers would have understood or identified their use of Scripture using the same categories. For example, New Testament writers probably never wondered

---

[2] I have drawn primarily on NA[28], appendix 4, for these references.
[3] Although 1 Enoch 1:9 is quoted in Jude 14-15, the citation describes the fate of the ungodly in the context of Jude's warning against ungodly, false teachers. The citation is not used as an authoritative support for a christological or theological argument. An implicit understanding of canonical Scripture can also be drawn from the Hebrew Scriptures that were eventually translated into Greek.

whether they should quote, allude to, echo, or draw out a typological correspondence from the part of Scripture that they were appropriating.[4] These writers were concerned with showing how the birth, life, death, resurrection, and ascension of Jesus of Nazareth clarified, developed, and extended God's former revelation through prophets (Heb 1:1-2) and other Old Testament writings.[5] Although some claim that New Testament writers treated Scripture as a source of prooftexts for their christological claims, the actual evidence does not support this. Instead, Scripture was the authoritative source that explained the significance of the person and work of Jesus Christ, who also became the lens by which to understand Scripture.[6] Thus the appropriation of Scripture often flows organically from inferences and developments that were already present in that particular Scripture, regardless of which appropriation method was employed.

For example, Peter looks to two Davidic psalms (Ps 69:25; 109:8) to explain Judas's betrayal. Peter saw correspondences between the ones (plural) who opposed David, the Lord's anointed one, and the one (singular, Judas) who betrayed Jesus, the Anointed One, the Messiah. Was Peter consciously thinking that he would use typology to draw out these correspondences? Most likely not. Yet he was clearly looking to Scripture to explain what Judas had done (Ps 69:25) and how the apostles should proceed (Ps 109:8). This thinking may feel farfetched to modern readers, but for those who were thoroughly steeped in Scripture and who were well-versed in the "patterned way"

---

[4]The term *type* (and related terms) has a wide range of meanings in contemporary research. I am using "typological" to indicate a correspondence of significance between a previous biblical event (e.g., the exile), institution (e.g., the priesthood), or person (e.g., David) and a later event, institution, or person. For example, in this chapter, the exile and the return from it anticipate certain events in Jesus' life.
[5]Elsewhere I describe this as a "hermeneutical worldview." See Dana M. Harris, "The Eternal Inheritance in Hebrews: The Appropriation of the Old Testament Inheritance Theme by the Author of Hebrews" (PhD diss., Trinity Evangelical Divinity School, 2009).
[6]This point is supported (in part) by the understanding that Scripture texts that were not considered messianic prior to Jesus' incarnation are so understood by NT writers and by the realization that not all citations serve only christological purposes but rather ecclesiological ones as well.

in which God worked in Israel's history, it was only natural to see the culmination of these patterns in the person and work of Christ.[7]

This is not to say that New Testament writers were completely unaware of various techniques that they could use to appropriate Scripture. Matthew, for example, frequently indicates that a certain event in Jesus' life fulfills a specific Scripture. The author of Hebrews uses Jewish midrashic techniques (e.g., the use of Ps 95 in Heb 3:7-19) and etymology (e.g., Heb 7:1-3) to develop his christological and soteriological arguments. Moreover, there is growing recognition that New Testament writers understood and intended to evoke the entire original context of the Scripture they appropriated.[8] Indeed, many New Testament writers appear to have understood that there was significant development of certain themes or patterns within Scripture (the OT) itself, such as the exodus typology developed extensively in Isaiah and elsewhere.

So, while it is helpful for modern interpreters to classify the various ways that New Testament writers appropriated Scripture, it is important to stress that these writers all understood that Scripture, in multiple ways, revealed that Jesus Christ fulfilled all of God's plans and purposes as recorded in Scripture. With this in mind, we can now consider how New Testament writers understood the contribution that Jeremiah made to this revelation about Jesus Christ.

---

[7]My gratitude to Lissa Wray Beal for this helpful concept.

[8]The seminal work in this regard is C. H. Dodd, *According to the Scriptures: The Sub-structure of New Testament Theology* (London: Nisbet, 1952). Subsequent works that confirm or extend Dodd's thesis include David Instone-Brewer, *Techniques and Assumptions in Jewish Exegesis before 70 CE*, TSAJ 30 (Tübingen: Mohr Siebeck, 1992) and Richard B. Hays, *The Conversion of the Imagination: Paul as Interpreter of Israel's Scripture* (Grand Rapids, MI: Eerdmans, 2005). I am indebted to Douglas S. Huffman for his helpful comments in private conversation in conjunction with his forthcoming volume on the NT use of the OT (Baker Academic), especially the former's respect for OT contexts.

Jeremiah and the Gospel of Matthew

Matthew's Gospel is the only one to refer to Jeremiah by name, although the prophet is quoted or alluded to in the other Gospels.[9] Two citations are ascribed to Jeremiah (Mt 2:17-18; 27:9-10), and he is mentioned by name in the disciples' response to Jesus' question at Caesarea Philippi (Mt 16:14). This section will focus on the citation in Matthew 2 and the reference in Matthew 16.[10]

Jeremiah 31:15 in Matthew 2:17-18. The citation of Jeremiah 31 in Matthew 2 occurs in the context of Jesus' birth and the magi's journey to him, the king of the Jews.[11] After (the illegitimate) King Herod calls for the magi and asks them to report to him the child's location (Mt 2:7-8), they are warned in a dream not to do so and instead return to their own country (Mt 2:9-12). Upon realizing that he has been tricked, Herod orders that all the baby boys two years old and younger in Bethlehem and the surrounding area be killed. This recalls the edict of Pharaoh to kill all the Hebrew baby boys in Exodus 1:15-16, 22, and presents Jesus as a new Moses. The ensuing unimaginable lament of the massacred baby boys is described by means of the citation of Jeremiah 31:15 in Matthew 2:18:

---

[9]This section focuses on Matthew's Gospel, which features Jeremiah more prominently than the other three Gospels. For other citations and possible allusions to Jeremiah in the Gospels and Acts, see NA[28], appendix 4.

[10]Although Mt 27:9-10 ascribes the citation to Jeremiah, it is from in Zech 11:12-13. There are, however, allusions to Jeremiah (Jer 19:1-13). See M. J. J. Menken, "The References to Jeremiah in the Gospel According to Matthew," *Ephemerides Theologicae Lovanienses* 60 (1884): 5-24, esp. 6-11; Michael Knowles, *Jeremiah in Matthew's Gospel: The Rejected-Prophet Motif in Matthaean Redaction*, JSNTSup 68 (Sheffield: JSOT Press, 1993), 60-81.

[11]Nicholas G. Piotrowski notes the seven explicit quotations ("prologue-quotations") in Matthew's prologue, which he delimits as Mt 1:1–4:16. He argues, "Matthew's prologue-quotations give shape to the narrative's christological and ecclesiological vision by drawing on the language of Israel's exile and restoration." Piotrowski, *Matthew's New David at the End of Exile: A Socio-rhetorical Study of Scriptural Quotations*, NovTSup 170 (Boston: Brill, 2016), 4. Each of these quotations concerns exile and restoration. "By evoking the images of exile and restoration (as a second exodus) Matthew introduces his *dramatis personae* in startling terms: a newly defined people of God (Mt 1:1, 21; 2:6, 10-11, 15; 3:8-9, 17; 4:3, 6, 4:16) is about to be restored by the last David (1:21-23; 2:2; 3:2-3; 4:12-17) while Israel's oppressors (2:3-4, 13, 16-18; 3:7-10) are about to face an aggravated exile if their rebellion persists (3:7 10-12)" (*Matthew's New David*, 13).

> A voice was heard in Ramah,
>   weeping and loud lamentation,
> Rachel weeping for her children;
>   she refused to be comforted, because they are no more. (ESV)[12]

The context of this verse in Jeremiah offers insights into its function in Matthew 2. Although much of Jeremiah contains judgment oracles concerning Judah's exile to Babylon, Jeremiah 30–31 (the Book of Consolation) offers oracles promising the eventual restoration of both Judah and Israel, including the well-known promise of a New Covenant in Jeremiah 31. The reference to Rachel and her weeping in Jeremiah 31:15 is somewhat unexpected, unlike Jacob, who is frequently referenced in this overall section of Jeremiah. Both, however, refer figuratively to the people of God.[13] Although Rachel died in childbirth, she became the personification of "grieving mothers in Israel."[14] Like the exiles, Rachel's children had to leave the land that had been promised to Abraham for Egypt.[15] In Jeremiah 31:15, Rachel weeps for the children who are no more because they have been carried off in captivity, whereas in Matthew she weeps for the slaughtered baby boys. This lament vividly contrasts with the overall focus on the hope of future restoration in Jeremiah 30–31.

The reference to Ramah is also somewhat unexpected. According to Genesis 35:19-20, Rachel was buried on the way to Ephrath, near Bethlehem and thus near Ramah (just north of Jerusalem) as well.[16] The connection to Ramah for Matthew, however, is more likely found in

---

[12]Bible citations are from the ESV, NIV, or NRSV, as noted. For a discussion of the source text from which Matthew quotes, see Knowles, *Jeremiah in Matthew's Gospel*, 36-38.
[13]Bob Becking, "A Voice Was Heard in Ramah," *BZ* 38 (1994): 229-42, here 238.
[14]Blomberg notes, "Thus it was natural to personify the grieving mothers in Israel as 'Rachel weeping for her children.'" Craig L. Blomberg, "Matthew," in *Commentary on the New Testament Use of the Old Testament*, ed. G. K. Beale and D. A. Carson (Grand Rapids, MI: Baker Academic, 2007), 1-109, here 9.
[15]Blomberg, "Matthew," 9.
[16]See Gen 48:7. Similarly, 1 Sam 10:2 locates Rachel's burial place in Zelzah, which is also near Bethlehem.

Jeremiah 40:1, where Ramah (north in Syria) was a point of departure for those who were being deported to Babylon.[17] This geographical connection likely also led Matthew to Jeremiah 31:15. The traditional interpretation is that Matthew saw a connection between the exile of Rachel's children to Egypt and Jesus' own exile to Egypt, although the parallels are not exact, since Matthew associated Rachel's weeping with the babies murdered by Herod not Jesus' exile. Additionally, the immediate context of Jeremiah 31:15 within Jeremiah, specifically Jeremiah 31:16-17, is important.[18] These verses foretell the return from exile and a future restoration of Rachel's children, in light of which present lament should be curtailed. Thus Matthew may have intended a connection to this larger Jeremiah context to suggest that there would also be a return from exile and future restoration associated with Jesus' birth. Indeed, Jeremiah 30–31 promises a return from exile, a restoration of Davidic rule, and a New Covenant through which sins are truly forgiven. Thus the citation of Jeremiah 31:15 in Matthew 2:18 sets up expectations for the fulfillment of these promises.

The citation from Jeremiah is closely linked to the citation of Hosea 11:1 in Matthew 2:15, which is best understood in terms of Jesus recapitulating Israel in both the exodus event and the exile, with the latter associated with Jeremiah and the former primarily with Hosea.[19]

---

[17] J. W. Mazurel, "Citations from the Book of Jeremiah in the New Testament," in *Reading the Book of Jeremiah: A Search for Coherence*, ed. Martin Kessler (Winona Lake, IN: Eisenbrauns, 2004), 181-89, here 183; see also Blomberg, "Matthew," 9.

[18] Jeremiah 31:16-17: "This is what the LORD says: 'Restrain your voice from weeping and your eyes from tears, for your work will be rewarded,' declares the LORD. 'They will return from the land of the enemy. So there is hope for your descendants,' declares the LORD. 'Your children will return to their own land'" (NIV).

[19] Keith Campbell traces the numerous parallels to the exodus in Matthew: "(1) Pharaoh killed the male Hebrew babies (Exod. 1:22; cf. Matt. 2:16), (2) Moses fled Egypt because Pharaoh threatened his life (Exod. 2:15; cf. Matt. 2:13-15), (3) when Pharaoh died, Moses returned to Egypt (Exod. 4:19-20; cf. Matt. 2:19-20), and (4) Exodus typology is evident in Matthew's quote of Hos. 11:1 (Matt. 2:15)." Campbell then offers "significant linguistic agreements between Exodus 2 and Matthew 2." He concludes: "The Exodus, then, is absorbed into the life of Jesus." Keith Campbell, "Matthew's Hermeneutic of Psalm 22:1 and Jer. 31:15," *Faith and Mission* 24 (2007): 46-58, here 50.

Traditionally, Egypt has been identified as the place of exile and Judea as the place from which Jesus was exiled. Nicholas Piotrowski, however, makes a persuasive case for an unexpected reversal of this interpretation. His work focuses on the how "prologue-quotations" from Isaiah, Micah, Jeremiah, and Hosea in Matthew 1–4 create an "intertextual conversation" that establishes the interpretive frames of David and "end of exile" and raise the question of the identity of the "end-of-exile people" in relationship to Jesus. The citations from Hosea 11:1 and Jeremiah 31:15 recall the exodus and the exile. The placement of Herod between these citations recalls both Pharaoh and the Babylonians and their respective murders of Israelites.[20] Piotrowski argues that Jesus' movement away from Herod (the oppressor) to Egypt (the place of refuge) and back to Judea indicates that Israel's oppressors are not foreign but are its own rulers and leaders and identifies "the land Israel as the place of captivity."[21] Moreover, since the larger context of Jeremiah 30–33 speaks of restoration of house of David, Piotrowski argues that the intertextual conversation between Jeremiah, Hosea, and Matthew indicates that Jesus is the promised Davidic king who will inaugurate the New Covenant of Jeremiah and lead his people out of exile. In this way, the citation from Jeremiah 31 in Matthew 2 contributes significantly to revealing Jesus' identity and mission.

The reference to Jeremiah in Matthew 16:14. All three Synoptic Gospels record Peter's confession that Jesus is the Christ (Mt 16:13-20; Mk 8:27-30; Lk 9:18-21), although Luke does not specify the location. When asked by Jesus as to who people say the Son of Man is, all three Synoptic Gospels also list Elijah or "one of the prophets" as possible answers. Matthew alone, however, specifies Jeremiah "or one of the prophets" (Mt 16:14).[22]

---

[20]Piotrowski, *Matthew's New David*, 114-16.
[21]Piotrowski, *Matthew's New David*, 122.
[22]Bruce T. Dahlberg lists additional elements of this pericope that are unique to Matthew. Dahlberg, "Typological Use of Jeremiah 1:4-19 in Matthew 16:13-23," *JBL* 94 (1975): 73-80, here 73-74.

This reference to Jeremiah has been variously understood, including seeing Jeremiah as the typical prophet or representative of the prophetic corpus. Yet, as Michael Knowles observes, Isaiah is more prevalent in Matthew's Gospel, which would argue against these views.[23] Some suggest that Jeremiah was understood as some type of messianic forerunner, although suggestions along these lines are speculative.[24] Another possibility is a typological connection between Jeremiah and Jesus, which has been explored extensively by Bruce Dahlberg, who draws on Jeremiah 1:4-19. Dahlberg compares Jeremiah's and Peter's respective commissioning, noting that each receives divine authority from Yahweh and Jesus, respectively (e.g., breaking down and building up for Jeremiah, and the keys of the kingdom for Peter).[25] He also compares the opposition that both Jeremiah and Jesus experience from rulers in Jerusalem.[26] Yet, as others note, the point of comparison in Matthew 16:14 concerns Jesus, not Peter.

Perhaps more convincing is the work of M. J. J. Menken, who extensively traces the understanding of Jeremiah as the prophet who suffered for the message he brought to his own people in Jewish and early Christian writings.[27] This accords well with Jesus' prediction of his death following Peter's confession. More recently, Mark Whitters argues,

> In the first century C.E., Jeremiah represented the stereotypical "rejected prophet," ostracized and persecuted by his own people. Further, Jeremiah was a prophet of doom and disaster because of his association with the Babylonian captivity. These characterizations of Jeremiah resemble what the reader finds in the Gospel of Matthew, for Jesus is

---

[23]Knowles, *Jeremiah in Matthew's Gospel*, 82-83; see also D. R. Law, "Matthew's Enigmatic Reference to Jeremiah in Mt 16,14," in *The Book of Jeremiah and Its Receptions: Le Livre de Jérémie et sa Réception*, ed. A. H. W. Curtis and T. Römer (Leuven: Leuven University Press, 1997), 277-302, esp. 286-90.

[24]Law, "Matthew's Enigmatic Reference," 280-86.

[25]Dahlberg, "Typological Use of Jeremiah 1:4-19," 75.

[26]This is ominously anticipated in the comment that "all Jerusalem" is troubled with Herod at the magi's report (Mt 2:3).

[27]Menken, "References to Jeremiah," 17-21; see also Law, "Matthew's Enigmatic Reference," 290-96.

simultaneously one who was rejected and persecuted by his own people even to the point of death and one who predicted the doom of his people.[28]

Thus the reference to Jeremiah presents Jesus as a suffering, rejected prophet to Matthew's audience and suggests that the prophet Jeremiah was instrumental in Jesus' self-understanding.[29] This identification is supported by the citations from Jeremiah at the beginning (Mt 2:15) and end (Mt 27:9-10) of Matthew's Gospel, which also occur in connection with significant opposition (Herod and Judas) against Jesus.[30] Knowles notes that several key allusions to Jeremiah in Matthew's Gospel further present Jesus as the prophet of judgment (e.g., Jer 7:11 in Mt 21:23) and the prophet of the New Covenant (Jer 31:31-34 in Mt 26:28).[31]

JEREMIAH AND THE PAULINE EPISTLES

There are several direct citations of Jeremiah in the Pauline Epistles as well as numerous allusions. I will first briefly discuss the citation of Jeremiah 9:23-24 in 1 Corinthians 1:31 and 2 Corinthians 10:17.[32] I will

---

[28] Mark F. Whitters, "Jesus in the Footsteps of Jeremiah," *Catholic Biblical Quarterly* 68 (2006): 229-47, here 230. For additional biographical parallels between Jeremiah and Jesus, see 231-32. He adds regarding Matthew's use of typology: "While many have seen this technique in subtle references to Moses, fewer have recognized the writer's gaze upon Jeremiah. Although the reader encounters Jeremiah as a model for Jesus directly in the middle of the Gospel (16:14), Jeremiah's presence is more opaque and cited less frequently than that of Moses. It is nonetheless at least as ubiquitous" (247).

[29] See esp. Knowles, *Jeremiah in Matthew's Gospel*. Blomberg suggests that Matthew may "see Jesus as a new and greater Jeremiah (i.e., a suffering prophet, who also spent time in Egypt [Jer 43-44])" ("Matthew," 10).

[30] Menken, "References to Jeremiah," 9. See also Whitters: "There are two other direct references to the Book of Jeremiah in the Gospel, one at the beginning of Jesus' life, the other at the end. Taken together, these three references lie at strategic points in the narrative, and they hint at some thread that binds the life of Jesus to the memory of Jeremiah" ("Jesus in the Footsteps," 230).

[31] Knowles, *Jeremiah in Matthew's Gospel*, 173-76, 207-9; Law, "Matthew's Enigmatic Reference," 297-302. See esp. Craig A. Evans, "Jeremiah in Jesus and the New Testament," in *The Book of Jeremiah: Composition, Reception, and Interpretation*, ed. Jack R. Lundbom, Craig A. Evans, and Bradford A. Anderson, VTSup 178 (Boston: Brill, 2018), 303-19.

[32] Additional allusions include Rom 1:22 (Jer 10:14); Rom 2:29 (Jer 4:4); Rom 9:21 (Jer 18:6); Rom 11:34 (Jer 23:18); Rom 14:11 (Jer 22:24); 1 Cor 2:16 (Jer 23:18); 2 Cor 10:8 (Jer 24:6); and 1 Thess 5:3 (Jer 6:14).

then discuss possible ways in which Jeremiah influenced Paul's self-understanding as an apostle.

Jeremiah 9:23-24 and 1 Corinthians 1:31 and 2 Corinthians 10:17.
In 1 Corinthians, in the context of Paul's rebuke to the Corinthians concerning the factions that had arisen in the church, Paul quotes an adapted citation of Jeremiah 9:24. First Corinthians 1:31 reads as follows: "Therefore, as it is written, 'Let the one who boasts boast in the Lord'" (NIV). The citation from Jeremiah 9:23-24 reads as follows: "Thus says the LORD: 'Let not the wise man boast in his wisdom, let not the mighty man boast in his might, let not the rich man boast in his riches, but let him who boasts boast in this, that he understands and knows me, that I am the LORD who practices steadfast love, justice, and righteousness in the earth. For in these things I delight, declares the LORD'" (ESV).

In the larger context of 1 Corinthians 1, this citation underscores the reality that things that appear to be wise and powerful according to worldly standards are actually foolishness in God's sight, and conversely the wisdom and strength of God, especially as they are revealed on the cross, appear as foolishness to those who have not been called (1 Cor 1:18-30). As one reads this passage, the language of Jeremiah 9:23-24 permeates Paul's writing, where the true nature of wisdom, power, and wealth are contrasted with the world's (and the Corinthians') false perceptions concerning these same things.[33]

Paul's appropriation of the Jeremiah text appears to consider its original context, where the prophet, speaking the Lord's words, similarly condemns those who put their trust in their own wisdom, power, and wealth, and reveals the true object of boasting, namely, boasting in the Lord. Similar wording to Jeremiah 9:23-24 occurs in the LXX translation of 1 Samuel 2:10 (1 Kingdoms 2:10), where Hannah praises the

---

[33] Thus, in addition to the direct citation, the surrounding context of 1 Corinthians is affected by the vocabulary from the Jeremiah citation.

Lord, who will bring down those who boast in their own wisdom, strength, and wealth, which Paul may have also had in mind.[34]

Paul again cites the adapted text from Jeremiah 9:24 in 2 Corinthians 10:17, where he is defending himself against the Corinthian so-called super-apostles. It seems likely that this citation is intended to recall its earlier citation in 1 Corinthians 1:31. Earlier in 2 Corinthians 10:8, there is an allusion to Jeremiah 24:6, where Paul draws on the "building up" and "tearing down" language of this passage in Jeremiah.[35] Second Corinthians 10:8 reads as follows: "Now, even if I boast a little too much of our authority, which the Lord gave for building you up and not for tearing you down, I will not be ashamed of it" (NRSV). Hetty Lalleman draws out the significant parallels between Jeremiah and Paul, noting that each confronted false teachers (either false prophets or false apostles) who did not confront the people's sin, as both Jeremiah and Paul did.[36] She concludes: "In this respect Jeremiah can be seen as a forerunner not only of Jesus Christ, but also of the apostle Paul, the apostle to the nations. Both Paul and Jeremiah were involved in the battle of false versus true messengers of God and both saw their mission questioned and rejected by their own people (Jer. 11.21; 12.6)."[37] This point naturally leads to Jeremiah's contribution to Paul's self-understanding.

Jeremiah and Paul's self-understanding. Numerous scholars draw attention to the parallels between Jeremiah and Paul, including their respective understanding of their calling from birth and their need to

---

[34] Roy E. Ciampa and Brian S. Rosner, "1 Corinthians," in Beale and Carson, *Commentary on the New Testament Use*, 695-752, here 699.

[35] Hetty Lalleman, "Paul's Self-Understanding in the Light of Jeremiah: A Case Study into the Use of the Old Testament in the New Testament," in *God of Faithfulness: Essays in Honour of J. Gordon McConville on His Sixtieth Birthday*, ed. Jaime A. Grant, Allison Lo, and Gordon J. Wenham (New York: T&T Clark, 2011), 96-111, here 107. She adds that the context in Jeremiah is also significant: "The phrases in Jeremiah which contain the terms 'building up' and 'tearing down' are summaries of the calling and the commissioning of the prophet, the content of his message and the effect of his ministry" (107).

[36] Lalleman notes: "Chapters 10-13 in 2 Corinthians do not reveal much about the false apostles but the fact that Paul repeatedly defends himself against the charge that his approach is negative suggests that these rival leaders did not tackle sins in the way he did" ("Paul's Self-Understanding," 108).

[37] Lalleman, "Paul's Self-Understanding," 110.

contend against false teachers who claimed to be either true prophets or true apostles. Henry J. Boekhoven asserts, "Paul saw his example in Jeremiah."[38]

Lalleman asks the following questions: "Did Paul understand himself as being a prophet in the tradition of Jeremiah? Was his self-understanding shaped by Jeremiah's mission and ministry?"[39] She answers both questions affirmatively. Like others, she draws on Paul's wording in Galatians 1:15-16: "But when God, who set me apart from my mother's womb and called me by his grace, was pleased to reveal his Son in me so that I might preach him among the Gentiles" (NIV). Compare this with Jeremiah 1:5, which states: "Before I formed you in the womb I knew you, before you were born I set you apart; I appointed you as a prophet to the nations" (NIV). She concludes, "Both Jeremiah 1 and Galatians 1 underline the authority of the person who is commissioned not by human beings, but by God. As a consequence of this commissioning, Jeremiah is a 'true prophet' and Paul is a 'true apostle.'"[40] Like Jeremiah, Paul suffered greatly and was rejected by his own people.[41] She further notes parallels between Jeremiah as a prophet to the nations (Jer 1:5) and Paul as an apostle to the Gentiles (Gal 1:15-16; see Rom 11:13).[42] She concludes with a discussion of the reference to uprooting, tearing down, destroying, overthrowing, building, and planting in Jeremiah 1:1:10 and Paul's use of similar terms in 2 Corinthians (e.g., 2 Cor 10:4-5, 8; 13:10).

---

[38]Henry J. Boekhoven, "The Influence of Jeremiah upon New Testament Literature," *Reformed Review* 14 (1960): 37-43, here 39. He also notes Acts 18:9 (alluding to Jer 1:8) and Acts 26:16-18 (alluding to Jer 1:7) ("Influence of Jeremiah," 39-40).
[39]Lalleman, "Paul's Self-Understanding," 98.
[40]Lalleman, "Paul's Self-Understanding," 106.
[41]Lalleman, "Paul's Self-Understanding," 110-11. She summarizes: "The parallels between the two thus include their divine calling, their message of 'tearing down and building up,' their life experiences and the need to defend themselves against a multitude of adversaries who claimed to be true messengers of God. It was only God's grace and power which sustained them both" (111).
[42]Lalleman, "Paul's Self-Understanding," 106.

Jeremiah and the Epistle to the Hebrews

As noted, the longest citation of any Old Testament text in the New Testament is the citation of Jeremiah 31:31-34 (LXX 38:31-34) in Hebrews 8:8-12. The last two verses of the extended citation are appropriated again in Hebrews 10:16-17. The promise of the New Covenant is alluded to by Jesus in Luke 22:20 and by Paul in 1 Corinthians 11:25 and 2 Corinthians 3:6; additionally, the promise of having the law written on believers' hearts is referred to in Romans 2:15.

The context of this prophecy concerning the future restoration of both Israel and Judah in Jeremiah 30–31 has already been discussed. Although only Jeremiah 31:31-34 is referenced in Hebrews, some echoes of Jeremiah 31:35-37 may be possible.[43] In his work on Jeremiah 30–31, Bob Becking notes parallels between Jeremiah 31:31-34 and Jeremiah 31:35-37. For example, each passage looks to God's past faithfulness, either in terms of his taking his people by the hand to lead them out of Egypt (Jer 31:32) or in terms of "the reliability of reality" as manifest in the regularity of the rising sun, the heavens, and other aspects of creation. He comments, "The hymnic depiction of YHWH as the guarantor of the regularity of the forces of nature functions as the central motivation for the implied oracle of salvation: YHWH guarantees the endurance of the people of Israel which cannot be threatened by forces of nature or human wrongdoings."[44] Although the author of Hebrews does not appear to draw on Jeremiah 31:35-37, the emphasis on the reliability of God's promises runs throughout Hebrews (see esp. Heb 6:13-20). It is not clear, however, that the author of Hebrews was consciously drawing on Jeremiah 31:35-37.

The citation of Jeremiah 31 in Hebrews 8 occurs in the center of the central section of Hebrews, which begins in Hebrews 5:1 and extends through Hebrews 10:18. In this section, the author of Hebrews

---

[43] Becking, "Voice Was Heard," 247.
[44] Becking, "Voice Was Heard," 263, 268. He adds, "The reliability of reality as met with in time and space, stands as a metaphor for the reliability of God's promise" (272).

methodically compares the Son with the core elements of the Levitical order and demonstrates Christ's superiority to that system. He begins with the Levitical priesthood and demonstrates the superiority of Christ's priesthood since it is eternal and depends on his resurrected life (Heb 5:1-10; 7:1-28), drawing out key inferences from the account of Melchizedek in Genesis 14:17-20 and Psalm 110:4. In this discussion, he demonstrates that this change of priesthood necessitates a change of the law, thus revealing the ultimately temporal nature of the Levitical law. Throughout this discussion, the author refers to a "better hope" (Heb 7:19), a "better covenant" (Heb 7:22), and the perfection that is achieved by Christ's superior priesthood and sacrifice (Heb 7:26-28).[45] In this way, the author anticipates the discussion of the New Covenant in Hebrews 8, which is founded on "better promises" (Heb 8:6). The "better promises" recalls the Abrahamic promises (Heb 6:13-20), which were the bases of the Sinaitic covenant. Just as the Abrahamic promises pointed typologically to the "better promises," so also the Mosaic covenant pointed typologically to the New Covenant.[46]

The focus on Christ as the perfect high priest in Hebrews 7 shifts to Jesus as the mediator of a New Covenant, which is introduced in Hebrews 8:1-6 and developed in Hebrews 8:7-13 and Hebrews 9:1-28. In Hebrews 8:6, the author concludes that just as Christ's priestly ministry is superior to the Levitical one, so also is the covenant of which he is the mediator superior to the covenant associated with the Levitical priesthood.

The mediator of the Sinaitic covenant, Moses, is not mentioned here, although an implied allusion to Moses could point typologically to the

---

[45] The significance of Christ's self-sacrifice is developed in terms of sanctuary, covenant, and sacrifice—"a symphony in three movements": Heb 8:1-13; 9:1-22; 9:23–10:18, each of which begins with sanctuary, focuses on sacrifice, and ends with covenant. See G. L. Cockerill, "Structure and Interpretation in Hebrews 8:1–10:18: A Symphony in Three Movements," *BBR* 11 (2001): 179-201.

[46] Although the LXX uses "covenant" (*diathēkē*) to refer to several OT covenants (e.g., Abrahamic and Davidic), Hebrews uses "covenant" only to refer to in the Sinaitic, or first, covenant and the New Covenant of Jer 31.

superior mediator, Christ. That this typological connection is not explicitly stated in Hebrews likely indicates the profound difference between the two covenants—unlike the first covenant, which depended on two parties (i.e., God and Israel), the power of the New Covenant is that it depends only on God.

The logic of Hebrews 8:7—"for if there had been nothing wrong with that first covenant, no place would have been sought for another" (NIV)—has already been introduced in several earlier sections of the epistle. For example, in the discussion of the Levitical priesthood, the author argues that if the Levitical priesthood had been able to bring about perfection, then why would there be mention of another order of priesthood, namely, the Melchizedekian one (Heb 7:11)?[47] This same logic applies to the summary statement in Hebrews 8:13 following the citation of Jeremiah 31, namely that by calling this covenant "new," God has revealed that the first covenant is now "obsolete."[48] Although this could be understood as an example of supersessionism, the approach in Hebrews is to show the incomplete and anticipatory nature of the former order such that it is pointing beyond itself to its final fulfillment in Christ.

The reference to "the days that are coming" (Heb 8:8) recalls the references to "these last days" in Hebrews 1:2. The limitation of the first covenant (as indicated by Jer 31:32 in Heb 8:9) recalls the earlier focus on the faithlessness of the wilderness generation in Hebrews 3:7–4:11, namely that human sin could (and did) invalidate the first covenant. The reference to both the people of Israel and the people of Judah implies that the New Covenant will bring about the reunification of the divided kingdom.

The extended citation from Jeremiah 31:31-34 (LXX 38:31-34) in Hebrews 8:8-12 reveals the nature of the "better promises" (Heb 8:6), yet

---

[47]See also the use of "day" in Heb 3–4.
[48]Most contemporary Jewish writings maintained the everlasting nature of the Sinaitic covenant (e.g., Sirach 17:12). The author of Hebrews draws inferences from the language of "new" in Jeremiah: "As soon as God promised a 'new' covenant, the Old was 'near passing away'" (Cockerill, "Structure and Interpretation," 370).

the application of these promises is delayed until Hebrews 10:15-18. The better promises include the internalization of the law and the reaffirmation that the people are God's people (Heb 8:10), drawing on language that expresses the core of God's covenantal relationship with his people. Hebrews 8:11 talks of a greater, more intimate knowledge of the Lord. But the most important of these promises is the one that God will remember the people's sins no more (Heb 8:12). These promises, and especially this last one, anticipate Hebrews 9:1–10:18, which describes the fulfillment of the New Covenant in terms of Jesus' fully efficacious sacrifice, which finally enabled the complete cleansing of the worshiper's conscience—something the first covenant could not do.

The citation from Jeremiah 31:31-34 is reappropriated in Hebrews 10:15-17. The immediate context in Hebrews 10 is the contrast between the repetitious and inefficacious nature of the Levitical priesthood in Hebrews 10:11 and the fully efficacious sacrifice of Christ in Hebrews 10:12-13. The re-citation of Jeremiah 31 in Hebrews 10 is significantly abbreviated, citing only Jeremiah 31:33-34, with several variations from its citation in Hebrews 8:10. For example, "to them" replaces "the house of Israel," perhaps to indicate the more extensive scope of the New Covenant. The author has thus summarized the promises of the New Covenant by re-citing the first and last promises enumerated in the full citation of Jeremiah 31:33-34 in Hebrews 8, without denying the intervening promises.[49]

The first citation of Jeremiah 31 in Hebrews 8 established that Scripture itself had prophesied about the Mosaic covenant's limitations and eventual end. Following the author's exposition of Christ's sacrifice as the penalty paid for the broken Mosaic covenant and inauguration the New Covenant, the citation of Jeremiah 31 again in Hebrews 10, at the conclusion of the author's main argument, makes explicit that Christ is the means by which Jeremiah's prophecy is fulfilled. The

---

[49]Cockerill, "Structure and Interpretation," 456.

internalization of God's laws and the complete forgiveness of sins with the resultant cleansed conscience promised in Jeremiah 31 have now been achieved by Christ's efficacious sacrifice and eternal exaltation. The focus in Hebrews 10 is thus on the application of the author's main argument to his audience.[50]

The connection to the New Covenant is also significant for the citation of Psalm 40 in Hebrews 10:5-7, which precedes the Jeremiah citation in Hebrews 10:15-18. The psalm citation shows that because of Jesus' incarnation and his willing self-sacrifice, the promise of the New Covenant, namely, the internalization of the law and the remembrance of sin no more, is now achieved through the Son's complete obedience to the Father's will.

In summary, the citation of Jeremiah 31 in Hebrews 8 and Hebrews 10 plays a vital role in revealing how Christ fulfills Jeremiah's prophecy and thereby inaugurates a new priesthood in the heavenly sanctuary that makes possible true worship, which was not possible with the first covenant.

Conclusion

It is evident, even from this brief survey, that Jeremiah had a significant influence on New Testament writers.[51] Citations are used to establish typological connections in the life of Jesus to previous events in the history of Israel, such as the exile. These connections also show that Jesus is the promised Davidic king, the true king of Israel, who will regather his people and lead them out of their exile. Citations and biographical parallels between Jeremiah and both Jesus and Paul appear to have been influential in each of their self-understanding. This self-understanding included an awareness of the suffering and rejection that each would experience at the hands of their own people. Yet

---

[50]See Cockerill, "Structure and Interpretation," 453-54.
[51]Even more contributions from Jeremiah occur with the other citations and the numerous allusions that were not discussed here due to space constraints.

Jeremiah also anticipates the perseverance and obedience of both Jesus and Paul. Finally, the extended citation of Jeremiah 31 in Hebrews plays a pivotal role in the author's exposition of the superiority of Christ. The promises of Jeremiah's New Covenant can only be fulfilled by the incarnation, sacrifice, and exaltation of Jesus Christ. His willing sacrifice paid the price for the broken Sinaitic covenant and inaugurated the New Covenant. His faithful obedience and exaltation confirmed him as the mediator of the new, eternal covenant.

The presence of Jeremiah is felt throughout the New Testament. Regardless of any hermeneutical technique that New Testament writers might have used to appropriate Jeremiah, it is clear that his person and his prophecies exerted a profound influence on the ways that New Testament writers understood the person and work of Christ, the way that Jesus likely understood his own life and work, and the way that Paul understood his own mission. May this influence draw us all back to the text of Jeremiah so that our own appreciation of his influence on the New Testament might be enriched.

7

WE ARE NOT APOSTLES

Limits on Reading Jeremiah Like the Apostles

GARY E. YATES

JEREMIAH'S MESSAGE CONCERNING THE NEW COVENANT (Jer 31:31-34) has sparked significant controversy over the relationship between the Old and New Testaments. Historical-critical readings often view Jeremiah's oracles as related only to the more immediate future and Israel's return to the land that occurred in the postexilic period, and have tended to view the New Testament and Christian theology as misappropriating the prophetic promise of the New Covenant for the church. Canonical readings from a two-testament perspective have rightly paid attention to New Testament developments and reappropriation of Jeremiah's New Covenant message but often minimize the historical details of Jeremiah's message and the role of Israel in God's redemptive plan. Christopher Wright reminds us of the challenge this prophecy presents for Christian readers: "This familiarity with the phrase 'new covenant'... is exegetically dangerous since it can tempt us to read the words of Jeremiah immediately through the lens of their New Testament quotations, rather than through the eyes and ears of those who first heard them or read them in his edited book."[1]

Christian readings of Jeremiah 31:31-34 also often operate on the assumption that Jeremiah's prophecy of the New Covenant applies principally or even exclusively to the church.[2] Louis Stulman observes, "Christian commentators often treat Jer 31:31-34 in complete isolation from its literary and historical setting. That is to say, they read this text as the exclusive property of Christians. Such exegesis creates a rigid dichotomy between Jews and Christians, relegating Judaism to the inferior province of the 'old covenant.'"[3]

Such readings are particularly inadequate because of how they largely overlook Jeremiah's New Covenant prophecy as a promise of a restored and spiritually renewed Israel. The restoration and renewal of Israel would include the blessing of the nations, as promised in the original Abrahamic covenant, but not apart from Israel or merely through the medium of a new spiritual or multinational Israel. In Jeremiah's New Covenant, Yahweh promises to renew and transform the Sinai covenant with his people Israel, providing a new administration of the covenant with the grace and enablement needed to guarantee the future fidelity of his people. Because this covenant remains specifically between God and Israel, the message of Jeremiah affirms Israel's special status and its enduring place in the working out of redemptive history.

---

[1] Christopher J. H. Wright, *The Message of Jeremiah: Against Wind and Tide*, BST (Downers Grove, IL: IVP Academic, 2014), 323.

[2] Hermann Ridderbos gives a standard expression of this form of supersessionism: "The church, then, as the people of the New Covenant has taken the place of Israel, and national Israel is nothing other than the empty shell from which the pearl has been removed and which has lost its function in the history of redemption." Ridderbos, *Paul: An Outline of His Theology* (Grand Rapids, MI: Eerdmans, 1997), 354-55.

[3] Louis Stulman, *Jeremiah*, Apollos Old Testament Commentary (Nashville: Abingdon, 2005), 272.

The Promise and Nature of the New Covenant in Jeremiah 31:31-34

Jeremiah's promise of the New Covenant (Jer 31:31-34) is part of the larger Book of Consolation in Jeremiah 30–33. Stulman explains that Jeremiah 1–25 highlights the prophet's message of judgment concerning the dismantling of Israel's old world order, which was founded on temple, covenant, and the privileged position of the house of David. Jeremiah 26–52 then emphasizes the hope of a new order that emerges out of the ruins of the past with the promise that the people will return from exile to repopulate their land and rebuild their cities.[4] The promise of the New Covenant in Jeremiah 31:31-34 assures that Yahweh's election of Israel and his covenantal commitments to Israel remain secure even as the old order collapses. The New Covenant will reverse the failures of the past covenantal arrangement by securing for all Israel the internalization of the Torah (Jer 31:33), personal knowledge of Yahweh, and the forgiveness of sins (Jer 31:34).

One of the major issues surrounding Jeremiah 31:31-34 is the relationship of this New Covenant to the prior Mosaic or Sinaitic covenant. David Peterson notes, "Commentators have long argued about whether the New Covenant is simply a renewal of the previous covenant or not."[5] The existence of both continuities and discontinuities between the two covenants has complicated the issue so that some interpreters have seen the New Covenant as nothing more than a renewal of the Mosaic covenant, while others view Jeremiah as announcing the end of the Mosaic covenant and the institution of an entirely new covenantal arrangement. The root $ḥdš$ is flexible enough to cover that which is both "new" and "renewed."[6] Additionally, continuity with the past is

---

[4]Stulman, *Jeremiah*, 260-62.
[5]David G. Peterson, *Transformed by God: New Covenant Life and Ministry* (Downers Grove, IL: IVP Academic, 2012), 29.
[6]Walter C. Kaiser with Tiberius Rata, *Walking the Ancient Paths: A Commentary on Jeremiah* (Bellingham, WA: Lexham, 2019), 369.

reflected in Jeremiah 31:23-26 and Jeremiah 31:35-38, which emphasize how Israel's future in the land will be like former times and that Yahweh's commitment to Israel is as enduring as the cycles of nature.[7]

The greater emphasis in Jeremiah's announcement, however, seems to fall on the radical newness of this arrangement. The use of *ḥādāš* in connection with the verb *bārā'* in Jeremiah 31:22 highlights "the creative newness" of the covenant, and Jeremiah 31:32 explicitly states that it will not be like the one made at Sinai.[8] Discontinuity between old and new is further highlighted by the repetition of "no more" (*'ôd*) in Jeremiah 31:34 (see Jer 31:29, 40).[9] The recurring "days are coming" (*yāmîm bā'îm*) in Jeremiah 31:27, 31, 38 also points to how the future will be different from the past.[10] This New Covenant offers more than simply a renewal and resumption of the Mosaic covenant in spite of its clear continuities with the arrangement made at Sinai.

Mark Boda offers a careful nuancing of the continuities and discontinuities reflected in the New Covenant when he states that this covenant remains the Sinai covenant but that its newness results from the "radically new means" by which the covenant will be administered.[11] John Goldingay similarly states that the making of a New Covenant does not necessarily imply the annulment of the previously existing one but rather that Yahweh "recognizes the necessity to improve how the covenant works in order to achieve the aim of having a people that does keep its side of the relationship."[12] Divine grace and enablement are needed in a new way as the impetus for fidelity on the part of the people.

---

[7]Peterson, *Transformed by God*, 29.
[8]Paul R. Williamson, *Sealed with an Oath: Covenant in God's Unfolding Purpose*, NSBT 23 (Downers Grove, IL: IVP Academic, 2007), 153.
[9]Williamson, *Sealed with an Oath*, 153.
[10]Peterson, *Transformed by God*, 29.
[11]Mark J. Boda, *A Severe Mercy: Sin and Its Remedy in the Old Testament*, Siphrut 1 (Winona Lake, IN: Eisenbrauns, 2009), 250.
[12]John Goldingay, *Old Testament Theology*, vol. 1, *Israel's Gospel* (Downers Grove, IL: IVP Academic, 2003), 378n17.

There are substantial changes associated with the coming of this New Covenant. The first essential variation is that the law will be permanently inscribed on the hearts of the people, unlike the Sinai covenant, which was written on stone (Ex 31:18). Laws written on stone could be broken (Ex 32:19), and the law itself could be lost (2 Kings 22:8), burned (Ex 36:23), or drowned (Jer 51:63).[13] The larger problem was that laws written on stone addressed the people from the outside in demanding obedience but did not provide the enablement for them to obey.[14] In contrast, the internal inscribing of the law on the hearts of the people will overwrite the sin and rebellion etched into their hearts (Jer 17:1). The people will have both the desire and capacity to obey Yahweh's commands, and this arrangement will break the endless cycle of sin and punishment that characterizes Israel's past (Jer 32:38-40). The people will truly "know" the Lord, not merely in terms of personal relationship but even more in the practice of obedience and fidelity to his commands and standards of justice (Jer 22:16; see Jer 9:23).

The nature and extent of forgiveness promised in Jeremiah 31:34 also transcends what was experienced under the Mosaic covenant. Jack Lundbom states that the promise of forgiveness in Jeremiah 31:34 reflects that the New Covenant is "grounded in a wholly new act of divine grace."[15] The divine promise not to remember sins is a direct reversal of Jeremiah 14:10.[16] Unlike in the old covenant, sacrifice and atonement appear to play no part in securing this forgiveness.[17] The *kî* introducing the

---

[13]T. Rata, "Covenant," in *Dictionary of the Old Testament Prophets*, ed. Mark J. Boda and J. Gordon McConville (Downers Grove, IL: IVP Academic, 2012), 104.

[14]Robert B. Chisholm Jr., *Handbook on the Prophets* (Grand Rapids, MI: Baker, 2002), 195.

[15]Jack R. Lundbom, *Jeremiah 21–36: A New Translation with Introduction and Commentary*, AB 21.2 (New York: Doubleday, 2004), 466.

[16]Leslie C. Allen, *Jeremiah*, OTL (Louisville, KY: Westminster John Knox, 2008), 356.

[17]Andrew G. Shead notes that "there is nothing normal about the forgiveness of 'iniquity'" (עָוֹן) under the old covenant. Sacrifices cleansed the sanctuary and priests of the guilt that came on them as a result of the people's sin (see Num 18:1), but regular sacrifices could not "atone for the iniquity of regular sin." See Shead, *A Mouth Full of Fire: The Word of God in the Words of Jeremiah*, NSBT 29 (Downers Grove, IL: IVP Academic, 2012), 200. Such sin required the sinner to be "cut off" from the people (see Lev 19:8; 1 Sam 3:13-14), and the scapegoat was needed on the Day of Atonement to carry away the people's iniquity (see Lev 16:21-22).

subordinate clause focusing on the forgiveness of sins in Jeremiah 31:34 stresses the innovative idea that divine forgiveness will be the underlying cause of the internal transformation provided within the New Covenant.[18]

The New Covenant as Renewal of God's Covenant with Israel

In spite of these significant innovations, there is also an essential continuity between Jeremiah's New Covenant and the past covenants Yahweh had made with Israel, particularly the Mosaic or Sinaitic covenant. Walter Kaiser estimates that "almost three-fourths of the contents of the new covenant are but a repetition of what was in the earlier covenants."[19] Daniel Block more categorically states that none of the features in the New Covenant were "absolutely new" and that "everything promised in the New Covenant had already been promised in the Old."[20] This overriding continuity indicates that Jeremiah envisioned the renewal of the old covenant rather than the institution of a brand-new arrangement, with the critical difference being that Yahweh now "guarantees that the ideals of the Old would be finally and fully realized."[21]

The primary feature of continuity in the New Covenant is that the partners in this arrangement remain the same—this covenant is specifically between Yahweh and Israel. Walter Brueggemann emphatically argues that "nothing could more distort" the message of Jeremiah 31 than to read into this passage a rejection of Israel in light of the fact that the prophet conveys "a divine declaration that Yhwh will begin again with Israel and restore a covenantal relationship that has been lost in the debacle of disobedience and destruction."[22] Terence Fretheim

---

[18]Shead, *Mouth Full of Fire*, 199.
[19]Kaiser, *Walking the Ancient Paths*, 369.
[20]Daniel I. Block, *The Triumph of Grace: Literary and Theological Studies in Deuteronomy and Deuteronomic Themes* (Eugene, OR: Cascade, 2017), 79.
[21]Block, *Triumph of Grace*, 79.
[22]Walter Brueggemann, *The Theology of the Book of Jeremiah*, Old Testament Theology (Cambridge: Cambridge University Press, 2006), 126.

similarly highlights the specificity of the New Covenant as an arrangement between God and Israel:

> Unless the new covenant is God's promise for the sake of the future of this very specific group of people, it is a promise for no one else. And certainly, those responsible for transmitting this promise understand the new covenant to be a promise God has given to this people, a people who will *never* be rejected by God (vv. 35-37). The promise of a new covenant is thus given to a particular people within a specific geographic locale; to interpret this text in individualistic, universalistic, or narrowly spiritual terms violates its context.[23]

Jeremiah even goes so far as to ground God's promises to Israel in the creational or Noahic covenant (Jer 31:35-37; 33:25-26), which indicates that his relationship with Israel is as enduring as the creation and that his redemptive purposes for Israel are inseparably linked to his universal plan of redemption. The prophet emphatically stresses that Yahweh's relationship with Israel is "beyond disruption."[24] Jeremiah's use of the alternate "everlasting [*'ôlām*] covenant" to describe the arrangement guaranteeing Israel's forgiveness and restoration (Jer 32:5; 50:5; see Jer 50:20) further emphasizes the perpetuity of the relationship between Yahweh and Israel.[25]

Some interpreters argue against the national or ethnic particularity of the references to Israel and Judah in Jeremiah 31. Peter Lee states, "The references to the 'house of Israel' and the 'house of Judah' in Jeremiah 31:27, 31 (cf. 30:3-4) are examples of prophetic idiom, where old covenant terms are used to express a new covenant reality—in this case, the church."[26] Paul Williamson also views the "house of Israel and house of Judah" in Jeremiah 31:27, 31 as referring to "the universal

---

[23]Terence E. Fretheim, *Jeremiah*, Smyth & Helwys Bible Commentary (Macon, GA: Smyth & Helwys, 2002), 442.
[24]Brueggemann, *Theology of the Book of Jeremiah*, 128.
[25]Williamson, *Sealed with an Oath*, 165.
[26]Peter Y. Lee, "Jeremiah," in *A Biblical-Theological Introduction to the Old Testament: The Gospel Promised*, ed. Miles V. Van Pelt (Wheaton, IL: Crossway, 2016), 294-95.

people of God."²⁷ Andrew Shead similarly argues that these references to Israel and Judah no longer refer to "a narrowly ethnic Israel" but rather to "a new Israel drawn from every nation."²⁸

Despite these proposed redefinitions or reconfigurations of Israel in the book of Jeremiah, none of the six other uses of the phrases "house of Israel" and "house of Judah" outside Jeremiah 31 employ these designations for any group other than ethnic or national Israelites (see Jer 3:18; 5:11; 11:10, 17; 13:11; 33:14).²⁹ The mention of "house of Israel" and "house of Judah" in Jeremiah 31:31 directly connects this oracle to the larger message of the Book of Consolation in Jeremiah 30–33, which is a specific and historically focused message regarding the restoration of Israel, the return of the Jews to their homeland from Babylonian captivity, and the rebuilding and repopulation of the cities of Israel.³⁰ Framing references in the Book of Consolation to "my people Israel, and Judah" (Jer 30:1) and "Israel and Judah" (Jer 33:26) highlight the specific focus of this section on the ethnic people and political nation of Israel. In Jeremiah 30–33, there are references to Israel as a distinct "people" (ʿam; Jer 30:3, 22; 31:1, 2, 7, 14, 33; 32:21, 38, 42; 33:24) and "nation" (gôy; Jer 31:36; 33:24). There are further specifying references to the "descendants" (zeraʿ) of Abraham, Isaac, Jacob, Israel, David, and the Levites (Jer 30:10; 31:36-37; 33:22, 26) and to the "families" (mišpāḥôt) of Israel/Judah (Jer 31:1; 33:24). The prophet anticipates that Israel in its restoration will become "the greatest of nations" (rōš haggôyîm, Jer 31:7), suggesting that Israel will remain a political entity with its own boundaries and national identity.³¹ In Jeremiah 30–33, the only specific focus on other nations is either as the agents or objects of divine judgment (see Jer 30:8-11; 32:26-35).³²

---

²⁷Williamson, *Sealed with an Oath*, 153.
²⁸Shead, *Mouth Full of Fire*, 196.
²⁹Femi Adeyemi, *The New Covenant Torah in Jeremiah and the Law of Christ in Paul*, Studies in Biblical Literature 94 (New York: Peter Lang, 2006–2007), 47.
³⁰Fretheim, *Jeremiah*, 441.
³¹Allen, *Jeremiah*, 358. See also W. Rudolph, *Jeremia*, Handbuch zum Alten Testament (Tübingen: Mohr Siebeck, 1968), 204.
³²Block, *Triumph of Grace*, 78.

The promise of Israel's restoration and New Covenant in Jeremiah 31:27-40 closely parallels the promise of Israel's restoration and spiritual transformation via the "everlasting covenant" (*bərît ʿôlām*) in Jeremiah 32:36-44. Both passages deal with specifics related to Israel's return to the land. The first passage focuses on the rebuilding of Israel's walls and cities (Jer 31:38-40), while the second anticipates the purchasing of fields in the land (Jer 32:43-44). Both passages promise that Yahweh will "plant" (*nṭʿ*) his people in the land (Jer 31:28; 32:41).[33] Like the New Covenant, the everlasting covenant envisions spiritual transformation on a national level that guarantees the fidelity of the people to Yahweh. Yahweh will place the fear of himself in the people's hearts so that they will never turn away from him and so that he can always do good for them as blessing for their obedience (Jer 32:39-40). Jeremiah's sign-act involving the purchase of family property at Anathoth in Jeremiah 32 reflects the inseparable connection between Israel's land promises and this new and everlasting covenant.

To view "house of Israel" and "house of Judah" in Jeremiah 31:31 as an idiom for the church or even as depicting a "new Israel" consisting of both Jews and Gentiles disconnects the New Covenant oracle in Jeremiah 31:31-34 from the literary and historical context in which it is firmly anchored. Lundbom states, "There is nothing to suggest that this new covenant will be made with an expanded Israel, including Gentiles. It was so interpreted by the Christian Church, but the promise as given is not that inclusive."[34] Block concurs and states, "It is obvious that in this 'new covenant' text, Jeremiah was concerned primarily—if not exclusively—with his own people Israel, and their relationship to God and the land they once occupied."[35]

---

[33] See B. J. Oropeza, "New Covenant Knowledge in an Earthenware Jar: Intertextual Reconfigurations of Jeremiah in 2 Corinthians 1:21-22, 3:2-11, and 4:7," *BBR* 28 (2018): 411.
[34] Lundbom, *Jeremiah 21–36*, 466-67.
[35] Block, *Triumph of Grace*, 77-78.

Even in those passages in Jeremiah that reflect the leveling of God's relationships with Israel and the nations or that promise Gentile inclusion in the blessings of future salvation, Israel and the nations retain their separate identities. The first oracle of hope in Jeremiah 3:14-18 portrays "all nations" making pilgrimage to worship Yahweh in Jerusalem (see Is 2:2-4; Zech 14:15-19), but there will also be an end to the historic division between the northern and southern kingdoms of Israel and Judah.[36] In Jeremiah 12:14-17, the neighboring "evil nations" that experience an "uprooting" in judgment such as Judah also receive the same offer of restoration given to Israel, but the prophet explicitly elaborates that, just like Israel, these nations will be restored "to their own lands and their own country" (Jer 12:16). In Jeremiah 18:7-10, the opportunity to avert threatened judgment (uproot, tear down, destroy) and to experience blessing (plant, build up) through repentance is extended to any "nation or kingdom" and not simply Israel alone. Jeremiah 30–33 highlights that Yahweh will "restore the fortunes" (*šûb šəbût*) of exiled Israel and Judah, and this same promise is extended to certain foreign nations as well (see Jer 48:47; 49:6, 39).[37]

Equating Israel/Judah with the church in Jeremiah 31 or understanding the prophet as envisioning a new Israel made up of Jew and Gentile is anachronistic and imposes later canonical developments on the message of Jeremiah. Craig Blaising explains, "The kingdom predicted in the Tanak ... is consistently a multinational kingdom. It is not a uninational kingdom made up of peoples drawn from multiple nations. Rather, it is a kingdom composed of multiple nations, one of which is Israel."[38] The

---

[36] Kaiser, *Walking the Ancient Paths*, 72.

[37] The reversal of fortunes for Moab, Ammon, and Elam (and Egypt in Jer 46:26) is clearly nationalistic in nature, and these particular nations are likely selected as recipients of these promises in Jeremiah MT because they would experience exile and return to their land just like Israel (see Jer 46:19; 48:7, 11, 46; 49:3). See Allen, *Jeremiah*, 468, 501-2.

[38] Craig Blaising, "Biblical Hermeneutics: How Are We to Interpret the Relation Between the Tanak and the New Testament on This Question?," in *The New Christian Zionism: Fresh Perspectives on Israel and the Land*, ed. Gerald R. McDermott (Downers Grove, IL: IVP Academic, 2016), 89.

book of Isaiah highlights the inclusion of foreigners in the blessings of the future kingdom even more so than Jeremiah, but even in Isaiah, the emphasis seems to be on a multinational kingdom in a manner that maintains the distinctiveness of Israel.[39]

Jeremiah takes his cues concerning the inclusion of the Gentiles in the blessings of Israel's restoration from the promise of the Abrahamic covenant that Abraham's descendants will become a blessing to all peoples (see Gen 12:1-3).[40] In Jeremiah 4:1-2, Israel's faithful swearing by Yahweh will not cause the other nations to become a part of Israel but rather to be blessed in the same manner as Israel. The universal aspects of the Abrahamic covenant in the Hebrew Bible are complementary to and not in conflict with the national and ethnic promises that God made to Israel.[41] With reference to the church, Kaiser explains that God does not make the New Covenant directly with the church, but instead "the church reaps the benefits of the Abrahamic-Davidic new covenants as she too participates in the roots and the trunk of the one olive tree rooted in the promises of God to the patriarchs of Israel (Rom 9–11). The church has no grounding and no vitality except through the promises made to Israel."[42]

Other Elements of Continuity in the New Covenant

There are other elements of continuity in the New Covenant consistent with the idea that the New Covenant is a renewal of the Sinai covenant

---

[39] For further development of the idea of a multinational eschatological kingdom in Isaiah, see Andrew H. Kim, *The Multinational Kingdom in Isaiah: A Study of the Eschatological Kingdom and the Nature of Its Consummation* (Eugene, OR: Wipf & Stock, 2020), esp. 50-150.

[40] Kim offers an extended critique of the view that the Abrahamic covenant promises the formation of a single "great nation" that consists of a worldwide kingdom (*Multinational Kingdom*, 58-61). The original promise that God gives to Abraham is not that the people groups of the world "will become the 'great nation' that will come from Abraham" but rather that God will bless both the "great nation" and the "families of the earth" through Abraham (Gen 12:1-3). This distinction continues throughout the OT canon in affirmations of the Abrahamic covenant and prophetic portrayals of its fulfillment (see Gen 26:4-5; 28:13-14; Is 19:24; Zech 8:13).

[41] Blaising, "Biblical Hermeneutics," 87.

[42] Kaiser, *Walking the Ancient Paths*, 370.

between God and Israel. Even though the prophet does not specify the exact nature of the internalized law in the New Covenant, the most natural assumption is that "it will be the law at the heart of the Sinai covenant."[43] The demands of the covenant will remain the same.[44] Brueggemann explains, "The purpose of the new covenant, like the purpose of the old covenant, is to shape a people in obedience to the commands of Sinai. Given the tone of the Book of Jeremiah, it is likely that the 'Torah' here in purview is the tradition of Deuteronomy."[45] In his own preaching, Jeremiah reiterates the specifics of the Decalogue in his temple sermon (Jer 7:6-9), condemns Israel's long history of disobedience to the Torah (Jer 7:22-26), and prioritizes Sabbath observance (Jer 17:19-27). He further castigates deceptive scribes who altered the "law of Yahweh" (Jer 8:8). All of the ten other uses of *tôrâ* in Jeremiah outside Jeremiah 31:34 refer to Yahweh's "law/instruction" as something that was previously given to the people even if all of these references are not exclusively to the Mosaic law (see Jer 2:8; 6:19; 8:8; 9:13; 16:11; 18:18; 26:4; 32:23; 44:10, 23).

The difference with the New Covenant lies not in the content of the law but in the enablement provided for obedience to its directives. Even heart transformation and the internalizing of the law were spiritual realities for Israel under the old covenant. In the book of Deuteronomy, the calls for Israel to love Yahweh with the heart (Deut 6:5; 10:12-13) and to "circumcise" their hearts (Deut 10:16) reflect that internal fidelity was the expected norm.[46] Michael Grisanti explains, "The 'loyalty language' of Deuteronomy . . . gives abundant evidence that Yahweh's covenant

---

[43]Lundbom, *Jeremiah 21–36*, 467-68.
[44]Contra Adeyemi, *New Covenant Torah in Jeremiah*, 65-68, and F. B. Huey, *Jeremiah, Lamentations*, NAC 16 (Nashville: B&H, 1993), 286. Chisholm explains that later revelation helps to clarify that the New Covenant community would fulfill the law "by obeying it (see Matt 5:17-20), not in the contextualized time-bound particulars of the Mosaic code, but in its essence as articulated by Jesus (see Matt 22:26-30)" (*Handbook on the Prophets*, 196).
[45]Brueggemann, *Theology of Jeremiah*, 128.
[46]John Kessler, *Old Testament Theology: Divine Call and Human Response* (Waco, TX: Baylor University Press, 2013), 251.

demands of His covenant nation were primarily internal."[47] Individual Israelites could speak of having God's law on their hearts (see Ps 37:31; 40:8 [MT 40:9]).[48] In Psalm 119, the psalmist repeatedly declares his love for the law of God (Ps 119:97, 102, 113, 127, 163, 165) and prays for God's teaching and enablement so that he might carry through on his good intentions to obey (Ps 119:29, 73, 80, 108, 117).

Commenting on the continuity between the New Covenant promises and the spiritual realities of the past, Block explains,

> There had always been new covenant Israelites who had the Torah of God in their hearts/minds (Gen 26:5; Num 14:24; Deut 6:6; Ps 119:11); who delighted in covenant relationship with God (Exod 29:45; Lev 26:12); who knew God (Exod 33:13; cf. Judg 2:10); and who rejoiced in the knowledge of sins forgiven (Lev 4:20, 26, 31, 35; 5:10, 13, 16, 18, 26[6:7]; 19:22).[49]

This expectation and availability of heart transformation under the old covenant is what makes the people's defection from Yahweh so egregious in the book of Jeremiah.[50] The promises that Yahweh will give a new heart to his people (Jer 24:7; 32:39) or write his law on their hearts (Jer 31:34) in the future restoration are merely expressing what should have been the reality for faithful Israel under the old covenant.

The New Covenant will specifically be effective in a way that the old was not because every person belonging to the covenant will experience this internal transformation, and the covenant community will no longer consist of a mixed group of those who genuinely knew the Lord and those who do not.[51] Block explains that in the past, "true

---

[47]Michael A. Grisanti, "Was Israel Unable to Respond to God? A Study of Deuteronomy 29:2-4," *Bibliotheca Sacra* 163 (2006): 192.

[48]Shead, *Mouth Full of Fire*, 198.

[49]Block, *Triumph of Grace*, 79.

[50]The corruption of the people's "hearts" is a recurring theme in Jeremiah (see Jer 3:17; 5:23; 7:24; 9:26; 11:8; 13:10; 16:12; 17:1, 5, 9).

[51]Peter J. Gentry and Stephen J. Wellum, *Kingdom Through Covenant: A Biblical-Theological Understanding of the Covenants* (Wheaton, IL: Crossway, 2012), 510.

covenant relationship had been experienced by only a few, the righteous remnant, for the masses the covenant remained an external reality, written on tablets of stone, but not on their hearts."[52] Jeremiah's promise for the New Covenant is that "all" (*kōl*) of Israel will come to know Yahweh in the transformative way that was true of only a portion of the people in the old covenantal arrangement (Jer 31:34).

The extraordinary forgiveness of the New Covenant will take what was exceptional under the old covenant and make it the norm, but there is still continuity between the covenants in the experience of divine forgiveness. The promise in Jeremiah 31:34 that Yahweh will "forgive" (*sālaḥ*) the "iniquity" (*'ăwōn*) and not "remember" (*zākar*) the "sin" (*ḥaṭṭā't*) of his people in Jeremiah 31:34 (see Jer 33:8) recalls Moses' request for "forgiveness" (*sālaḥ*) of Israel's sin in response to Yahweh's declaration of his attribute of "forgiving" (*nāśā'*) "iniquity" (*'ăwōn*), "transgression" (*peša'*), and "sin" (*ḥaṭṭā't*) when Israel worshiped the golden calf in Exodus 34:6-9. Yahweh remained faithful to his relationship with Israel when they egregiously broke the covenant (Ex 32:19) because of his prior covenantal commitments to the patriarchs (Ex 32:13). Similarly, even though Jeremiah stresses the totality and finality of how Israel and Judah have "broken" (*pārar*) their covenant with Yahweh (Jer 31:32; see Jer 11:1-13), God's covenantal commitments to Israel remain in place. Even the dissolution of Israel and Judah and the judgment of exile will not mean the end of God's covenant relationship with Israel.

---

[52]Block, *Triumph of Grace*, 79. See also Grisanti, "Was Israel Unable to Respond?," 191. The inclusion of nonbelievers within this covenant is why Israel is frequently described as "hard-hearted" (see Ps 95:8; Ezek 3:7; Zech 7:12), "stiff-necked" (see Deut 9:6, 13; 10:16; 31:27; 2 Kings 17:14; Jer 7:26; 17:23; 19:15), and "stubborn" (see Neh 9:29; Is 30:1; 65:2; Jer 6:28; Hos 4:16; 9:15; Zech 7:11).

Jeremiah's New Covenant and Other Prophetic Promises of Covenant Renewal

Jeremiah's theology concerning the restoration of Israel aligns with the larger restoration theology of the Old Testament prophets. Like Jeremiah, the prophets Isaiah and Ezekiel refer to the future covenantal arrangement between Yahweh and Israel as an "everlasting/enduring [ʿôlām] covenant" (see Is 55:3; 61:8; Ezek 16:60; 37:26). Ezekiel 16:59-63 is the passage among these "everlasting covenant" passages that most closely corresponds to Jeremiah 31:31-34, with both using the verb *pārar* to refer to the breaking of the old covenant (Ezek 16:59; Jer 31:32) but also promising a future covenant renewal (Ezek 16:60; Jer 31:31) that accompanies the forgiveness of sins (Ezek 16:63; Jer 31:34).[53] Ezekiel assures that "remembrance" (*zākar*) of the past covenant will lead to the "establishment" (i.e., renewal; *hiphil* of *qûm*) of this new and enduring covenant (Ezek 16:60, 62).[54]

Important parallels to Jeremiah's New Covenant prophecy also appear in Ezekiel 11:19; 36:25-27 and Isaiah 59:20-21. Ezekiel 36:25-27 promises that Yahweh will give the people "an undivided heart" (Ezek 11:19), a "new heart" (Ezek 36:26), and a "new spirit" (Ezek 11:19; 36:26). Yahweh will replace the old "heart of stone" that is rebellious with a new "heart of flesh" that is responsive and compliant (Ezek 11:19; 36:26). This transformation of the people's hearts will come from God placing his Spirit within them (Ezek 36:27; 37:14; 39:29), and the Spirit will empower and enable Israel's obedience to the divine commands. In Isaiah 59:20-21, Yahweh also promises a covenant that provides redemption, a turning of the people from sin, and the placement of his Spirit and words in the people's mouths as part of Israel's restoration and renewal (see Is 60–62, esp. Is 61:8-9). The prophets strategically

---

[53] Daniel I. Block, *The Book of Ezekiel Chapters 1–24*, NICOT (Grand Rapids, MI: Eerdmans, 1997), 516-17.

[54] For discussion of the prevailing use of the *hiphil* of *qûm* + *bərît* to indicate the renewal of a previously existing covenant, see Gentry and Wellum, *Kingdom Through Covenant*, 155-61.

emphasize the enduring nature of Yahweh's covenantal commitments to Israel at a time when Israel's very existence as a people and nation is in grave danger and anticipate divine enablement and transformation for all of Israel that will break the past cycle of rebellion and judgment.

MOVING TO THE NEW TESTAMENT

The emphasis of this chapter on the idea that "we are not apostles" is not intended to deny or disparage canonical readings of Jeremiah and the New Covenant. The apostles were divinely inspired interpreters of the Hebrew Scriptures and our hermeneutical guide for how to understand the fulfillment of Old Testament prophecies. The apostles bring out the full meaning and significance of the prophets' message as intended by the divine author of Scripture from the vantage point of progressive revelation and the inauguration of God's eschatological kingdom through the first coming of Christ.[55] The emphasis here is simply to offer the reminder that these canonical readings should not mute the distinctive historical message of the prophets and should not be viewed as terminating the specific and concrete covenantal promises that God made to Israel as part of his redemptive plan for salvation history.

With respect to Jeremiah's New Covenant, the New Testament provides ample testimony to the fact that the death of Jesus inaugurated this covenant and that the church inherits the promises of this covenant as the people of God. The quotation of Jeremiah 31:31-34 in Hebrews 8:8-12 and Hebrews 10:16-17 appears in the larger context of Hebrews 8:3–10:18, which teaches that Jesus has inaugurated the New Covenant through the superior sacrifice of his sinless life that transcends the offerings and institutions of the old covenant.[56] The

---

[55]On the importance of this *sensus plenior* approach to Scripture based on its divine and human authorship, see further Matthew Barrett, *Canon, Covenant, and Christology: Rethinking Jesus and the Scriptures of Israel*, NSBT 51 (Downers Grove, IL: IVP Academic, 2020), 1-201.

[56]George H. Guthrie, "Hebrews," in *Commentary on the New Testament Use of the Old Testament*, ed. G. K. Beale and D. A. Carson (Grand Rapids, MI: Baker Academic, 2007), 970-72.

prominence of the New Covenant for the Christian gospel is reflected in Jesus' promise at the institution of the Lord's Supper—"this cup is the new covenant in my blood" (Lk 22:20; 1 Cor 11:25). In this manner, the promise of New Covenant fulfillment "is embedded in the ritual most central to community identity" for the Christian church.[57]

The present fulfillment of New Covenant blessings in the church leads the New Testament writers to offer figural and typological readings of Jeremiah's original prophecies concerning the New Covenant and Israel's restoration. Perhaps the most fully developed of these reconfigured readings of Jeremiah appears in 2 Corinthians 1–7, as Paul presents his gospel ministry as a fulfillment of the New Covenant. In 2 Corinthians 3, Paul affirms that he is a "minister of the new covenant" (2 Cor 3:6) and that the working of God's Spirit through this covenant is what brings real and lasting transformation into the lives of those who believe the gospel. In the larger context of 2 Corinthians 1–7, Paul reimagines the story of Jeremiah's sign-act of purchasing family property as a sign guaranteeing Israel's future restoration and renewal in MT Jeremiah 32 (LXX Jer 39) to show how believers in Jesus now inherit these promises as well. Believers have the "sealing" (*sphragizō*) of the Holy Spirit on their hearts as a guarantee of their future inheritance in the same way that Jeremiah "sealed" (*sphragizō*) the title deed that assured Israel's future inheritance (LXX Jer 39:10-11; 2 Cor 1:22). The Corinthian believers are written on Paul's heart, just as Jeremiah promised that the Torah would be written on the hearts of God's people (Jer 31:33). Through the presence of the Spirit in their lives, believers now have God's glory in "clay" (*ostrakinos*) jars (their bodies) so that others can see Christ in them, just as Jeremiah placed the deed of future inheritance in a "clay" (*ostrakinos*) jar (LXX Jer 39:14; 2 Cor 4:6-7).[58]

---

[57]Jason A. Staples, "What Do the Gentiles Have to Do with 'All Israel'? A Fresh Look at Romans 11:25-27," *JBL* 130 (2011): 379.
[58]Oropeza, "New Covenant Knowledge," 405-24.

The present fulfillment of the New Covenant promises is clear in the progress of biblical revelation, but these partial fulfillments and typological reconfigurations of the New Covenant in the New Testament do not preclude the likelihood of more literal fulfillments in the future for ethnic or national Israel. As Michael Vlach explains, the typology of Jesus as the new Israel does not "remove or transcend national Israel's significance. The opposite is true. Jesus' role as the true Israelite involves the restoring of Israel as a nation (Is 49:3-6; Rom 11:26-27)."[59] The sustained focus of the Hebrew prophets on Israel's return to the land and national renewal suggests that they form the substance of biblical eschatology and not merely a typological foreshadowing of the kingdom realities developed and clarified in the New Testament. Israel's historical return from exile fell far short of prophetic expectation, and Richard Hess correctly notes that the normal expectation that ancient prophetic pronouncements would come to pass as promised leads to the inescapable conclusion "that many elements specific to the restoration of Israel are yet awaiting fulfillment."[60]

Jesus comes to redeem Israel (Lk 2:25, 38) and sends his disciples on a mission to reclaim the "lost sheep of the house of Israel" (Mt 10:6), but there will be more judgment before the final restoration occurs. Jesus ultimately reactivates Jeremiah's temple sermon as he announces the impending destruction of Jerusalem and the coming of a second exile (see Mt 21:13; Mk 11:17; Jer 7:11).[61] Like Jeremiah, Jesus weeps over the impending destruction of Jerusalem (see Mt 23:37-39; Lk 13:34; 19:41-44). Unlike Paul's positive reconfiguration of the sign-act

---

[59]Michael J. Vlach, "A Non-typological Future-Mass-Conversion View," in *Three Views on Israel and the Church: Perspectives on Romans 9–11*, ed. J. Compton and A. D. Naselli (Grand Rapids, MI: Kregel, 2018), 23.

[60]Richard S. Hess, "The Future Written in the Past: The Old Testament and the Millennium," in *A Case for Historic Premillennialism: An Alternative to "Left Behind" Eschatology*, ed. C. L. Blomberg and S. W. Chung (Grand Rapids, MI: Baker Academic, 2009), 35.

[61]For the extensive Jeremiah typology in Matthew's portrayal of Jesus, see Michael Knowles, *Jeremiah in Matthew's Gospel: The Rejected Prophet Motif in Matthean Redaction*, JSNTSup 68 (Sheffield: JSOT Press, 1993).

concerning the purchase of the field in Jeremiah 32, instead Matthew 27:9-10 negatively portrays the purchase of the field in Jeremiah 32 by connecting this passage, along with references to the potter in Jeremiah 19:1, 11 and Zechariah 11:12-13, to Judas's betrayal of Jesus as demonstration of Israel's continued unbelief.[62] Rather than connoting hope, the purchase of the field symbolizes judgment that results from unbelief and the shedding of "innocent blood" (*haima athōon*, Mt 27:3-8), but ironically, it was also the shedding of the blood of Jesus that initiated the fulfillment of the blessings of the New Covenant that Jeremiah promised (Mt 26:28).[63]

Jeremianic typology and intertextuality in the New Testament point in the direction of a now and not-yet fulfillment of the New Covenant promises, with the Israel-specific aspects of the covenant finding an eschatological fulfillment in connection with the second coming of Christ. New Testament eschatology reflects a specific Jewish focus and concentration informed by the Old Testament prophets.[64] Joel Willitts highlights Matthew's theme of a "turfed kingdom," in which the kingdom of God "is somewhere on earth" and "the 'somewhere' is most likely the land of Israel" (see Mt 8:11).[65] In both Matthew and Luke, Jesus promises the Twelve that they will sit on thrones judging the "twelve tribes of Israel" in the future day of renewal (Mt 19:28; Lk 22:29-30). The specific mention of the twelve tribes indicates a likely reference to ethnic or national Israel, rather than the church (see Mt 8:11-12; 21:43; 22:7; 23:32-36; 27:25).[66] Jesus portrays Israel's renewal

---

[62]On the combined citation of Jeremiah and Zechariah in Mt 27:9-10, see Craig L. Blomberg, "Matthew," in Beale and Carson, *Commentary on the New Testament Use*, 95-97.

[63]See the references to the shedding of "innocent blood" (*haima aiōn*) in LXX Jer 19:4; 33:15.

[64]See, for example, McDermott, *New Christian Zionism*, 107-94; Isaac W. Oliver, *Luke's Jewish Eschatology: The National Restoration of Israel in Luke–Acts* (Oxford: Oxford University Press, 2021); Matthias Konradt, *Israel, Church, and the Gentiles in the Gospel of Matthew*, trans. Kathleen Ess, Baylor–Mohr Siebeck Studies in Early Christianity (Waco, TX: Baylor University Press, 2014).

[65]Joel Willitts, "Zionism in the Gospel of Matthew: Do the People of Israel and the Land of Israel Persist as Abiding Concerns for Matthew?," in McDermott, *New Christian Zionism*, 124-28.

[66]Robert H. Gundry, *Matthew: A Commentary on His Handbook for a Mixed Church Under Persecution* (Grand Rapids, MI: Eerdmans, 1994), 393. See also Konradt, *Israel, Church, and the Gentiles*, 260-63.

in the context of a messianic kingdom on earth and envisions the fulfillment of what is promised concerning the rule of the "Son of Man" involving corporate Israel in Daniel 7:9-27.[67]

Luke–Acts gives more specific expression of this hope for Israel's future restoration. Jesus clarifies in Luke 21:24 that the captivity of Israel and judgment of Jerusalem will have a termination point when the "times [*kairoi*] of the Gentiles" are completed (Lk 21:24). Further references to "time(s)" (*kairos* and *chronos*) in Acts 1:6-8 and Acts 3:19-21 elaborate further on the timing and nature of Israel's restoration.[68] Just prior to Jesus' ascension into heaven, the disciples are not wrong in asking about Israel's "restoration" (*apokathistēmi*), a term used in the LXX with reference to Israel's future return and renewal (see Hos 11:11; Jer 16:15; 24:6) but are misinformed as to its timing.[69] The gospel will first have to be preached to the whole world (Acts 1:7-8) as the means by which Messiah's kingdom will expand to all nations.[70] Acts 3:19-21 assures that Israel's restoration (*apokatastasis*) still awaits future fulfillment and will occur when Israel turns to God, who will then send Jesus the Christ from heaven.[71]

The clearest expression of God's ongoing commitment to his covenant with Israel and the promises of Israel's future restoration and renewal is found in Paul's teaching on the working out of God's redemptive purposes for Israel in Romans 9–11. Paul frames this section of the letter with expressions of his confidence in the abiding covenantal relationship between God and Israel (Rom 9:4; 11:29). In Romans 11, Paul is explaining how the present fracture between the "Israel according to the promise" (the present believing remnant

---

[67] Gundry, *Matthew*, 393.
[68] Mark S. Kinzer, "Zionism in Luke–Acts," in McDermott, *New Christian Zionism*, 151, 162-63.
[69] Kinzer, "Zionism in Luke–Acts," 151, 162-63.
[70] Oliver, *Luke's Jewish Eschatology*, 68.
[71] Note Peter's emphasis on how this specific hope has its source in the message of the OT prophets—Moses (Acts 3:22-23) and Samuel and his successors (Acts 3:24). See Mark J. Boda, *The Heartbeat of Old Testament Theology: Three Creedal Expressions* (Grand Rapids, MI: Baker Academic, 2017), 109.

in Rom 11:1-6) and "Israel according to the flesh" (the "rest" of nonbelieving Jews in Rom 11:7-10) will be healed through an overpowering demonstration of God's faithfulness.[72] In addition to the present Jewish remnant coming to faith in Christ (Rom 11:5-6), Paul envisions a future time in Romans 11:26 when "all Israel shall be saved" in conformity with Jeremiah's expectation in the New Covenant that "all" in Israel will truly know the Lord (Jer 31:34). Block states, "Paul's vision of Israel's future is refracted through the lens of Jer 31:31-40."[73] Paul has not eliminated Israel's distinctive place in redemptive history, but he has instead reversed the order of blessing envisioned by the prophets so that the inclusion of Gentiles leads to the blessing of Israel.

Conclusion

Jeremiah's promise of the New Covenant assures that Yahweh's relationship with the people of Israel and his covenantal commitments to them are permanent and enduring. Israel's unfaithfulness will not terminate the covenant, and the New Covenant offers assurance of a divine work of grace that will enable all Israel to know Yahweh and obey his commands. If the covenant could survive the first exile prophesied by Jeremiah, then it only stands to reason that the covenant will also survive the exile that Jesus warns would come against nonbelieving Israel. The church's present experience of the New Covenant blessings is anticipatory of God's future saving work on Israel's behalf and the fulfillment of the covenantal promises concerning Israel's restoration and renewal. Recognition of both this present and future fulfillment is essential for a fully canonical and apostolic reading of Jeremiah's New Covenant prophecy.

---

[72] Michael F. Bird, *Romans*, Story of God Bible Commentary (Grand Rapids, MI: Zondervan, 2016), 305.
[73] Block, *Triumph of Grace*, 334.

8

EMULATING THE APOSTLES

*Reading Jeremiah as Christian Scripture
in the Footsteps of the Apostles*

Lissa M. Wray Beal

In Luke's account of the Last Supper, Jesus proclaims, "This cup is the new covenant in my blood, which is poured out for you" (Lk 22:20 NIV). The passage is so familiar that when Christians initially encounter the less familiar New Covenant passage (Jer 31:31-34), they might be startled at how Lukan it sounds. While further reflection corrects the error, an additional misconception may remain: that Jeremiah is Christian Scripture because the New Testament quotes and alludes to it.[1] That faulty assumption must be hastily corrected. Read as part of the Christian Scriptures of the Old and New Testaments, Jeremiah is intrinsically a Christian book.

---

[1] Besides Luke, the New Testament frequently quotes or alludes to this Jeremiah passage (e.g., 1 Cor 11:25; 2 Cor 3:5-14; Heb 8:8-12; 10:16-17).

But *as* Christian Scripture, how is Jeremiah to be read? This chapter reads with the sensibility brought to Jeremiah by the apostolic witness and New Testament authors; that is, it reads in the footsteps of the apostles. Three working examples are here presented. Each considers first the passage's Old Testament context before offering reflections arising from the context of a two-testament canon. An initial, longer engagement of Jeremiah's New Covenant (Jer 31:31-34) is followed by briefer engagements with Jeremiah's polemic against idolatry (Jer 10:1-16) and his first lament (Jer 11:18-19).

Each example works with key assumptions.[2] First, Jeremiah is part of the Christian canon composed of the Old and New Testaments; neglect of either constituent part makes its Christian witness incomplete. However, such reading does not force the New Testament's mode of witness on the Old. Rather, it affirms the triune God is revealed within the discrete witness of the Old Testament, speaking in many and varied ways before speaking through his Son (Heb 1:1-2). Thus reading after the apostles does not neglect to read Jeremiah within its own cultural and literary context.

Second, while the Old Testament witnesses to the character and work of the triune God, this witness finds its telos in Jesus Christ. It is a telos the Old Testament writers did not fully understand (1 Pet 1:10-12). The New Testament writers did, guided by Christ's own direction (Lk 24:25-27, 44-46) and the Spirit's illumination of Christ's life, death, and resurrection. These hermeneutical guides directed them to the Old Testament as revealing Christ, while also anticipating his full revelation in the New Testament. Together, these first two assumptions affirm the necessity of "allowing the first witness the scope to do its peculiar and distinctive work in the One God's economic and ontological life with Israel and the church and all creation. Not fusing the witnesses, not

---

[2]The intent of this chapter is to provide working examples of reading after the apostles, and therefore only brief comments on hermeneutical assumptions are included.

ranking them, but allowing their distinctive contribution to sound forth to those of us who stand outside the circle of their specially mediated life with God."[3]

A third assumption affirms that the Old Testament is both ontologically and economically trinitarian and that the God revealed in its pages is the God and Father of the Lord Jesus Christ. If the same God acts across both testaments, it is not surprising that one observes in different moments of time similar patterns of thought and action, expressive of God's unchanging character and goals. Whether labeled as types or figurations, such patterns attest across both testaments to God acting as God does.[4] A basic helpful framework considers theological patterning (that is, "networks of recurring, corresponding depictions of the God-human-world relationship") as an umbrella category within which typology and figuration fit.[5] Figuration might be simply described as "discerning how the workings of the triune God in the OT bear witness to God's ways in Christ," while typology has a "limited focus on 'events, persons, or places' that correspond with later realities."[6] This third assumption does not require the employment of typological or figural methodologies but acknowledges such patterns as they appear across the Old and New Testaments.

---

[3]Christopher R. Seitz, *The Elder Testament: Canon, Theology, Trinity* (Waco, TX: Baylor University Press, 2018), 48.

[4]The definition and delineation of types, patterns, and figurations is complex, without wholesale agreement. See Stanley D. Walter, ed., *Go Figure! Figuration in Biblical Interpretation*, Princeton Theological Monograph Series (Eugene, OR: Pickwick, 2008); Christopher R. Seitz, *Figured Out: Typology and Providence in Christian Scripture* (Louisville, KY: Westminster John Knox, 2001); David L. Baker, *Two Testaments, One Bible: The Theological Relationship Between the Old and New Testaments* (Downers Grove, IL: IVP Academic, 2010).

[5]Andrew T. Abernethy, "Theological Patterning in Jeremiah: A Vital Word Through an Ancient Book," *BBR* 24, no. 2 (2014): 151.

[6]Abernethy, "Theological Patterning," 152.

Reading the New Covenant Within the Book of Jeremiah

The context of the New Covenant: Literary and historical. To read Jeremiah's New Covenant in the footsteps of the apostles is to be attentive to the text's historical and literary context.[7] The New Covenant is found in the Book of Consolation (Jer 30–33; hereafter "the Book"), which collects hopeful oracles and narratives into one scroll (Jer 30:1-3).[8] Together they proclaim God's plans to restore his people.[9]

The Book proclaims a multifaceted restoration that includes the people to their land and future hope (Jer 30:3, 10, 20; 31:8-9, 10-14, 16-17, 21-23; 32:15, 37; 33:6-7), the land's fruitfulness and animals (Jer 31:5, 12-13, 27; 33:12-13), the city and temple (Jer 30:18; 31:6, 23-24; 33:9-11, 18-22), and the king (Jer 30:9, 21; 33:16-17, 21-22). The New Covenant prophesies the restoration of covenant relationship, a theme that is apparent elsewhere in the Book (Jer 30:22; 31:1, 20, 36-37). Coming as it does at the end of Jeremiah 31 as the poetic oracles conclude, the New Covenant "provides an initial climax within the 'Book of Consolation.'"[10]

---

[7] Mark S. Gignilliat discusses reading that "takes seriously the events of the text and their initial reception but does not limit the text's purview or provenance to immediate historical reception. . . . The community of faith's continued wrestling with its Sacred Scriptures, while seeking to identify God and his will in fresh theological insights and acts of obedience, is most assuredly in the purview of the canonical text as well." Gignilliat, *Reading Scripture Canonically: Theological Instincts for Old Testament Interpretation* (Grand Rapids, MI: Baker Academic, 2019), 50. It is just such attention to historical particularity *and* ongoing insights that underlies this chapter's reading.

[8] Despite the difference of genre between Jer 30–31 (poetry) and Jer 32–33 (narrative), the chapters are typically considered a redacted whole. See Jack R. Lundbom, *Jeremiah 21–36*, AB 21B (New York: Doubleday, 2004), 368; J. A. Thompson, *The Book of Jeremiah*, NICOT (Grand Rapids, MI: Eerdmans, 1980), 551; Terence E. Fretheim, *Jeremiah*, Smyth & Helwys Bible Commentary (Macon, GA: Smyth & Helwys, 2002), 413. Others consider Jer 30–31 alone to comprise the Book. So Kathleen M. O'Connor, *Jeremiah: Pain and Promise* (Minneapolis: Fortress, 2012), 103.

[9] Such oracles are infrequent elsewhere in Jeremiah (see Jer 3:14-18; 16:14-15; 23:3-8; 24:6-7). Jeremiah's message is primarily of judgment (Jer 1:10, "to uproot and to tear down, to destroy and overthrow"), although restoration is not neglected ("to build and plant"). Note: translations of the Old Testament in this chapter are the author's own, unless otherwise specified.

[10] J. G. McConville, *Judgment and Promise: An Interpretation of the Book of Jeremiah* (Leicester, UK: Apollos, 1993), 98. Walter Brueggemann speaks of a "massive assurance of YHWH's unilateral decision to enact a wondrous, joyous future for those who return to Jerusalem." Brueggemann, *The Theology of the Book of Jeremiah* (Cambridge: Cambridge University Press, 2007), 121.

The focus on restoration in the Book is in stark contrast to the majority of Jeremiah. The book as a whole spotlights covenant failure and ensuing judgment in many ways, including oracles outlining Israel's sin and its judgment (Jer 2-10), the failures of kings and prophets (Jer 21-24), the release of Yahweh's wrath (Jer 25), and accounts of the last days of the kingdom and the fall of Jerusalem (Jer 37-39). Throughout, Yahweh's people refuse to attend to Jeremiah and his message, causing him to lament over his ministry (Jer 11-20) and setting him in opposition to kings, leaders, and prophets (Jer 26-29). There is little to relieve the picture of failure and judgment. In the midst of such bleakness, the Book and its New Covenant provide an astounding message of hope and restoration, of life renewed out of death. The juxtaposition to the surrounding chapters is, as Gordon McConville notes, a non sequitur, an illogicality.[11]

Within the final structure of Jeremiah, the Book stands at its heart as a word of hope. Not only does the Book provide a counterpoint to covenant failure, but it injects a message of hope vis-à-vis the account of Jerusalem's fall. While Jeremiah repeatedly references the coming fall of Jerusalem and the nation (e.g., Jer 1:15; 4:5-6, 19-21, 31; 6:1-6; 10:17-22), the event is not narrated until Jeremiah 39. Yet before this narration, the Book gives assurance that the nation's death is not the final word; restoration will come. The Book's placement highlights that "this salvific work of God was seen to be already at work in the midst of judgment . . . [revealing what God] had in mind for [his] own people."[12]

To summarize, within Jeremiah the Book and its climactic New Covenant promise provide astounding hope in the midst of covenant

---

[11]McConville, *Judgment and Promise*, 94. Corrine Carvalho notes that the poems of Jer 30-31 "sing a counter-vision to that of a smoldering landscape strewn with corpses" and read like "a fantasy or dream of an idyllic life." Carvalho, *Reading Jeremiah: A Literary and Theological Commentary* (Macon, GA: Smyth & Helwys, 2016), 93, 95. O'Connor calls them an "unbidden, unexpected revelation of divine love" that surprises with its "explosive beauty" (*Jeremiah: Pain and Promise*, 103).

[12]Fretheim, *Jeremiah*, 413. Carvalho notes that the chapters "remind the reader of Judah's corporate identity, even in the midst of their destruction" (*Reading Jeremiah*, 95-96).

failure and coming disaster, death, and destruction. Its position before the account of the city's fall structurally communicates God's grace, even before that moment of irredeemable loss.

The content of the New Covenant. The New Covenant anticipates a future event of blessing in keeping with but surpassing the blessings already enumerated in Jeremiah 30–31. The passage begins by saying that "days are coming," a phrase that elsewhere in Jeremiah can anticipate judgment (Jer 7:32; 9:25 [24]; 19:6; 48:12; 49:2; 51:47, 52) but in the Book always signals blessing and restoration (Jer 30:3; 31:27, 31, 38; 33:14).[13] This unnamed future time is for the "house of Israel and the house of Judah" (Jer 31:31), a designation that indicates the possible existence of an original northern oracle. In its present context it designates "all the families of Israel"—the whole Old Testament people of God (Jer 31:1).[14] It is for this reason unsurprising that the rhetoric reverts to name only the "house of Israel" in Jeremiah 31:33. Thus, the New Covenant prophesies a future for the whole people, Israel. This does not deny that the New Testament expands the blessings of this prophecy to all peoples—Jew and Gentile—in Jesus Christ. However, inclusion of the Gentiles does not negate the covenant's continuing and primary reference to Israel. Access for Gentiles occurs only through the engrafting work of Christ (Rom 10–12).[15]

---

[13] The phrase also occurs in Jer 16:14; 23:5, 7-8, a doublet anticipating the blessings in the Book.
[14] See Fretheim, *Jeremiah*, 414, 428, who notes several designations in Jer 31:2-22 suggest an original northern provenance (e.g., Israel, Samaria, Ephraim [but note the reference to Zion in Jer 31:6, 12]) but concludes all Israel is now in view. See also Samuel Hildebrandt, *Interpreting Quoted Speech in Prophetic Literature: A Study of Jeremiah 2.1–3.5*, VTSup 176 (Leiden: Brill, 2017), 80-81; R. Abma, *Bonds of Love: Methodic Studies of Prophetic Texts with Marriage Imagery (Isaiah 50:1–3 and 54:1–10, Hosea 1–3, Jeremiah 2–3)*, Studia Semitica Neerlandica (Assen: Van Gorcum, 1999), 237. Joshua N. Moon notes the phrase is "likely formulaic, perhaps emphasizing the totality of the breaking of the covenant." Moon, *Jeremiah's New Covenant: An Augustinian Reading*, Journal for Theological Interpretation, Supplements 3 (Winona Lake, IN: Eisenbrauns, 2011), 227.
[15] Fretheim states, "Unless the new covenant is God's promise for the sake of the future of this very specific group of people, it is a promise for no one else" (*Jeremiah*, 442). Walter Brueggemann shows the error of a supersessionist reading that "ignores the text itself . . . [and] in fact asserts the rejection rather than the reconstitution of Israel, a point not on the horizon of these oracles." Brueggemann, *A Commentary on Jeremiah: Exile and Homecoming* (Grand Rapids, MI: Eerdmans, 1998), 292.

The covenant is a *new* covenant, a designation unique in the Old Testament. Elsewhere Jeremiah calls this covenant "everlasting" (Jer 32:40; 50:5) and within Jeremiah 31 speaks of the "new thing" God is creating (Jer 31:22).[16] In Jeremiah 31:32 the New Covenant is contrasted to the Sinai covenant, which it is "not like." Yet the New Covenant is not sui generis, for it stands in significant continuity with the Sinai covenant.[17]

First, both covenants are contextualized within God's deliverance. Exodus from Egypt led to the covenant at Sinai (Ex 19:1–24:8), and deliverance out of Babylon is the context of the New Covenant (Jer 31:23-24, 27-28). The correlation of exodus to return from Babylon is made explicit in Jeremiah 16:14-15, which considers the exodus out of Babylon as greater than that out of Egypt: "Yet behold, days are coming, declares Yahweh, when it will no longer be said, 'As Yahweh lives, who brought up the children of Israel from the land of Egypt,' but 'As Yahweh lives, who brought up the children of Israel from the land of the north and from all the lands where he scattered them.' For I will restore them to their land which I gave to their ancestors."[18]

Second, both covenants are concerned with impartation of the law, or *tôrâ* (Jer 31:33). The content of the New Covenant's law is variously understood as the written law of Sinai, the Ten Commandments only, the whole of the Pentateuch, or more broadly as God's general will for human life.[19] What is pertinent to the discussion at hand is, however, merely the centrality of the law to both covenants.

---

[16] Ezekiel similarly describes a "new heart" and "new spirit" (Ezek 36:26).

[17] See the discussion of the covenant's continuity with Sinai, as well as its newness, in Daniel I. Block, *Covenant: The Framework of God's Grand Plan of Redemption* (Grand Rapids, MI: Baker Academic, 2021), 280–286. Block concludes the covenant is a "renewal and ultimate realization of the same covenant that God had made long ago with Abraham, established with the exodus generation of his descendants at Sinai, and renewed with the conquest generation on the plains of Moab."

[18] The verse (with slight variations) appears again in Jer 23:7-8. Like the Book, Jer 16:14-15 and Jer 23:7-8 speak of restoration to the land.

[19] Discussions of these options are found in Fretheim, *Jeremiah*, 443; Lundbom, *Jeremiah 21-36*, 467-68.

Finally (and tellingly), the New Covenant uses the covenant formula, "I will be their God, and they will be my people" (Jer 31:33; see also Jer 30:22; 31:1). Ubiquitous in the Old Testament, it defines the relational heart of Sinai's covenant (Ex 6:6-7; Lev 26:12-13; Deut 29:12-13 [11-12]).[20] The New Covenant's use of this formula implies that the covenant relationship broken by Israel's sin will be repaired and restored.[21]

In these significant ways the New Covenant is continuous with the Sinai covenant. Yet the New Covenant *is* new and marked by difference. For instance, as already noted, the exodus of the New Covenant exceeds the exodus out of Egypt. Other differences also mark the New Covenant. First, in the New Covenant God himself sets the law directly into the hearts and minds of his people. At Sinai, the law was written on stone and still needed to make the connection into people's hearts. The point here is not to draw a contrast between an *only* external law at Sinai and a new *internal* law under the New Covenant.[22] While the Sinai law was written externally on stone, it was capable of being internalized, and to this God's people were called (Deut 30:14). Indeed, Jeremiah assumes the possibility of internalization when he calls Israel to

---

[20] The formula appears with some variation throughout the OT. For a full discussion see Mark J. Boda, *The Heartbeat of Old Testament Theology: Three Creedal Expressions* (Grand Rapids, MI: Baker Academic, 2017), 53-75.

[21] Moon argues, "Common as the formula is to the Old Testament, it represents nothing more than that desired relationship between Yhwh and the people: what always ought to have been the case, but came to an end in some real way in the judgment in the book of Jeremiah.... What we find in 31:33c is that Yhwh will restore things to what they always ought to have been. And at the center of that restoration lies the (old) formula that frames the core of the covenant between Yhwh and his people" (*Jeremiah's New Covenant*, 239).

[22] Leslie C. Allen argues that the "writing on the seat of the human will contrasts with an external writing on tablets at Sinai." Allen, *Jeremiah*, OTL (Louisville, KY: Westminster John Knox, 2008), 356. Moon argues instead that "having the law on stone tablets is *not* the contrast to having the law on the heart. Rather the contrast to the law on the heart is having a 'stubborn and rebellious heart' (or we might say, as Augustine, to have the law *only* on stone tablets)" (*Jeremiah's New Covenant*, 232). Moon's volume counters the strong tradition of reading two eras of salvation signified as the old era (external law of Sinai) and the new era (internal law of the New Covenant). The tradition does not account for OT saints whose faith was internal *before* the New Covenant's institution. Moon's approach traces a less-common Augustinian reading of the passage by which the New Covenant contrasts not an external versus an internal law but two subjective states: unbelief versus faith.

circumcise its heart. He is calling them to an internal disposition toward the law (Jer 4:4).

Jeremiah reveals that this newness was necessitated by the people's heart. It was "evil" (Jer 3:17; 7:24; 16:12), "uncircumcised" (Jer 4:4; 9:26 [25]), "stubborn" (Jer 3:17; 5:23 [here, also rebellious]; Jer 7:24; 9:14 [13]; 11:8; 13:10; 16:12; 18:12; 23:17), and "turned away" (Jer 17:5). Israel's heart, a hard tablet engraved with sin (Jer 17:1), was one of infidelity, incapable of receiving the law. God's New Covenant promise to set his law within hearts and minds addresses the problem posed by hard, unreceptive hearts.

The state of Israel's heart underlies the second significant difference between the two covenants: the New Covenant is not like the old, "which they broke" (Jer 31:32). The book of Jeremiah delineates fulsomely the broken covenant but pointedly does so in Jeremiah 11. In Jeremiah 11 the prophet presents Israel's persistent covenant failure as a failure to listen and obey. By such failure God asserts Israel has "broken my covenant" (Jer 11:10). In Jeremiah, the assertion's phrasing appears only in Jeremiah 11:10 and Jeremiah 31:32, joining the passages linguistically and thematically.[23]

Covenant continuance requires "recognition of Yahweh as Lord, and continuing obedience to the terms of the covenant (Jer. 11:1–8)."[24] On both counts, Israel breaks the Sinai covenant. The new cannot be so broken because it is written by God on his people's heart. Thus, the newness of the New Covenant is discerned not so much in asking *what* is new, but in asking "*why* each part of the oracle is called 'new.' And the answer, once asked, is found on nearly every page of the book: because this people have broken the covenant; because this people are unfaithful—do not have Yhwh's law on their heart; because this people

---

[23] The assertion is "Israel has broken my covenant" (root *prr* [*hiphil*] + *bərîtî*). Note that Jer 33:20-21 uses the root *prr* (*hiphil* and *hophal*) + *bərîtî* but in a hypothetical sense. Allen recognizes that the radical breaking of the covenant in Jer 31:32 "consciously reiterates 11:10" (*Jeremiah*, 356).
[24] Thompson, *Jeremiah*, 580.

do not know Yhwh; and because this people are reaping Yhwh's judgment upon their sins."[25]

The unbreakable nature of the New Covenant attests to God's gracious action toward recalcitrant, undeserving Israel. It arises by God's unilateral initiative as he announces in first-person forms, "the covenant I will make. . . . I will set my law within them. . . . I will write it on their hearts" (Jer 31:33).[26] The New Covenant is inscribed by Yahweh on hearts so that it can be heard and obeyed by all his people.

Finally, from this new inscribed reality flow particular benefits; two are here mentioned. First, Yahweh will "forgive their iniquity and remember their sin no more." It is a reversal of his commitment to remember his people's sins (Jer 14:10). In the context of Jeremiah, these are sins by which Israel broke the covenant and for which it is judged and exiled. It is not that forgiveness is extended here for the first time; forgiveness has long been part of Yahweh's covenant with Israel.[27] Rather, forgiveness of those sins by which the covenant was broken is God's gracious means of releasing Israel to experience all the promised blessings of the New Covenant.

Second, in this new gracious reality there will no longer be need for instruction to promulgate knowledge of Yahweh. It is an astounding statement in the midst of a book in which the prophet has repeatedly sought to teach Israel to embrace covenant relationship with Yahweh. Now, through the implanted law, all people will be open to Yahweh, knowing him and his will. By this they will embrace the intended

---

[25] Moon, *Jeremiah's New Covenant*, 243.

[26] This unilateral initiative is further described by Block, *Covenant*, 283, who notes that "Jeremiah recognized the monergistic nature of the 'new covenant' with his focus on the divine actions involved in its implementation." Block cites various aspects of this divine action: Yahweh alone sets the time for the covenant's implementation, and determines its occurrence, nature, and partners.

[27] McConville comments, "The promise of forgiveness of sins . . . is sometimes seen as the essentially new thing in the new covenant, but the argument depends on a low evaluation of other texts. The forgiveness promised here is not introduced as a new concept; rather it comes in the wake of new possibilities which YHWH is creating by transforming the people themselves" (*Judgment and Promise*, 98).

covenant relationship.[28] The two covenant benefits regarding forgiveness and instruction interact with each other. As the New Covenant imparts knowledge of Yahweh inscribed on hearts, there is the hope of new possibilities of covenant faithfulness, thus impinging positively on any need for forgiveness.

In summary, within the context of Jeremiah the New Covenant is unilaterally extended to Israel at a time of apparent hopelessness. The people are revealed as persistent covenant breakers whose hardened hearts prevent them listening to either the *tôrâ* or Yahweh's prophet. Jeremiah reveals that their fate is exile (Jer 5:9, 29; 9:9 [8]; 13:18-19). At this time of seemingly no hope, God demonstrates his *ḥesed* toward Israel, extending (beyond hope!) the gift of a New Covenant and restoration of all that was lost due to sin.

Within the postexilic community, the promises of the New Covenant begin to find realization. The greater exodus occurs as the people return to the land and rebuild the city and temple. The returnees seek to be a community of renewed commitment to God (Neh 8:1–10:39), but despite this not all know Yahweh and hard hearts are not done away. Yet however imperfect was this taste of the New Covenant, "We should not for that reason underestimate the new thing God did. . . . These great prophecies did indeed have a measure of fulfilment . . . in the restored community of Judah."[29]

READING THE NEW COVENANT IN THE FOOTSTEPS OF THE APOSTLES

Inaugurating the New Covenant. As noted earlier, the New Testament alludes to and quotes the New Covenant. This chapter now turns to Jesus' statement that the New Covenant is inaugurated by his blood

---

[28]Note that Jer 31:34 is not a statement against religious/theological instruction per se. The focus here is on changed hearts that are open to and have received knowledge of God.

[29]Christopher J. H. Wright, *The Message of Jeremiah*, BST (Downers Grove, IL: InterVarsity Press, 2014), 335.

(Lk 22:20; see 1 Cor 11:25). Without specifically identifying a *new* covenant, Matthew and Mark also correlate Jesus' blood to the covenant (Mk 14:24; Mt 26:28). In his discussion of the Markan passage, Craig Evans observes that the connection presupposes a "collocation of related covenant texts (Ex 24:8; Jer 31:31; Zech 9:11)," with the Sinai covenant primarily in view (Ex 24:1-8) and the modifier *new* referencing Jeremiah.[30]

Of particular interest is Evans's description of the relationship of Jesus' blood to the New Covenant: "The covenant of which Jesus speaks concerns the promise of the coming kingdom of God, the new covenant promised by Jeremiah. Jesus will give his own blood *to effect the new covenant*, the restoration of Israel, and the kingdom of God 'having come in power' (cf. Mark 9:1)."[31]

The language of effecting the covenant is helpful. It acknowledges the promise of Israel's restoration but also addresses the promise's fulfillment through the shed blood of Jesus.[32] Thus the crucifixion becomes the moment and means by which the New Covenant promises are set in motion, effected, or inaugurated into a new and greater reality than that experienced for postexilic Israel.[33] This understanding of effect or inauguration informs the following discussion.

---

[30] Craig A. Evans, *Mark 8:27–16:20*, WBC 34B (Nashville: Thomas Nelson, 2001), 393.
[31] Evans, *Mark 8:27–16:20*, 394, emphasis added.
[32] Citing the effecting, enacting, or fulfillment of the New Covenant in Christ does not negate that it was made with and continues for Israel. As noted earlier, there is no supersession by the church, a point Fretheim addresses: "Having used the word 'obsolete' for the old covenant (Heb 8:13) . . . Hebrews seems not to draw any negative conclusions regarding the relationship of the Jewish people to God. . . . Even though the Sinai covenant is broken or obsolete, God's promises to Abraham remain, and to those promises the faithful (see Heb 11) could cling. In this light, the formulation in Hebrews regarding the new covenant might mean that Christians are now drawn into the new relationship with God of which Jeremiah speaks, not unlike the manner in which Paul speaks of being ingrafted into the vine (Rom 11)" (*Jeremiah*, 449-50).
[33] While the promises are effected or inaugurated through Christ's blood, there remains yet a fuller eschatological fulfillment of them. Wright conceptualizes this as three horizons: the first is the historical and literary (post)exilic context, the second is the greater fulfillment through Christ, and the third is "when, in the new creation, the redeemed people of God will live with God in perfect intimacy, free from sorrow, free from sin, and the relational heartbeat of the covenant will beat for all eternity" (*Jeremiah*, 337).

Woven through the New Covenant's inauguration through Jesus' blood are patterns or "networks of recurring, corresponding depictions of the God-human-world relationship" that figurally connect its promise in Jeremiah to its inauguration in Jesus' blood.[34] Through these patterns, we see God working similarly in the New Covenant's promise and its inauguration, now making Christ's sacrifice central to the covenant's fullness: "Entrance into or participation in the 'new covenant—which is fidelity to God's covenant—becomes tied to a participation in the sacrifice of Jesus Christ. . . . The climax of the covenant has come, and fidelity to that covenant now centers on the sacrifice of Jesus Christ."[35]

Figural patterns and the New Covenant. Examination of three such patterns opens further understanding of the character and work of God. First, the promise and its inauguration arise solely out of God's gracious ḥesed. The New Covenant, gifted to recalcitrant Israel even before the final judgment of exile, reveals God's gracious commitment to his people. Beyond deserving, Israel receives the promise of New Covenant. Through it is effected abundant restoration of all that was intended under the Sinai covenant. Similarly, it is God's loving mercy that stands behind Christ's sacrificial death, proffering restoration not only to Israel but to Gentiles and all creation (Eph 2:11-13; Rom 8:20-21). By this, the great promise given Abraham—that through his seed all nations would find blessing—is brought to completion. In New Covenant promise and inauguration, God similarly acts with ḥesed to fulfill his purposes.

Second, the New Covenant is promised to Israel. In the Book, Israel is referenced in various ways, including as God's "firstborn son" (Jer 31:9) and his "dear son" (Jer 31:20).[36] The nation Israel—God's

---

[34]Citing Abernethy, "Theological Patterning," 151, as noted earlier in this chapter.
[35]Moon, *Jeremiah's New Covenant*, 255.
[36]Other designations include Israel and Judah (Jer 30:3, 4; 31:27, 31), Israel (Jer 31:7, 33, 36, 37), Jacob (Jer 30:7, 18; 31:7, 11), my son Ephraim (Jer 31:9, 20), Ephraim (31:18), Virgin Israel (Jer 31:4, 21), yoked cattle (Jer 30:8), servant (Jer 30:10), an outcast (Jer 30:17), well-watered garden

son—will be punished and brought to the death of exile.[37] Only after this punishment is the son restored. In a similar way, the inauguration of the New Covenant involves another Israel as God's son. Christ comes as the true Israel, the Son of God (Mt 2:15).[38] As the Son, he is brought to death, just as Israel is brought to death in exile. Here the patterning includes not only parallel (Christ is the true Israel; the son Israel dies) but reversal. Israel the nation is the son who sins and is punished; the true Israel—Christ—is the Son who has not sinned but bears punishment for all.

Finally, the New Covenant passage appears in Jeremiah before the account of the city's fall and the nation's ultimate demise in exile (chaps. 39, 52). These events are the full expression of Jeremiah's message of "uprooting, tearing down, destroying, and overthrowing" (1:10). It is a gracious mark of hope that the New Covenant—a full expression of Jeremiah's message of "building and planting" (1:10)—is given before the book recounts the darkness and despair of exile in a foreign land. In a similar way, during the Last Supper Jesus speaks the hopeful words of the New Covenant in his blood. This supper occurs before his own exile into a foreign land of darkness that he voluntarily enters to rescue his people and deliver them into a kingdom of light (Col 1:13). In both cases, God's prior, gracious, and sure word of promise endures through exile and even speaks in the midst of its darkness and despair.

The inauguration of the New Covenant echoes the covenant's promise through several parallels and reversals. These patterns attest to a similarity of God's working in Jeremiah's time and in Christ.

(Jer 31:12), Rachel's children (Jer 31:15, 17), unruly calf (Jer 31:18), daughter Israel (Jer 31:22), and wife (Jer 31:32).

[37]Donald E. Gowan proposes exile as the nation's death, and return as its resurrection: Gowan, *Theology of the Prophetic Books: The Death and Resurrection of Israel* (Louisville, KY: Westminster John Knox, 1998).

[38]He is also one of the group of "sons" over whom Rachel weeps in Mt 2:18. By God's warning to Joseph the son is saved out of the Bethlehem massacre.

Together the patterns point to ways in which Jeremiah's New Covenant reveals the God who Jesus is, and they anticipate his inauguration of the New Covenant.

READING OTHER JEREMIAH TEXTS IN THE FOOTSTEPS OF THE APOSTLES

Jeremiah's New Covenant, read in the footsteps of the apostles, seeks to attend to the text's witness within its own context and the context of a two-testament canon. The patterning considered between Luke's account and the Jeremianic New Covenant provides some paradigmatic signposts for reading Jeremiah when the New Testament proffers little or no engagement of the prophet. Attentive to continuity and discontinuity between the testaments, and to patterns of God's faithfulness, one sees the book of Jeremiah provides rich material for such reading, and two further examples are here briefly presented.

Jeremiah and the idols (Jer 10:1-16): Patterns of idolatry and worship. Jeremiah early on calls attention to the futility of idols, stating in Jeremiah 2:5 that they are worthless (*hebel*), and those who worship them likewise become worthless.[39] This is a sentiment taken up again in Jeremiah 10, where the idolatry of the nations is described as worthless (Jer 10:3, 8). Israel is warned against making idols, objects of wood and precious metal that cannot stand, walk, or do good.[40] The description of this futility is interspersed with doxologies lauding Yahweh's incomparability (Jer 10:6-7, 10, 12-13, 16). Yahweh is the Creator of all, an eternal king of the nations, before whose great name all bow.

Jeremiah 10's focus on idols provides a sadly fitting conclusion to the judgment oracles in Jeremiah 2–10 as it reveals the sins that judgment addresses. Through its folly Israel has become as worthless as what it

---

[39]This truth is clearly stated in Ps 115; 135. See also G. K. Beale, *We Become What We Worship: A Biblical Theology of Idolatry* (Downers Grove, IL: IVP Academic, 2008); Richard Lints, *Identity and Idolatry: The Image of God and Its Inversion*, NSBT 36 (Downers Grove, IL: IVP Academic, 2015).

[40]A similar polemic appears in Is 40:18-31; 41:7; 44:6-20; 46:5-13; Hab 2:18-20.

worships and has shown its so-called wisdom to be true folly (Jer 8–10). Indeed, in the creation of idols and the rejection of the true Creator, humanity has become less than human. For the exilic community, living in a land where Bel and Marduk are worshiped (Jer 50:2; 51:44), the chapter is a cautionary tale: the way of wisdom does not lie in the worship of any god but Yahweh.

Jeremiah's warning speaks powerfully to New Testament believers, who, belonging to the Lord of life, can still in futility fashion idols in their own image: "The old gods may have changed their names or lost their personal names altogether in favor of more abstract concepts and phrases (patriotism, the free market, economic growth, national security, etc.), but they can still wield enormous power."[41]

If the folly of idolatry speaks within the New Testament context as powerfully as within Jeremiah's own context, so too does his laudatory descriptions of Yahweh, the true God, whom the New Testament reveals incarnate. Honoring the Son is to honor to the Father for as true God, Christ answers the prophet's doxological description at every point: Creator of all things (Col 1:15-19), a king (Mt 2:1-6; Acts 4:23-26) whose name is great and before whom all bow (Acts 3:6, 16; Phil 2:9-11). Jeremiah's cautionary tale continues to speak to the church in its own sojourning as an alien in a foreign land: the way of wisdom does not lie in the worship of any god but Yahweh.

Jeremiah as a gentle lamb led to slaughter (Jer 11:18-19): Typology and the suffering servant. As Yahweh's prophet, Jeremiah mediates God's message to the people through oracles and sermons. But Jeremiah in a way unique among the prophets also embodies that message through enacted symbolic messages (Jer 13:1-11; 19:1-13; 27:1-7) and through his life situation (Jer 16:1-9; 32:6-15). Jeremiah not only

---

[41]Christopher J. H. Wright, *"Here Are Your Gods": Faithful Discipleship in Idolatrous Times* (Downers Grove, IL: IVP Academic, 2020), 23. Wright's volume provides a helpful overview of false gods as primarily human constructs from within the created order or the imagination of our own hearts.

communicates God's word through speech; he *embodies* it "in the sense that everything he says and does is a declaration of the word of God among his people."[42] The same embodied message is true also of Jeremiah's laments (Jer 11–20). Irreducible to simply a window into the prophet's psyche, they too are a declaration of God's word.

On its own, the embodied nature of Jeremiah's message opens a typological anticipation of Christ: both are embodied Word of God (while of course of significantly different order). The typological connection is sharpened by Jeremiah's first lament (Jer 11:18-19). Recognizing plots against him, he cries out, "I was like a pet lamb brought to slaughter. I did not know that they devised schemes against me." One can readily imagine Jeremiah's words in Christ's mouth in his own trial of suffering: both are embodied Word of God; both cry out in suffering.

The figural potential of Jeremiah's cry is heightened in light of Isaiah's suffering servant, who is also "like a lamb led to slaughter" (Is 53:7).[43] The connection between Jeremiah and the servant is furthered by eight additional linguistic connections and broader parallels between the two passages (for instance, both are shamed, beaten, and then vindicated).[44] An intentional intertextual referencing seems certain.

---

[42]Andrew G. Shead, *A Mouth Full of Fire: The Word of God in the Words of Jeremiah*, NSBT 29 (Downers Grove, IL: IVP Academic, 2012), 138. See also Carol Dempsey, *Jeremiah: Preacher of Grace, Poet of Truth*, Interfaces (Collegeville, MN: Liturgical Press, 2007), 38-53; Lissa M. Wray Beal, "Prophetic Ministry in Jeremiah 20.7-18: 'Violence and Destruction,' and Paradoxical Hope for a Shattered Community," in *Violent Biblical Texts: New Approaches*, ed. Helen Paynter and Trevor Laurence (Sheffield: Sheffield Phoenix, 2022), 170-72.

[43]"Like a lamb led to slaughter" employs different nouns for "lamb," but verbs and object are the same. Jeremiah: *kəkebeś . . . yûbal liṭbôaḥ*; the servant: *kaśśê laṭṭebah yûbāl*.

[44]Benjamin D. Sommer notes several parallels between Jeremiah and the suffering servant, including eight linguistic connections: "and Yahweh" (*wayhwh*), "by his/our hand(s)" (*bəyādô*), and shared roots such as "to see" (*rʾh*), "to think (thoughts)" (*ḥšb*), "to do justice" (*ṣdq*), "to destroy" (*šḥt*), "to die" (*mwt*), and "to reveal" (*glh*). Sommer, *A Prophet Reads Scripture: Allusion in Isaiah 40–66*, Contraversions: Jews and Other Differences (Stanford, CA: Stanford University Press, 1998), 65-66. While Sommers posits a late Isaiah that relies on Jeremiah, these dating conclusions do not obscure the textual parallels. See also Gary E. Yates, "Intertextuality and the Portrayal of Jeremiah the Prophet," *Bibliotheca Sacra* 170 (2013): 293-95; Kathleen M. O'Connor, "Figuration in Jeremiah's Confessions with Questions for Isaiah's Servant," in *Jeremiah Invented: Constructions and Deconstructions of Jeremiah*, ed. Else K. Holt and Carolyn J. Sharp, LHBOTS 595 (London: Bloomsbury T&T Clark, 2015), 71-72.

The New Testament presents the suffering servant as a type of Christ (Mt 8:17; Lk 22:37; Jn 12:38; Acts 8:32-33; Rom 10:16; 1 Pet 2:22-25).[45] Given the embodied nature of Jeremiah's ministry and the several parallels to the suffering servant, a typological reading of Jeremiah and his cry seems warranted.[46] Such a reading reveals that Jeremiah's situation parallels that of the suffering servant (and by extension Christ). Both Jeremiah and the suffering servant are innocent sufferers at the hands of those who resist their message. Both are vindicated by God and as survivors "express and mirror traumatic sufferings . . . and augur hope for survival" for the exilic community.[47] However, Jeremiah also presents contrasts to the suffering servant (and Christ). The servant is silent before his oppressors (Is 53:7-8), while Jeremiah decidedly is not, calling for God's judgment against them (Jer 11:20; 12:3; 15:15; 18:20-23; 20:12).[48] There is no word of forgiveness or prayer offered for his tormentors. It is a stark contrast to Christ, who on the cross prays, "Father, forgive them" (Lk 23:34).

Jeremiah's embodiment of God's word and the parallels and contrasts to the servant provide, when reading "after the apostles," material for a strong typological reading of Christ. Jeremiah and the servant

---

[45]Consensus on this understanding is not complete, as evidenced by Morna D. Hooker's *Jesus and the Servant* (London: SPCK, 1959). The issues are complex and the bibliography vast. For an accessible and succinct statement of the main approaches to the question see John N. Oswalt, *The Book of Isaiah 1–39*, NICOT (Grand Rapids, MI: Eerdmans, 1986), 49–52, and John Goldingay, "Servant of Yahweh" in *IVPDOTP*, 700-707.

[46]So Wright (*Jeremiah*, 146) and commonly in premodern interpreters. See Jerome, *Commentary on Jeremiah*, ed. Christopher A. Hall (Downers Grove, IL: IVP Academic, 2011), 75; Dean O. Wenthe, ed., *Jeremiah, Lamentations*, Ancient Christian Commentary on Scripture Old Testament 12 (Downers Grove, IL: IVP Academic, 2009), 98-99, citing Jerome, Cyril of Jerusalem, and Origen. Fretheim acknowledges the link to Is 53:7 but does not pursue it, crediting the metaphor as indicative of innocent (but not vicarious) suffering (*Jeremiah*, 190). R. E. Clements considers it "mistaken . . . to compare Jeremiah's action with that of Jesus almost six centuries later." Clements, *Jeremiah*, Interpretation (Atlanta: John Knox, 1988), 80. Yet the New Testament draws typological relationships between other characters (e.g., the servant and Christ) and events (e.g., the Red Sea and baptism) that are separated by centuries.

[47]O'Connor, "Figuration in Jeremiah's Confessions," 64.

[48]Of note, Jeremiah also laments and challenges God (Jer 15:18; 17:17; 20:7), as does Jesus ("My God, why have you forsaken me?"; Mt 27:46; Mk 15:34). Whether Jesus' lament is similarly a challenge is less certain.

bring depth and nuance to an understanding of Christ, the innocent victim led like a lamb to slaughter. Like the servant, Christ too is silent, and the contrast to Jeremiah's protestations and cries for vengeance strengthens this depiction. Both the parallels and the contrasts work within the two-testament canon to illuminate Christ, the righteous, silent sufferer, whose vindication comes from God.

Conclusion

Reading Jeremiah as Christian Scripture is a hermeneutical imperative within a two-testament canon. This chapter considers Jeremiah's message within its own context and its New Testament context with attention to figural and typological resonances. In the New Covenant, God's gracious promises to a needy people are given before their hour of death. This illuminates the similar context of the promise's inauguration as the new Israel prepares to give himself to death. At both moments the exile of death is overshadowed. Hope of resurrection and life, and of the restoration of covenant relationship lightens the darkness. In Jeremiah's polemic on idolatry, the folly of fashioning and worshiping false gods is descriptive of his time, as of ours. In both contexts wise worship is only of the true and living God, who is Creator, king, and lauded Lord now revealed in Jesus the Christ. Finally, Jeremiah speaks and also embodies Yahweh's word. His suffering, like that of a lamb led to slaughter, connects intertextually with the suffering servant. Together these characters typologically anticipate *the* suffering servant, who imbues their innocent suffering with heightened nuance and meaning.

The hermeneutical imperative of this chapter's reading strategy adds depth to the New Testament's portrait of Christ. It also provides new contours to our reading of Jeremiah. In Jeremiah we see God in grace, longsuffering, and covenant faithfulness amid his people. The triune God is revealed in this historical context, informing a Christian understanding of the God who is later incarnated. Additionally, observed figural and typological resonances need not be partitioned off for consideration until a reading of the New Testament. Rather, they glimmer behind one's reading of Jeremiah, infusing it with the knowing and yearning of the now-and-not-yet. There is the prophet and the promises made true for Israel and inaugurated in Christ. There is the Christian experience of the blessings of the New Covenant alongside the anticipation of their eschatological fullness. In such reading, ancient prophet and ancient word are a place where past, present, and future collide and blend. Such is God's word in Jeremiah, which spoke, speaks, and now calls us into the hope of God's future.

9

THE HISTORY OF INTERPRETING JEREMIAH AS CHRISTIAN SCRIPTURE

Patristic Interpretation and Its Modern Legacy

Andrew G. Shead

THE NEW COVENANT focus of this volume diverts us from considering how time and place have shaped the interpretation of specific issues (e.g., divine impassibility, political theology) to examine the nature of Christian interpretation itself. Jeremiah 31:31-34 leads into this subject because, rightly or wrongly, the two covenants have always been closely related to the two testaments. As Henri de Lubac remarks,

> The Christian tradition understands that Scripture has two meanings. The most general name for these two meanings is the literal meaning and the spiritual ("pneumatic") meaning, and these two meanings have the same kind of relationship to each other as do the Old and New Testaments to each other. More exactly, and in all strictness, they constitute, they *are* the Old and New Testaments.[1]

I shall have cause to challenge this statement, but it is a good place to start. My focus is the patristic period because most major interpretive issues were addressed by the fifth century. It was not until the modern era that a genuinely new question entered the debate: How important is it for Christian interpretation to reconstruct the world and worldview of Jeremiah's first readers?

A history of interpretation enables us to reflect on the following questions: Is "what the text originally meant" the proper basis for Christian reading? Or does the fact of Scripture's divine inspiration mean that the letter, read as part of a canonical whole, speaks out of its own sufficiency to disclose eternal truths to Spirit-filled readers? If so, what controls the process? Is it simply salvation history and the typology it generates, or may Christ be found by other means?

Before we go further, I should clarify the terms *literal* and *spiritual*. Today we associate *literal meaning* with the modern notion of authorial intention. A more helpful synonym is *plain meaning*. "The plain sense is 'the way the words run' for a community in the light of that community's techniques for following the argument of texts."[2] A third synonym, frequent in Jerome, is the *historia*, meaning the grammatical meaning of the text in its literary context, including its moral significance. The *historia* was the way a Jewish reader might have understood Jeremiah.

---

[1] Henri de Lubac, *Medieval Exegesis*, trans. Mark Sebanc (Grand Rapids, MI: Eerdmans, 1998), 1:225.

[2] Lewis Ayres, *Nicaea and Its Legacy: An Approach to Fourth-Century Trinitarian Theology* (Oxford: Oxford University Press, 2004), 33.

The *spiritual sense* refers to the text's Christian meaning. It is discerned by reading figurally, in the light of the New Testament, so as to illuminate "an aspect of the incarnate Word's mission."[3] The figures that point to Christ can include metaphor, typology, allegory, hyperbole, and so on.

Old and New Covenant in the Second Century

Barnabas, Justin, Irenaeus. The pseudepigraphal Epistle of Barnabas,[4] probably written in Alexandria before AD 138, is a radical treatise on Christian interpretation from a time when Christianity was still working to define itself over against Judaism. The newness of the law of Christ lies in its transforming power, not its content (Barnabas 6.11). The Law and the Prophets describe the life, death, and resurrection of Jesus. This extends even to the food laws, whose true meaning was only ever spiritual: "Because of their fleshly desires the people accepted [the precepts of Moses] as though they referred to actual food" (Barnabas 10.9).[5]

Completed in Rome, Justin Martyr's *Dialogue with Trypho* (ca. 160) seeks to convince his Jewish interlocutor that Jesus is the God of the Old Testament.[6] Unlike Barnabas, Justin does not deny the validity of plain reading. Circumcision, for example, is a sign both of the old covenant and of future righteousness in Christ (*Dialogue* 15). However, the New Covenant, toward which the Sinai covenant points, is now the only means by which anyone, Jew or Gentile, may approach the God of the Old Testament (*Dialogue* 11). Justin's main point is that the God of Abraham is the only God and that we approach him through Jesus.

---

[3] Ayres, *Nicaea and Its Legacy*, 37.
[4] Michael W. Holmes, *The Apostolic Fathers: Greek Texts and English Translations*, 3rd ed. (Grand Rapids, MI: Baker Academic, 2007), 380-441.
[5] This is so startling that Coxe's translation in *The Ante-Nicene Fathers* qualifies it. See Alexander Roberts and James Donaldson, eds., *The Ante-Nicene Fathers* (Grand Rapids, MI: Eerdmans, 1993), 1:143. However, the adversative construction in Barnabas 10.9 "finally confirms [the implication of Jer 10:2] that the law's demands were issued with respect not to the Jews, but to the Christians." Ferdinand R. Prostmeier, *Der Barnabasbrief*, Kommentar zu den Apostolischen Vätern 8 (Göttingen: Vandenhoeck & Ruprecht, 1999), 380, my translation.
[6] *ANF* 1:194-270.

In *Against Heresies* (Lyons, ca. 185) Irenaeus confronts those who taught that the God of the Old Testament was a lesser deity.[7] He moves from the New Testament to the Old to demonstrate that the God of the Old Testament is Jesus, the author of both covenants (*Against Heresies* 4.9.1). The patriarchs, righteous by faith, already had "the meaning of the Decalogue written in their hearts." When this heart-righteousness faded in Egypt, God instituted the Sinai covenant to caution Israel by "prohibitory mandates" (4.16.2-3). These "laws of bondage" were eventually "cancelled by the new covenant of liberty," because Christ's people are freed from slavery to sin by their adoption as sons. Like the patriarchs, they keep the Decalogue (which Christ extends, 4.16.4) and obey God's "natural and noble" laws from the heart (4.16.5).

Irenaeus lifts his conclusion that Christ is the author of both covenants into a hermeneutical principle. Because the prophets saw Christ and announced "that liberty which distinguishes the new covenant," the spiritual reader will locate each of the prophets' statements within the "dispensation of the Lord" (*dispositionis Domini*)[8] and "the entire system [*integrum corpus*] of the work of the Son of God, knowing always the same God, and always acknowledging the same Word of God" (*Against Heresies* 4.33.14-15).

Christ in all Scripture. Each of these apologists parses the relation between the covenants differently. For Barnabas, the New Covenant *is* the old covenant, written on renewed hearts. Its content was always and only Christ. For Justin, the New Covenant *abrogates* the old covenant. The content of the old was commands; the content of the new is Christ, through whom all—even Jews—must approach the God of Israel. For Irenaeus, the New Covenant *fulfills* the old covenant. The old

---

[7] *ANF* 1:462-525 (book 4).
[8] That is, the economy of salvation fixed by the Father to his Son in the universal dispensation of human blessing. See Antonio Orbe, "Cinco exegesis ireneanas de Gen 2,17b adv. haer. V, 23,1-2," *Gregorianum* 62, no. 1 (1981): 98.

commands condemned Israel and prophesied Christ. They are fulfilled in people—whether living before Moses or after Christ—who give him filial respect and love. The Old Testament is a fully Christian book.

At the same time, all three apologists find Christ throughout the Old Testament with what strikes modern readers as extravagant freedom. They have no worked-out system of typology or allegory; they simply find credible ways to display Christ as the principal subject of Scripture. For Barnabas, the plain meaning *is* the spiritual meaning. For Justin, the plain meaning attests to Christ by means of *typoi*, "events in which the Holy Spirit enacted a picture of the future," and *logoi*, "verbal prophecies of future events"; but Justin does not always pursue a deeper meaning.[9] For Irenaeus, the plain meaning always has a spiritual meaning. His overarching scheme of history creates patterns and recurrences by which later events can give spiritual meaning to earlier ones. Despite these differences, for each of them the New Covenant attests before anything else to Christ's identity with the God of Israel.

The Third to the Fifth Centuries

Commentary on Jeremiah survives from three major scholars of this period: Origen of Alexandria, whose extant homilies include selections from Jeremiah 1–20 and 50–51 (ca. 240); Theodoret of Cyrus, whose brief Jeremiah commentary (445) represents the school of Antioch; and Jerome, whose late and unfinished commentary (414–419) is influenced by both schools without being a product of either. In addition, Augustine's treatise *The Spirit and the Letter* (412) includes a lengthy exposition of Jeremiah 31:31-34.

Origen. Biblical commentary begins with Origen. His system for unpacking Scripture's spiritual message while avoiding arbitrary spiritualizing is sophisticated, internally consistent, and grounded in

---

[9]Gerald Bray, *Biblical Interpretation Past and Present* (Downers Grove, IL: IVP Academic, 1996), 81.

Scripture.¹⁰ He does not always follow his system, but in general Origen begins with clear, well-attested typologies, such as the people of God, who anticipate the church (when they are faithful), or Israel, that is, Jews who reject Jesus (when they are not). Then, within and controlled by this larger typological frame, he considers features of the text that seem arbitrary, gratuitous, unreasonable, fanciful, or impossible, and seeks the spiritual truths God must have included them to reveal. These truths are principally christological: "The doctrines concerning God and His only-begotten Son; of what nature the Son is, and in what manner he can be the Son of God, and what are the causes of his descending to the level of human flesh and completely assuming humanity" (*First Principles* 4.2.7). The plain meaning keeps spiritual interpretation in check. Origen's mammoth work of textual criticism, the *Hexapla*, demonstrates the seriousness with which he treated the letter of Scripture.

Two examples will give a taste of Origen's method.¹¹ On Jeremiah 15:5-6, "Who will spare you Jerusalem? And who will feel sad for you? . . . You have turned away from me," Origen begins with the plain meaning.¹² When a great king condemns somebody, that person's friends hide their grief, lest they express disapproval of the king's judgment. So then: Jerusalem (the *literal* city) killed Jesus. And when God destroys Jerusalem (in AD 70) the angels show no pity but turn their backs on the city they once protected. Second, Jerusalem has a deeper *moral* significance, found in the etymology of its name, Jebus, "what has been trampled" (this tradition of etymologizing comes from Philo). It represents the soul of one who has "trampled upon the Son of God" (Heb 10:29), whose apostasy places them beyond pity. Finally, Jerusalem points *heavenward*. The city that "turned away from me" is

---

¹⁰Origen, *On First Principles*, trans. G. W. Butterworth (London: SPCK, 1936), 4.2.1-3.
¹¹Origen, *Homilies on Jeremiah; Homily on 1 Kings 28*, trans. John Clark Smith, Fathers of the Church 97 (Washington, DC: Catholic University of America Press, 1998).
¹²All biblical quotations in this section are Origen's, as translated by John Clark Smith.

a synecdoche for the Jewish people as a whole, who turned away from Christ and back to Egypt. Christians must rather strain forward to what lies ahead. Methodologically, Origen points out that "with each meaning of *Jerusalem*, the next also agrees"; in other words, the plain sense is never left behind (*Hom. Jer.* 130-34).

Origen more often confines himself to two levels of meaning. His homily on Jeremiah 18:1-16 is a textbook example of his method, demonstrating its robustness and restraint. "What then these words portend we will consider first in an overview, then ... word by word" (*Hom. Jer.* 188). Origen's overview begins with the plain meaning: an initial vision concerning a malleable pot capable of being remade into a fresh pot (Jer 18:1-4), and a second vision concerning finished pots, hardened into earthenware (Jer 18:5-10). He then summarizes the spiritual meaning: humans are formed and re-formed during this life into better creatures; but humans beyond the present age "become whatsoever we become by being put through fire, either under the fire of the 'flaming darts of the evil one' or under the fire of God, 'since also our God is a consuming fire.' ... We are not remade nor does our constitution admit of bettering" (*Hom. Jer.* 189).

Origen then examines "by reason" eye-catching details of the text, beginning with Jeremiah going *down* to the potter's house (*Hom. Jer.* 190-192). As opposed to Moses, who went *up* the mountain to learn of things above, Jeremiah is being taught about things below. There is a wisdom peculiar to each realm, and Christ has been in both. (The anthropological focus of the whole directs Origen's mind as he reflects on the parts.) He next considers the vessel that "fell from his hands" (LXX Jer 18:4), which implies human capacity for negligence within God's sovereign will, before turning from these literal truths to the text's deeper meaning via the commonly held view that the remade pot speaks of the resurrection body (*Hom. Jer.* 193). Origen does not disagree but points out that Jeremiah speaks of the fate of this remade pot in terms of "two nations, the former one named whom the Word threatens, and the second, to whom he promised." These nations are Israel and the church, respectively. "Scrutinize all of Scripture and you will discover that most passages concern these two nations" (*Hom. Jer.* 194). Origen surveys the history of Israel from the patriarchs to the exile—a history of repeated divine warnings, which finally ended when Israel crucified Jesus and "God selected another nation" (*Hom. Jer.* 195). Jeremiah speaks of each nation changing its path and God changing his mind, and this conundrum is Origen's final concern, a question of theology he teases out in a combination of exegesis, reasoning, and comparison with other texts.

Origen's exegesis is bold and unfamiliar, but the spiritual meaning of the whole, typologically understood—that is, understood in terms of the significance Scripture gives to events through the relationships it creates between them—constrains the way he extracts meaning from the details. If Scripture is divinely inspired at the level of its words, and the message those words combine to communicate is a Christian message, then how can we know when to stop pressing the words for Christian meaning? Perhaps this is a matter not just of literary or hermeneutical judgment but of spiritual discernment. "For Origen the text yields its message in degrees as purity of heart and attention to the Logos grows."[13]

Theodoret. As an Antiochene exegete, Theodoret prioritizes grammatical subtleties, the explanation of images, historical fulfillment, precise theology, and a minimum of paraenesis.[14] Only occasionally and briefly does he consider Christian meaning (see Jer 31:22, a prophecy that there will be new growth through daughter Israel, fulfilled by "the apostles that sprang from her"). His exposition of Jeremiah 31:31-34 is a noteworthy exception. The God of old and new

---

[13] Ayres, *Nicaea and Its Legacy*, 22.
[14] Robert Charles Hill, "Introduction," in Theodoret of Cyrus, *Commentary on the Prophet Jeremiah*, trans. Robert Charles Hill (Brookline, MA: Holy Cross Orthodox Press, 2006), 10-15.

covenants is one and the same lawgiver, Jesus Christ. The typological patterning of salvation history makes this clear:

> The only-begotten Word of God was the source of the evangelical goods for us, he being the one who freed Israel from the slavery of the Egyptians. He was therefore the one who in speaking to Moses said, "I am he who is." . . . On leading the sacred apostles up the mountain, instead of giving them stone tablets he inscribed the divine laws on their hearts and proposed the Beatitudes to those who practice virtue. (*Commentary on the Prophet Jeremiah* 117)[15]

For Theodoret the law may describe either the Mosaic law or the moral law inscribed on Christian hearts by the Spirit. Their difference is taken as read; their similarity derives from the eternal Son, whose character they both reflect. Jesus Christ is shown by his ministry to be the God of Israel. While more modest than Origen in his interpretation (Theodoret's longer Isaiah commentary is more adventurous), he finds Christ in the Old Testament with the same directness and shares the same convictions about the substance of Jeremiah's spiritual message, which principally (though not exclusively) concerns the person of Christ.

Jerome. Jerome advocated Origen's method until the mid-390s, when controversy over Origen's unorthodox views drove Jerome to repudiate him. In theory, at least, Jerome stayed close to the plain meaning, which he called the *historia*. Jeremiah 31:31-34 provides Jerome with a hermeneutical key. Following its use in Hebrews 8–9, the church recognizes "that these things were fulfilled in the first advent of the Savior and that the New Testament (that is, the Gospel) has succeeded the Old Testament. The law of the letter was replaced by the law of the spirit, so that everything—including the sacrifices, circumcision and the sabbath—was fulfilled spiritually."[16]

---

[15]It is unclear whether Theodoret discerns a Christophany in Ex 3:14 or simply the inseparable operations of the Trinity.

[16]Jerome, *Commentary on Jeremiah*, trans. Michael Graves, Ancient Christian Texts (Downers Grove, IL: IVP Academic, 2011), 201.

Jerome's conclusion draws on the traditional understanding of 2 Corinthians 3:3, but the basis of his exegesis lies in Jeremiah 31:31. For Jerome "the house of Israel" coincides with "the lost sheep of the house of Israel" to whom Jesus preached but who rejected him, so that eternal life was then offered to the Gentiles (Acts 13:46). The spiritual meaning of Jeremiah 31:33-34 is thus to be found in the life of the church, whose members do not teach one another with Jewish teaching or human traditions (Jer 31:34) but are taught by the Holy Spirit. Thus, the old covenant was both *replaced*, when the Jews rejected Jesus, and *fulfilled*, as first Jews and then Gentiles became children of God through faith in Christ.

For Jerome, as for Origen, the Old Testament's plain meaning is its Jewish meaning, including its Jewish fulfillment in the time of Jesus, culminating in the temple's destruction in AD 70. Jerome explains that Jeremiah 30–32 contains

> mystical promises that the Jews and our Judaizers think will be fulfilled at the consummation of the world. . . . But we, following the authority of the apostles and evangelists—and above all the apostle Paul—will show that whatever was promised carnally to the people of Israel has been fulfilled spiritually in us and is being fulfilled today. Between Christians and Jews there is no other conflict than this. (*Comm. Jer.* 183)

The point where *historia* ends and spiritual reading begins can be seen in Jerome's treatment of the wicked shepherds (Jer 23:1-4). According to the plain sense, they correspond to the scribes and Pharisees. With the spiritual meaning, Jerome's horizon of interpretation leaves Israel behind, and the shepherds become church leaders unworthy to govern, teachers of heresy (*Comm. Jer.* 137-138).

When Jerome's spiritual readings—which he sometimes labels "tropology" or "anagogy," without clear distinction in meaning—grow more adventurous, he secures them in the *historia* by a number of techniques, including (1) attention to the literary context, (2) confirmation of typology from elsewhere in Scripture, or (3) multiple points of less obvious correspondence. An example of the first comes in Jeremiah 24:1-10, the good and bad figs. Jerome contests Origen's interpretation by taking all ten verses as one pericope and by using Jeremiah 24:3-10 to ground spiritual readings of Jeremiah 24:1-2 in the events that follow (*Comm. Jer.* 149-50). Using the second technique, Jerome can take the "first-ripe figs" (Jer 24:2) to represent the patriarchs and Moses, because the same image is used in Hosea 9:10. With the third technique, using Jeremiah 22:24, multiple points of correspondence allow Jerome to follow Origen for once: "Origen referred this passage to Christ, because he [like King Jeconiah] was torn from the hand of God the Father like a ring, and he was sent to the land of captivity through the Valley of Weeping" (*Comm. Jer.* 135).

Despite his repudiation of Origen, once the spiritual meaning of a passage is established in broad outline, Jerome is prepared to interpret its details spiritually as well. On Jeremiah 22:13-17 he reproduces Origen's exegesis, unacknowledged.[17] Jehoiakim's palace points spiritually to the evil church built by heretics. Within this straightforward typological frame, the heretical church is "measured, not great and wide"; with airy upper rooms "carried about with every wind of doctrine"; with windows, "since they do not have a lasting structure"; with cedar, which rots under the stormy rains of persecution; "and so on with the rest of the passage" (*Comm. Jer.* 134). Behind this practice lies the conviction that every God-breathed word is there for a reason. This same conviction underlies Jerome's meticulous text-critical work. When the versions contain different readings, Jerome may reject the Septuagint if he judges it faulty but frequently uses both (as do Origen and Theodoret). The Hebrew, Septuagint, and Theodotion all differ at Jeremiah 15:10b, but Jerome argues that each can be read Christianly, deriving "the sense out of the *persona* of Christ" (*Comm. Jer.* 96). The

---

[17]See *Fragments from the Catena* 13, in Origen, *Homilies on Jeremiah*, 285.

Christian meaning of Scripture as a whole secures the meaning of each part from straying into heresy.

The importance of doctrine for controlling spiritual interpretation can be seen in Jerome's polemics against Origen and Pelagius. We have seen Jerome borrow from Origen's allegories, but Jerome only ever uses the word *allegory* when he considers the result heretical.[18] Origen had entertained unorthodox speculations about the transmigration of souls by referring Jerusalem to a heavenly reality (Gal 4:26) and Egypt and Babylon to other spiritual locations where certain souls are held captive.[19] So Jerome counters "[him] who always interprets allegorically, fleeing the truth of the *historia*" (*Comm. Jer.* 167) by providing plain readings of texts such as Jeremiah 24:1-10; 27:2-4, 9-11. Nevertheless, Jerome allegorizes Jeremiah 2:6 to attack the Pelagian heresy. He begins with typology: the journey through the wilderness prefigures the Christian journey to heavenly perfection. Within this frame, "the 'impassable' land . . . shows the difficulty of the journey; 'through a land of thirst' [shows that] we always desire more . . . ; and the image (or 'shadow') of death . . . [shows that] everywhere the devil sets his traps" (*Comm. Jer.* 9-10). Christian reading means letting Christ illumine the text, so that the truth about him shows us what the text may and may not mean.

Finally, the living text can speak prophetically to Jerome's audience. On the promise of Jeremiah 16:14-15, where "according to the spiritual understanding he is describing things that were going to be completed more truly and more perfectly in Christ," the land of Israel is a type of the church, and those who come "out of all the countries" are first the Gentiles, and then "all Israel" (Rom 11:25-26). The end-time horizon of this fulfillment brings Jerome's readers into the frame: "We can also relate this passage to the persecutions that befell our people from the

---

[18]There is one exception, where Jerome declares himself open to a suggestion by "allegorical interpreters" about Jer 25:15-17 (*Comm. Jer.* 157).
[19]Origen, *On First Principles* 4.3.8-11.

days of Nero. . . . Just as the Lord had compassion on his people, and brought them back to their land, he will surely bring his people back to the church, which he gave to their 'fathers,' who are the apostles and apostolic men" (*Comm. Jer.* 102).

Augustine. In *The Spirit and the Letter* Augustine counters the Pelagian belief that God's grace assists us by showing us how to please him. The New Covenant is necessary because mere possession of the law was not enough to save Israel. Human sinfulness turns it into "the letter that kills." The New Covenant fulfills the same law that was given to Moses, so its newness does not lie in its content; rather, it is "new with the newness of the Spirit, which heals the new man from his old failing." A Christian's love of neighbor may look the same as an Israelite's, but the similarity is superficial. The newness of the Christian heart makes every action an expression of love, not fear, and hence quite distinct from its old covenant counterpart. Finally, the reward of the New Covenant is not the land but God himself ("They shall all know me"). It is a reward we do not fully enjoy until "the Word, which took flesh to appear to flesh, shall show himself to his lovers," and we become like him.[20]

Emerging consensus. Perennial questions surround the interpretation of the New Covenant prophecy. By the fifth century varying degrees of consensus emerged around the most important of them.

- The relationship between the covenants: If the contents of the covenants are the same, why do Christians not keep Jewish laws? For Irenaeus, we are bound by the Decalogue but not "prohibitory mandates." For Jerome, we keep all the laws spiritually through their fulfillment in Christ. Augustine agrees and adds that New Covenant behavior such as not stealing is "a good of the heart itself," hence deeply different from its old covenant correlate.

---

[20]John Burnaby, ed., *Augustine: Later Works*, Library of Christian Classics (Philadelphia: Westminster, 1955), 195-250.

- Present versus future fulfillment: If the New Covenant is in force, why do Christians still (seemingly) teach one another to know the Lord? Jerome insists that because the promise of forgiveness has been fulfilled, Jeremiah 31:34a must mean Jewish teaching. Theodoret allows that Scripture can "mix" prophecies, and so Jeremiah 31:34a describes "the future life." For Augustine, it describes the New Covenant's ultimate reward—"the most blessed contemplation of God himself"—and is now experienced only in part (*The Spirit and the Letter* 223).[21]

- Hermeneutics: When and how far may details be pressed for meaning? None of the Fathers entirely rules out allegory, though there are frequent disagreements on specifics. However, when an interpreter is judged to have gone too far, the circular objection that their exegesis is unorthodox is avoided; rather, it is shown that their reading has lost a proper connection to the letter of the text.

Two Early Modern Developments

The formalization of the *quadriga*, or four senses of Scripture, encouraged medieval exegetes to discover layers of meaning without reference to salvation history.[22] Only late in this period did two scholars reject the habit of allegory. Thomas Aquinas (1225–1274) argues from Aristotle that one cannot divorce the spirit of the text from the letter, as allegory so often did.[23] His answers to the abovementioned perennial questions are thoroughly Augustinian.[24] Nicholas of Lyra's *Literal Postill [Commentary] on Jeremiah* (ca. 1330) is equally Augustinian on the New Covenant and features an overt salvation-historical framework.[25] This strong patristic

---

[21] Burnaby, *Augustine: Later Works*, 223.
[22] See de Lubac, *Medieval Exegesis* 1:1-9.
[23] Bray, *Biblical Interpretation*, 142.
[24] Thomas Aquinas, *In Jeremiam prophetam exposito* (Parmae, 1863), lectio 10, www.corpusthomisticum.org/cph.html.
[25] Joy Schroeder, trans. and ed., *The Book of Jeremiah*, The Bible in Medieval Tradition (Grand Rapids, MI: Eerdmans, 2017), 251-52.

tradition continued into the Reformation; at the same time, however, interpretation of Jeremiah 31 took a fresh turn.

Luther. In his occasional references to Jeremiah 31:31-34 Martin Luther speaks in a new way about the law written on the heart. Uncontroversially, he interprets the act of writing as the regenerating work of the Spirit; however, in a 1519 lecture on Galatians 2:19 he equates what is written ("my law") not with acts of righteousness but—in a kind of metonymy—with faith in Christ, which springs from regeneration and which produces obedience.[26]

How does Luther connect his spiritual reading of Jeremiah to the letter? In his polemic against Emser (1521), Luther denies that letter and spirit constitute two discrete levels of meaning. Scripture's only indispensable meaning is its literal meaning; the only true spiritual meanings are those the Spirit shows us in the New Testament.[27] Yet in a nonpolemical context Luther exercises considerable interpretive freedom. In a sermon on Deuteronomy 16 (1523) he speaks of "an allegory of the Spirit" by which Christians daily celebrate the Sinai festivals, including Pentecost, "when we receive the new Law, the Spirit, into our hearts (Jer 31:33) through the ministry of the Word."[28] The literal sense has expanded to include the meaning the text has in the context of its typological recurrence in Christ. Jerome would call this a spiritual reading or tropology.

The real difference between Luther and Jerome lies in Luther's focus on the work of Christ in the life of the believer. By setting faith in the place of obedience, he highlights the discontinuity between the covenants, and the role of forgiveness in the New Covenant for maintaining a person's righteousness in law. In terms of the meaning of Jeremiah 31:33, however, this is surely an allegory of the Spirit.

---

[26]Martin Luther, "Lectures on Galatians 1519," trans. Richard Jungkuntz, *LW* 27:234.
[27]Martin Luther, "Concerning the Letter and the Spirit," in *Martin Luther's Basic Theological Writings*, 2nd ed., ed. Timothy F. Lull (Minneapolis: Fortress, 2005), 78.
[28]Martin Luther, "Lecture on Deut 16:8," *LW* 9:156-57.

Calvin and beyond. In his Jeremiah commentary (1563) Calvin reaffirms the patristic reading of the New Covenant prophecy but introduces a new and influential way of speaking about the relationship of the covenants, in terms of form and substance. Their *substance* is the same, for "God in the gospel brings forward nothing but what the Law contains": the same doctrine, the rule of a perfect life, the way of salvation, and—by types and figures pointing to Christ—the same remission of sin. The newness of the covenant lies in its *form*: no longer words only but Christ, who "really fulfilled what God had exhibited under types"; regeneration by the Spirit, so that the letter penetrates to the heart "and really forms us for the service of God"; and the "outward mode of teaching," whereby "God speaks to us now openly, as it were face to face, and not under a veil."[29]

The recovery of typologically controlled spiritual reading, from Aquinas to Calvin, was not sustained consistently after the Reformation, and it is not uncommon to find interpretation in the seventeenth and eighteenth centuries tipping over into full-blown allegory.[30] There was a growing interest in "general truths of religion," explored by means of "a general study of symbols and pictures."[31] In Gerhard von Rad's assessment, this spelled the beginning of the end for typology as a respectable hermeneutical technique.

THE MODERN PERIOD

During the nineteenth century, European Old Testament scholarship abandoned theological inquiry, devoting itself exclusively to historical investigation. "History" in this modern sense uses multiple sources to create an alternative account of the past, by which

---

[29]John Calvin, *Commentaries on the Prophet Jeremiah and the Lamentations*, trans. John Owen, Calvin's Commentaries 10 (Grand Rapids, MI: Baker, 2009), 4:125-28.
[30]See for example John Mayer, *A Commentary Upon all the Prophets both Great and Small* (London: Abraham Miller and Ellen Cotes, 1652), 368, on Jer 11:16.
[31]Gerhard von Rad, *Old Testament Theology*, trans. D. M. G. Stalker (San Francisco: Harper & Row, 1965), 2:366.

interpreters may supplement, modify, or displace a plain reading of Scripture. To see what became of the patristic legacy in such a milieu, we turn to the contrasting proposals of two German scholars in the mid-twentieth century.

Wilhelm Vischer. When the Old Testament came under attack in Germany as a Jewish book, few Old Testament scholars were equipped to provide a theological response.[32] A rare exception was Vischer, whose 1934 book on the Old Testament's witness to Christ used typology to eliminate the distance between the Testaments. As Vischer covers the events of 2 Kings 23–25, he artfully weaves together recently translated Babylonian chronicles and the book of Jeremiah to create a gospel-shaped narrative, into which he places the New Covenant promise. He avoids allegory, but his typology can wax extravagant. Josiah's death at Megiddo (referred to in Jer 22:10) is perplexing, given that he acted out of the "obedience of faith" in seeking to keep Pharaoh at bay. However, Megiddo is the location of two great victories of God over the nations, one at each end of Scripture (Judg 5:19; Rev 16:6), and in this context Josiah's death points to the death of the Son of David as the true victory of God.[33]

Vischer, like Jerome, grounds Christian reading in the *historia* rather than the history constructed by scholars from events underlying the biblical account. He readily incorporates recent historical findings but uses them to confirm and embellish Scripture's "plain meaning." Ultimately, every verse derives its Christian meaning from the same context: all of Scripture. In a 1935 review, von Rad objects to Vischer's "way of deducing the testimony to Christ from the Old Testament by reducing the Old Testament utterances in every case to the greatest possible generality, or common denominator, so that the true meaning

---

[32]See Rolf Rendtorff, "Christological Interpretation as a Way of 'Salvaging' the Old Testament? Wilhelm Vischer and Gerhard von Rad," in *Canon and Theology: Overtures to an Old Testament Theology*, trans. and ed. Margaret Kohl (Edinburgh: T&T Clark, 1994), 76-91.

[33]Wilhelm Vischer, *Das Christzeugnis des Alten Testaments*, 2nd ed. (Zürich: Evangelischer Verlag A. G. Zollikon, 1946), 2:529.

of the texts is levelled out to the point of unrecognizability."[34] For a proper scholarly context for interpretation, Israel's history and religion must first be reconstructed.

Gerhard von Rad. The history of Israel has been rewritten endlessly since von Rad's *Old Testament Theology* (1957–1960), but when it comes to interpreting the Old Testament as Christian Scripture von Rad stands on the cusp of the era in which we live. This is the era in which the text's meaning in the minds of its authors and first readers— its *historical* meaning—becomes the starting point for Christian interpretation. Many scholars today resist reading the Old Testament theologically, but Israel's history as von Rad reconstructed it (both the events and Israel's beliefs about them) is a theological history. Von Rad pushed behind the text to establish as far as possible what actually happened and how Israel interpreted what happened. This produced a sequence of events with promises attached to them, that is, saving events. These are continually reinterpreted by Israel, and their incompleteness makes them continually open to the future. This openness paves the way for a typology that is properly grounded in the discipline of history.[35]

Von Rad's Old Testament therefore has no unifying point. The focal point of its diverse witness lies outside it, in the saving event of Christ. This is demonstrated by typological correspondence, "a typology based not on myth and speculation, but on history and eschatology." The New Covenant promise is a good example, for its newness, its openness to the future, is something that both negates the saving events of the past and resignifies them. The old covenant will be both actualized (continuity) and repeated on the basis of a new saving event (discontinuity). This typological process "holds true in principle for all Old Testament texts."[36]

---

[34]Cited in Rendtorff, "Christological Interpretation," 83.
[35]Von Rad, *Old Testament Theology* 2:357-87.
[36]Von Rad, *Old Testament Theology* 2:365, 384.

How does this differ from Vischer's reading? Consider the interpretation of Jeremiah's personal confessions. To avoid Vischer's "all of Scripture" approach to interpreting every text, von Rad not only situates Jeremiah's ministry in its seventh- through sixth-century context but creates a fresh account of the history of Israel's prophetic tradition, within which the *book* of Jeremiah witnesses to something new: a "shift of the centre of interest from the message to the messenger." The historical particularity of this phenomenon keeps the interpreter from blandly generic readings. It is only because the personal voice of the prophet achieves a representative quality that his confessions have "a typical significance for Israel."[37]

To find what is new about the New Covenant von Rad must identify the point where Israel is freshly reinterpreting its past. This is not the content of the New Covenant or even the concept of obedience from the heart (Deut 10:16). What is new is the act of writing, for this does away with the question of obedience. The human's will is replaced by God's. "What is here outlined is the picture of a new man, a man who is able to obey perfectly because of a miraculous change of his nature." Whatever "perfect obedience" may have meant to Jeremiah, its Christian meaning only emerges retrospectively, through "reinterpretation . . . in the light of Christ's appearance on earth."[38]

Four Reflections on Christian Interpretation Today

History serves the letter, not the spirit. It is noteworthy how little von Rad's theological conclusions about the New Covenant differ from patristic discussions of continuity and discontinuity or the Reformers' interest in anthropology. He is aware of this:

> The only difference between ancient exegesis and that of the present day is that the former took as its starting point this final meaning

---

[37] Von Rad, *Old Testament Theology* 2:197, 204.
[38] Von Rad, *Old Testament Theology* 2:213-14, 333.

which the ancient words gained in Christ, whereas we, who have a keener eye for history, realise that two possible ways of understanding them are open, the Christian interpretation of the Old Testament and the pre-Christian one.[39]

It should be clear by now how strongly patristic exegetes would object to this. The pre-Christian meaning of Jeremiah, the *historia*, was always their starting point; it is rather a matter for von Rad of going back to reconstruct the history behind the book of Jeremiah and its precursors. But the message of Jeremiah is not the sum of the messages of its parts, whenever and however they were written. Moreover, Jeremiah's theological message arises not from history as we might reconstruct it but from his prophetic interpretation of history (compare Jer 39:1-10 with the more "interpretive" Jer 21:4-10). Von Rad's interpretation remains Christian because he built his theology on Israel's beliefs about their history and not simply what he believed to be Israel's actual history. Nonconfessional scholarship has pressed hard into that gap to assert that saving history is a literary fiction, leaving Christian interpretation behind altogether. Instead, one must reconstruct the competing ideologies that one discerns behind the complex process of Old Testament book formation and criticize them from one's own theological standpoint.

In today's world we must begin with history. Recent shifts away from modernism have not lessened the apologetic importance of establishing the happenedness of the Bible's saving history. However, when it comes to the Christian meaning of Jeremiah, historical investigation is the servant of exegesis, not theology; the letter of the text, not its spirit. History can enrich our appreciation of things the text already tells us and clarify the meaning of its words but cannot expand its message. Archaeology teaches us that the *baqbuq* jar Jeremiah uses in Jeremiah 19:1 was beautiful and costly; but since Jeremiah makes

---

[39] Von Rad, *Old Testament Theology* 2:385.

nothing of this fact, playing on the pot's name (Jer 19:7) rather than its value, this piece of history contributes nothing to Jeremiah's *historia*. We are not expected to figure out what we would have seen if we were there but to take Jeremiah's prophetic account as a piece of whole cloth, which represents reality in a way designed to reveal the invisible hand of God moving all things to their destined end. This is and has always been the book's original and plain meaning.

Every word serves the Christian meaning but may not have a Christian meaning. The difference between ancient and modern exegesis that von Rad fails to mention is the ancient—and orthodox— conviction that every word of Scripture comes from the mouth of God. It is this conviction that allows Vischer to find a *sensus plenior* in Josiah's death, or Origen to seek Christian meaning in tiny details. In the end, von Rad's Bible is not quite the same object as theirs, for the independence of its human witness to God's actions does not permit us to invest its words with the same direct divine authority.

Augustine strikes the right balance when he insists that while the New Covenant prophecy conveys a spiritual truth, and many historical narratives have suprahistorical significance, spiritual meaning should never be claimed at the expense of the plain meaning:

> People are far too rash when they consider that everything recorded there carries allegorical significance.... However, I do not condemn those who have been able to devise a spiritual meaning for each historical event recorded there, just so long as, first of all, they preserve the truth of the history itself. On the other hand, with regard to any statements that cannot possibly apply to any historical event, ... anyone who could, would certainly interpret them in a spiritual sense.[40]

Covenants have hermeneutical priority over testaments. According to patristic exegesis of Jeremiah 31:31-34, it is not that the Old

---

[40] Augustine, *The City of God, XI–XXII*, trans. William Babcock, Works of Saint Augustine 1.7 (Hyde Park, NY: New City, 2013), 17.3.

Testament is fulfilled in the New but that the old *covenant* is fulfilled in the New. The plain, old covenant meaning of Jeremiah is the *historia* that emerges from its narrative logic. This *historia* derives its meaning from within the larger narrative of the Christian canon, as it partakes in patterns of promise and fulfillment. Modern readers ask what the text *meant*, but the distinction between this and what the text *means* is not particularly helpful theologically. The plain meaning of Jeremiah 31:33-34 was and still is that Yahweh promises to write the Mosaic torah on the hearts of his people, in a realization of his ancient plan that will be achieved by an act of forgiveness made visible in the return from exile. That the return from exile did not achieve transformed hearts (Neh 13:15-22; see Jer 17:19-27) extends Jeremiah's *historia* into the Gospels and Epistles, where the Israel to whom Jesus came is the same Israel that Jeremiah 52 left in exile.

Christ fulfills Jeremiah's historical, old-covenant meaning by fulfilling Israel's history, and Jeremiah's Christian meaning must always be anchored in the plain meaning of the text, with its prophetic interpretation of events. But having seen those events fulfilled in Christ, we can speak of Jeremiah itself as possessing spiritual, or New Covenant, meaning. The person and work of Christ, his continued activity in the church, and his second advent provide the antitypes that reveal the previously hidden dimension of the original meaning of Jeremiah.[41]

"Reading Christ back in" can be an act of Christian meditation. In modern terms, we might say that the Fathers read Jeremiah both christotelically, for its plain meaning, and christocentrically, as they brought Christ to bear on the text, illuminating its Christian meaning in light of its Christian fulfillment. This can be a dangerous practice. At its worst it can make every text say the same thing. However, this final act of reading Christ back in was never arbitrary or divorced from

---

[41] The question of the availability of this hidden spiritual meaning to the faithful Old Testament reader takes us beyond the scope of this chapter.

history and the gospel—at least in theory; and there is an art to reading back in a way that enriches the Christian imagination. This is the aspect of patristic interpretation that is most foreign to us and might better be thought of as Christian meditation. We may not always be able to follow them, but the church fathers are just as likely to expose the shallowness of our reflection, if we are willing to hear them in a humble spirit.

10

PREACHING JEREMIAH AS CHRISTIAN SCRIPTURE

Philip Ryken

Admittedly, not everyone thought it was a great idea at first—including the senior minister. But, undaunted by the complexity of the Bible's longest book, I took our evening congregation on a two-year journey through the book of Jeremiah, preaching the entire corpus chapter by chapter and verse by verse.

It takes a certain type of church to hear sixty-five sermons on an Old Testament prophet. I was fortunate to serve in those days as the associate minister of preaching for Philadelphia's Tenth Presbyterian Church, under the leadership of James Montgomery Boice. Sustaining such a long sermon series also takes a particular conviction about the Scriptures of the Old Testament, namely that they are purposely designed for proclaiming the gospel of Jesus Christ.

Given the chance, I would preach the whole book all over again. After the first sermon, Boice came up to tell me cheerfully that preaching Jeremiah might not be such a bad idea after all. A month or two later, one of my congregants said that the prophet's message was so relevant for his daily job in Center City that sometimes he wondered whether Jeremiah worked in his office. But most gratifying as a preacher and most nourishing to my soul was the opportunity to experience the good news in a totally fresh way—the gospel according to Jeremiah.[1]

As I preached this great book of the Bible—which in effect is the scrapbook of Jeremiah's prophetic ministry—I repeatedly found myself agreeing with nineteenth-century Baptist minister F. B. Meyer, who writes:

> Jeremiah has always a fascination to Christian hearts because of the close similarity that exists between his life and that of Jesus Christ. Each of them was "a man of sorrows, and acquainted with grief"; each came to his own, and his own received him not; each passed through hours of rejection, desolation, and forsakenness. And in Jeremiah we may see beaten out into detail, experiences which, in our Lord, are but lightly touched on by the evangelists.[2]

CONVICTIONS FOR PREACHING THE OLD TESTAMENT AS CHRISTIAN SCRIPTURE

Before presenting the New Covenant in Jeremiah 31 as a test case, I wish to make explicit some of my core convictions about preaching the Old Testament as Christian Scripture, as well as to give hermeneutical guidance for preaching this way faithfully and responsibly.

I begin with the total unity of the Bible as it unfolds the narrative of redemption, which is made possible only by the inspiration of the

---

[1] These expositions are collected in Philip Graham Ryken, *Jeremiah and Lamentations: From Sorrow to Hope*, Preaching the Word (Wheaton, IL: Crossway, 2001).
[2] F. B. Meyer, *Jeremiah: Priest and Prophet*, rev. ed. (Fort Washington, PA: Christian Literature Crusade, 1993), 7.

Holy Spirit. While believing fully in the authenticity and personality of the various human authors who wrote the sixty-six books of the Bible—including that man Jeremiah—I also maintain that every word of the Bible was breathed out personally by the one Spirit of God (2 Tim 3:16).

One of the most compelling confirmations of the Holy Spirit as the divine author of Scripture comes from a direct quotation of our test passage. Hebrews 10:16 reads, "This is the covenant that I will make with them after those days, declares the Lord: I will put my laws on their hearts, and write them on their minds." The following verse continues, "I will remember their sins and their lawless deeds no more" (Heb 10:17). The author of Hebrews clearly has Jeremiah in mind. Thus, we might have expected him to introduce his scriptural quotation by mentioning the prophet explicitly. "According to Jeremiah," he could have begun. Instead, he tells us that "the Holy Spirit also bears witness to us" by what he "says" in Jeremiah 31:33 and then "adds" in Jeremiah 31:34. God the Holy Spirit is the author of Jeremiah, as he is of everything in the Old and New Testaments.

The Holy Spirit's sole divine authorship of sacred Scripture gives the Bible its fundamental unity. Always and everywhere—whether implicitly or explicitly—the Spirit's design is to reveal to us the divine-human person and creative-redemptive work of Jesus Christ. As evangelical scholars affirm in the Chicago Statement on Biblical Inerrancy, "The Person and work of Jesus Christ are the central focus of the entire Bible," and one of the ways we put our creed into practice and "believe in the Holy Spirit" is by preaching the gospel he revealed in the Scriptures of the Old and New Testaments.

Some scholars use the term *Christotelic* to describe the relationship between the Old Testament and the gospel. Jesus Christ is the end goal of biblical prophecy—not always seen in the Old Testament but revealed in his advent.[3] These scholars tend to emphasize the Bible's human authorship and wish to bracket their reading of the Old Testament from christological interpretations they believe the original authors did not have in mind.

Others—such as Richard Gaffin—prefer to use the term *Christocentric* to describe *both* the Old and New Testaments. These scholars prioritize the Bible's divine authorship and believe that in revealing the Old Testament, the third person of the Trinity constantly had the second person of the Trinity in mind. Christ is not only the endpoint of Scripture but also its starting point. Gaffin writes:

> Scripture is Christotelic just because it is Christocentric. It is Christotelic only as it is Christocentric, and as it is that in every part, the Old Testament included. Or, as we may, in fact must put the issue here in its most ultimate consideration, Christ is the mediatorial Lord and Savior of redemptive history not only at its end but also from beginning to end. He is not only its omega but also its alpha, and he is and can be its omega only as he is its alpha.[4]

Another way to say this is that because the Old Testament is Christocentric, it is not merely Christotelic but also *Christobasic*. The person and work of Jesus Christ are foundational to the message of the Old Testament. John the Evangelist thus identifies Jesus Christ as "the Lamb who was slain [before the foundation of the world]" (Rev 13:8). The apostle Peter claims further that the "lamb without blemish or spot," who redeemed us by his "precious blood" and was "made manifest in the last times" for the sake of our faith and hope, was also "foreknown before the foundation of the world" (1 Pet 1:19-20). It should not surprise us, then, that the whole Bible is Christian Scripture,

---

[3] See, for example, Peter Enns, *Inspiration and Incarnation: Evangelicals and the Problem of the Old Testament* (Grand Rapids, MI: Baker, 2005).
[4] Richard Gaffin, "WRF Member Westminster Theological Seminary Responds to Clair Davis's Comments Regarding the 'Retirement' of Doug Green," World Reformed Fellowship, June 30, 2014, https://wrf.global/blog/blog-2/theological-education/wrf-member-westminster-theological-seminary-responds-clair-daviss-comments.

as it reveals Jesus Christ and his saving gospel. We are not limited to the Gospel according to Matthew, Mark, Luke, and John, therefore, but also have at our disposal the Gospel according to Moses, David, Isaiah, and Jeremiah.

What Jesus and the Apostles Believed About Preaching the Old Testament

When Jesus interpreted the Old Testament for his disciples on the road to Emmaus (Lk 24:25-27) and afterward (Lk 24:44-47), he did not regard the sufferings, death, resurrection, and glorification of the Christ as obscure or unexpected but as obvious and pervasive. He had no need to read his ministry *into* the Pentateuch, the Psalms, or the Prophets; he could read it *out of* them. "They bear ... witness about me," he claims (Jn 5:39), and this is confirmed at various points in the Gospel of John where Abraham (Jn 8:56), Moses (Jn 5:46), and Isaiah (Jn 12:41) celebrate the Christ they revealed.

Although we do not have a reliable audio recording of the Easter sermons of Jesus Christ, we do have functional transcripts. The Gospel that John wrote, the sermons Peter preached in Acts, and the epistles these men penned were based in part on the mental notes they took during their final seminar with Jesus Christ—his capstone course on reading and preaching the Old Testament as Christian Scripture.

Peter, for one, understood that a Christ-centered way of interpreting and applying the Scriptures depended on the ministry of the Holy Spirit. When he describes the careful inquiry the biblical prophets made into the coming of salvation, Peter explains that it was "the Spirit of Christ in them" who indicated and predicted both "the sufferings of Christ and the subsequent glories" (1 Pet 1:10-11). The literary unity and gospel centrality of the Bible are not accidental but intentional. The same indwelling Holy Spirit who empowered Peter to proclaim the good news first inspired the prophets to predict his saving grace: "To him all the prophets bear witness that everyone who believes in him receives forgiveness of sins through his name" (Acts 10:43).

We find the apostle Paul employing a similar method in 1 Corinthians 10, where he shares the outline for a canonical-theological sermon we might title "The Gospel According to the Exodus." Paul begins with the particulars of the biblical text: the pillar of cloud, the Red Sea crossing, the manna in the wilderness, and the water that flowed from the rock. Then he makes an astounding claim: "that Rock was Christ" (1 Cor 10:4). His rationale for this claim is a subject for another occasion. For our present purposes it is sufficient to point out that Paul plainly does not understand himself to be reading anything into the Old Testament but instead is showing us what is already there. Then—as any good preacher would—he applies the lessons of the exodus to the church in a practical and grace-filled way. The things that happened back then are "examples for us" (1 Cor 10:6; see Rom 15:4); they are meant for our conversion and sanctification today.

Here I have mentioned only the passages in the New Testament where a method for preaching the Old Testament as Christian Scripture is made transparent. What is striking about these examples is how natural it is for Jesus and the apostles to read the Old Testament in a Christ-centered way. It is *obvious* to them that "Moses and the Prophets" (Lk 16:29) are divinely intended to make people "wise unto salvation through faith in Jesus Christ" (2 Tim 3:15). Thus Luke and Corinthians are only the beginning. The Old Testament has a pervasive presence in the New Testament, and everywhere it bears connection to the gospel of Jesus Christ.

Nor should we feel constrained to see christological connections only in the places where Jesus and the apostles explicitly call them to our attention. These examples would be sufficient to satisfy our souls. But the sense we get from the abundance of quotations from, allusions to, and implications drawn from the Old Testament is that the New

Testament is overflowing with intimations of Christ. The fecundity of biblical Christology gives us the freedom to proclaim Christ and apply its gospel from all the Scriptures.

We may conclude that the apostolic proclamation of a Christ-centered Old Testament is not merely exemplary; it is normative. When the New Testament authors draw lines from the Old Testament to the gospel, they are doing something more than giving us a limited and well-defined set of Christ-centered passages to preach on Sunday morning. They are giving us a *Christobasic* way of reading the Bible that teaches us to draw *Christotelic* conclusions beyond the ones they model for us.

While we are neither prophets nor apostles (at least in some biblical senses of these terms), we are nonetheless called to build on their foundation (see Eph 2:20). This holds true not only in our faith and worship but also for our biblical exegesis, our reading of redemptive history, and our proclamation of the gospel.

Controls for Preaching Christ Responsibly

By now it should be evident that I am not a minimalist but a maximalist when it comes to preaching Christ from both testaments. Raymond Brown popularized the phrase *sensus plenior* to describe the "fuller sense" or "fuller meaning" that goes beyond what an Old Testament prophet may have intended.[5] The prophets spoke better than they knew. Because this *sensus plenior* comes under the inspiration of the Holy Spirit, it is a *sensus divinus*, or divinely intended meaning. It is also a *sensus evangelisticus*, or gospel meaning, which helps us understand the good news of Jesus Christ.

Such maximalism raises certain exegetical concerns. The more we talk about seeing Christ in the Old Testament, the more anxious careful scholars will be about careless preachers drawing arbitrary connections

---

[5]Raymond E. Brown, *The Sensus Plenior of Sacred Scripture* (Eugene, OR: Wipf & Stock, 2008).

to Christ that are neither grounded in the biblical text nor sensitive its historical context.

Happily, I am not here to bury the grammatical-historical method; I am here to praise it. The authentic preaching of the gospel according to the Old Testament begins with a proper understanding of the biblical text, using all the tools of biblical exegesis. As the author of sacred Scripture, the Holy Spirit does not reveal Christ to us apart from grammar and history but through the particularities of the biblical text. Thus, a close reading of each Old Testament passage is indispensable to understanding the unique contribution that it can make to our understanding of the gospel.

To proclaim Christ in ways that are true to the meaning of Scripture, we will need some hermeneutical controls. Here I rely on the insights of Edmund Clowney—especially his seminal book *Preaching Christ in All of Scripture*.[6] What Clowney wants to avoid are allegorical interpretations that demonstrate the preacher's ingenuity but hardly help us to understand the Bible's own way of proclaiming the gospel. This happens when preachers reach back into the Old Testament, lay hold of a scriptural particular, and come up with some gospel connection that bears no intrinsic connection to the original meaning.

According to Clowney, the way to avoid this pitfall is to contemplate the symbolic function of an Old Testament person, event, or institution in its biblical context and discover there the truth that it teaches about God's way of salvation. This transcendent truth can then be carried forward to its specific fulfillment in Jesus Christ, before the preacher finally applies it in a gospel way to the spiritual needs of a contemporary congregation. When preachers short-circuit this hermeneutical process by failing to understand the inherent symbolism of the Old Testament, they are in danger of allegorizing (attaching the five smooth stones of David to five Christian virtues, for example); if they bypass

---

[6]Edmund P. Clowney, *Preaching Christ in All of Scripture* (Wheaton, IL: Crossway, 2003).

the cross and the empty tomb on their way to practical application, never explaining a spiritual principle's vital connection to the crucified and risen Christ, they will be guilty of moralizing ("You, too, can slay your own Goliath!").

How the Apostles Preached the Old Testament

Whether they were fully conscious of it or not, something like this hermeneutical method undergirds the apostolic preaching of the gospel. At times, the apostles may appear simply to draw a straight line from the Old Testament to Jesus: "that Rock was Christ." But their gospel connections were always securely grounded in the details of the biblical text—their meaning in the original context and in the flow of redemptive history. "That Rock was Christ" because it was the source of life, signifying God's sustenance, struck in judgment to bring forth living water.

Clowney helps us to see that the apparently direct line of typology in fact depends on several steps of biblical exegesis and theological reflection—all presupposing God's authorship of Scripture and sovereignty in salvation. This way of preaching the gospel, he writes, is divinely designed:

> There is continuity, for it is God who begins His work of salvation long before He gives His Son. Yet there is discontinuity, too. Salvation in Christ is not simply an improvement on Old Testament salvation. It is not just the final phase of God's dealings with His people. It is rather the ground of Old Testament salvation. God's call to Israel presupposes the sending of Jesus Christ. Salvation in Christ is the only real salvation, the only salvation with ultimate and eternal meaning.[7]

Clowney is not the only scholar to offer reliable methods for preaching the Old Testament as Christian Scripture. In *Preaching Christ from the*

---

[7] Edmund P. Clowney, "Preaching Christ from All the Scriptures," in *The Preacher and Preaching: Reviving the Art in the Twentieth Century*, ed. Samuel T. Logan Jr. (Phillipsburg, NJ: Presbyterian & Reformed, 1986), 174.

Old Testament and other books, Sidney Greidanus amplifies Clowney's basic method and applies it to many parts of the Old Testament.[8] Graeme Goldsworthy goes beyond people, events, and institutions to show how the various epochs of Old Testament history also have christological implications.[9] Patrick Fairbairn's classic work *The Typology of Scripture* can still be read with profit.[10] More recently, John Currid outlines four principles for faithful typology, which must (1) be grounded in biblical history; (2) demonstrate historical and theological correspondence between type and antitype; (3) display intensification, so that the type finds its culmination in the antitype; and (4) show evidence that the type is divinely ordained to foreshadow the antitype.[11]

I mention these authors and the hermeneutical controls they provide—however briefly—to nuance my desire to make room for a *sensus evangelisticus* in reading and preaching the Old Testament. The apostles were not minimalists in their reading of Scripture. But even when they did not show their work, the connections they drew between various passages in the Old Testament and specific aspects of Christ's saving work were never arbitrary. The more we read the New Testament, the better we understand the Old Testament, and vice versa. Upon reflection, we can see how the apostolic proclamation of the gospel grew out of a thorough understanding of the biblical text and careful thought about its connection to Christ.

While we do not want to read more into the Bible than is really there, neither do we want to miss its message by getting less out of it than we really should. Having proper hermeneutical controls gives us greater

---

[8] Sidney Greidanus, *Preaching Christ from the Old Testament: A Contemporary Hermeneutical Method* (Grand Rapids, MI: Eerdmans, 1999).

[9] Graeme Goldsworthy, *Preaching the Whole Bible as Christian Scripture: The Application of Biblical Theology to Expository Preaching* (Grand Rapids, MI: Eerdmans, 2000).

[10] Patrick Fairbairn, *The Typology of Scripture; Or, The Doctrine of Types Investigated in Its Principles, and Applied to the Explanation of the Earlier Revelations of God, Considered as Preparatory Exhibitions of the Leading Truths of the Gospel* (Edinburgh: Thomas Clark, 1845).

[11] John Currid, "Recognition and Use of Typology in Preaching," *Reformed Theological Review* 53, no. 3 (1994): 121.

homiletical freedom to preach each passage the way it is uniquely designed to proclaim the good news.

Jeremiah's New Covenant as a Test Case

With these theological and methodological considerations in mind, we are ready to consider Jeremiah 31:31-34 as a test case for preaching the Old Testament as Christian Scripture. These famous promises of a New Covenant come near the end of the Book of Consolation, in which the prophet comforts the people of Judah by foretelling the end of their exile. Up to this point, Jeremiah has been dominated by divine judgment. God's people have failed to keep the covenant that God made with them through Moses. This is stated fairly explicitly in Jeremiah 5:4-5, for example, and indicated implicitly in passages too numerous to mention.

But at the end of Jeremiah 31, in a series of bold proclamations introduced with the words "the days are coming" (Jer 31:27, 31, 38), Jeremiah prophesies the advent of a New Covenant. This new covenant seems imminent and feels climactic, especially since this is the only passage in the Old Testament that speaks of a "new covenant" in so many words. Going back to Clement of Alexandria, this phrase was so significant for the Christian understanding of the canon that it became the conventional title for the books from Matthew to Revelation: "New Testament."[12]

What is surprising and seemingly contradictory about the promises in Jeremiah 31 is that despite being characterized as a "new" covenant, they are familiar from earlier parts of the Old Testament. Having a law written on the heart, knowing God and belonging to him as a people, experiencing forgiveness—these precious gifts were all given already at Mount Sinai, when God brought his people out of the land of Egypt

---

[12]See J. Andrew Dearman, *Jeremiah and Lamentations*, NIVAC (Grand Rapids, MI: Zondervan, 2002), 289n20.

(Jer 7:22-23; 11:4). Yet Jeremiah insists that this new covenant is "*not like*" the covenant that God made with their forefathers (Jer 31:32) and that its practices "*no longer*" pertain (Jer 31:34).

What specifically, then, is so new about the New Covenant?

There are reasonable answers to this question in the new exodus event of Judah's return to Jerusalem from Babylon. Perhaps most notably, any deficiency with the old covenant does not lie in that covenant itself but rather in the inability of God's people to keep it (see also Heb 8:7-8). As Christopher Wright points out, "Up to now, the only way Jeremiah had ever spoken of the covenant was to say that it was broken, shattered—lying in ruins as Jerusalem itself now was."[13] Here in Jeremiah 31 the prophet identifies it as the "covenant that they broke" (Jer 31:32). What they need, therefore, is not so much a New Covenant as a new capacity to keep it. The end of their exile—which geographically display their spiritual distance from God—comes with the hope of a renewed relationship.

Yet a fuller understanding of the newness of the New Covenant comes in Jesus Christ. The New Testament makes relatively frequent use of Jeremiah 31:31-34, which "constitutes the longest continuous quotation of any Old Testament text in the New."[14] This usage makes the passage comparatively easy to preach as Christian Scripture. The Evangelists and the apostles are here to help us.

New forgiveness for sin through the cross of Christ. The New Covenant is—perhaps most simply and importantly—the covenant that Christ purchased with his own precious blood. Jesus makes this connection at the Last Supper when he declares, "This cup that is poured out for you is the new covenant in my blood" (Lk 22:20; see Mt 26:28). The New Covenant that God has made for us in Jesus Christ comes with blood-bought remission of our sins—a more complete atonement than

---

[13]Christopher J. H. Wright, *The Message of Jeremiah*, BST (Downers Grove, IL: IVP Academic, 2014), 324.
[14]Wright, *Message of Jeremiah*, 323.

Jeremiah may have understood, but not less than he prophesied. To express this christological connection the way a preacher might say it in a sermon aimed from the outset at personal application: *through the cross of Christ there is new forgiveness for your sins.*

Perhaps it seems backward to start with forgiveness, since this theme comes at the end of Jeremiah 31:31-34. But forgiveness is the foundation for all the other blessings of the New Covenant. At the heart of the New Covenant is such full atonement for our iniquities that they are remembered no more. The apostle Paul draws a similar inference in Romans 11:27, where he writes, "This will be my covenant with them when I take away their sins"—another allusion to Jeremiah 31:34. The New Covenant is not a new demand for our obedience but a renewed promise to take away our sin. Based on this passage, John Chrysostom declares that "on his coming, Christ would also pardon the transgressions of all people and no more remember their sins. What could be clearer than this?"[15]

The clear declaration of the New Covenant in Christ's blood comes as the culmination of redemptive history. Remember the occasion: Jesus is celebrating Passover with his disciples. Remember also the source of his cross-reference: he is referring to Jeremiah's promise of an end to exile. At this redemptive-historical turning point, both the *exodus* and the *exile* are within our field of vision—the two great saving events of the Old Testament. Both of these dramatic deliverances suffered from the same limitation: the stiff-necked, hardhearted people of God could not keep covenant. But the full atonement that Christ announced brings both a greater exodus and a final return from spiritual exile. His blood of the covenant is everything salvation could be—the "once and for all" putting away of sin "by the sacrifice of himself" (Heb 9:26).

---

[15]John Chrysostom, *Against the Pagans*, in *Jeremiah, Lamentations*, ed. Dean O. Wenthe, Ancient Christian Commentary on Scripture Old Testament 12 (Downers Grove, IL: IVP Academic, 2009), 218.

New life in God's Word by the Holy Spirit. Here is something else that is new in God's covenant with us in Christ: an inward experience of the Word of God that causes us to know God more deeply and that spiritually empowers us to live in fuller obedience. *By the Spirit of Jesus,* a preacher might say, *you have a new heart for living God's Word.*

Once again, Jeremiah's promise contains elements of both continuity and discontinuity. The knowledge of God is one of the primary purposes for every covenant that God has ever made with his people. When he cut a covenant with Abraham under the desert sky (Gen 17:7), and again when he met with Moses on the mountain (Ex 19:5-6), God wanted his people to know him as their God. He still wants us to know him as our God (2 Cor 6:16) and always will (Rev 21:3). Yet this is precisely where Judah and Israel failed. Jeremiah diagnoses God's people as having an incurable heart condition (Jer 30:12-15). One of his saddest laments is that due to their stubborn and deceitful hearts, they do not keep covenant, they do not know God (Jer 3:17; 9:14; 11:18; 13:10; 16:11-12; 18:12). Given his emphasis on this theme, we might think of Jeremiah as the J. I. Packer of the Old Testament.[16]

The covenant knowledge of God was never meant to be merely a form of mental cognition; it was always intended to be a heartfelt affection that made a practical difference in daily life. Knowing God in the biblical sense meant "relating to him in love, loyalty and obedience."[17] When Jeremiah says that we do not know God, therefore, he is saying that we do not live for him the way we should (Jer 2:8; 4:22; 9:3).

Enter the Holy Spirit . . . literally. Jeremiah prophesies that one day God will take his divine word—the torah, or "law," which expressed his holy will—and put it right inside his people by writing it on our very hearts (Jer 31:33). What is new here is not the law but the location of its inscription. Or, to say this in a different way, what is new

---

[16] See J. I. Packer, *Knowing God* (Downers Grove, IL: InterVarsity Press, 1973).
[17] Wright, *Message of Jeremiah,* 329.

is not the law but the people. The covenant breakers will become promise keepers.

Earlier Jeremiah prophesied, "I will give them a heart to know that I am the LORD, and they shall be my people and I will be their God, for they shall return to me with their whole heart" (Jer 24:7; see Jer 30:22; 32:38). Here in Jeremiah 31 the prophet plays up the contrast between the giving of the law to Moses, which was engraved on tablets of stone (Ex 31:18; 32:15-16), and a New Covenant, in which God's Word is written so directly on the human heart that it becomes part of who we are.[18] In the words of the venerable Jerome, when the truth finally comes in Jesus Christ, God's "covenant will be written not on stone tablets but on tablets of embodied hearts."[19] God always wanted his Word in his people's hearts (e.g., Deut 30:5-6). To get it there, he needed to write it there himself, and in this way to grant us "a new ability, from within, to live in accordance with the essence of the law God has given."[20]

The deeper, more permanent inscription of this everlasting covenant (see Jer 31:35-37; 32:40; 50:5) is a gift of God the Holy Spirit. If we need apostolic warrant for drawing this pneumatological connection, we find it in 2 Corinthians 3. There Paul—writing as the minister of "a new covenant" (2 Cor 3:6) and thus referring to Jeremiah 31—describes the church in Corinth as "a letter from Christ delivered by us, written not with ink but the Spirit of the living God, not on tablets of stone but on tablets of human hearts" (2 Cor 3:3).

Although the third person of the Trinity is present from the first moment of creation, the Spirit did not descend forever in the fullness of his indwelling presence until the day of Pentecost. When that Spirit conveyed the life-changing gift of regeneration, nonbelieving hearts were changed from sinful rebellion to loving obedience. New believers

---

[18]There is also an implied contrast with Jer 17:1, where Judah's sin "is engraved on the tablet of their heart" with "a point of diamond."
[19]Jerome, *Six Books on Jeremiah*, in Wenthe, *Jeremiah, Lamentations*, 215.
[20]Wright, *Message of Jeremiah*, 328.

no longer needed their neighbors and family members to evangelize them by saying, "Know the Lord" (Jer 31:34). They *did* know the Lord. They *all* knew the Lord, personally and communally.

The covenant first made "with the house of Israel and the house of Judah" (Jer 31:31)—that is to say, with God's united people—is fulfilled for both Gentiles and Jews in the body of Christ. Jeremiah's promise pertains to the whole people of God. Now we know the Lord because his Spirit has come to reside inside us. When God pours his love "into our hearts through the Holy Spirit who has been given to us" (Rom 5:5), his will is so internalized that it becomes part of our spiritual operating system. As Calvin writes in his commentary on Jeremiah 31, the gospel "penetrates into the heart and reforms all the inward faculties, so that the obedience is rendered to the righteousness of God."[21] From the moment that we first believe until forever, we are thus empowered to live in heartfelt obedience to God.

New intimacy with God through the love of Jesus. The depth of God's New Covenant relationship with his new people in Christ is further intimated by his self-description in Jeremiah 31:32 as Israel and Judah's husband. Here I take the Hebrew word *baʿal* specifically as "husband," not more literally as "master." I do this in part because the metaphor in the first part of the verse—where God takes his people "by the hand"—suggests a closer relationship. This marital bond finds its consummation in Christ as the bridegroom for the beautiful people of God. To express this New Covenant promise as a preaching proposition, and thus to complete a simple, exegetically grounded, christologically focused, and practically oriented sermon outline for Jeremiah 31:31-34, *through the love of Jesus you have new intimacy with God.*

The love match between God's Son and God's people is one of the grand themes of salvation history. The romance of redemption starts

---

[21]John Calvin, *Commentary on Jeremiah*, in *Jeremiah, Lamentations*, ed. J. Jeffery Tyler, Reformation Commentary on Scripture Old Testament 11 (Downers Grove, IL: IVP Academic, 2018), 307.

in early Genesis—where the first man goes on a blind date with the first woman (Gen 2:21-23)—and ends with the last chapters of Revelation, when a beautiful bride descends from heaven (Rev 21:2) and sits down for the marriage supper of the Lamb (Rev 19:6-9).

Like most romantic relationships, God's love match with his people has had many ups and downs—especially downs. Tim and Kathy Keller wryly describe God as trapped "in the longest-lived, worst marriage in the history of the world."[22] It certainly seemed that way to Jeremiah. In Jeremiah 2–3 the prophet portrays God as filing for divorce on the legitimate grounds of spiritual adultery. There God argues his devastating case by amassing evidence of Israel and Judah's covenant infidelity. To put the matter as bluntly as Jeremiah does, the virgin bride (Jer 2:2) has become a lusty whore (Jer 2:20).

Strange to say, although God had every reason to go his separate way, he never finalized the divorce. Jeremiah hints at this by describing Judah once again as God's "virgin bride" (Jer 31:4)—notwithstanding her proven adultery. Hints of restored purity become a promise of renewed intimacy in our test passage, where God reassures his people that he will be their loving and faithful husband.

This promise finds its fulfillment in the Gospels, where suddenly the groom walks into the room (e.g., Mt 9:14-15). Jesus Christ is many things to his people: Savior, Shepherd, Redeemer, King. He is also our husband and the lover of our souls. Although the New Testament never makes explicit reference to marital imagery from the book of Jeremiah, this theme is part of the deep structure of our salvation. This is how literature works: through patterns of images that convey meaning. God's romance with his people, culminating in covenant vows of eternal matrimony, is one of the main story lines of Scripture. Thus, one gospel way to interpret and apply Jeremiah 31:31-34 is to connect its New Covenant promises to our love relationship with Jesus Christ.

---

[22]Timothy Keller and Kathy Keller, *On Marriage* (New York: Penguin, 2020), 69.

As we survey the promises in this passage, it is important to see that each action is divinely initiated. God says, "I will make . . . I will put . . . I will forgive." Derek Kidner observes that not until the coming of Christ do we fully recognize the *sacrifice* that fulfilling each of these promises requires. It was only "when Jesus inaugurated his new covenant" in the blood he poured out for many that we could see how "each of these divine gifts was a costly *self*-giving."[23] Complete forgiveness for our sins, regenerate obedience to the Word of God, loving intimacy with God's beautiful Son—these covenant gifts came at the cost of our Savior's blood.

Other Ways to Preach the Gospel According to Jeremiah

This essay is a plea for the Christ-centered proclamation of Jeremiah. When preached with careful attention to the rich variety of ways that it points us to Christ, this book can sustain a congregation's interest. To that end, I offer a brief taxonomy of strategies for preaching the gospel according to Jeremiah in all its saving and sanctifying power.

Some sections of Jeremiah are as straightforward for proclaiming the gospel as Jeremiah 31 because they, too, are *passages fully or partly quoted in the New Testament*. The promise of Jeremiah 6:16, for example—which offers rest for weary souls who walk in the way of the Lord—provides the background for the rest that Jesus promises to people who bear his easy yoke (Mt 11:28-30). The connection between the prophet's famous temple sermon in Jeremiah 7 and the cleansing of the temple in Mark 13 is more explicit. When Jesus claims that Jerusalem's religious leaders have turned God's house of prayer into "a den of robbers" (Mk 11:17), he is not only quoting Jeremiah 7:11 but also repeating the prophet's cry against injustice. Nor can we fully grasp the desperation in our Savior's plea for his Father to "remove this cup from

---

[23]Derek Kidner, *The Message of Jeremiah*, BST (Downers Grove, IL: IVP Academic, 1987), 110.

me" (Lk 22:42) unless we read it against the backdrop of the command that God once gave to Jeremiah: "Take from my hand this cup of the wine of wrath" (Jer 25:15). Paul's teaching on "vessels of wrath" in Romans 9:19-23 gives us yet another example of a close semantic and thematic connection, drawing as it does on Jeremiah's visit to the potter's workshop and his subsequent prophetic act of destroying an earthenware vessel (Jer 18–19). Or consider the apostle's teaching on wisdom and folly, weakness and strength in 1 Corinthians 1:18-31, which critiques Greek and Jewish culture but also echoes the prophet's "boast in the Lord" in Jeremiah 9:23-24.

Here it should be emphasized that when Jesus, an apostle, or an Evangelist quotes from Jeremiah or some other prophet, he is not simply appropriating an isolated prooftext; rather, he is calling to mind an entire biblical context. The citation of Jeremiah 31:15 in Matthew 2:17-18—in which the Evangelist calls to mind not only Rachel's despairing tears but also her ultimate consolation—is a powerful example of *metalepsis*, which Richard Hays defines as "the practice of citing a fragment that beckons readers to recover more of the original subtext in order to grasp the full force of the intertextual link."[24]

Another way to preach the gospel according to Jeremiah is to explore *strong prophetic images that provide the necessary background for gospel teaching*. For example, Jeremiah's reference to figs that wither on the tree in Jeremiah 8:13 and his contrast in Jeremiah 24 between the "very good figs" that submit to the Babylonian exile and the "very bad figs" that escape to Egypt provide the biblical context for the divine judgment that Jesus pronounces against Israel when he curses the fig tree in Mark 11:12-14. Similarly, Jesus trades on Jeremiah's imagery of vineyards and vines (e.g., Jer 2:21; 8:13) when he describes his purposes for Israel (e.g., Lk 20:9-18). The apostle Paul presumably has passages such as Jeremiah 11:16 in mind

---

[24]Richard B. Hays, *Reading Backwards: Figural Christology and the Fourfold Gospel Witness* (Waco, TX: Baylor University Press, 2014), 42.

("a green olive tree, beautiful with good fruit") when he describes how both Jews and Gentiles will be grafted into the church of Jesus Christ like natural branches and wild olive shoots that together "share in the nourishing root of the olive tree" (Rom 11:17). Nor should we miss the important connection between the fishermen that bring God's people out of spiritual exile in Jeremiah 16:14-18 and the fishers of men whom Jesus summons in Mark 1:16-20. Or the way Jesus comforts the prophet's lament for the lost sheep of Israel in Jeremiah 50:6-7 by sending his disciples to "the lost sheep of the house of Israel" (Mt 10:5-6; see Mt 15:24) and later by telling the story of the Good Shepherd who looks for every last lamb until he finds it (Lk 15:1-7; see Jer 23:1-4).

The New Testament has Jeremiah more in mind than many people realize. By allusion as well as quotation, it draws on the prophet's metaphors of judgment and salvation to help us recognize the pattern of the gospel and understand God's purposes in Jesus Christ. As Hays also writes, the Gospels "create a narrative world thick with scriptural memory," in which "scenes are played out on a stage with scenery familiar to the reader who remembers the biblical drama."[25]

Beyond direct quotations and broad allusions, Jeremiah makes *clear predictions of the coming Messiah*, even if they never get quoted in the biblical accounts of his nativity, ministry, or final passion. For example, Jeremiah promises more than once that God will raise up "a righteous Branch" for David (Jer 23:5; 33:15). The latter prophecy adds that healing, joy, prosperity, and thanksgiving will return to the people of God specifically when shepherds are keeping watch over their flocks in the hill country of Judea (Jer 33:12-13; see Lk 2:8). For readers who know their Gospels, Christ is revealed as the direct fulfillment of such prophecies.

Sometimes Jeremiah sets up an opportunity to *proclaim the gospel of Jesus Christ by way of contrast or negation*. The prophet poses some

---

[25]Hays, *Reading Backwards*, 59.

apparently insoluble problem or confronts a seemingly insurmountable limitation for which the only ultimate answer is the saving work of the Son of God. There may be "no balm in Gilead," as Jeremiah once lamented (Jer 8:22), but Jesus of Nazareth brings humanity's healing cure. Although on more than one occasion the prophet is strictly forbidden to pray for God's sinful people (Jer 7:16; 11:14; 14:11-12)—so severe is God's judgment against them—Jesus "always lives to make intercession" for us (Heb 7:25; see 1 Jn 2:1). At the beginning of Jeremiah 5 the prophet goes on a quest to find one good man in Jerusalem—someone so true, so just, and so righteous that God will pardon his promise-breaking people. The quest is futile, of course—"None is righteous, no, not one" (Rom 3:10)—but Jeremiah's failure exposes our crying need for a Savior perfect enough to secure our pardon.

Finally, we should note that the flawed prophets, foolish priests, and failed kings we meet in Jeremiah help us to *preach Jesus Christ in his prophetic, priestly, and kingly offices*. They do this by helping us to see what kind of Savior we need and what kind of Savior God has given. Keeping a careful eye on these three offices—which is one example of the figural reading of the Old Testament for which Hays advocates in *Reading Backwards*—suggests many lines of christological connection for homiletical application.

Preaching the Gospel Newly from the Old Testament

These are only some of the many ways to preach Jeremiah as Christian Scripture. Indeed, when it comes to proclaiming the gospel, Jeremiah has as much to offer as Isaiah.

Admittedly, there are some wrong ways to interpret and apply Holy Scripture. Sometimes preachers proclaim the gospel in ways that are not according to the Old Testament after all; they are inauthentic to the biblical text or inconsistent with the proper trajectories of redemptive history. But there are also many right ways to preach the gospel from Jeremiah—not inventing interpretations that are alien to the biblical text but elucidating the meanings that are truly there. Every passage in the Bible has its own way of presenting the gospel. When a pastor (or a Bible scholar) preaches Christ from any part of the Old Testament in the way that it was uniquely and divinely designed to present the gospel, this refreshes the preacher's soul and enables God's people to see Jesus Christ in a way perhaps they have never seen him before.

The best way to learn how to preach this way is to follow the example of the apostles and the Evangelists. We start with the examples they have set in their many quotations from and allusions to the Old Testament. But we also have the freedom to follow their hermeneutical and homiletical methods to our own christological conclusions. First, we learn their basic moves, the way a beginner might learn the simple steps for a square dance. But soon this becomes more intuitive, and once we get our feet under us we can step out with the gospel and start to swing. Finding this homiletical freedom his honors the apostles, who always intended for us to do much more than simply repeat their exegetical and expository steps; they wanted us to learn how to dance. More importantly, this way of preaching honors the risen Lord Jesus Christ, whose Spirit compels us to study "Moses and all the Prophets" and then teach "the things concerning himself" that we are sure to find there (Lk 24:27).

11

HOW THE APOSTLES READ EZEKIEL AS CHRISTIAN SCRIPTURE

Alicia R. Jackson

"O DRY BONES, hear the word of the LORD!" (Ezek 37:4). As in the Garden of Eden when the word of the Lord brought order from chaos, light from darkness, and life from nothing (Gen 1), so the word of the Lord in Ezekiel's vision of the valley of dry bones turns a morgue into a militia (Ezek 37:1-14). As unique as the prophet himself, Ezekiel's visionary experience of resurrection life resounds throughout centuries of Jewish and Christian reception history, and with good reason. Even today, as visitors exit Yad Vashem (the Holocaust Memorial Museum in Jerusalem), the last words they read on the memorial arch exit are from Ezekiel 37:14, "And I will put my Spirit within you, and you shall live, and I will place you in your own land." The Spirit of the

Lord who transformed Ezekiel's valley of dry bones into a living, breathing army is also the same Spirit of the Lord who raised Jesus Christ from the dead and even now indwells the physical bodies of believers (Rom 8:11), as a down payment guaranteeing that death is not the Christian's final destiny (Eph 1:13-14).

While Ezekiel 37:1-14 remains symbolically iconic and theologically significant for both Jews and Christians, it is somewhat surprising that the apostles do not directly quote this portion of Scripture. However, the message of life from death that propels the literary structure of the book of Ezekiel from judgment (Ezek 1–32) to restoration (Ezek 33–48) also permeates the gospel message throughout the New Testament in the person and presence of Jesus, who declares to Martha, "I am the resurrection and the life" (Jn 11:25). How this messianic hope of resurrection finds its fulfillment in Jesus relates to our topic of how the apostles read the book of Ezekiel as Christian Scripture.[1] This chapter begins by observing some hermeneutical approaches likely employed in the apostles' readings of the book of Ezekiel, progresses by exploring the apostles' allusions to and quotes from the book of Ezekiel, and concludes by considering how apostolic readings of the book of Ezekiel challenge Christians to live faithfully.

How Then Did They Read It?

It is important to begin this study by acknowledging three key hermeneutical principles.[2] First, the apostles were Jews reading Ezekiel as Jewish Scripture, anticipating the coming of a Jewish Messiah (Ezek 34:23-24; 37:24-25) and the restoration of the nation of Israel (Acts 1:6). The apostles did not view themselves as heralds of a new religion replacing Judaism but as ministers of the gospel announcing the inauguration of God's kingdom, encompassing the inclusion of

---

[1] For more on beliefs in early Judaism regarding resurrection and restoration of the nation, see George W. E. Nickelsburg, *Resurrection, Immortality, and Eternal Life in Intertestamental Judaism and Early Christianity*, 2nd ed. (Cambridge, MA: Harvard University Press, 2006).

[2] While it would be anachronistic to project modern hermeneutical approaches onto the first-century Jewish world, the following observations emerge from their readings of Ezekiel.

Gentiles in the New Covenant (Acts 15) and the restoration of the nation of Israel (Acts 1:1-8; Rom 9–11). Second, the apostles understood that they were reading Ezekiel's reading of Torah and other Jewish prophets, hearing echoes of Israel's history and covenantal identity, with Ezekiel's priestly emphasis on Levitical purity. Third, the apostles were reading the book of Ezekiel in its own historical, literary, and canonical context, and they likely would have expected their Jewish and Christian readers to do the same. It is important for Christian readers to remember that when the apostles quote, allude to, or expand on a theological theme in Ezekiel, they are doing so with the entire literary and historical context in mind, evoking the text's original intended meaning, and *not* (as some would argue) creatively taking Ezekiel's message out of context and applying it ad hoc in an unanticipated way to Christ or to the church.

The apostles also read with awareness of Ezekiel's theological placement in the metanarrative of redemption history. Not only is Ezekiel situated historically and geographically in the middle of the Babylonian exile (586–539 BC), but theologically and canonically, his book functions as a biblical hinge between Genesis and Revelation. It intentionally employs similar metaphorical imagery as it looks back historically in light of Israel's unfaithfulness while also looking forward eschatologically in light of Yahweh's faithfulness. Two frequently repeated phrases encapsulate Ezekiel's main message, which is God's presence with his people: (1) the recognition formula "then they will know that I am Yahweh their God," and (2) the covenant formula "and I will be their God, and they will be my people."

It is also important to note that the apostles understood the *eschatological* and *apocalyptic* nature of Ezekiel's writings, pointing toward the inauguration of a new age and the coming of God's kingdom.[3] In this

---

[3]For more on Jewish eschatological and apocalyptic literature, see Anathea E. Portier-Young, *Apocalypse Against Empire: Theologies of Resistance in Early Judaism* (Grand Rapids, MI:

light, my study will explore how the apostles read Ezekiel as Christian (and Jewish) Scripture according to the following thematic categories of Ezekiel's writings: (1) eschatological visions in light of divine presence, (2) eschatological judgment in light of divine purity, and (3) eschatological restoration in light of divine promises.

Eschatological visions in light of divine presence. Though separated by approximately five hundred years, Ezekiel and the apostle John record visions revealing the timeless continuity of eternal heavenly realities centered on the *kəbôd*, "glory," of Yahweh and the worship of the Lamb.[4] Ezekiel and John share similarities in the ways which they receive and relay their visions, with a strong emphasis on encounters with the Spirit (*rûaḥ* in Ezek MT and *pneuma* in Ezek LXX and NT, both of which can also be translated "wind" or "breath").[5] Ezekiel emphasizes connections between the hand of Yahweh, the *kəbôd* of Yahweh, and the activity of the Spirit, such that Yahweh's hand, as Rebecca Basdeo Hill expresses, is "homologous with the activity of the Spirit in relation to divine revelation and the prophetic word."[6] The Spirit acts by coming into Ezekiel, raising him to his feet (Ezek 2:2; 3:24), and lifting him up and taking him to various locations (Ezek 3:12, 14; 8:3; 11:1, 24; 37:1; 43:5). Likewise, John receives his visions when he is "in the Spirit on the Lord's day" (Rev 1:10), or simply "in the Spirit" (Rev 4:2; 17:3; 21:10).[7]

Visions of the heavenly throne room. Both Ezekiel and John see a hand holding a scroll with writing on the front and back (Ezek 2:9-10; Rev 5:1).

Eerdmans, 2014); and John J. Collins, *The Apocalyptic Imagination: An Introduction to Jewish Apocalyptic Literature*, 2nd ed. (Grand Rapids, MI: Eerdmans, 1998).

[4] See G. K. Beale, *John's Use of the Old Testament in Revelation*, JSNTSup 166 (Sheffield: Sheffield Academic Press, 1998).

[5] Of the 378 references to *rûaḥ* in the Old Testament, 52 occur in Ezekiel, making Ezekiel the OT prophetic book with the greatest number of references to the Spirit. See Daniel I. Block, "The Prophet of the Spirit: The Use of Rwh in the Book of Ezekiel," *JETS* 32, no. 1 (March 1989): 28; Alicia R. Jackson, "The Spirit of Yahweh in Ezekiel," *Pneuma* 43, no. 3-4 (December 2021): 377-83.

[6] A. Rebecca Basdeo Hill, *Visions of God in Ezekiel: Pentecostal Explorations of the Glory and Holiness of Yahweh* (Cleveland, TN: CPT, 2019), 72.

[7] See Melissa L. Archer and Robby Waddell, "The Spirit in John's Apocalypse: Vision, Prophecy, Discernment," *Pneuma* 43, no. 3-4 (2021): 561.

When commanded to eat the scroll, it tastes like honey in their mouths (Ezek 3:1-3; Rev 10:9-10), and yet it creates bitterness of spirit for Ezekiel (Ezek 3:14) and bitterness of stomach for John (Rev 10:9-10). They both describe living creatures surrounding the heavenly throne, identified as cherubim, in great detail (Ezek 1:5-10; 10:1; Rev 4:6-7). Ezekiel's creatures each have *four* faces (of a human, a lion, an ox, and an eagle), while John sees four creatures, which each have *one* face (of a human, a lion, an ox, and an eagle).[8] The cherubim worship close to the throne, with fiery torches blazing between them (Ezek 1:13) and before the throne (Rev 4:5), and whose wings sound like many waters (Ezek 1:24; Rev 14:2; 19:6).

Ezekiel describes the heavenly throne as sapphire, while John compares it to jasper and carnelian stone, surrounded by the radiance of Yahweh's kəbôd like a rainbow or an emerald (Ezek 1:26-28; Rev 4:2-3). Ezekiel falls on his face before the radiance of Yahweh's kəbôd (Ezek 1:28), just as John lays prostrate as though dead at the feet of the resurrected Christ (Rev 1:17). John's description of this glorified Son of Man, with his face shining like the sun (Rev 1:13-15), resembles Ezekiel's depiction of one seated on the throne, appearing in the likeness of a man and shining with the radiance of amber and fire (Ezek 1:26-27).

Visions of a new temple and a new city. God's presence, enthroned eternally in heaven, also inhabits holy space on earth. Just as God's presence filled Solomon's temple at its dedication (2 Chron 7:1-3), so Ezekiel watched his presence depart in a vision before the temple's destruction (Ezek 10). Yet in Ezekiel's eschatological vision of a new temple (Ezek 40–48), he witnesses the return of Yahweh's kəbôd to the temple through the eastern gate of the city (Ezek 43:4-5). The Gospels record this same return of the embodied divine kəbôd as he rides humbly on a donkey, descends the Mount of Olives, and enters the eastern gate of the city (Mt 21:1-11; Mk 11:1-11; Lk 19:28-44; Jn 12:12-19).

---

[8]David L. Thompson, *Ezekiel*, Cornerstone Biblical Commentary: Ezekiel & Daniel (Carol Stream, IL: Tyndale House, 2010), 46.

Ezekiel and Revelation close with visions of a new temple (Ezek 40–48) and a new city (Rev 21–22), emphasizing God's presence with his people (Rev 21:3).[9] Ezekiel and John experience transportation to a high mountaintop, from which they both see a city, identified by John as Jerusalem descending from heaven (Ezek 40:2; Rev 21:10). In Ezekiel's vision, a river of life flows from the temple, and in John's vision, a river of life flows from the throne of God and of the Lamb (Ezek 47:1; Rev 22:1). Beth Stovell explains the significance of the river's source in Ezekiel:

> By locating the source of the river as the temple, Ezekiel 47 is playing on the conception of the temple as the place of God's presence. Thus, the waters that give life and restoration are the waters that come from the place of God's presence in the Temple. The ultimate source of these living waters which grant nourishment and healing (Ez 47:12) is God's presence.[10]

John explains why the river does not flow from the temple in his vision of the heavenly city: "And I did not see a temple in it, for the Lord God All-Powerful is its temple, and the Lamb" (Rev 21:22 LEB). Melissa Archer highlights the significance of John's river flowing from the *throne* instead of from the *temple*: "The coupling of God and the Lamb that has been so characteristic throughout the Apocalypse has its climax here: God and the Lamb is the temple!"[11]

The centrality of this message for John—in its connection to God's presence dwelling in the tabernacle and the temple historically—is evidenced by the opening of his Gospel as he writes, "The Word became

---

[9]John employs a version of the covenant formula here. For a treatment of the covenant formula in the biblical canon, see Rolf Rendtorff, *The Covenant Formula: An Exegetical and Theological Investigation*, trans. Margaret Kohl, Old Testament Studies (Edinburgh: T&T Clark, 1998).
[10]Beth M. Stovell, "Fruit for Food, Leaves for Healing: Archaeobotany, Conceptual Metaphor, and Ezekiel 47," in *Nature Imagery and Conceptions of Nature in the Bible*, ed. Mark Boda and Dalit Rom-Shiloni (New York: T&T Clark Bloomsbury, forthcoming), 11-12.
[11]Melissa L. Archer, *"I Was in the Spirit on the Lord's Day": A Pentecostal Engagement with Worship in the Apocalypse* (Cleveland: CPT Press, 2015), 278-79.

flesh and dwelt among us," literally *eskēnōsen*, "tabernacled," among us (Jn 1:14). This aligns with John's understanding of what Jesus means when he says, "Destroy this temple, and in three days I will raise it up!" (Jn 2:19 LEB). John wants to clarify for his readers that when Jesus referred to his own body as the temple, he intentionally pointed back to the Mosaic tabernacle, to Solomon's temple, and to Ezekiel's eschatological temple as the dwelling place(s) of God, while just as intentionally pointing forward to the eternal heavenly reality, in which the Lamb himself would be the temple, the presence of God among his people.

Visions of the tree of life, healing leaves, and living water. Ezekiel and John both envision fruit-bearing tree(s) lining the banks of the river, which John identifies as the "tree of life" (Rev 22:2; Ezek 47:12). The "tree of life" metaphor functions canonically as an *inclusio* (Gen 2:9; Rev 22:2), accentuating its theological significance throughout the biblical text. In the Old Testament, images of fruit-bearing trees or vines often refer to Israel and Judah (e.g., Ezek 15:2-7; 17:5-10; Hos 9:10; Jer 2:21). Likewise, Jesus curses the fruitless fig tree because it is not fulfilling its function as a life-giving source, just as Israel's corrupt religious leaders are not bearing fruit as God intended (Mt 21:18-22; Mk 11:12-25; Lk 13:6-9). Although the tree of the nation of Israel was cut down in the judgment of exile, from the stump would grow a branch (Is 11:1, 10; 53:2; Jer 23:5; Rom 15:8-9, 12)—Jesus, the Messiah, the true Vine (Jn 15).

Ezekiel and John employ the dual metaphors of eating from fruit-bearing trees and drinking living water. While Ezekiel explains that the leaves of the trees are for healing (Ezek 47:12), John adds that the leaves are "for the healing *of the nations*" (Rev 22:2). Ultimately, this life-giving source is to flow from the nation of Israel to all nations, so that, as in John's account of Jesus' words to the Samaritan woman, "whoever drinks of this water which I will give to him will never be thirsty for eternity, but the water which I will give to him will become in him a well of water springing up to eternal life" (Jn 4:14 LEB).

Conclusion. The apostles read Ezekiel's eschatological visions with an understanding of his emphasis on divine presence, interpreting various ways in which the person of Jesus Christ—God's temple and divine presence among them—inaugurated the fulfillment of Ezekiel's visions. In his Gospel, John explains that the Word who became flesh and tabernacled among them is God's temple and presence with his people (Jn 1:14). Gospel authors describe the return of Yahweh's *kəbôd* in Jesus' triumphal entry through the eastern gate of the city, as Ezekiel envisions. The close correlation of John's visions in the apocalypse with Ezekiel's heavenly visions emphasizes eternal worship in God's presence. John's visions expand the worship depicted in Ezekiel's visions to include all peoples worshiping Yahweh and the Lamb eternally. Just as the apostles read Ezekiel's eschatological visions in light of divine presence, so also they read Ezekiel's eschatological judgment oracles in light of divine purity.

Eschatological Judgment in Light of Divine Purity

Ezekiel's revelation of Yahweh's holiness (Ezek 1) lays the theological foundation for his emphasis on covenantal purity, expressed by obedience to Yahweh's commands. The Hebrew word for judgment (*mišpāṭ*) can be translated both "judgment" and "justice," which flows from the holiness and purity of Yahweh's character.[12] Ezekiel prophesies judgment for three distinct groups of people: (1) the nations, (2) Israel and Judah, and (3) Israel and Judah's corrupt leaders.

Ezekiel's oracles of judgment for the nations. Readers of the Apocalypse hear John's echoes of Ezekiel's judgment oracles against Tyre and Sidon (Ezek 26–28; Rev 17–18). Just as the leader of Tyre is adorned with precious stones and possesses beauty beyond compare (Ezek 28:13; 31:8-9), so the woman seated on the beast and the great city of Babylon are clothed with scarlet, gold, precious stones, and pearls (Rev 17:4;

---

[12]Basdeo Hill, *Visions of God*, 132.

18:16). Their jubilant songs will be silenced (Ezek 26:13; Rev 18:22), while the princes of the sea, kings of the earth, merchants, sailors, and inhabitants of the coastlands will mourn over their destruction (Ezek 26:16-17; 27:22, 27-29, 30-36; Rev 18:9, 11-13, 15-19). Similarly, Paul compares the haughty words of Tyre's leader with the words of the coming man of lawlessness, both of whom will sit in the seat or temple of God, proclaiming themselves as God (Ezek 28:1-2; 2 Thess 2:4).

The apostles also refer to Ezekiel's imagery depicting the darkening of sun, moon, and stars in the context of judgment against the pharoah of Egypt (Ezek 32:7-8). Ezekiel's language is reminiscent of Joel's portrayal of the day of the Lord, before which the sun will turn to darkness and the moon to blood (Joel 2:2, 10, 30-31).[13] Matthew, Mark, and Luke record Jesus' warning of coming signs in the sun, moon, and stars preceding a time of great tribulation (Mt 24:29; Mk 13:34; Lk 21:25), and John similarly describes heavenly lights darkening and falling in his visions of the seals and the trumpets (Rev 6:12-13; 8:12).

John repeats some of Ezekiel's judgment language against Gog of Magog (Ezek 38–39), applying it as well to the beast, the false prophet, and the kings of the earth and their armies (Rev 19:11-21; 2:7-10). Ezekiel 39:4, 17-20 and Revelation 19:17-21 contain parallel accounts of the gruesome aftermath of a fierce battle against God's enemies, while Ezekiel 38–39 and Revelation 20:7-10 depict battle scenes against Gog and Magog.[14] In Ezekiel, Gog is a person and Magog a place where he ruled, but in Revelation, Gog and Magog symbolize nations from the four corners of the earth that wage war against God.[15] These eschatological

---

[13] Scholars acknowledge some similarity in language between Ezekiel and Joel but debate the direction of dependence. See Gary Edward Schnittjer, *Old Testament Use of Old Testament: A Book-by-Book Guide* (Grand Rapids, MI: Zondervan Academic, 2021), 377.

[14] For a thorough treatment of thematic and verbal parallels in Ezekiel 39:4, 17-20 and Revelation 19:17-21, see Sverre Bøe, *Gog and Magog: Ezekiel 38–39 as Pre-text for Revelation 19:17-21 and 20:7-10*, WUNT 2/135 (Tübingen: Mohr Siebeck, 2001), 274-99.

[15] Rebecca Skaggs acknowledges evidence for identifying Gog and Magog with historical nations but concludes that the wisest interpretation is to understand them as symbolic names that represent the forces of evil, noting that these names were employed symbolically in apocalyptic

scenes of final victory over God's enemies likely would have encouraged Ezekiel's audience of Babylonian exiles and John's audience of first-century believers, both of whom were suffering hardship and persecution.[16] Ezekiel and John encourage their readers to remain faithful during trials, knowing that God will perform justice on their behalf through the final eschatological judgment of all evil powers.[17]

Ezekiel's oracles of judgment for Israel and Judah. Ezekiel warns Jerusalem's survivors of Yahweh's four judgments: the evil sword, famine, a fierce animal, and plague (Ezek 14:21). John presents similar imagery in his vision of the fourth seal, in which death—depicted as a rider on a pale horse—kills one-fourth of the earth by sword, famine, plague, and wild beasts (Rev 6:8). In this instance, John employs imagery that Ezekiel relegates to Jerusalem's survivors and applies it to the inhabitants of the entire world. Yet for both Ezekiel and John, there is hope in the midst of judgment, because God will protect and preserve for himself a righteous remnant among his people—those who lament over their sin, according to Ezekiel (Ezek 9:4), and those whom John describes as "the slaves of our God" (Rev 7:3), believers who remain faithful to the Lamb.

In the judgment depicted by both John and Ezekiel, the righteous will be distinguished from the wicked by a mark or a seal on their foreheads (Ezek 9:4; Rev 7:3; 9:4), which John appears to later identify as the name of the Lamb and the name of his Father (Rev 14:1). Ezekiel describes how judgment begins in the sanctuary, wherein those without the mark on their foreheads are killed (Ezek 9:6). Peter clearly alludes to this text when he writes, "For it is the time for the judgment to begin

---

literature. See Priscilla C. Benham and Rebecca Skaggs, *Revelation*, Pentecostal Commentary Series (Blandford Forum, UK: Deo, 2008), 209-10.

[16]G. R. Beasley-Murray, *Revelation*, New Cambridge Bible Commentary (Grand Rapids, MI: Eerdmans, 1974), 298.

[17]Keener views this entire section of Scripture as a reminder for believers to remain faithful and vigilant; if the "camp of the saints" needs to remain vigilant following the millennium, Keener argues, how much more do saints in the present time need to display vigilance? See Craig S. Keener, *Revelation*, NIVAC (Grand Rapids, MI: Zondervan, 2000), 469.

out from the household of God" (1 Pet 4:17 LEB). While Ezekiel's judgment was specifically for the Jerusalem survivors of the sixth-century Babylonian siege, Peter now includes both Jewish and Gentile believers in the household of God as potential recipients of divine judgment. The context for Peter's allusion to Ezekiel is a call for Christians to live holy lives despite persecution for their faith (1 Pet 4:17). In the book of Ezekiel, the nation of Israel, originally called to stand out among the nations as the household of God, is called "the house of rebellion who has eyes to see and they do not see; they have ears to hear, and they do not hear" (Ezek 12:2 LEB). Peter's point is that just as ancient Israel and Judah were called to a standard of holiness in relationship with Yahweh, so Christians are called to suffer on account of righteousness instead of suffering because of sin.

Similarly, Mark records Jesus' quotation of Ezekiel when the apostles mistake his warning against the yeast of the Pharisees and of Herod as an admonition for forgetting to bring bread: "Although you have eyes, do you not see? And although you have ears, do you not hear? And do you not remember?" (Mk 8:18 LEB). While it may seem harsh for the modern reader to realize that Jesus intentionally used Ezekiel's rebuke of rebellious Israel and Judah to reprimand his own disciples for their spiritual blindness, the point Jesus makes here in Mark's Gospel is that even followers of Jesus must stand before the purifying gaze of divine judgment.

Jesus' warnings against nonbelieving Galilean cities, recorded by Matthew and Luke, also refer back to Ezekiel's judgment oracles against Tyre and Sidon (Ezek 26–28; Mt 11:21-22; Lk 10:13-14). The apostles understood that Jesus viewed ancient Tyre and Sidon—deemed ripe for judgment in the book of Ezekiel—as possessing more faith than some of the Jewish inhabitants of first-century Galilee. If readers miss Jesus' allusion to Ezekiel and his ensuing shocking contrast, they may miss the severity of his rebuke.

Ezekiel's oracles of judgment for Israel and Judah's corrupt leaders. As Ezekiel was a watchman for the house of Israel (Ezek 3:17), Yahweh held Ezekiel personally accountable for delivering divine warnings. The author of Hebrews alludes to Ezekiel's watchman role as a positive example for godly spiritual leaders, who "keep watch over your souls as those who will give an account" (Heb 13:17 LEB). God tells Ezekiel that *if he warns the people* and they do not repent, their blood will be on their own heads. However, *if he does not warn* the people, their blood will be demanded from his—the watchman's—hand (Ezek 33:1-6). This theme of blood being on someone's head (Ezek 33:5) goes back to Mosaic law (Lev 20:9-16) and continues by allusion in Matthew's account of Pilate's washing his hands and declaring, "I am innocent of the blood of this man" (Mt 27:24 LEB).[18] Jennifer Rosner presents an alternate interpretation of Matthew's allusion to Ezekiel 33:5 in the people's response to Pilate, "His blood be on us and on our children!" (Mt 27:25 LEB), arguing that these words "are no longer read as a self-imposed curse, but as an unwitting prophecy of the redemptive power of Jesus' death in relation to His own people."[19] Indeed, the heart of the gospel message is that the blood of Jesus on his Jewish people—and even on the Gentiles—brings redemption and salvation for all of humanity.

Just as God held Ezekiel accountable as a watchman, so the prophets and leaders of Israel were called to account. False prophets, whom

---

[18] Craig L. Blomberg, "Matthew," in *Commentary on the New Testament Use of the Old Testament*, ed. G. K. Beale and D. A. Carson (Grand Rapids, MI: Baker Academic, 2007), 97.

[19] Jennifer M. Rosner, *Finding Messiah: A Journey into the Jewishness of the Gospel* (Downers Grove, IL: InterVarsity Press, 2022), 141. Unfortunately, gross misinterpretation of these verses has contributed toward the lie "the Jews killed Jesus," used to justify antisemitism and violence against the Jews throughout church history. Michael Brown counters this charge by arguing that (1) Jesus willingly laid down his own life (1 Cor 15:3; Rom 5:6-8), (2) God himself ordained Jesus' death (Rev 13:8), and (3) Jesus himself prayed for forgiveness for those crucifying him, since "they do not know what they are doing" (Lk 23:34). See Michael L. Brown, *Answering Jewish Objections to Jesus*, vol. 4, *New Testament Objections* (Grand Rapids, MI: Baker, 2007), 55; Brown, *Our Hands Are Stained with Blood: The Tragic Story of the Church and the Jewish People*, rev. and expanded ed. (Shippensberg, PA: Destiny Image, 2019).

Ezekiel likens to foxes among ruins and flimsy, whitewashed walls, lead the people of Israel astray by saying, "Peace!" when there is no peace (Ezek 13:1-16). Paul alludes to Ezekiel's metaphorical portrayal of false prophets at least two times: (1) after Ananias strikes Paul in the face during his testimony before the Sanhedrin, Paul replies, "God is going to strike you, you whitewashed wall!" (Acts 23:3 LEB); and (2) warning the Thessalonians of the coming day of the Lord, Paul writes, "Whenever they say, 'Peace and security,' then sudden destruction will overtake them like the birth pains of a pregnant woman, and they will not possibly escape" (1 Thess 5:3 LEB).

Matthew also alludes to Ezekiel when Jesus calls the Pharisees "whitewashed tombs" that appear pure on the outside but contain decay on the inside (Mt 23:27-28). Israel's false prophets and leaders, depicted by Ezekiel as false shepherds (Ezek 34:1-11; Jer 10:21; 23:1-2), scattered and slaughtered the flock instead of protecting and providing for it. Ezekiel recalls the phrase "scattered, without a shepherd" (Ezek 34:5 LEB; Zech 10:2) from Micaiah's vision of Israel's defeated army (1 Kings 22:17; 2 Chron 18:16).

Conclusion. The apostles read Ezekiel's judgment oracles as Christian Scripture by holding the first-century Jewish community and the believing Jewish and Gentile community to the same standard of holiness and faith that God expected from ancient Israel and Judah. The believing remnant of Israel and Judah in the apostles' day, including Gentile believers, were called to live holy lives in light of divine purity as a light to the nations surrounding them. Modern Christian readers, living in a time when preaching about sin and judgment is less than popular in many churches, would do well to heed Ezekiel's and the apostles' warnings of eschatological judgment for all of humanity in light of divine purity.

Eschatological Restoration in Light of Divine Promises

Following the pronouncement of judgment against Israel's false shepherds (Ezek 34:9-22), Ezekiel records Yahweh's promises to bring restoration in the true shepherd-king—the Messiah—(Ezek 34:23-25, 37:24-26), restoration with a new heart and a new Spirit (Ezek 36:26-28), and restoration by resurrection (Ezek 37:1-14).

Restoration in the shepherd-king. Yahweh's answer to the abuse of the false shepherds is twofold: (1) Yahweh himself will be their shepherd (Ezek 34:11-22), and (2) Yahweh will establish his servant David as shepherd-king over them (Ezek 34:24; 37:24-25; Mic 5:4).[20] Ezekiel's description of transition in leadership also initiates the covenant of peace (Ezek 34:25; 37:26), Ezekiel's equivalent of Jeremiah's prophesied New Covenant (Jer 31:31-37), which the author of Hebrews explicitly identifies as the New Covenant in Christ (Heb 8:1-8). Jesus' self-identification as the Good Shepherd (Jn 10:14-15) reminds his listeners of Ezekiel's Davidic shepherd but also of Ezekiel's judgment warnings for Israel's false shepherds, clearly paralleled with the hired hand and the wolf, the false shepherds and false teachers of Jesus' day (Jn 15:12-13). Matthew also portrays Jesus as Ezekiel's Davidic shepherd, motivated by compassion for the crowds, who were "weary and dejected, like sheep that did not have a shepherd" (Mt 9:36 LEB; Ezek 34:5; 1 Kings 22:17; 2 Chron 18:16; Zech 10:2).

Finally, John envisions the resurrected Messiah as both Ezekiel's Davidic shepherd and as the rider on the white horse (Rev 19:11-16) in his second coming. For Ezekiel, the role of shepherding is visualized by the stick in Yahweh's hand (Ezek 37:19), and for John, the role of shepherding is visualized by the rod of iron in the rider's hand (Rev 19:15), particularly because the word in Revelation 19:15 often translated "rule"

---

[20] Ancient Near Eastern literature abounds with examples of kings and gods described as "shepherds." See G. R. Driver, *Canaanite Myths and Legends* (Edinburgh: T&T Clark, 1956), 67; *ANET* 41, 69, 72, 337.

(*poimanei*) can also be translated "shepherd."²¹ John expands the covenant people of God over whom Yahweh and the Messiah rule and shepherd from the reunited nation of Israel and Judah (Ezek 37:19, 27) to all the nations of the world who welcome their Messiah by faith and submit to his lordship (Rev 19:15).

Ezekiel's employment of the shepherd-king metaphor indicates the type of king this Messiah will be, as one who serves and cares for the flock with justice (Ezek 34:25; 37:25).²² Naming the Messiah "king" after the shepherd-king David is ironic, given the prophet Nathan's parabolic rebuke of David, thereby indicting him as one of Israel's false shepherds (2 Sam 12:1-25; Ezek 34:1-11). April Westbrook connects David's abuse of power to his ensuing abuse of Bathsheba and the nation, reminding the reader of Samuel's prophetic warning against human kingship (1 Sam 8:10-18):

> The major point is clear—David, the irresponsible king, has come to a place in his life in which he feels quite empowered to avoid what he does not want (to fight in battle) and to take what he does want (Bathsheba), regardless of the impact of these choices on others.... By recognizing Bathsheba's experience as a reflection of Israel's destiny, the reader is pressed to face an ugly picture. The human king will use the power given to him to take from the nation whatever he may want. He will destroy his own people on a whim because he can, and even his admission of guilt before the deity will not undo the damage he has done.²³

---

²¹In the ancient Near Eastern world, the shepherd's crook was often representative of a royal scepter, as is evidenced by the use of the shepherd's crook as the Egyptian pharaoh's earliest insignia. Therefore, while the stick in Yahweh's hand (Ezek 37:19) can be seen as a royal scepter, it can just as easily be understood to represent a shepherd's staff. See William C. Hayes, *The Scepter of Egypt, Part 1* (New York: Metropolitan Museum of Art, 1953), 28, 285-86.

²²See Beth M. Stovell, "Yahweh as Shepherd-King in Ezekiel 34: Linguistic-Literary Analysis of Metaphors of Shepherding," in *Modeling Biblical Language: Papers from the McMaster Divinity College Linguistics Circle*, ed. Stanley E. Porter, Gregory Fewster, and Christopher Land, Linguistic Biblical Studies (Leiden: Brill, 2016), 230; Stovell, *Mapping Metaphorical Discourse in the Fourth Gospel: John's Eternal King*, Linguistic Biblical Studies 5 (Leiden: Brill, 2012), 221-54.

²³April D. Westbrook, *"And He Will Take Your Daughters...": Woman Story and the Ethical Evaluation of Monarch in the David Narrative*, LHBOTS 610 (New York: Bloomsbury T&T Clark, 2015), 141.

The Messiah is called "David" (Ezek 34:25; 37:25) not because he is *like* David but rather because he is *unlike* David; he fulfills the divine promises of the Davidic covenant (2 Sam 7:16; Mt 1:6; Lk 3:31) and succeeds as the perfect shepherd-king where David failed. The selfish taking of Bathsheba and slaughter of Uriah (2 Sam 12:9) contrasts the selfless sacrifice of the cross, on which Jesus is designated "king of the Jews" (Jn 19:2, 12, 19-20). As king of the Jews from his birth (Mt 2:2) to his death (Mt 27:11, 29-30; Mk 15:2, 17-19; Lk 23:3; Jn 18:33), Jesus in his earthly life and ministry showed the world what it looks like when God is king, in all of his glory and holiness (Ezek 34:24-25; 37:24-26; 1 Sam 8:7; Mt 6:9-10).[24]

Restoration with a new heart and a new Spirit. Sometimes called Ezekiel's gospel, this spiritual restoration is enacted by heart transplant from hearts of stone to hearts of flesh, by heart cleansing with water, and by implantation of the Spirit of Yahweh into the hearts of the people (Ezek 36:27) so that they will obey his commandments (Ezek 11:19-20; 16:60-63; 34:25; 36:26-27; 37:26-28). It should be no surprise, then, that when Jesus explains spiritual rebirth to Nicodemus—a Pharisee who would have been familiar with Ezekiel's words—he emphasizes the necessity of being born again of water and of the Spirit (Jn 3:5), alluding to Ezekiel's cleansing by the sprinkling of water and heart transformation by the Spirit (Ezek 36:25-27).[25] Stovell unpacks John's theological connection between birth and cleansing: "This differentiation between spirit and flesh is consistent with John's theology elsewhere, and, as is typical of John, this is more than a simple differentiation between spiritual and physical birth. It is clarifying our need to be born anew through cleansing."[26]

---

[24]Jesus describes the rule, or kingdom (*basileia*), of God through numerous parables in the Gospels. In his parable of the mustard seed (Mt 13:32; Mk 4:32; Lk 13:19), Jesus alludes to two of Ezekiel's parables: (1) the parable of the two eagles and the vine (Ezek 17:22-24) and (2) the parabolic depiction of Egypt in its splendor as a tree in which the birds nested (Ezek 31:6).

[25]Andreas J. Köstenberger, "John," in Beale and Carson, *Commentary on the New Testament Use*, 434; Grant Osborne and Philip W. Comfort, *John and 1, 2, and 3 John*, Cornerstone Biblical Commentary 13 (Carol Stream, IL: Tyndale House, 2007), 54.

[26]Beth M. Stovell, "The Birthing Spirit, the Childbearing God: Metaphors of Motherhood and Their Place in Christian Discipleship," *Priscilla Papers* 26, no.4 (Autumn 2012): 18.

The apostle Paul recognizes Ezekiel's prophecy of implantation of God's Spirit in human hearts not only as spiritual resurrection and rebirth but also as a mark of sonship and adoption (Gal 4:6). Ezekiel's imagery recalls Mosaic prophecy of heart circumcision (Deut 10:16), which the apostle Paul describes as "circumcision. . . of the heart, by the Spirit" (Rom 2:29) and as "the circumcision of Christ" (Col 2:11), so that the law, as Jeremiah envisions, will be written on human hearts (Rom 2:15; Jer 31:33; Heb 8:10).

Restoration by resurrection. Just as the Spirit enacts restoration for Israel via heart transplant and Spirit implantation in Ezekiel 36:25-27, so the Spirit takes a prominent role in the spiritual and national resurrection of Israel, pictured by Ezekiel's vision of the valley of dry bones coming to life in Ezekiel 37:1-14. Ezekiel prophesies to the *rûaḥ*, "wind," and the *rûaḥ*, "breath," enters the dry bones and resurrects them by the *rûaḥ*, "spirit," evoking the face-to-face intimacy of creation, when Yahweh breathed into Adam's nostrils (Gen 2:7; Ezek 37:1-14).[27] Lisa Ward encapsulates the Spirit's salvific activity in Ezekiel's resurrection imagery: "Ultimately, this vision portrays a promise that YHWH will bring life out of death; a new spirit in exchange for an old spirit; and hope for the hearts of Israel to receive YHWH's indwelling Spirit as a means of empowering them to become obedient to YHWH as their Lord."[28]

Beneath the New Testament accounts of resurrection stands a belief in resurrection grounded in the Old Testament, with Ezekiel 37:1-14 figuring significantly. Even before Jesus' resurrection, the apostles portray Ezekiel's vision of dry bones coming to life with Lazarus's resurrection (Jn 11:1-44), with the resurrection of Jairus's daughter (Mt 9:18-26; Mk 5:21-43; Lk 8:40-56), with the resurrection of the widow of Nain's son (Lk 7:11-17), and with the resurrection of saints in

---

[27] Gerald L. Borchert, *John 1-11*, NAC 25A (Nashville: Broadman & Holman, 1996), 173-74; Daniel I. Block, *The Book of Ezekiel, Chapters 25-48*, NICOT (Grand Rapids, MI: Eerdmans, 1998), 360-61.

[28] Lisa R. Ward, *A Pentecostal Encounter with Ezekiel's Visions: The Spirit, Power, and Affectivity* (Cleveland, TN: CPT Press, 2021), 208.

Jerusalem at the moment of Jesus' crucifixion (Mt 27:52-53).[29] Jesus defines himself as the source of resurrection life envisioned in Ezekiel 37:1-14 when he declares to Martha just before the resurrection of Lazarus, "I am the resurrection and the life" (Jn 11:25 LEB). Jesus' explanation to Nicodemus of being born of the Spirit in John 3, which he compares to the wind blowing wherever it wishes, also undoubtedly echoes Ezekiel's visionary encounter of the Spirit blowing life into dry bones with resurrection power (Jn 3:6-8; Ezek 37:1-14).[30]

Ezekiel's resurrection vision in Ezekiel 37:1-14 pictures both a spiritual and national rebirth for Israel, enabling reconciliation between Israel and Judah as they are united under messianic leadership in the covenant of peace (Ezek 37:15-28). As Jacqueline Grey writes, the Spirit works "to achieve the re-creation of the despairing community through the words of the prophet, inspiring hope and life."[31] By reading Ezekiel 37:1-14 as Christian Scripture, the apostles lived in expectation of a time when not only individual resurrections would occur but also Israel and Judah would be reunified and resurrected as a nation restored permanently to its land.

Even after the resurrection of Jesus, the apostles still anticipate Ezekiel's national "dry bones" resurrection for Israel when they ask, "Lord, is it at this time you are restoring the kingdom to Israel?" (Acts 1:6 LEB). Jesus does not seem surprised by their question, nor does he rebuke them for it. Rather, he answers, "It is not for you to know the times or seasons that the Father has set by his own authority" (Acts 1:7 LEB), possibly implying that this national restoration may be yet to come. Even after the day of Pentecost and the outpouring of the Spirit, Luke explains that the restoration of all things *is yet to come* (Acts 3:19-21), allowing for the possibility of future national regathering

---

[29]Block, *Ezekiel, Chapters 25–48*, 389-91.
[30]See Craig S. Keener, *The IVP Bible Background Commentary: New Testament* (Downers Grove, IL: InterVarsity Press, 1993); Jn 3:5-8; 20:22; Stovell, "Birthing Spirit," 19.
[31]Jacqueline Grey, "Acts of the Spirit: Ezekiel 37 in the Light of Contemporary Speech-Act Theory," *Journal of Biblical and Pneumatological Research* 1 (Fall 2009): 70.

and restoration for Jewish people in the land of Israel, never again to be removed or scattered (e.g., Ezek 28:25-26; 37:21-25; 39:28; Jer 24:5-6; Amos 9:14-15; Mic 4:6-7; Zeph 3:19-20).[32]

Jesus' last words to the apostles before ascending to heaven, "But you will receive power when the Holy Spirit has come upon you" (Acts 1:8 LEB), vividly recall Yahweh's promise recorded by Ezekiel, "And I will not hide my face again from them when I pour out my Spirit over the house of Israel" (Ezek 39:29 LEB). Verena Schafroth explains, "The reference to God hiding His face is usually connected to His wrath in Ezekiel (cf. 7:8; 9:8; 20:8; 30:15; 36:18)."[33] Additionally, Ezekiel 39:29 is the only instance in which the prophet uses the language "pour out" in a positive sense.[34] As Schafroth argues, Ezekiel transforms typical judgment language into anticipation of "God's restorative activity."[35] Basdeo Hill connects this divine outpouring of the Spirit (Ezek 39:29) with the river of life (Ezek 47): "The allusion depicts YHWH pouring out 'my Spirit' as water is poured out from a vessel. Thus, the river flowing out of the temple may be another expression of the life-giving presence of YHWH, particularly YHWH's רוּחַ (*rûaḥ*)"[36]

The outpouring of the Spirit prophesied by Ezekiel is inaugurated on the day of Pentecost (Joel 2:28-29; Acts 2:1-21) and continues as Jews and Gentiles receive the Spirit. This is why Paul declares that "all Israel will be saved," referring back to the spiritual resurrection of the nation of Israel envisioned by Ezekiel (Rom 11:25-27 LEB) and extending the gospel to all nations, so that even Gentiles can be "grafted in" to the people of God (Rom 11:13-24).

---

[32] See Darrell L. Bock, "Biblical Reconciliation Between Jews and Arabs," in *Israel, the Church, and the Middle East: A Biblical Response to the Current Conflict*, ed. Darrell L. Bock and Mitch Glaser (Grand Rapids, MI: Kregel, 2018), 173-77.

[33] Verena Schafroth, "An Exegetical Exploration of 'Spirit' References in Ezekiel 36 and 37," *Journal of the European Pentecostal Theological Association* 29, no. 2 (2009): 73.

[34] Schnittjer explains, "When Ezekiel speaks of 'giving the spirit' positively elsewhere, he uses the verb 'give' (נתן *nātan*) (Ezek 11:19; 36:26, 27; 37:14)" (*Old Testament Use of Old Testament*, 337).

[35] Schafroth, "Exegetical Exploration of 'Spirit,'" 73.

[36] See Basdeo Hill, *Visions of God*, 144; Ward, *Pentecostal Encounter*, 223-24, 267.

Conclusion: How Then Shall We Live?

Apostolic readings of the book of Ezekiel challenge Christians to live faithfully in light of divine presence, divine purity, and divine promises. First, the apostles' reading of Ezekiel calls Christians to live in awareness of God's presence, both in the majesty of his eternal heavenly throne and in the mundanity of human brokenness and suffering. Both John and Ezekiel received their heavenly visions in the context of exile, disappointment, and persecution; thus they invite their readers to encounter God's presence not only in life's glorious spaces but perhaps more significantly in the spaces and places where they may need him the most and yet expect him the least. God surprised Ezekiel and John with dramatic divine encounters in times of their greatest despair, and so Christians should not be surprised when their gentle shepherd-king pursues his sheep in their valley of the shadow of death.

Second, the apostles' reading of Ezekiel calls Christians to live in light of God's purity and holiness, from which his perfect justice flows. This divine purity allows believers to discern rightly and to live wisely. Just as Israel was held accountable for living in light of its covenant relationship with Yahweh, and just as Israel's leaders—both in Ezekiel's and in Jesus' day—received judgment for failing to shepherd with justice, so Christians are called to holy living by walking in covenant relationship with the Holy One.

Finally, the apostles' reading of Ezekiel calls Christians to remain hopeful because of God's promises of restoration and resurrection. For the exilic survivors, the dream of being united as one nation in their own land under one shepherd must have seemed impossible as they looked at the dry bones surrounding them. They needed the reminder that God was the God of restoration and resurrection and that he had promises yet to be fulfilled for Israel. For first-century Christians, the dream of worshiping openly without persecution, suffering, and death must have seemed impossible as they lost homes, loved ones, and their very lives. They needed the reminder that the Lamb who was slain has overcome death and all the forces of evil and that the eternal heavenly realities of God's presence and glory would soon outweigh even their most horrific suffering for allegiance to the Lamb.[37] Perhaps all Christians need this final reminder from the apostles' reading of Ezekiel: our God is still the God of the impossible, the God of restoration, and the God of resurrection life—and this is not the end of our story.

---

[37] Archer, "I Was in the Spirit," 304.

12

WE ARE NOT APOSTLES

Limits on Reading Ezekiel as Christian Scripture

John W. Hilber

Before addressing the topic at hand, I need to qualify my title somewhat. The first part of the title, "We Are Not Apostles," sets up a distinction between how the apostles were authorized to read the Old Testament and how subsequent Christian readers are more constrained in their interpretive method. This is a binary choice to which I do not personally subscribe. I think there is a distinction between us and the apostles at the level of interpretive *infallibility*. But regarding exegetical *method*, I do not maintain any distinction between us and the apostles. Christians today read the Old Testament the same way as the apostles did, but our interpretations are not safeguarded as infallible. I do subscribe to a *sensus plenior* hermeneutic that is informed by a communication model called relevance theory, which I will explain below. So we, together with the apostles, are free to discover deeper meaning in the Old Testament that the *human* authors may not have appreciated at the time of writing but was intended all along by the *divine* author.

As for the second half of my title, the "Limits on Reading Ezekiel as Christian Scripture," relevance theory also constrains Christian interpretation. The original meaning, intended by the human author and understood by the original audience, was never set aside by the apostles, nor can it be disregarded in the Christian reading of the Old Testament. In this essay, I will first explain the hermeneutical foundation for my position by describing relevance theory. Second, I will apply this hermeneutic to the interpretation of Ezekiel's vision in Ezekiel 37:1-14. Finally, in order to illustrate how to read Ezekiel as Christian Scripture, I will discuss briefly other passages from Ezekiel that are actually used in the New Testament.

READING SCRIPTURE WITH RELEVANCE THEORY

Introducing relevance theory. Relevance theory is a communication model that explains how audiences arrive at interpretive conclusions.[1] While used in biblical studies for several decades, recently it has garnered the attention of New Testament scholars who grapple with the use of the Old Testament in the New.[2] In contrast to older models of

---

[1] This section of the essay adapts portions of John W. Hilber, *Old Testament Cosmology and Divine Accommodation: A Relevance Theory Approach* (Eugene, OR: Cascade, 2020), 7-13.

[2] For diverse treatment in biblical studies, see Ernst-August Gutt, *Relevance Theory: A Guide to Successful Communication in Translation* (New York: Summer Institute of Linguistics and United Bible Society, 1992); Stephen Pattemore, *The People of God in the Apocalypse: Discourse, Structure and Exegesis*, Society for New Testament Studies Monograph Series 128 (Cambridge: Cambridge University Press, 2004); Harriet Hill, *The Bible at the Crossroads: From Translation to Communication* (Manchester, UK: St. Jerome, 2006); Karen H. Jobes, "Relevance Theory and the Translation of Scripture," *JETS* 50 (2007): 773-93; Gene L. Green, "Relevance Theory and Biblical Interpretation," in *The Linguist as Pedagogue: Trends in the Teaching and Linguistic Analysis of the Greek New Testament*, ed. Stanley E. Porter and Matthew Brook O'Donnell (Sheffield: Sheffield Phoenix, 2009), 217-40; Green, "Relevance Theory and Theological Interpretation: Thoughts on Metarepresentation," *Journal of Theological Interpretation* 4 (2010): 799-812; Green, "Lexical Pragmatics and the Lexicon," *BBR* 23 (2012): 315-33. For helpful essays applying relevance theory specifically to the NT use of the OT, see Peter S. Perry, "Relevance Theory and Intertextuality," in *Exploring*

communication that focus on decoding dictionary meanings of words and their grammatical relationships, relevance theory attends to the role of contextual inference. Paul Grice observes that from assumptions shared between speaker and audience, listeners infer implications from a speaker's utterance.[3] From Grice's insight about inference, Paul Sperber and Deirdre Wilson developed their contribution to understanding how communication works.[4] For them, the crucial link between listeners and the inferences a speaker intends them to draw is contextual relevance. As this chapter explores the interpretation of Ezekiel 37, the spotlight will be on those assumptions shared between the prophet and his audience (their shared contextual relevance). But first, the terms *context* and *relevance* need further explanation.

Context. A cognitive environment is whatever a person is *capable* of being aware of. It could be something in the physical environment, the verbal context of a present discussion, religious beliefs, memories, or cultural assumptions. Within that environment, a context includes all the assumptions from that cognitive environment that a person draws on for interpretation.[5] In other words, *context* refers to the subset of the cognitive environment that is pertinent to a particular communication event. For example, the concept "stars" can be understood as galactic fusion reactors, celebrity persons, the ratings earned by a hotel, or even deities. All of these possibilities are aspects of cognitive environment. The ancient Near Eastern person could never imagine stars as galactic fusion reactors, and the average modern

---

Intertextuality: Diverse Strategies for New Testament Interpretation of Texts, ed. B. J. Oropeza and Steve Moyise (Eugene, OR: Cascade, 2016), 207-21; Steve Smith, "The Use of Criteria: A Proposal from Relevance Theory," in *Methodology in the Use of the Old Testament in the New: Context and Criteria*, ed. David Allen and Steve Smith (London: T&T Clark, 2020), 142-54.

[3] H. Paul Grice, "Logic and Conversation," in *Studies in the Way of Words* (Cambridge, MA: Harvard University Press, 1989), 1-143.

[4] Dan Sperber and Deirdre Wilson, *Relevance: Communication and Cognition* (Cambridge, MA: Harvard University Press, 1995).

[5] Sperber and Wilson, *Relevance*, 15-16, 38-40; Green, "Relevance Theory and Biblical Interpretation," 235.

scientist might not associate stars with deities. Their cognitive environments are quite different.

These examples illustrate how the mental accessibility of an object, event, or idea is important in communication. An individual's perception of something from the environment will vary from person to person, and some ideas are more manifest or salient than others for mental processing. For our study of Ezekiel 37, what matters to the meaning of the text is not only the words used but also the contextual assumptions shared between Ezekiel and his audience. What was foremost on the mind of Ezekiel's audience in the original context? This leads to consideration of relevance.

Relevance. Listeners expect to hear new information, support for existing beliefs, or correction of mistaken ideas, and they attempt to maximize the cognitive benefit from what they hear.[6] The speaker accommodates the listener's expectation of relevance. But in good communication, the speaker also crafts their utterance optimally. That is, they choose sufficient words to guide the audience to infer their meaning, but they avoid too many words so as not to place an undue burden on the listener. So Sperber and Wilson argue that good communication is *optimally relevant*. Sufficient words guide an audience so that they attend to a particular context (subset) of their cognitive environment, limiting the scope to a mutually understood pool of assumptions from which to infer meaning.[7] It is important to distinguish between *relevance* as the term is used in this communication model and *significance*, which is often used in hermeneutics for subsequent applications.[8] Relevance theory's term *relevance* identifies what is significant to the *original* speaker and audience but not necessarily subsequent audiences. Making associations beyond those imagined by the

---

[6]Ernst-August Gutt, *Translation and Relevance: Cognition and Context* (Manchester, UK: St. Jerome, 2000), 29.
[7]Sperber, and Wilson, *Relevance*, 61-63.
[8]See E. D. Hirsch Jr., *Validity in Interpretation* (New Haven, CT: Yale University Press, 1967), 8.

author is better called *external* relevance. But *meaning* pertains to the significance for the original audience only.

"Optimal" communication also leads to the prediction of how an audience arrives at a correct interpretation. In Sperber and Wilson's words, an audience "will follow a path of least effort in computing cognitive effects: [they will] Test interpretive hypotheses (disambiguations, reference resolutions, implications, etc.) in the order of accessibility [i.e., what first comes to mind]," and processing will "stop when [their] expectations of relevance are satisfied (or abandoned)."[9] They add, "When a hearer following the path of least effort arrives at an interpretation that satisfies his [or her] expectations of relevance, in the absence of contrary evidence, this is the most plausible hypothesis about the speaker's meaning."[10] Experimental testing has confirmed the outcomes predicted by relevance theory.[11] This principle is fundamental to assessing the most plausible interpretation of the meaning of Ezekiel 37, both in its original context and for the apostolic community, as discussed below.

Implicit versus implicated assumptions. For this essay, one other helpful concept related to contextual relevance is the distinction between contextual assumptions that are only *implicit* in the background of an idea and those that are *implicated* in the meaning of a specific text. I illustrate this with the utterance "There is a tree." Many assumptions are attached to the notion "tree." Trees are wood, have leaves, grow near water, provide shade, and lend themselves to climbing for a better view. If we are walking across a field in the heat of the day, and I say, "There is a tree," I am fully communicating the suggestion that we might find

---

[9]Deirdre Wilson and Dan Sperber, "Relevance Theory," in *The Handbook of Pragmatics*, ed. Laurence R. Horn and Gregory L. Ward (Oxford: Blackwell, 2004), 614; Dan Sperber and Deirdre Wilson, "Pragmatics," in *The Oxford Handbook of Contemporary Philosophy*, ed. Frank Jackson and Michael Smith (Oxford: Oxford University Press, 2005), 474-75.
[10]Wilson and Sperber, "Relevance Theory," 614.
[11]Jean-Baptiste van der Henst and Alexander Sperber, "Testing the Cognitive and Communicative Principles of Relevance," in *Meaning and Relevance*, ed. Deirdre Wilson and Dan Sperber (Cambridge: Cambridge University Press, 2012), 279-306.

shade from the sun underneath the tree. The assumption of shade is *implicated*. But other assumptions about trees regarding wood, water, leaves, or height are only *implicit* in the background but not brought into the intended meaning of my statement. These other assumptions are implicit but not implicated. All of the assumptions remain true, but the intended meaning of the utterance changes based on context. As discussed below, the distinction between implicit assumptions and implicated assumptions is essential to correctly understanding why bodily resurrection is *not* taught in Ezekiel 37.

Covenantal Assumptions Underlying Ezekiel's Message

The biblical covenants provide the relational framework through which God asserts his rule over creation and blesses humanity. Expressed in different terms, this means that the covenants mediate salvation history; all books of the biblical canon relate in a subordinate way to this purpose. It is the grand story of the universe: God's redemption of his creation to refashion a world in which he rules in fellowship with his creatures. In biblical terms, this is the irruption (inbreaking) of God's kingdom (Mt 3:2; 4:17; Mk 1:15; Acts 1:6; 28:31; Col 1:13; Rev 1:6; 11:15); and it unfolds through the covenants. The covenants set forth God's blueprint for how he is restoring the corruption of his creation.

After the catastrophic fall of humanity (Gen 3), culminating in the flood (Gen 6), Yahweh reestablished the order of creation through a covenant with Noah (Gen 8:20–9:17). This covenant preserves creation while God's redemptive plan unfolds. The rebellion of humanity continued, culminating in the debacle at Babel (Gen 11), after which Yahweh again intervened redemptively to call Abraham through the Abrahamic covenant (Gen 12:1-3; 15). This covenant provided for blessings to Abraham and his descendants, including a promised homeland, as well as blessings to all nations. The blessing on Abraham's descendants (eventuating in the nation Israel) became mediated through the Mosaic covenant, inaugurated on Mount Sinai (Ex 19–24, esp. Ex 19:5-6). Through the Mosaic covenant, God mediated his rule and blessing to humanity through the nation Israel. The establishment of a tabernacle/temple among God's chosen people facilitated the key ingredient of the Mosaic covenant—God's presence.

Also within the context of Israel's Mosaic covenant (Deut 17:14-20), the promise to Abraham of "kings" (Gen 17:6) unfolded as the Davidic covenant (2 Sam 7), which established David's descendants as the representatives of God's rule over the earth. But neither the Mosaic nor Davidic covenant provided the means by which the nation (or kings) might fulfill its covenantal responsibilities. God once again intervened through the New Covenant to ensure the ultimate consummation of his promises to Abraham (Jer 31; Ezek 36). The New Covenant provides what none of the other covenants entailed, the means by which people cling faithfully to God and walk in his ways so as to receive the blessings of the other covenants.

The reason this summary of the comprehensive covenant package is necessary is that the prophet Ezekiel alludes to these expectations in the announcement that follows the vision of dry bones. The covenant expectations and the resurrection of dry bones are contextually connected, since these expectations form the contextual assumptions drawn into the promised restoration of Ezekiel 37.

Contextual Relevance in Ezekiel 37:1-14

The vision of dry bones in the structure of the book. The general flow of Ezekiel's message through the book might be traced as follows: Ezekiel 1–24 is dominated by a message of judgment against God's rebellious people, both in exile and back home in Jerusalem. The prophet turns his attention against foreign nations in Ezekiel 25–32, warning that Israel's covenant Lord is the sovereign God of history, who will prevail. Therefore, Israel (and everyone else) must trust in him alone. Ezekiel 33 returns to the opening call to the prophet to be a watchman for the nation, calling it to repentance and trust (see Ezek 3). This functions as a sort of bookend capping off the judgment section of the book of Ezekiel, with Ezekiel 33:33 declaring vindication for the prophet when news arrives of the destruction of Jerusalem (Ezek 33:21).

After this point, Ezekiel's message turns from doom to hope; but he begins with cleanup of the leadership in Ezekiel 34. Yahweh will replace Israel's failed leadership with his own gentle presence. Within this context, covenant restoration is anticipated in the repeated naming of Israel as "my people" (see Exod 3:7, 10; Lev 26:12; Ezek 37:13, 27). The blessing of life in the land receives center stage in Ezekiel 35. But in order to make the way for restoration of physical blessing to Israel, the problem of the nation's characteristically rebellious heart must be resolved. In the covenant program of God, he promises through the prophets that God's Spirit will renew the hearts of his people to repair them spiritually as he restores them physically (Deut 30:1-6). As a corollary to physical restoration, spiritual transformation must also happen for God's name's sake (Ezek 36:22-23, 32). While Ezekiel speaks of physical promises to the nation in Ezekiel 35–36, this comes into primary focus in Ezekiel 37.

The inbreathing of S/spirit into the lifeless bones of Ezekiel's vision (Ezek 37:1-14) is a graphic illustration of the work of the Spirit in Ezekiel 36, and so Ezekiel 37 is a continuation of that message. After the vision of dry bones, Ezekiel 37 continues with a brief description of the whole covenant package—restored national unity under the blessing of Davidic leadership and the assurance of God's permanent presence among his people (Ezek 37:28). This presence is the absolute core of the covenant relationship. But before taking up that theme in the climactic temple vision of Ezekiel 40–48, the eschatological destruction of chaos embodied in Gog/Magog (Ezek 38–39) offers final assurance of God's capacity and commitment to remove forever the threats to Israel's well-being. Let us examine more carefully the place of Ezekiel 37:1-14 in context, using the lens of relevance theory.

Contextual relevance for Ezekiel's contemporaries. What was the contextual relevance of Ezekiel's vision of dry bones for his contemporaries? The traumatic awareness of Ezekiel's contemporaries, that life back home was destroyed, cast a shroud of vanished hope over their heads. In relevance-theory terms, this trauma was the most accessible assumption in the cognitive environment of the exilic audience. If one were expecting relevant speech from a prophet of God, it was any word that would address their trauma. Was there any hope of restoration for them or their children? Recall that listeners will stop processing information as soon as their expectations of relevance are met. In the context of Ezekiel 37:1-10 there is explicit reinforcement of their expectations of news about restoration, seen in the interpretation of the vision in Ezekiel 37:11-14. The vision is about restoration to the land. Other promises in context with Ezekiel 37:1-14 also cohere with this expectation. The vision of dry bones illustrates the work of the Spirit promised in the preceding Ezekiel 36 to vindicate God's reputation by restoring the exilic community. The vision is followed in Ezekiel 37:15-28 by more detailed description of national restoration under full covenantal blessing.

What about an expectation of bodily resurrection? In order for Ezekiel's vision to make any sense to his contemporaries, the concept of individual resurrection must have already been imaginable to them.[12] So the question is not whether a doctrine of individual resurrection existed in Ezekiel's cognitive environment. Rather, the question is *how* Ezekiel implicated that assumption in Ezekiel 37:1-14. Did he do so in

---

[12]Other texts suggest this was in the cognitive environment of ancient Israel, including resuscitation from death (1 Kings 17:17-24; 2 Kings 4:18-37; 13:20-21), disembodied emergence from the grave (1 Sam 28:8-14), and embodied restoration from the grave (Is 26:19; possibly Hos 6:1-3; Ps 49:14-15). See Daniel I. Block, *The Book of Ezekiel: Chapters 25–48*, NICOT (Grand Rapids, MI: Eerdmans, 1998), 386-87.

order to teach the doctrine of resurrection, or did he merely use the concept as a metaphor for his message about national restoration from exile? As noted above, the contextual relevance for Ezekiel's exilic audience was national restoration. The original audience would have understood the vision of dry bones as an illustration of physical restoration to covenant blessing because that is what satisfied their expectation of relevance and coheres with other language in the literary context. When Cyrus allowed exiled peoples to return to their homelands, the historical outworking confirmed this expected relevance for Ezekiel's immediate audience.

An important point for this essay is that a biblical text can mean *more* than what the original audience fully understood, but it cannot mean *less*. This point is fundamental to everything that follows. Exilic expectations of relevance from the book of Ezekiel cannot be disregarded by later communities without doing violence to the intended meaning of the text. If expectations for restoration to the blessings of the Mosaic and Davidic covenants were never to be realized, *as understood by the original audience of exiles*, then we are faced with a problem of divine deception. More on this below.

Contextual relevance for Ezekiel's canonical audience. The original audience of Ezekiel's preaching and writing is only the first horizon of communities for whom his prophecies were intended. Ezekiel spoke to his contemporaries and wrote for their benefit directly. But Ezekiel's prophecies were gathered and preserved into book form for secondary audiences as well, in what we might call a second horizon. This second horizon is composed of those who receive the book in its final form in contexts of living that differ from the original audience. This essay considers horizons of the postexilic community, the apostolic community, and the faith community today.[13]

---

[13] Due to space limitations, I have regretfully passed over the reception of Ezekiel in the ancient, medieval, Reformation, and early modern church; no small oversight, to be sure. But the apostolic and contemporary church queries satisfy the need of this essay. The dominant

Postexilic community expectations. Could the historical restoration from exile in the aftermath of Cyrus's decree have fully satisfied the original audience's expectations? There was return from exile and the rebuilding of a sacred city with a temple. The allusion to Ezekiel's temple vision (Ezek 40:2-4) in Zechariah 2:1-2 is one demonstration of continuity between the exilic and postexilic communities' expectations for physical restoration in the land, whether a reconstructed temple or a blessed city.[14] But postexilic prophecy and history is sufficient to show that as generations passed on, the nation as a whole, as envisioned in Ezekiel 36, was not careful to obey God's statutes (Ezek 36:27). So the exiles who returned to the land did experience the prophetic promises in some measure, but other contingencies played out historically so as to delay the consummation of promise.[15] In contemporary parlance, the gap between what the believing community experiences immediately and what they continue to wait for is framed as the "now but not yet" tension.

Apostolic community expectations. As with all of the Old Testament, it is important to read the book of Ezekiel in view of the incarnation, death, and resurrection of God in Jesus the Messiah (Lk 24:27). Did the apostolic experience with Jesus and his teaching change in any way their expectations of relevance from that of the exilic faithful or

---

interpretation of the ancient church viewed Ezek 37:1-14 as a prophecy of bodily resurrection. See, e.g., Kenneth Stevenson and Michael Glerup, eds., *Ezekiel, Daniel*, Ancient Christian Commentary on Scripture: Old Testament 13 (Downers Grove, IL: IVP Academic, 2008), 120-24. The Reformation tradition, in its recapture of meaning intended in the original context, considered both resurrection and restoration of Israel to the land and ultimately to faith. See, e.g., Carl Beckwith, ed., *Ezekiel, Daniel*, Reformation Commentary on Scripture: Old Testament 12 (Downers Grove, IL: IVP Academic, 2012), 178-87.

[14]See Mark J. Boda, *The Book of Zechariah*, NICOT (Grand Rapids, MI: Eerdmans, 2016), 172-76; Michael R. Stead, *The Intertextuality of Zechariah 7–8*, LHBOTS 506 (London: T&T Clark, 2009), 109-13. I thank Julie Dykes for directing me to Stead's book.

[15]On the subject of contingent prophecy, written by someone thoroughly committed to a Calvinist framework, see Richard L. Pratt Jr., "Historical Contingencies and Biblical Predictions," in *The Way of Wisdom: Essays in Honor of Bruce K. Waltke*, ed. J. I. Packer and Sven K. Soderland (Grand Rapids, MI: Zondervan, 2000), 180-203. More broadly considered is the important article by Chisholm. See Robert B. Chisholm Jr., "When Prophecy Appears to Fail, Check Your Hermeneutic," *JETS* 53 (2010): 561-77.

subsequent postexilic community? Perhaps most telling is the question the apostles asked Jesus shortly before his ascension: "Will you at this time restore the kingdom to Israel?" Jesus answers, "It is not for you to know times or seasons that the Father has fixed by his own authority" (Acts 1:6-7). In relevance-theory terms, the apostles had no other assumptions on which to draw other than what had been handed down to them, namely, physical restoration of national Israel. More telling is that Jesus did not correct any of these assumptions; rather, he placed the fulfillment of such expectations of relevance into the future. Relevance theory predicts that communication offers new information, support for existing assumptions, or correction. Jesus does not correct the content of the apostles' expectations but rather their assumption as to the time of fulfillment.[16]

The sermon preached by Peter not long after Pentecost expresses the same expectation: "Repent therefore, and turn back, that your sins may be blotted out, that times of refreshing may come from the presence of the Lord, and that he may send the Christ appointed for you, Jesus, whom heaven must receive until the time for restoring all the things about which God spoke by the mouth of his holy prophets long ago" (Acts 3:19-21). The promises spoken by God through the prophet Ezekiel about restoration from exile to covenant blessing are included here. Recall that the language used of covenant blessing in Ezekiel 37 could contain *more* meaning than understood by the original audience, but it cannot mean *less*. Like Ezekiel's original audience, the apostles still expected kingdom life in the land for Israel with a Davidic king who mediated peaceful prosperity, enjoyed in the presence of God. Without contrary clarification from the language of Peter's sermon, his audience would have shared the same expectations for a restored kingdom as Ezekiel's audience. Recall the quotation of Wilson and

---

[16]See Darrell L. Bock, *Acts*, Baker Exegetical Commentary on the New Testament (Grand Rapids, MI: Baker, 2007), 62, 177 for Acts 3:19-21 below.

Sperber cited above, that "when a hearer following the path of least effort arrives at an interpretation that satisfies his [or her] expectations of relevance, *in the absence of contrary evidence*, this is the most plausible hypothesis about the speaker's meaning" (emphasis added).

Faith community today. There are two common but quite opposite interpretive traditions in the contemporary church regarding Israel's restoration.[17] One approach follows from a belief that ethnic Israel has been superseded as the special people of God by the church, who are now the heirs of Abraham by spiritual descent (e.g., Rom 9:8; Gal 6:16; 1 Pet 2:9), without geopolitical expectations. In this view, the physical-land promises to national Israel are no longer expected, contrary to what Ezekiel's audience had hoped. So, the Bible has no bearing on the question of modern Israel's right to a national homeland. But as stated above, there needs to be satisfaction of expected relevance for Ezekiel's contemporaries, the postexilic community, and the apostles. This necessitates restoration of the Promised Land inhabited by physical Israel. There may be *more* enriched meaning than imagined even by Ezekiel himself, but meaning cannot be diminished or rendered *less* than what the original speaker and audience legitimately inferred. Anything *less* constitutes divine deception.

Another view regarding Israel's future is that some sort of physical restoration of ethnic Israel to the land promised to Abraham is not only necessary but that modern-day Israel is the first stages of this fulfillment. But this application to contemporary international politics is more complicated than typically assumed. First, only a genuine prophet has the authority to declare what God is doing in current events. The United Nations authorization of a national homeland for Jews may or may not be a stage in the fulfillment of Old Testament promises. More important is the realization that modern-day Israel is a secular state,

---

[17]The following two paragraphs reproduce with minor changes the sidebar "Modern Israel in the Land," in John W. Hilber, *Ezekiel: A Focused Commentary for Preaching and Teaching* (Eugene, OR: Cascade, 2019), 211-12.

and from the standpoint of Christian theology, the people as a whole have no allegiance to Israel's Messiah, Jesus. Consequently, the nation is not following covenantal stipulations necessary to rightfully enjoy blessing (see Ezek 36:16-38).

Those who advocate a permissive political posture toward modern-day Israel should be as eager to apply Old Testament legal and prophetic expectations of covenant faithfulness and justice as they are to declare blessing. What of the prophetic pronouncement of covenant curses for faithlessness and injustice? Faithful Christian preaching requires application of God's Word without respect to person or nation (e.g., Acts 7:1-53). Consequently, without contemporary, prophetic authorization on how to configure political boundaries *today*, in the Middle East or on any continent, Christians must exercise caution before declaring what God is or is not doing on the geopolitical landscape. What is clear from Scripture is the mandate to uphold in a consistent manner the Bible's message of righteousness and justice. In linguistic terms, this modern interpretation makes an unwarranted reference assignment from reconnected dry bones in Ezekiel 37 to the modern state of Israel. Furthermore, it derives modern policy decisions based on an interpretation of the biblical text that is not warranted by expectations of Ezekiel and his contemporaries. This popular view confuses the meaning of the text and its application. Even if modern Israel's restoration is the first stage anticipated by Ezekiel, the significance of this for international policy is not as simple as carte blanche approval of whatever modern-day Israel does.

Ezekiel 37:1-14 and Theological Reflection: Resurrection Revisited

How does relevance theory explain theological reflection on Old Testament texts in the light of New Testament revelation? Relevance theory predicts that listeners or readers interpret an oral or written discourse so as to maximize relevance. Unless enlightened by the speaker with new information, the audience draws on whatever assumptions are available from their cognitive environment in order to infer meaning, and they stop mental processing when their expectations of relevance are met. But as the community of God's people experiences more and more of redemptive history, as well as new revelation, they acquire a broader and deeper set of assumptions about the nature of God's past activity and revelation as well. Their cognitive environment has expanded, allowing inferences not possible to earlier generations of believers. The old texts can be read with enriched meaning.

A modern analogy is a *Looney Tunes* cartoon. The children laugh at what the script writers have put in the cartoon, and the parents watching alongside their children also laugh, but with a much broader and more mature set of assumptions from which to infer meaning. The parents laugh at things intended by the script writers that are missed by the children because of their lesser contextual experience. One might say that the meaning of the script is fuller (*sensus plenior*) for the adults. That does not negate what is understood by the children. Let us apply this to Ezekiel 37 and the question of the resurrection. While bodily resurrection is not implicated in the text, can the text be read theologically so as to affirm the necessity of bodily resurrection?

In *eschatological perspective*, the regathering and restoration of Israel necessarily involves individual, bodily resurrection in order to satisfy the hope of Ezekiel and his contemporaries, together with the myriads of faithful Jews reading Ezekiel who died since the return from exile. While Ezekiel 37 does not implicate this meaning in the original context, such a belief is consistent with Ezekiel's message and could be drawn in as secondary support for the doctrine of eschatological resurrection. Ezekiel's informative intention was not to teach individual, bodily resurrection. But, as history played out and the generation of returned exiles did not experience the full promised restoration of Ezekiel 37, subsequent generations of believers down to the present day correctly inferred the necessity of a promise of bodily resurrection, especially in the aftermath of Jesus' resurrection. In the absence of explicit allusion to Ezekiel 37 for resurrection teaching in the New Testament, we could still derive a reasonable, albeit not infallible, theological construct. But the use of Ezekiel 37–48 in John's Apocalypse (Rev 20–22) renders such theological inference more reliable, even if it is rather surprising that more explicit allusion to Ezekiel 37 in conjunction with bodily resurrection is not found in the New Testament.

Ezekiel in the New Testament

The book of Revelation. As just noted, the cluster of events described in Revelation 20–22 follows a similar sequence to images in Ezekiel 37–48. This eschatological reading of these chapters from Ezekiel extends the Old Testament prophet's visions into the distant future, beyond the near-term expectations of the prophet Ezekiel's community. Since I do not interpret Ezekiel's temple vision in its original context as referring to a physical temple, the spiritualized interpretation in Revelation 21–22 is not problematic for my view.[18] The defeat of Gog and Magog in Ezekiel is similarly couched in highly symbolic language, the historical referents of which are highly underdetermined, and the forces of chaos more generally are primarily in focus.[19] But these are not the only allusions to the book of Ezekiel in John's Apocalypse.

John's vision of the throne room in Revelation 4–5 corresponds in numerous respects to Ezekiel's visionary experiences.[20] The vision given John accommodates his expectations of such an encounter based on his knowledge of Ezekiel. However, the revelation of the character

---

[18] Hilber, *Ezekiel*, 244-46.
[19] Hilber, *Ezekiel*, 233-37.
[20] G. K. Beale and Sean M. McDonough, "Revelation," in *Commentary on the New Testament Use of the Old Testament*, ed. G. K. Beale and D. A. Carson (Grand Rapids, MI: Baker Books, 2007), 1107-9.

of God is appropriately expanded in John's vision to incorporate trinitarian aspects. The resurrection of the two witnesses in Revelation 11:11 possibly alludes to Ezekiel 37:9-10, but the nature of historical reference and fulfillment of Ezekiel's imagery is more difficult to determine. But the teaching here is clear that resurrection hope encourages bold witness to the gospel today.

The Gospels. The most explicit correlation between the ministry of Jesus and the book of Ezekiel pertains to the image of shepherd from Ezekiel 34. Jesus identifies himself with Ezekiel's promised shepherd (Jn 10:1-18; see Mk 6:34), an identification that unites in one person both the expectation for Yahweh himself as shepherd and the expectation of a descendent of David (esp. "I myself," Ezek 34:11, 15, 20; and "you are my sheep . . . I am your God," Ezek 34:31; "David," Ezek 34:24; see Ezek 37:24-25). Unlike the self-serving leaders of Ezekiel's day, Jesus feeds his sheep and lays down his life for them. The point for modern preaching is that the character issues addressed in Ezekiel's critique of leaders, as well as God's promise to help, are the same today.

Not only do the promises of Ezekiel find enriched meaning in the light of the New Testament, but words of judgment can also apply. This is clear from Jesus' rebuke of his generation recorded in Mark 8:18. His rebuke corresponds in formula to Ezekiel's accusation of his contemporaries in Ezekiel 12:2. This is not fulfillment language; rather, it illustrates how the things that angered God in the days of ancient Israel continue to anger him regardless of which generation. The revelation of the character of God as judge in Ezekiel finds application to new horizons of audiences. This is not a change in meaning. It is an application of new significance where the dynamics of the divine-human relationship remain similar across the ages. This dynamic works for accusations of judgment against Christians whenever their behavior is analogous in some way to the enemies of the kingdom in the Old Testament. There is "no condemnation," to be sure (Rom 8:1), but there is divine displeasure (Eph 4:30) and the possibility of discipline (1 Cor 11:29-30; Heb 12:7-11).

The same principle of analogy applies to the gospel call. Jesus' words to Nicodemus allude to language from Ezekiel 36–37. The heart must be transformed by the Spirit and metaphorically cleansed as if by water (Ezek 36:25-27; Jn 3:5). The Spirit blows from wherever he comes to enliven the spiritually dead (Ezek 37:9-10; Jn 3:6-8). What was true of ancient Israelites remains true by analogy of every person today.

Letters of Paul. The apostle Paul cites Ezekiel in several passages, and his use of the Old Testament provides further illustration of valid application for today. For example, Paul applies Ezekiel's promises that the God of glory will dwell among his people as a temple (2 Cor 6:16; Ezek 37:27). This is not a denial of relevance to the descendants of the exilic community, but it is a startling inclusion of Gentiles into the community of God's people.[21] This is an example of how the text can mean *more* but not *less* than understood by the original audience. In 1 Thessalonians 4:8, Paul calls the Christian community to moral purity (holiness), a similar concern using purity language as expressed by Ezekiel.[22] It is possible that Paul cites Ezekiel 37:14 here, which would be an analogous application of Ezekiel's vision of restoration. In both contexts God sends the Holy Spirit to his people for their sanctification (see Titus 2:14).[23]

Lessons for Preaching and Teaching Today

Rooted in linguistics, relevance theory supports interpretations that honor the expectations of relevance held by Ezekiel's original audience. In none of the examples cited above do the apostles allude to Ezekiel in

---

[21]Peter Balla, "2 Corinthians," in Beale and Carson, *Commentary on the New Testament Use*, 770, 773.
[22]Jeffrey A. D. Weima, "1–2 Thessalonians," in Beale and Carson, *Commentary on the New Testament Use*, 878.
[23]Philip H. Towner, "1–2 Timothy and Titus," in Beale and Carson, *Commentary on the New Testament Use*, 914-15.

a way that denies these expectations. We can practice the same interpretive method as the apostles, only without the same assurance of infallibility for our interpretation. The "not yet" aspects of Ezekiel's promises were still expected at the time of the apostles, albeit deferred to the future, with surprising enrichment for Gentile believers. But the promises expected by Old Testament Israel were not diminished. The New Testament shows that new significance in application is found for analogous circumstances but not change in meaning.

1. The accusations against sin are as applicable today as they were in Ezekiel's day. What defiled the name of God in ancient days (Ezek 36:22-23, 31-32) and led to the condition of Israel's judgment in Ezekiel 37 continues to damage his reputation and leads to judgment of all humanity today.

2. The vision of dry bones illustrates the desiccated condition of God's human creatures both physically and spiritually. By the prophet Ezekiel's and Israel's own admission, their condition was hopeless (Ezek 37:3, 11), and so is ours apart from the action of God's Spirit. Spiritual restoration is concomitant with any restoration—we must be born again.

3. The promises of God for Israel's restoration have elements directly applicable to Abraham's physical descendants who, like Abraham (Gen 17:1), sought after God in order to walk in his ways. As just noted, the consummation of these promises is necessary in order to vindicate God in the eyes of all humanity (Ezek 36:23, 36). But there are aspects to his redemptive work that either directly or by analogy apply to every man and woman today. Israel's Davidic king is our king (Ezek 37:24-25; Mt 2:2). The New Covenant provides the renewing work of the Spirit for all who believe, both Jew and Gentile (Ezek 37:9-10; 2 Cor 3:6; Rom 8:2-4). In this covenant, Israel's ultimate peace is the assurance of our peace (Ezek 37:26; Eph 2:15). By way of theological inference, their restoration to the land necessitates a bodily resurrection of the faithful of all ages, including our hope of resurrection.

4. The spiritual and physical restoration of Israel is the starting point for the restoration of the entire created order, alluded to with Eden imagery in Ezekiel 36 (Ezek 36:35; see Ezek 47) and so included in their hope of covenant consummation. At the center of the whole new creation is the presence of the Lord, promised in Ezekiel 37:28 (see Ezek 48:35) and alluded to in Revelation 22:1-5. This is the ideal world that Ezekiel projects onto our screens, so to speak. We are invited to step into that world now, in order to live in the hope of the things not yet seen.[24]

---

[24]The notion that Scripture projects God's ideal world is developed by Abraham Kuruvilla, *Privilege the Text!* (Chicago: Moody, 2013), especially 39-54.

13

EMULATING THE APOSTLES

Reading Ezekiel as Christian Scripture in the Footsteps of the Apostles

WILLIAM R. OSBORNE

I ONCE HEARD THE STORY of a seminary professor who took his class to a graveyard for a field trip. The point of the trip was to have each student preach for a few minutes staring out at the tombstones. The professor then wrapped up the lesson gathering by everyone together and saying, "This, friends, is the challenge of preaching. Proclaiming the word of God over dead people, believing that *this* word can produce new life." Whether the account was apocryphal or not, I cannot say. However, the revised modern-day reenactment based on Ezekiel 37:1-14 reveals the way these significant verses have worked their way deeply into Christian life and imagination.

The Christian community maintains long and various traditions of interpreting the prophet's valley vision.[1] Indeed, Jerome writes in the

---

[1] Note the examples provided by Iain Duguid in this volume.

fifth century, "The vision is a famous one and is celebrated by being read in all the churches of Christ."[2] Perhaps the variation of readings stems from the rich imagery and symbolism of the passage, along with the fact that the text is not explicitly referenced in the New Testament. We might say the vision is clearly in the key of Christian theology, but the christological melody is polyphonic. It is precisely for these same reasons that the passage makes an excellent case study for the present project exploring how to read Ezekiel as Christian Scripture. Indeed, the challenge for Christians in reading and studying Ezekiel is quite real. Having taught semester-long courses on the book for several years now, I can attest to the regular disorientation experienced by my Christian students as they wrestle with notions of divine judgment, striking metaphorical imagery, and arresting visions of the glory of God. As we explore Ezekiel 37:1-14, along with a few other passages, my hope is that this chapter and even this section of the book will help students of the prophets grow in their ability to navigate some of the theological challenges encountered in the book and reflect more deeply on how Ezekiel bears witness to the Father, Son, and Holy Spirit.

CAN WE READ LIKE THE APOSTLES?

Given the varied approaches to the Old Testament Scriptures in the New Testament, it is perhaps a little dangerous to draw quick-and-dirty principles about how the New Testament authors read the Old Testament. However, there are consistent patterns that are helpful for guiding our approach to Ezekiel 37.

1. The New Testament authors believed the Old Testament Scriptures were fulfilled in Christ, both in their present days and the eschaton.[3]

---

[2]Kenneth Stevenson and Michael Glerup, *Ezekiel-Daniel*, Ancient Christian Commentary on Scripture Old Testament 13 (Downers Grove, IL: IVP Academic, 2008), 122.

[3]"The New Testament's modification of Jewish apocalyptic rested upon the perception that in the mission, death, and resurrection of Jesus the Messiah the age to come, the future kingdom of God, had become present in hidden form in the midst of the present evil age, although its public

2. The New Testament authors believed that the story of Israel found its fulfillment in Jesus, to the extent that Jesus redefined the people of God as those responding in faith to the gospel.

3. The New Testament authors believed that the Old Testament Scriptures were God's authoritative revelation of himself and therefore theologically pointed toward the future unfolding of his redemptive plan.

4. The New Testament writers perceived solidarity between Old Testament Israel and the New Covenant people of God, in that both are held together in the fulfilling and founding work of Jesus the Christ, applied respectively.

5. These foundational theological commitments led the New Testament writers to freely read the Old Testament Scriptures—persons, events, and institutions—as being typologically fulfilled or figuratively corresponding to realities perceived and understood in the New Covenant era.

I would argue that not only can we read like the apostles, but we must. Some have raised hesitation to reading the Old Testament prophets through the same apostolic lenses mentioned above for various reasons. Those reading with a more dispensationalist approach might argue that to take the Old Testament seriously historically (and literally) is to see the prophetic word given to Israel as only to be fulfilled in Israel (either in the past or in some eschatological fulfillment for a future Jewish community). Others state that we can see that Jesus fulfills these promises given to Israel, but only the apostles have the authority as inspired authors to assert such "deeper meanings" or "extra theological layers" (i.e., *sensus plenior*) to a text that does not appear to clearly point toward these

---

manifestation awaited the Parousia of Jesus." See E. Earle Ellis, *History and Interpretation in New Testament Perspective*, Biblical Interpretation Series 54 (Atlanta: Society of Biblical Literature, 2001), 114.

connections.[4] I think here of Paul's assertion that Christ is the Rock in Exodus 17 (1 Cor 10:4), or perhaps Peter's use of temple imagery applied to the New Testament people of God as "living stones" (1 Pet 2:4). Knowing what they knew about Jesus as the Messiah, Paul and Peter reflected on the Old Testament Scriptures in ways that provided a christological intention to a text that would not necessarily be evident on first glance. It was only through a further, christological reflection on their sacred Scriptures that such interpretations emerged.

So, are we—twenty-first-century Christians—permitted to read the Old Testament finding these types of christological parallels? If so, how do we know if we have gone too far? Can you go too far? Are we prepared to accept the view of a particular biblical scholar I recently heard say something like, "If someone's reading of the Old Testament gets them to Jesus, I'm not sure we can say that it is a 'bad' reading"?

To say that we are free to read like the apostles is not to embrace a hermeneutical posture of anything goes. The New Testament authors are not freestyling their way through the Old Testament in some kind of desperate attempt to demonstrate who Jesus is and how the kingdom has come. Their engagement with the Old Testament is rooted in a tripartite hermeneutical configuration that moves through the categories of historical situatedness of God's providential acts through and for his people, intertextual engagement with the revealed and authoritative Word of God, and theological development focused on Jesus as God's Messiah.[5] These hermeneutical categories are not always in a

---

[4]See Richard N. Longenecker, *Biblical Exegesis in the Apostolic Period*, 2nd ed. (Grand Rapids, MI: Eerdmans, 1999), 188.

[5]Kevin J. Vanhoozer and Daniel J. Treier present a three-part interpretive framework: canon, creed, and culture. The three categories espoused in this chapter seem to be wrapped up, however, in their first two components of theological exegesis—canon and creed. Culture, in their framework, speaks more to the historical awareness and presuppositions of the modern church interpreting the text. See their helpful chapter on theological interpretation of Scripture in *Theology and the Mirror of Scripture: A Mere Evangelical Account* (Downers Grove, IL: IVP Academic, 2015), 158-91.

fixed sequence or three easy steps to follow, but they are perpetually present in the apostolic reading of the Old Testament.[6]

Too often in discussions about reading the Old Testament as Christians, history and theology end up pitted against each other in the hermeneutical ring. Some would argue that reading the Old Testament with an eye to Christ devalues the "discrete witness of the Old Testament," and the theological interpretation of the Old Testament presents a fundamental challenge to the historical nature of the text.[7] Others would contend that historical inquiries (both authorial and textual) are mere holdovers of a lingering historical positivism that needs to be put to rest. However, neither of these extremes is necessary or helpful in approaching the Old Testament as Christian Scripture. As D. A. Carson helpfully writes, "*Historical* reading is determinative for a great deal of *theological* interpretation."[8]

Carson's care and caution in not positioning history and theology against each other is laudable and likely reveals that, for evangelical interpreters, the greater misunderstanding is with the concept of history than theology. Christians have been reading the Old Testament theologically for millennia; it is only within the past few hundred years that our understanding of history has been significantly defined or redefined. Kevin Vanhoozer and Daniel Treier note, "The real challenge concerns how much modern academic history-writing tends toward naturalism, affecting biblical theology's treatment of historical texts and events."[9] A Christian—that is, confessional—approach to the Major Prophets requires a theological ascent to the incarnation: God

---

[6]See William R. Osborne, "Introduction," in *The Law, the Prophets, and the Writings: Studies in Evangelical Old Testament Hermeneutics in Honor of Duane A. Garrett* (Nashville: B&H Academic, 2021), 1-27.

[7]Brevard Childs, *Biblical Theology of the Old and New Testaments: Theological Reflection on the Christian Bible* (Minneapolis: Augsburg, 1993). Note the concerns raised in John C. Poirier, "'Theological Interpretation' and Its Contradistinctions," *Tyndale Bulletin* 61, no. 1 (2010): 105-18.

[8]D. A. Carson, "Theological Interpretation of Scripture, Yes, But . . . ," in *Theological Commentary: Evangelical Perspectives*, ed. Michael Allen (London: T&T Clark, 2011), 189-90.

[9]Vanhoozer and Treier, *Theology and the Mirror of Scripture*, 172-73.

became flesh and dwelt among us. In many ways, the prophetic word of the Old Testament prepares the ways for a divine word embodied in a human vehicle (see Ezek 2–4; Heb 1:1-2). Such theological positions drive Christians toward a view of the world that is divinely infused and theologically committed. Epistemologically, there is no neutral ground—history is theological.

How then, do we read like the apostles? Is there anything distinct about approaching the text in this way, over against common contemporary evangelical interpretations? In answer to these questions, the next section walks through Ezekiel 37:1-14 attempting to demonstrate the importance and significance of holding fast to the apostolic commitment to text, history, *and* theology. Intentional effort has been made not to subdivide the sections based on history and theology, in an effort to reduce the supposed categorical separation between them. Indeed, Ezekiel 37:1-14 was a profoundly *theological message* from its origin in the sixth century BC. Following the structural elements of the canonical text, we will explore the historical, intertextual, and theological nature of this iconic passage.

Reading Ezekiel 37:1-14 Like the Apostles

Ezekiel 37:1-10: The valley vision. The people of God, in this passage referred to by the historic moniker "Israel," are cut off from the land of promise granted to them by their God. We hear the desperation of the people in their voiced complaint in Ezekiel 37:11: "They say, 'Our bones are dried up, and our hope is lost; we are indeed cut off.'" Reading the vision in light of this statement, we understand the bones of the valley are Israel's bones—laid bare and dry. The image of bones scattered around has already been employed in the book, as the prophet describes the coming judgment of the people for their worship of idols in Ezekiel 6:5. In the ancient world, the idea of a death without burial was frequently associated with covenant curses, not unlike those spelled out in Deuteronomy 28.[10] The vision captures the resultant covenant curses of Judah's idolatry and the horrific theological reality that follows—spiritual death.

The Lord asks Ezekiel, "Can these bones live?" Perhaps struggling to make sense of the divine inquiry, the prophet's answer appears somewhat noncommittal, or even evasive, "Oh Lord, you know."[11] But Ezekiel may not be trying to sidestep a painful question as much as confess his belief in the God who has proven himself to be truly inscrutable. Looking out on a valley of death in the midst of exile as God's chosen people is disorienting enough to lead anyone to begin to question all of their assumptions. Instead of viewing the question as a test of Ezekiel's faith in "with God all things are possible" theology, we are perhaps on firmer ground to see Ezekiel's response as one of absolute certainty in the God who gives life and takes it away.[12]

The initial command is to prophesy over the bones—"hear the word of the Lord." The people's choice to ignore God's word led them into exile, but hearing it will be the only thing to bring them out—the word of God work's in concert with the breath of God. Throughout Scripture the word of God is associated with the work of the Spirit. Even in the opening chapters of Ezekiel, the prophet is commanded by the word of God and then propelled to obedience by the Spirit. The word *rûaḥ* is a significant term throughout the book, and perhaps nowhere is this more evident than Ezekiel 37, where it is employed ten times in Ezekiel 37:1-14. The full semantic range of the Hebrew term is employed as the vision describes the "breath" of the army, the four "winds" of the earth, and the "spirit" of God that will be placed in his people. The vitality and life of this new people ultimately flows from the source of all power and life—God.

---

[10]Daniel I. Block, *Ezekiel 25–48*, NICOT (Grand Rapids, MI: Eerdmans, 1998), 77-78.
[11]Leslie C. Allen, *Ezekiel 20–48*, WBC 29 (Dallas: Word, 1990), 185.
[12]Christopher J. H. Wright, *The Message of Ezekiel: A New Heart and Spirit*, BST (Downers Grove, IL: IVP Academic, 2001), 305.

Many commentators have noted the two-part structure of the vision; Block writes, "Despite some significant differences in the two parts, the parallelism between vv. 4-8 and 9-10 is obvious."[13] While the structure may be obvious, its significance is not. Are we to understand this as a climactic or rhetorical device? Or simply observe that it makes for good drama?[14] If there is any prophet that tends toward the dramatic, it would be Ezekiel. Or is the vision guiding our attention back to the foundations of creation in Genesis 2, where God forms and then breathes his animating breath into the man's nostrils? Both of these aspects of the passage are valid, and neither are they mutually exclusive. There is a rhetorical development that highlights the reception of the divine Spirit as a shocking and unexpected act of re-creation.

The two-part structure of the vision is also reminiscent of the two-part nature of the old and new covenants—or, as Robert Jenson says, "A penultimate act of God and the ultimate act of God are seen together."[15] Israel—created by God—lived as God's people for generations without knowing him and recognizing him as their God. They were a covenant people set apart but not indwelled by the Spirit of God. The first act of re-creation demonstrates the power but incompleteness of this image of God's people. Ever since the fall of creation, humanity has been characterized by mortality and death. Here, the dead bones of Israel come to represent destruction that will befall all those who rebel and reject the covenant-making God. As Wright states, "Resurrection for Israel anticipated resurrection for all."[16] An

---

[13] Block, *Ezekiel 25–48*, 375.

[14] Michael V. Fox states: "One is reminded of the magician who invariably 'fails' once or twice in attempting his grand finale in order to intensify suspense and to focus attention on the climactic success to follow." Fox, "The Rhetoric of Ezekiel's Vision of the Valley of Bones," *Hebrew Union College Annual* 51 (1980): 11.

[15] Robert W. Jenson, *Ezekiel*, Brazos Theological Commentary on the Bible (Grand Rapids, MI: Brazos, 2019), 284. Interestingly, Odell also notes that the language points toward a two-stage process, only she posits the stages are the exodus from Egypt compared to the settlement in the land. See Margaret S. Odell, *Ezekiel*, Smyth & Helwys Commentary (Macon, GA: Smyth & Helwys, 2005), 455.

[16] Wright, *Message of Ezekiel*, 310.

amazing transformation takes place from bones to corpses, but the work is still unfinished.

The second prophecy calls forth the breath/wind from the "four winds" to enter the dead bodies and produce life. The previous chapter has already addressed Yahweh's future intentions in transforming his people by causing his Spirit to dwell in them (Ezek 36:22), and it is not coincidental that they will also receive a heart of flesh alongside this transformation. The imperative given to the prophet to summons the "four winds" highlights the creative and universal power of God to harness what seems uncontrollable for his own sovereign purposes. The army of corpses is transformed by the prophetic word, as the divine breath/wind (i.e., Spirit) fills them and brings them to their feet, similar to what Ezekiel experienced in earlier visions (e.g., Ezek 2:1; 3:24). The arrival of the Spirit as a source of life finds its parallel in Ezekiel 37:12-14 as the prophet offers further reflection on the dry-bones vision and response to Israel's complaint.

Ezekiel 37:12-14: A new life for a restored people. The final element of the current passage is the declaration to the people that God is going to bring them out of their graves. The prevailing notion of resurrection in the ancient world is that the idea was developed in later Judaism through interactions with Persia and Zoroastrianism.[17] Still others propose an earlier association, perhaps associated with dying-and-rising gods of Canaan. The ministries of Elijah and Elisha certainly speak to the power of the spirit-endowed prophet to bring life out of death (1 Kings 17:17-24; 2 Kings 4:31-37; 13:20-21), and Hannah's song in 1 Samuel 2:6 declares, "The LORD kills and brings to life; he brings down to Sheol and raises up."[18]

Needless to say, the preexilic traditions of the Old Testament leave much to be desired in the way of answering questions about the

---

[17] See Block's helpful survey of proposed backgrounds for Ezekiel's view of resurrection (Block, *Ezekiel 25-48*, 384).

[18] See Shaul Bar, "Resurrection or Miraculous Cures? The Elijah and Elisha Narrative Against Its Ancient Near Eastern Background," *Old Testament Essays* 24, no. 1 (2011): 9-18.

afterlife, but it seems likely that Sheol was not perceived to be the eternal destiny of the righteous, whose future was inseparably tied to the presence of God.[19] Indeed, Leilah Bronner notes, "Diverse expressions of the resurrection motif were already present as early as the Ninth and Eighth Centuries, becoming increasingly explicit and more fully developed beginning in the exilic period of the Sixth Century."[20] While the idea of bodily resurrection is not prevalent in the Old Testament, it would be incorrect to believe that the notion is completely absent.[21]

The vivid resurrection language of Ezekiel 37:12-14 perhaps drives us the with the greatest force to reflect on this passage as Christian Scripture. But the question that faces interpreters is, How and when is this picture of resurrection fulfilled? Is this a prophetic statement about the regathering of Judah to Jerusalem after the exile? Or, as Walther Zimmerli writes with pronounced clarity, "In contrast to all these later interpretations of Ezek 37 it must now once more be finally and unambiguously stated that Ezek 37:1-14 . . . expresses the event of the restoration and the regathering of the politically defeated all-Israel."[22]

While Zimmerli's conclusion about the original setting of the vision appears in many ways correct, it is left to be determined what the restoration and regathering of all Israel looks like and when it takes place. Does a national reading of the vision preclude any further implications about bodily resurrection? In the ancient mind, did the categories of corporate life and individual life separate as cleanly as they do today? Were the restoration of a nation and belief in life from death such separate cognitive domains that they had to be forged together metaphorically?

---

[19]T. Desmond Alexander, "The Old Testament View of Life After Death," *Themelios* 11, no. 2 (1986): 45.
[20]Leila Leah Bronner, "The Resurrection Motif in the Hebrew Bible: Allusions or Illusions?," *Jewish Bible Quarterly* 30 (2002): 145.
[21]Block, *Ezekiel 25–48*, 387.
[22]Walther Zimmerli, *Ezekiel 2*, trans. J. D. Martin, Hermeneia (Philadelphia: Fortress, 1983), 264.

The statement in Ezekiel 37:11 indicates that Ezekiel's audience already understood that their national status was best reflected by the terms of physical death. In his study "The Origin of the Idea of Resurrection," Leonard Greenspoon writes, "We have no doubt that those scholars are correct who see in Ezekiel's Vision a hope for national restoration addressed to his fellow exiles. We also have no doubt that they are incorrect when they limit Ezekiel's message to only this."[23] The vision of the recreated people finds its interpretation with the resurrection pronouncement in Ezekiel 37:12-14, with the latter explaining the former. While most commentators are quick to assume the passage delivers only a symbolic interpretation of the restoration of the nation of Israel, Jenson's comments counter this assumption:

> The promised return itself can be construed as simply an event of this age only by sheer determination to do so. It is plainly the same event as the return delineated in the previous chapter, whose features blatantly transcend what is possible within history as it now runs (→36:16–38). Moreover and decisively, the promised resurrection is identified, besides with a return to Judah, with an ineluctably eschatological event.[24]

The eschatological event Jensen speaks of is the giving of the Spirit of God to "my people." While some later rabbis argued that there were literal resurrections that occurred during Ezekiel's day, or later, when the people returned to Judah, many early interpreters believed the vision to be eschatological and referring to a bodily resurrection.[25] Hundreds of years after Judah resettled in the land, the Jews at Qumran appear to have read the valley vision through an eschatological expectation of resurrection, at least according to Pseudo-Ezekiel 4Q385.[26]

---

[23] Leonard J. Greenspoon, "The Origin of the Idea of Resurrection," in *Traditions in Transformation: Turning Points in Biblical Faith*, ed. Baruch Halpern and Jon D. Levenson (Winona Lake, IN: Eisenbrauns, 1981), 292.

[24] Jenson, *Ezekiel*, 284.

[25] Zimmerli, *Ezekiel 2*, 264.

[26] "It shows rather that the author [of 4Q385] meant it literally, thus indicating that he understood the vision as referring to a real resurrection of the righteous in the eschatological future.

When one turns to the New Testament in search of allusions, the clearest example of the reuse of the text is the apocalyptic vision of two witnesses rising from the dead in Revelation 11:10-13. While the text does point to resettling in the land, the inseparable presence of the Spirit of Yahweh gives the vision an eschatological scope. Such an eschatological interpretation dominated early church interpretations as well. The restoration is fundamentally future in orientation and eschatological in nature. That is, the prophetic message points to God's unswerving commitment to bring a people to himself out of the depths of covenant-breaking judgment, which looks like nothing less than bringing life from death.[27]

Ezekiel 37:1-14: Canonical reflections. If Ezekiel 37:1-14 is a passage composed in the key of Christology using multiple countermelodies, we are now in a position to reflection on those countermelodies and strive to better understand how they contribute christological shape of Ezekiel's message. There is little doubt that the visionary message communicated in these verses points toward the restoration of Israel after exile but that the passage cannot be restricted to a mere historical interpretation. However, it must be said that refusing to accept such limitations is not playing fast and loose with the way the text would have been originally received by the exilic community but extending it theologically through the apostolic pattern of seeing Christ and the church as the fulfillment of the Old Testament Scriptures. The text reveals the melodies of restoration, new life by the Spirit of Yahweh, resurrection, and the

---

Pseudo-Ezekiel, then, constitutes the earliest witness for such an understanding of *Ezekiel* 37.1-14, an understanding which later became widespread among Jews and Christians." Devorah Dimant, "Ezekiel, Book Of: Pseudo-Ezekiel," in *Encyclopedia of the Dead Sea Scrolls*, ed. Lawrence H. Schiffman and James C. VanderKam (Oxford: Oxford University Press, 2000), 283.

[27]Steven Tuell comments, "Verses 1-14 portray a symbolic vision of exile and restoration as the national death and resurrection of Israel. However, the image proved too powerful to be restricted to that single, historical interpretation. Indeed, the resurrection of the dead becomes the dominant mode for understanding life beyond this life in Judaism and Christianity." Tuell, *Ezekiel*, Understanding the Bible Commentary (Grand Rapids, MI: Baker, 2008), 254.

eschaton. Each of the melodies contributes to the New Covenant realities picked up by the New Testament writers, even though the passage is never directly quoted.

So, if Ezekiel's audience indeed perceived a divine all-Israel resurrection as part of the eschatological enterprise of restoration, two possible questions arise: (1) Does this mean that Christians should anticipate a literal resurrection of Jews in an eschatological restoration of national Israel? (2) If we read Ezekiel 37:1-14 as speaking to a future resurrection, are we just saying the passage is pointing univocally to the resurrection of Jesus? Taking these questions in turn, if we look to the apostolic pattern, the New Testament frequently reads prophetic promises given to Israel as applied to Jesus and the church (consisting of the broader community of Jews and Gentiles). In a study examining John's use of the prophetic material in Revelation that was originally directed to national Israel, Alex Stewart writes, "John freely and consistently applied these passages to the new community of Jews and Gentiles centered on Jesus."[28] Jesus is the hinge on which John's interpretive method turns, and Jesus presents himself as the turning point in the Jewish understandings of resurrection.

In Ezekiel 37:12 the Lord states that he will return the people to the "land of Israel." While some might argue that this requires a literal fulfillment of placing the people once again in the land (which does happen, with limited spiritual results), this passage requires some historical understanding. Ezekiel frequently employs the language of the Mosaic covenant to both indict the people of Judah for their sins (e.g., the Levitical indictments of Ezek 22) and describe Yahweh's restoration. The language of the Mosaic covenant blessings, including life in the land, becomes the typological and eschatological reservoir from which the prophetic vision flows.

---

[28] Alexander Stewart, "The Future of Israel, Early Christian Hermeneutics, and the Apocalypse of John," *JETS* 61, no. 3 (2018): 565.

This vision flowed through the people of God for centuries. Through a combination of Old Testament ideas (possibly including Ezek 37:1-14) culminating in the work of Daniel, the Jews in the first century anticipated a bodily resurrection at the eschaton. This is evident in Jesus' interaction with Martha regarding the death of her brother Lazarus. When Jesus proclaims to Martha that her brother will rise again, her response confirms an orthodox belief that the eschaton will include the bodily resurrection of God's people: "I know that he will rise again in the resurrection on the last day" (Jn 11:24). But Jesus explains to her that the eschaton has arrived. "I am the resurrection and the life. Whoever believes in me, though he die, yet shall he live" (Jn 11:25).

With these words, Jesus does not deny the validity of an eschatological resurrection for the people of God, clarifying only that this end-time event is breaking into their present. Such a reality is demonstrated moments later as Jesus, the Lord over life and death, calls Lazarus out of the tomb. However, it is ultimately revealed in his own resurrection. The eschatological vision for a restored Israel vivified by the power of God's Spirit found its fulfillment in the resurrection of the true Israelite, the first resurrection of the eschaton. All that Israel was longing for in divine restoration and resurrection found its fulfillment in the person, work, and resurrection of Jesus Christ.

Addressing the second question—if we read Ezekiel 37:1-14 as speaking to a future resurrection, are we just saying the passage is pointing univocally to the resurrection of Jesus?—it is important to note that Ezekiel's vision of resurrection is an eschatological, corporate resurrection of the people of God, empowered by the Spirit. Glossing over such features of the text to assert merely that Ezekiel 37:1-14 is talking about Jesus oversimplifies the theological contribution of the passage and misrepresents reading the Old Testament Christianly. Ezekiel prophesies to the people a future resurrection for an exilic people, and Jesus' resurrection is the first of that order. So, in one sense Ezekiel's words do point toward the reality of Christ's resurrection, but only through the already/not-yet tension of the eschaton. However, that does not remove the people of God from the scope of the prophet's valley vision. Indeed, an eschatological resurrection continues to await the people of God, even as we, like exiles, anticipate the restoration of all things.

A Christian reading of the Scriptures hangs on the reality that Israel's Messiah has ushered in the eschaton—not in its fullness but with profound implications for the world nonetheless. Unlike the exiles from Jerusalem, the church now looks back to the first resurrection of the eschaton and eagerly anticipates the future one. While we have already experienced an eschatological transformation in our union with Christ that constitutes nothing less than life from death (2 Cor 4:11), we look forward to laying aside the broken and weak body of this present age to be raised anew with bodies imperishable (1 Cor 15:50-54).

It is no wonder that the language and imagery of Ezekiel 37:1-14 has affected the people of God throughout the ages. The passage truthfully speaks to God's people at various moments through redemptive history. The picture of life from death should have reminded a traumatized exilic community that God had not abandoned them in their current sojourn from the land. The Jewish community continued to find comfort and hope in the vision of eschatological resurrection up until the first century. Jesus proclaimed to his disciples that what they were longing for in the future had arrived in his resurrection, and their hope and faith in him would assure their participation in the resurrection in the age to come.

Finally, we read the words of the prophet as those trusting and hoping in the resurrected life of Israel's Messiah, though we too are exiled from our eternal home. The powerful image of the prophetic word transforming lifeless corpses to a vivified army continues to remind us of the power of the Spirit of God within the people of God. The Word and Spirit bring life—then, now, and forever.

Reading Other Passages in Ezekiel Like the Apostles

Ezekiel 1:27-28: The glory of Yahweh. The voice of Ezekiel ben Buzi opens the book with an autobiographical declaration concerning his "visions of God." Standing alongside the Chebar River, the prophet witnessed a great cloud coming from the north, surrounded with flashes of light. The language and imagery here are not dissimilar from the mythopoeic language found in Isaiah 14:12-14, where the divine mountain is portrayed in the north and above the clouds. Indeed, what would otherwise seem like metaphorical language in Psalm 104:3 seems to come to life before the prophet's eyes: "he makes the clouds his chariot; the one riding upon the wings of the wind [*rûaḥ*]" (author's translation). The book of Ezekiel begins with reverberations of the biblical tradition that views the visitation of the Lord as a means of both judgment and salvation.

Ezekiel once again directs his gaze toward the living creatures and sees something that looks like wheels within wheels, constructed of beryl or topaz, covered with eyes, and extending to the earth from each of the living creatures (Ezek 1:15-18). The prophet's gaze moves upward, and he witnesses an enormous expanse of a sparkling (either ice or crystal, *qeraḥ*) firmament above the heads of the creatures (Ezek 1:22). The wings of the creatures are located under the firmament and appear to function like a base for the throne sitting on the firmament (Ezek 1:26).

In the final verses of Ezekiel 1, Ezekiel continues to describe what he saw seated on the throne—a human-like, fiery, metallic-looking being, surrounded by an overwhelming rainbow of light. This, he declares, is the "appearance of the likeness of the glory of YHWH [*marʾēh dəmût kəbôd-yəhwâ*]" (Ezek 1:28, author's translation). Ezekiel's description is similar to the glory cloud of Yahweh in Exodus 24:16-17. There also we read of a fiery description of the "appearance of the glory of YHWH [*ûmarʾēh kəbôd-yəhwâ*]." But what did Ezekiel actually see? Is there any significance to the human-like appearance on the throne that is not present in the Mount Sinai account?

The Lord tells Moses in Exodus 33:20, "You are not able to see my face, for man shall not see me and live," and consequently Moses is hidden in the rock while the glory of Yahweh passes before him. Several other Old Testament texts allude to the reality that humankind cannot live in the presence of God (e.g., Gen 32:30; Deut 5:24; Judg 6:22-23; 13:22; Is 6:5). The early church fathers wrestled with this issue in their debates against Gnostics and Arians, seeking to defend the incomprehensibility of God. In his work *Against Heresies*, Irenaeus turns to the prophet's careful use of *appearance* and *likeness* to demonstrate that Ezekiel did not see the essence of God. However, the conclusion of Irenaeus and other early interpreters was that Ezekiel saw the Word—that is, the preincarnate Christ revealed in his glory.

We could similarly explore Isaiah's vision in Isaiah 6 and Daniel's night vision where he sees "one like a son of man" coming on the clouds of heaven (Dan 7:13). The apostle John interprets Isaiah's vision in Isaiah 6 as speaking to Christ. After paraphrasing Isaiah 6:9-10 with reference to those rejecting Jesus, John writes, "Isaiah said these things because he saw his glory and spoke of him" (Jn 12:41). Jesus himself takes up the words of Daniel 7:13 in describing his own eschatological victory to Pilate in Mark 14:62. Jesus' and John's christological interpretations of these Old Testament visions shed light on how we should think about the appearance of the glory of God in Ezekiel 1. However, a stronger New Testament case can be made for reading Ezekiel's vision christologically by looking at Revelation 4.

A quick read through Ezekiel 1–2 and Revelation 4 will reveal numerous thematic parallels, many of which become even clearer when comparing the New Testament text with the Greek Septuagint. Both visions include the appearance of one on a throne with a crystal-like expanse surrounded in a rainbow of light, flashing lightning, torches, and four eye-covered living creatures around the throne. In his commentary on Revelation, Greg Beale ably demonstrates that Ezekiel 1–2 and Daniel 7 serve as the Old Testament foundation for John's vision in Revelation 4. Wright comments, "Here, in anthropomorphic reversal, God appears in the likeness of a human being, albeit in glowing, fiery splendour that anticipates the transfiguration of the incarnate Son of God himself and certainly provided the imagery for John's great vision of the heavenly throne in Revelation 4."[29]

It is evident that the anthropomorphic imagery associated with the glory of Yahweh in this chapter troubled the early Jewish community. The early Aramaic translation of Ezekiel 1 in the Targums leaves the phrase *kəmar'ēh 'ādām* ("like an appearance of a man," Ezek 1:26) untranslated in the text, thus veiling it from public reading in the synagogue. However, the theological human-like vision of likeness of God's glory moves quite easily into the New Testament's portrayal of an incarnate Son of God perfectly reflecting the glory (*apaugasma tēs doxēs*, Heb 1:3) of Yahweh. What does this reveal about God? Both the glory of God and the divine presence of God come to Ezekiel in the form of a divine, otherworldly, human-like figure—a pattern quite consistent with the incarnation of the Messiah. What the revelation of the glory of the God in the New Testament reveals about these verses is that God would one day in fullness—not in appearance—take on human flesh and come to us into our own cursed exile. When Ezekiel is offered a personal prophetic glance into the revelation of Yahweh, he sees majesty, power, mystery, and humanity. Given the description of overwhelming light, majesty, and holiness, Ezekiel's response of falling on his face seems very appropriate. God's glory in these verses is characterized by his very presence.

Ezekiel 36:22-32: A new heart and God's Spirit. Perhaps one of the more surprising aspects of Ezekiel's prophecies is the depiction of restoration. While divine judgment dominates the language of the thirty-two chapters of the book and often leaves us to struggle with the dark

---

[29]Wright, *Ezekiel*, 51.

consequences of Judah's sin, at times the promised restoration after judgment appears just as unsettling. Ezekiel 36:22-32 reveals the beauty and spiritual immensity of God's work in transforming his people but also exposes any false notions as to why such a transformation happened in the first place. In Ezekiel 36:22 Yahweh clarifies his singular motivation for the spiritual transformation he intended to carry out among his people: "It is not for your sake . . . that I am about to act" (note also the *inclusio* in Ezek 36:32). Israel had profaned the name of God among the nations through their idolatry, wicked leadership, and violation of the covenant. The restoration program is motivated by Yahweh's concern for reputation among the nations ("the nations will know that I am YHWH . . . when I am consecrated among you before them," Ezek 36:23, author's translation), and his spiritual work among his people is a means to an end—the sanctification of his name among the nations of the earth.

God's holiness will be revealed as he and he alone restores his people. The following verses of this section reveal the monergistic portrait of Israel's salvation so often depicted in the book.[30] The first-person declarations take up the covenantal language and imagery that have shaped Israel's relationship with God since their formation as a nation. First, the passage draws from Israel's past exodus from Egypt but frames their future restoration within the image of a new exodus. God is once again going to regather his people from the nations where they have been scattered and bring them to dwell within the land that he gave to their fathers, so that "you shall be my people, and I will be your God" (Ezek 36:28; see Ex 6:7).

Second, the covenant language of Sinai permeates the imagery of the restored people. The imagery of the land is developed into a prophetic vision of prosperity and blessing in the land promised by the Lord. Ezekiel creatively draws on old covenant imagery to describe New

---

[30] Ronald E. Clements, *Ezekiel* (Louisville, KY: Westminster John Knox, 1996), 162.

Covenant realities.[31] Not only will a renewed Israel experience the covenantal blessings of prosperity in the land (e.g., Deut 11:13-32), but their spiritual transformation will include nothing less than divine empowerment to carry out the statutes and rules of God (Ezek 36:27). The generational plague of sin that characterized Israel's covenant history with its God will be finally addressed as God unilaterally transforms his people into the spiritual people they were always called to be. God will have a Shema people who love him with their whole heart and walk in obedience to his ways, and the presence of his very own Spirit will ensure that his will be done. The language of law obedience and land occupation need not be overly literalized here to mean that this text will be fulfilled only when the nation of Israel keeps torah and dwells once again in the ancient boundaries of the Promised Land. The eschaton changes everything!

The regenerating power of God's people is evident in Ezekiel 37:1-14. In this passage the Spirit indwells and transforms the hearts and wills of God's people. Paul Joyce rightly comments that the new Spirit is "the dynamic power of YHWH, which inspires judges, kings and prophets, and also evoke[s] the eschatological outpouring of that *rûaḥ* of YHWH." The Spirit points toward an eschatological moral transformation that will take place in the hearts of God's people. He goes on to state, "Although obedience is never the condition of restoration, right behavior is an integral part of the renewal."[32]

Ezekiel prophesies of an eschatological moment when God's people—Israel—will be morally transformed by the internalization of God's Spirit. This spiritual change will not only rewrite their futures but also deal with their pasts. God will cleanse them from their past uncleanness and idolatry and remove their lifeless stone heart. Yet, such a transformation

---

[31]Risa Levitt Kohn, *A New Heart and a New Soul: Ezekiel, the Exile and the Torah*, Journal for the Study of the Old Testament Supplement Series 358 (London: Sheffield Academic Press, 2002), 107.

[32]Paul Joyce, *Ezekiel: A Commentary*, LHBOTS 482 (London: T&T Clark, 2007), 204.

will not produce shouts of joy and acclamation, as one might expect, but rather disgust and sorrow (Ezek 36:31). While the reasoning for such associations with restoration might evade us at first, the New Testament reveals to us a Comforter who also convicts (Jn 16:8). The prophets, Jesus, and the Holy Spirit reveal to us that the path to salvation and restoration always goes directly through the reality of our sin—never around it. There is no repentance where there is no conviction. There is no redemption where there is no vicarious suffering. Ezekiel speaks to a New Covenant reality where God's people will experience a new exodus by the work of a greater Moses, who will not only call his people to holiness but empower them to live it by his Spirit.

Conclusion

This chapter has not presented a particular method of reading like the apostles as much as a desire to do so. Never disparaging the original intentions of the biblical author, Christian reflection on the Old Testament prophets demands a theological acuteness and sensitivity to the great redemptive work of God through Christ as played out in the Scriptures. It is not misguided to read Ezekiel expecting the book to reveal the trinitarian God. Ezekiel 1:27-28; 36:22-32; 37:1-14 show us the nature, character, and prophetic plan of the Father, Son, and Spirit to dwell with a people, restore them from their sin and iniquity, and bring them to a place of new life where they will dwell in his presence as his people. While readers and interpreters will continue to debate the finer points of this fascinating book, we can all reflect on and receive the good news according to Ezekiel.

14

THE HISTORY OF INTERPRETING EZEKIEL AS CHRISTIAN SCRIPTURE

Iain M. Duguid

THE BOOK OF EZEKIEL HAS offended different people in different ways since it was first written. Even prior to the production of the book, we know that the prophet's words were being countered and domesticated in a variety of ways. Some of his listeners dismissed him as merely a skillful singer of raunchy songs (*šîr ʿăgābîm*; Ezek 33:32; see Ezek 23:11): like much contemporary rap music, people listened to Ezekiel's preaching for entertainment—or perhaps for the shock value—but would not have dreamed of going to him for serious moral instruction any more than we would go to a rapper. Others paid lip service to Ezekiel's words but drained them of contemporary relevance by postponing their significance to some faraway time in the future, saying, "The vision that he sees concerns many years from now; he prophesies about distant times" (Ezek 12:27).¹ Not much has changed over the years: some interpreters continue to treat Ezekiel as a singer of pornographic songs ("porno-prophetics," as one scholar calls it), while others insist that much of his writing is only really relevant for times long after the days when he was preaching and writing.²

History of Interpreting Ezekiel

Early Jewish interpretation. Early Jewish interpreters also found Ezekiel a problematic text to interpret. According to Jerome, Jews under thirty years old were forbidden from reading the beginning and ending of the book, and the cautionary tale is recorded of a child who picked up a scroll of Ezekiel at his teacher's home and apprehended the true meaning of the obscure Hebrew word *ḥašmal*, the substance of which the divine figure appears to be composed of in Ezekiel 1:27.³ Instantly, fire came out from the *ḥašmal* and incinerated him (Babylonian Talmud Hagigah 13a).⁴ The visual nature of the depiction of God in this chapter was clearly challenging for some to incorporate into an aniconic faith.

A more symbolic understanding of this opening vision became prominent in Judaism after the fall of the Jerusalem temple in AD 70. It was perhaps natural that that cataclysmic event would cause Jewish people to turn back to the prophet of the previous destruction in 586 BC.

---

[1] Except as noted, all quotations of Scripture are from *The Christian Standard Bible* (Nashville: Holman Bible Publishers, 2017).
[2] Fokkelien van Dijk-Hemmes, "The Metaphorization of Woman in Prophetic Speech: An Analysis of Ezekiel XXIII," *VT* 43 (1993): 163-64; J. C. Exum, *Plotted, Shot and Painted: Cultural Representations of Biblical Women* (Sheffield: Sheffield Academic Press, 1996), 101-28; see also the response by Corinne L. Patton, "'Should Our Sister Be Treated Like a Whore?' A Response to Feminist Critiques of Ezekiel 23," in *The Book of Ezekiel: Theological and Anthropological Perspectives*, ed. M. Odell and J. T. Strong (Atlanta: Society of Biblical Literature, 2000), 221-38.
[3] Jerome, "Letter LIII: To Paulinus," in *A Select Library of Nicene and Post-Nicene Fathers of the Christian Church: Volume 6: St. Jerome: Letters and Select Works*, trans. Henry Wace (New York: Christian Literature Company, 1893), 8.
[4] Intriguingly, modern Hebrew uses *ḥašmal* as the word for "electricity," brilliantly capitalizing on this sense of danger. Wherever you go in Israel, you see signs saying "Caution: *ḥašmal*."

They found themselves once again without a temple, the visible symbol of the Lord's presence in their midst. In this situation, the vision of the Lord seated on his *merkābâ*, his throne-chariot, became a potent symbol of the Lord's transcendent power, along with his immanent presence with his people. Through this mobile presence, the sovereign Lord of all the universe could still dwell with his scattered people wherever they found themselves, as a "sanctuary for them for a little while" (Ezek 11:16 NASB).

At the other end of the book, the rabbis had problems with Ezekiel's temple vision in chapters 40–48. Here the difficulty lay in harmonizing Ezekiel's regulations with those prescribed by Moses. For example, Ezekiel's program calls for only two annual festivals, both very similar to each other, which was hard to align with the three quite different annual festivals (Passover, Weeks, and Tabernacles) that Moses established in his law (Ezek 45:18-25; see Lev 23). In addition, the temple building that Ezekiel describes has significantly different dimensions and features from the Solomonic temple (Ezek 40–42; see 1 Kings 6). Were it not for the work of Hananiah ben Hezekiah, who hid himself away in his attic and burned three hundred barrels of oil in his lamp in order to reconcile these different laws, the book of Ezekiel would have been excluded from the canon (Babylonian Talmud Shabbat 13b). Unfortunately, the fruits of Hananiah's work have not been preserved for us—the rabbis claim "because of our sins"—meaning that we will have to wait until Elijah comes for him to explain the apparent conflict (Babylonian Talmud Menah 45a).

Most early Jewish interpretations saw the prophecy of Ezekiel 37:1-14 as evidence for the literal resurrection of the dead. There was debate in Jewish circles about whether what Ezekiel saw was a vision or an actual event that took place while he looked on (compare Mt 27:51-53)—and if the latter, what happened subsequently to the bodies that had been resurrected. However, there were also some within Jewish circles who saw it to be a specific representation of the return of Israel from the exile, under the figure of a resurrection, building on the exiles' self-description in Ezekiel 37:11 as "dried up bones."[5]

Early Christian interpretation. In the early church there was a general acknowledgment that the prophets were among the more difficult biblical texts to interpret. Jerome says, "As for Isaiah, Jeremiah, Ezekiel and Daniel, who can fully understand them or adequately explain them?"[6] Of course, allegorical interpretation helped: for example, Irenaeus was the first to identify the four faces of the cherubim in Ezekiel 1:10—the lion, the man, the ox, and the eagle—as representing the fourfold picture of Christ revealed in the four Gospels (*Against Heresies* 3.11.8).

Jerome preached a series of sermons on parts of Ezekiel while Rome was under siege between AD 410 and 414. He reflects in the preface to his commentary on Ezekiel, dedicated to his friend Eustochium, "It seemed as though I was sharing the captivity of the saints." Gregory the Great (AD 540–604) preached a series of sermons on the book during a later siege of Rome, focusing on the first and last visions of the prophet—precisely the parts that the Jewish interpreters had found problematic (though his explanation of the temple vision is limited to Ezek 40). It is perhaps not coincidental that when a scholar/pastor's city was under siege, they turned to the parts of Ezekiel's work that were most formative for the book of Revelation, seeking help from a biblical writer who has shared their experience.

Where Jerome's line of interpretation of Ezekiel is grounded in a more literal mode, albeit with profound spiritual significance, Gregory the Great's approach could move quickly in an allegorical direction, in order to derive spiritual fruit from otherwise seemingly unprofitable

---

[5]See Moshe Greenberg, *Ezekiel 21–37*, AB (New York: Doubleday, 1997), 749-51.
[6]Jerome, "Letter LIII: To Paulinus," 8.

texts. Thus, in his homily on Ezekiel 40:6-8, Gregory identifies the east gate of the visionary temple as Jesus, the steps leading up to the gate as the merits of the virtues that lead to salvation, and the threshold of the gate as the ancestors of Jesus. The chamber inside the gate has length, which symbolizes longsuffering in expectation, and breadth, which symbolizes amplitude of charity.[7]

Our key text, Ezekiel 37:1-14, was not entirely neglected during this period. Indeed, as part of the liturgical calendar, it would have been read and preached on more frequently than most texts from the prophet. Jerome, as is typical, grounded his interpretation in the historical: the vision of the valley of the dry bones has an initial fulfillment in the return of the Jewish people of God from Babylon to their homeland in Israel, under the figure of resurrection. But for Jerome, this historical reality paves the way for a spiritual understanding of the text: the exile and return finds its fulfillment in the death and resurrection of Christ, by which we are delivered from the depths of hell.[8]

The passage was explained more generally as a prooftext for the resurrection of the body by Tertullian (*De carnis resurrection* 29-30) and many others in the early church.[9] Indeed, Tertullian saw the physical resurrection of the dead as its primary meaning, arguing that the metaphorical use in describing the return of Israel to its land necessarily presupposes the fact of the bodily resurrection; otherwise the analogy would not have made sense to its audience. Ezekiel 37:1-14 was also a frequent source of inspiration for Christian art during this period, especially on sarcophagi, which suggests a similar interpretation of the significance of the text.[10] Unlike the earlier Jewish interest in Ezekiel 1

---

[7] *The Homilies of Gregory the Great on the Book of the Prophet Ezekiel*, trans. T. Gray (Etna, CA: Center for Traditionalist Orthodox Studies, 1990), 179-85. It is not immediately clear how one could have a chamber that lacked length and breadth.

[8] F. Glorie, ed., *Commentariorum in Hiezechielem (Hieronymus); Libri XIV*, Corpus Christianorum: Series Latina 75 (Turnhout, Belgium: Brepols, 1964), 519-22.

[9] Tertullian was himself following in the footsteps of Justin Martyr and Irenaeus.

[10] See E. A. de Boer, *John Calvin on the Visions of Ezekiel: Historical and Hermeneutical Studies in John Calvin's Sermons Inédits, Especially on Ezek. 36-48* (Leiden: Brill, 2004), 16. In addition to

and patristic interest in Ezekiel 38–48, this interpretation did not flow out of an identification with the earlier saints experiencing trials so much as a more general apologetic interest in countering the arguments of Gnostics. Since Ezekiel 37:1-14 was part of the regular liturgical reading of the Scriptures, it attracted the attention of many writers who were not commenting specifically on the book of Ezekiel as a whole, which probably encouraged the tendency to read it in isolation from its surrounding context.[11]

Medieval interpretation. Much of the medieval work on Ezekiel was a reworking of earlier scholarship, especially the commentaries of Jerome for a more literal perspective and Gregory the Great for spiritual inspiration. Gregory's allegorical exegesis found a new life in the commentaries of Rabanus Maurus (ca. AD 780–856) and his contemporary Haimo of Auxerre, while Richard of Saint Victor (d. AD 1173) explored the literal sense of the prophet's words, especially his portrayal of the new temple. Richard's interest in architecture found expression in detailed drawings of the temple, attempting to work out exactly what it looked like, down to the angle of the mountain slope into which he thought it must be built. In the process, he virtually invented the art of architectural drawing, which had hitherto been almost unknown.[12] His focus on the literal meaning of the text reflected his greater access to and appreciation for Jewish interpretation of the Old Testament, most likely by means of Rashi's commentary.

This pattern was repeated throughout the medieval and Reformation period. Scholars such as John Calvin, who had access to medieval Jewish commentaries either directly or through compendia of sources, such as that developed by Nicholas of Lyra, tended to be much better

---

Christian artwork, the vision also formed the basis for part of the decorations of a third-century AD synagogue at Dura-Europos, in what is now Syria. See C. H. Kraeling, *The Synagogue: The Excavations at Dura-Europos; Final Report*, VIII/I (New Haven, CT: Yale University Press, 1956).

[11]De Boer, *John Calvin on the Visions of Ezekiel*, 180-81.

[12]See Walter Cahn, "Architecture and Exegesis: Richard of St. Victor's Ezekiel Commentary and Its Illustrations," *The Art Bulletin* 76 (1994): 53-56.

equipped to interpret difficult texts such as Ezekiel than those who did not. The latter were often forced to allegorize the text in order to get useful insights from it to make application of the text to their people.

One passage that attracted significant interest during the medieval period was Ezekiel 44:1-3, with its description of the closed east gate of the temple. Ratramnus uses this text to argue that in the incarnation, Christ entered the world in the normal way (*On the Parturition of Saint Mary*, 3.14), while Radbertus uses the same passage to argue that since Christ was able to pass through closed doors, he came into this world without any of the pain and suffering normally associated with childbirth (*De assumptione Sanctae Mariae Virginis*). For Thomas Aquinas, Ezekiel 44 was the classic prooftext for the perpetual virginity of Mary, since it clearly states that no man has passed through the east gate but only the Lord, after which it remains shut forever.[13] Once again, the text is interpreted largely in isolation from the wider context or message of the prophet.

Reformation interpretation. As we come to the turbulent times of the Reformation, there was a resurgence of interest in the more apocalyptic aspects of the prophet. Martin Luther first engaged Ezekiel when preparing his translation of the Bible into German. Strikingly, he published his translation of Ezekiel 38–39 separately, in advance of the rest of the Bible. Against the background of the imminent danger of invasion of Germany by the Turks, who threatened Hungary in 1527 and advanced as far as Vienna in 1529, Luther identified the Turks as the personification of Gog, while the church was the true Israel depicted under siege in the prophecy.[14]

Perhaps unsurprisingly, Luther also takes a strongly christological approach to interpreting Ezekiel: for example, the throne chariot in the opening vision is "the spiritual vehicle of Christ on which he rides in

---

[13]Thomas Aquinas, *Summa Theologica* 3 q. 28 art. 3. See de Boer, *John Calvin on the Visions of Ezekiel*, 57.
[14]Martin Luther, "On the War Against the Turk," *LW* 46:202.

this world," while the new temple in Ezekiel 40–48 pictures the kingdom of Christ surviving on the earth until its final day. Luther finds it impossible to correlate the temple design with the practical realities of Israelite geography, and so he insists that it must be spiritually understood with reference to Christ's kingdom. At the same time, unlike the allegorists, Luther is not concerned with making application out of all the various details of the temple vision, saying, "That we will save until that life, when we will see the whole building, then at last ready and accomplished."[15]

Though they broke with Rome, the Reformers did not completely reject medieval patterns of exegesis. Huldrych Zwingli follows Aquinas in seeing Ezekiel 44:1-3 as a prooftext for the perpetual virginity of Mary.[16] Yet Zwingli does not follow Luther in making contemporary application of Ezekiel 38–39, nor does he see it having a future referent; instead, he sees it as having been completely fulfilled in the oppression of the Jews in the days of Alexander the Great, with ongoing typological significance for the church.[17] This may be connected to his interpretation of Ezekiel 40–48 as applying to the kingdom of Christ from its beginnings until now: if that is the case, then it makes sense that Ezekiel 38–39 must have found its fulfillment before the coming of Christ.

Calvin never completed a commentary on Ezekiel, although he preached a complete series of sermons on Ezekiel in the 1550s—an achievement that may represent the first complete *lectio continua* series on Ezekiel recorded at that time.[18] Regrettably, Calvin began to write his commentary on Ezekiel only at the close of his life and left it

---

[15]Cited in de Boer, *John Calvin on the Visions of Ezekiel*, 69.
[16]Huldrich Zwingli. "Friendly Exegesis, That Is, Exposition of the Matter of the Eucharist to Martin Luther, February 1527," in *Selected Writings of Huldrych Zwingli: In Search of True Religion: Reformation, Pastoral and Eucharistic Writings,* trans. and ed. H. Wayne Pipkin (Eugene, OR: Pickwick, 1984), 2:275.
[17]Letter to Pierre Viret, 19 May 1540; cited in de Boer, *John Calvin on the Visions of Ezekiel*, 71.
[18]De Boer, *John Calvin on the Visions of Ezekiel*, 17. Though these sermons have never been published in English, de Boer's work sheds light on Calvin's approach.

unfinished at Ezekiel 20. His hermeneutical approach was more historical than Luther's, recognizing the context of the original readers in the Babylonian exile while still applying their message to Christ and his church. Thus, for Calvin, Ezekiel 37:1-14 is not primarily to be understood as a prophecy of the resurrection, as it was for some of the church fathers, but rather as a depiction of the captivity and restoration of Israel. As such, however, it also conveys a lesson of hope to the church and to individual Christians as they find themselves in similar circumstances, as well as shaping our understanding of the role of the prophetic word in building the church and the activity of the Spirit in regenerating God's people. Calvin is rather dismissive of Luther's more allegorizing approach: "Luther is not so much concerned with the proper meaning of the words and the circumstances of history; he is satisfied when some fruitful doctrine comes forth."[19]

Seventeenth-century exegetes showed significantly more interest in Ezekiel than Calvin had. Early scholar of apocalyptic Joseph Mede (1586–1639) identifies the New World as the true home of Gog. He believed that its Native American inhabitants were descended from the Scythians and would assault Europe in the last days.[20] Meanwhile in England, Puritan William Greenhill published five volumes of expository lectures on Ezekiel over 1645–1667, alternating between awareness of the original historical context and a desire for practical application that at times leads him into allegorical exposition, especially in the more obscure passages.[21] He resists the temptation to identify Gog as any contemporary foe; after surveying many different interpretations, he leaves the identity of this enemy of the church open. He confesses that he finds much of the detail in Ezekiel 40–48 virtually incomprehensible but asserts nonetheless that the overall message of

---

[19]De Boer, *John Calvin on the Visions of Ezekiel*, 71.
[20]See Jeffrey K. Jue, *Heaven upon Earth: Joseph Mede (1586–1638) and the Legacy of Millenarianism* (Dordrecht: Springer, 2006), 184-85.
[21]William Greenhill, *Ezekiel* (repr., Edinburgh: Banner of Truth, 1945).

this portion is a depiction of the Christian church and its worship under the figures and types of the old covenant.

Meanwhile, eighteenth-century American Cotton Mather interacted with Mede's conjecture about the identity of Gog. He takes the possibility of a Native American interpretation seriously but stresses rather the positive aspect of his New England forefathers' errand into the wilderness and the prospect of redemption even for this previously godforsaken land, seeing in the prophet's vision of a steadily increasing river in Ezekiel 47 an image of the progressive growth of Christianity throughout the generations.[22]

MODERN INTERPRETATION

More modern scholarship has gone in a multitude of different directions in interpreting the book of Ezekiel. Julius Wellhausen had little interest in Ezekiel, preferring to focus on texts such as Isaiah and Amos that could more easily be adapted to the goal of moral instruction in the universal fatherhood of God and the brotherhood of all humankind. For him, Ezekiel was complicit in the downward trajectory of Israel that started from the highpoint of the ethical monotheism of the eighth-century prophets and led through Ezekiel 44:6-8, which he understood to be prescribing a "downgrading" of the Levites from equality with the priests to a subservient state, onward to the ritualistic and legalistic P source, composed after the exile. That trajectory in turn led toward the formalism of Judaism and Catholicism rather than the freedom of the Spirit described in the New Testament.[23]

Still, the unity and fundamental authenticity of the book was affirmed by most scholars throughout the nineteenth century, culminating in S. R. Driver's comment that "the whole from beginning to end

---

[22]S. Bercovitch, "Cotton Mather," in *Major Writers of Early American Literature*, ed. E. Emerson (Madison: University of Wisconsin Press, 1972), 93-150.

[23]Wellhausen grew up in a pietistic Lutheran context and retained from it the sharp disjunction between law and freedom, even as he rejected much of its doctrinal basis.

[bears] the stamp of a single mind."[24] There were certainly many dissenting opinions in the twentieth century, ranging from those who defended the book's unity but placed its date much later (e.g., C. C. Torrey) to those who denied almost all of the book to the prophet and divided it into many different layers (e.g., Gustav Hölscher; Jörg Garscha).[25] But the book's unity has been remarkably robustly defended up until the present day.[26]

In the early part of the twentieth century, much of the theological interest in Ezekiel revolved around psychological questions. Many scholars saw Ezekiel as advancing a new religious insight, individual responsibility, over against older texts, which stressed the corporate responsibility of the people as a unity, especially in Ezekiel 18. This trend lent itself to reading Ezekiel 37 about hope for and the regeneration of individual souls rather than about the future of Israel as a nation, or even a future general resurrection of the dead. Yet more recent scholarship has recognized that Ezekiel 18 is more about generational responsibility than it is about individual responsibility: the history of any generation does not simply depend on the behavior of the father's generation but on that of their own generation.[27] Repentance and restoration is always an option for a community, not just for

---

[24]S. R. Driver, *An Introduction to the Literature of the Old Testament* (New York: T&T Clark, 1913), 279. G. B. Gray writes, "No other book of the Old Testament is distinguished by such decisive marks of unity of authorship and integrity as this." Gray, *A Critical Introduction to the Old Testament* (New York: Scribner's, 1913), 198.

[25]C. C. Torrey, *Pseudo-Ezekiel and the Original Prophecy* (New Haven, CT: Yale University Press, 1930); Gustav Hölscher, *Hesekiel; der Dichter und das Buch*, Beihefte zur Zeitschrift für die alttestamentliche Wissenschaft 39 (Giessen: Töpelmann, 1924); Jörg Garscha, *Studien zum Ezechielbuch* (Frankfurt: Peter Lang, 1974).

[26]Notably by Moshe Greenberg, who writes, "A consistent trend of thought expressed in a distinctive style has emerged giving the impression of a single mind.... The persuasion grows on one ... that a coherent world of vision is emerging, contemporary with the sixth-century prophet and decisively shaped by him, if not the very words of Ezekiel himself." Greenberg, *Ezekiel 1–20*, AB (Garden City, NY: Doubleday, 1983), 26-27. See also the magisterial two-volume commentary by Daniel Block, *Ezekiel 1–24* and *Ezekiel 25–48* (Grand Rapids, MI: Eerdmans, 1997, 1998). On the contours of the twentieth-century debate, see Iain M. Duguid, *Ezekiel and the Leaders of Israel* (Leiden: Brill, 1994), 3-8.

[27]Paul M. Joyce, *Divine Initiative and Human Response in Ezekiel*, Journal for the Study of the Old Testament Supplement Series 51 (Sheffield: JSOT Press, 1989), 46.

an individual, as is the case in Ezekiel 37:1-14, which addresses the exiles as a whole, not as isolated individuals.

Other popular writers have returned to Luther's speculative approach to identifying the actors in the final battle of Ezekiel 38–39 with modern people and nations, which in turn requires a more corporate interpretation of the bones of Ezekiel 37 as Israel. Hal Lindsay's bestseller *Late Great Planet Earth* was merely the most prominent publicity vehicle for a movement when it identified the Rosh of Ezekiel 38:2 with Russia, Meshech with Moscow, and Tubal with Tobolsk.[28] These ideas had already been put forward in the early part of the century in the notes of the dispensationalist *Scofield Reference Bible*, which itself draws on ideas circulating in nineteenth-century Germany in the context of the Russian expansionism that led to the Crimean War.[29] Lindsay developed these ideas into a complex jigsaw linking biblical names and places with current events around the world, which he then used to argue for the imminent rapture of the church and the end of the world, events that he said would almost certainly take place during the 1980s.[30]

In spite of the failure of Lindsay's detailed timelines and specific predictions, he and others have continued to argue in the same vein and have a large public following in fundamentalist and conservative evangelical circles. On this view, Ezekiel 37 is not about the resurrection of the dead or the immediate restoration of Israel following the exile to Babylon but rather the physical restoration of the Jews to their homeland in Israel in 1948, to be followed by a spiritual restoration (as the second stage in the resurrection described in Ezek 37), which will in turn trigger the countdown to the final cataclysmic war described in Ezekiel 38–39.[31]

---

[28]Hal Lindsay with C. C. Carlson, *The Late Great Planet Earth* (Grand Rapids, MI: Zondervan, 1970).
[29]The significance of that historical context for German lexicologist Wilhelm Gesenius, identifying *ro'sh* in Ezek 38:2 as a proper noun, which he then connected with Russia, should not be overlooked.
[30]See Hal Lindsay, *The 1980s: Countdown to Armageddon* (New York: Bantam, 1981).
[31]See Lindsay, *Late Great Planet Earth*, 51-52. In the process, Lindsay identifies the "they" of Ezek 37:11, who describe Israel's state as dry bones, as being the surrounding enemy nations at the time of restoration, rather than the exiles describing their own state in the sixth century BC.

Interpreting Ezekiel

The history of interpretation of the prophet Ezekiel shows us a number of mistakes and pitfalls into which it is easy to fall. First, we may note the danger of using Scripture in a disconnected way to provide prooftexts for doctrines. In some cases, theologians have strip-mined the Scriptures for propositions to support their theology in a way that isolates those texts from their original context and treats them like timeless truths. This is evident when Ezekiel 37:1-14 is used simply as a prooftext of a general resurrection of the dead at the end of the age. In reality, the prophet is not depicting the expectation of a universal resurrection. Otherwise, his answer to the question "Can these bones live?" would have been "Most certainly," or at the least, "I know they will rise again in the resurrection at the last day" (see Jn 11:24). The question posed by God to the prophet is not a universal philosophical one: "Will bones in general be resurrected?" In the context, it is the intensely particular historical question "Will *these* bones live?"[32] This is not to say that the text has nothing to say to that wider philosophical and theological question. If God is able to restore exiled Israel to life in this way, then certainly he is able to raise the dead to new life on the last day. Prooftexts have their proper place in theology. However, the general resurrection of the dead is a peripheral inference from the text, not its central focus.

Second, we may highlight the mistake of allegorical interpretation, whose roots (in the case of the prophet Ezekiel) go back to well before the time of Gregory the Great. Allegorical interpretation neglects the original historical context and literal meaning of the text and makes a leap in connecting the text to the current situation of the hearers in pursuit of spiritual edification. The driving force behind this approach

---

A more scholarly presentation of this premillennial interpretation may be found in Walter C. Kaiser Jr., *Preaching and Teaching the Last Things. Old Testament Eschatology for the Life of the Church* (Grand Rapids, MI: Baker, 2011), 31-38.

[32]See Iain M. Duguid, *Ezekiel*, NIVAC (Grand Rapids, MI: Zondervan, 1999), 429.

is undoubtedly the preacher's desire to do the congregation spiritual good, in accord with 2 Timothy 3:16, which teaches that all Scripture (and Paul was thinking specifically of the OT) is profitable for teaching, for rebuking, for correcting, and for training in righteousness. When faced with a biblical passage that on the surface does not seem very profitable for these things, such as the lengthy description of the gates of Ezekiel's visionary temple in Ezekiel 40, allegory provides an appealing method of providing spiritual food, even from these hard passages.

This approach is by no means restricted to the church fathers and the medieval church. Puritan William Greenhill finds significance in the windows of the visionary temple (Ezek 40:16) as denoting the spiritual light and joy that should be in the church of Christ. That there are windows also in the "little chambers" means that even the least churches and the least saints shall not be without light and joy, teaching and comfort.[33] The danger of such allegorizing preaching is that there is no real connection between the text and the application, other than the skill of the preacher's imagination, so we train people to see the Bible as a magician's hat out of which theological rabbits may be conjured, rather than a clear revelation of God that must be patiently studied to determine its true meaning. It almost inevitably leaves the congregation impressed by the cleverness and "spirituality" of the preacher rather than being equipped to feed themselves from the Word. They come out of church saying, "I would never in a million years have thought that the passage meant that," instead of, "How clear it all is now! How could I have missed what the passage was saying?"[34]

Yet simply claiming to follow a principle of literal interpretation does not exempt interpreters from the kind of free association we generally

---

[33] Greenhill, *Ezekiel*, 780.

[34] A good example of this may be seen in missionary Jim Elliot's palpable frustration over his own failure to derive profound spiritual benefit from the curtains and boards of the tabernacle, unlike the preachers and writers with whom he was familiar. Elliot blamed his own lack of spirituality rather than recognizing the problem lay with the preachers' allegorizing of the text. Elliot, *The Journals of Jim Elliot* (Old Tappan, NJ: Revell, 1978), 39-40.

associate with allegory. I discovered that reality in my study of the Song of Songs, where Tommy Nelson's *Book of Romance*—which interprets the Song literally, as being primarily about human relationships—is every bit as imaginative in its interpretation and application as anything written by Gregory the Great.

One way in which the historical context of the passage may be neglected, even while literal interpretation is being insisted on, is when the true meaning of the passage is deferred into the distant future from the perspective of the original audience. This problem is evident in the repeated attempts throughout the history of the church to identify the protagonists of Ezekiel 38–39 with the contemporary enemies of the church, from Ambrose through Luther and Mede to Hal Lindsay and his successors. Instead of asking first how this passage spoke to Ezekiel's original audience, an immediate application is made to the contemporary context of the interpreter—and in a world of much tribulation, there will always be agents of evil who can be made to line up sufficiently with the description of the biblical text.

Interpretations of Ezekiel 40–48 that—on the basis of a presumed literal interpretation—identify these chapters as containing a blueprint for a future millennial age with a new temple and an associated revival of the Old Testament cult seem to me to be open to similar challenge. They are faced with Hananiah ben Hezekiah's questions about how the restored cultus described in these chapters can possibly be harmonized with that prescribed by Moses—not to mention how future atoning temple sacrifices (*ləkappēr*; Ezek 45:15, 17, 20) can be harmonized with the book of Hebrews and the sufficiency of Christ's once-for-all sacrifice (Heb 9:27-28).

Such a futurist understanding of Ezekiel 34–48 ironically agrees with Ezekiel's critics in Ezekiel 12:27: "The vision that he sees concerns many years from now; he prophesies about distant times," removing any relevance for the original audience, whose concerns the prophet is explicitly addressing (Ezek 37:11; 43:10-11). In addition, it tends to remove personal relevance even for the contemporary audience, most of whom *ex hypothesi* would have been raptured before the millennial temple became a reality. If allegorical interpretation sacrifices literality for the sake of spiritual edification, this interpretation seems to sacrifice spiritual edification for the sake of a supposed literal interpretation.

In contrast to these approaches, a better interpretive model is provided by Scottish pastor Ebenezer Erskine, who preached a sermon on Ezekiel 37:1-14 at the Tollbooth church in Edinburgh in 1715. In line with the history of interpretation we have surveyed, Erskine saw three potential interpretations of the passage: (1) as a depiction and confirmation of the final resurrection of the body; (2) as a depiction of the resurrection of the soul from the grave of sin, effected through the Spirit as the effective cause by means of preaching as the instrumental cause; and (3) a representation of the resurrection of the (OT) church of God from its grave in Babylon, under which they were presently detained. He affirms that that third interpretation is the primary and immediate scope of the prophet's concern, but he goes on:

> However, seeing the deliverance of the children of Israel out of their Babylonish captivity, was typical of our spiritual redemption purchased by the Lord Jesus Christ upon the cross, and in a day of power applied by the mighty and powerful operation of the Holy Spirit of God; and seeing it is this redemption with which we under the gospel are principally concerned, therefore I shall handle the words that I have read under this spiritual sense and meaning.[35]

This spiritual interpretation of the passage is by no means allegorical, since it is rooted and grounded in Jesus' own instructions as to how to interpret the Old Testament in Luke 24:44-47:

---

[35] Ebenezer Erskine, *The Complete Works of the Rev. Ebenezer Erskine* (Edinburgh: Oliver & Boyd, 1871), 1:40.

"This is what I told you while I was still with you: Everything must be fulfilled that is written about me in the Law of Moses, the Prophets and the Psalms." Then he opened their minds so they could understand the Scriptures. He told them, "This is what is written: The Messiah will suffer and rise from the dead on the third day, and repentance and forgiveness of sins will be preached in his name to all nations, beginning at Jerusalem." (NIV)

For Jesus, the message of the prophets is always rooted and grounded in "the sufferings of Christ and the glories that would follow" (see 1 Pet 1:10-11).

The key to this gospel-centered interpretation lies in the biblical-theological connection between Old Testament Israel and the New Testament church, and between Israel's exile and return and the death and resurrection of Christ. As a result, it is sensitive to the inherent parallels and connections that the Scriptures themselves repeatedly urge us to make. It adopts the fundamental connection that the New Testament makes between the Old Testament people of God and the New Testament people of God, and observes that the sufferings and resurrection of Christ and the glories that will follow are the main theme of the entire Old Testament.[36]

This perspective is sometimes pejoratively mischaracterized as replacement theology by its critics, as if on this view the New Testament church replaces God's Old Testament people.[37] However, that is to misunderstand the position completely. It is not that the church replaces Israel; rather, Israel as a nation finds its telos in the person of Jesus Christ, who is himself the new Israel, the promised seed of Abraham (Gal 3:16). Thus the classic Old Testament image of Israel, the vine, is now used of Jesus (Jn 15). It is Jesus who is the focus of the one people

---

[36]See, e.g., Heb 8:8-13, where the New Covenant promised to the house of Judah and the house of Israel is applied to the church, or 1 Pet 2:9, where epithets that describe the OT people of God—"a chosen race, a royal priesthood, a holy nation, a people for his own possession" (ESV)—are applied to NT saints.
[37]E.g., by Kaiser, *Preaching and Teaching the Last Things*, 31.

of God of all times and places, who find their salvation not in their ethnic identity as Jews or as Gentiles but through union with him. The church—made up of *both* Jews and Gentiles—is the inheritor of the promises of God as they are united to Christ (Gal 3:28). Both Jews and Gentiles become true children of Abraham through faith in Christ, not through circumcision or other ethnic markers (Rom 4:11-12), and in that way they are grafted together into a single olive tree, the one people of God in all times and places (Rom 11:17-36).

Ezekiel 37:1-14 thus encouraged the original audience of Babylonian exiles that they were not cut off from God forever and without hope because of their exiled condition. The God whom they served was able to bring the driest of bones back to life and could restore his people also to himself. His promises had not been abandoned because of human unfaithfulness but would reach their promised goal through a resurrection of Israel to new life, foreshadowed by the immediate return to Judah in 538 BC but culminating in the resurrection of Christ.

At the same time, the condition of the exiles was also emblematic of the condition of all people outside Christ. On the most fundamental level, all human beings share by nature the hopelessness of Israel's situation in exile. As Paul tells us in Ephesians 2, through Adam's sin, we all enter this world spiritually dead, as helpless as the bones that Ezekiel saw. Can such spiritually dead people be brought back to life? The answer cannot be a glib "Of course." If we are to live, God must intervene—and though God certainly has the power to do so, does he have the desire? After all, we are born not merely spiritually dead but spiritually rebellious, haters of God and lovers of ourselves and of sin. Will God really raise people like us from our deserved spiritual death?

Conclusion

Thanks be to God, the answer is positive for us, as it was for exiled Israel. In Christ, there is life from the spiritually dead: as Paul tells the Colossians: "You, who were dead in your trespasses and the uncircumcision of your flesh, God made alive together with [Christ], having forgiven us all our trespasses, by canceling the record of debt that stood against us with its legal demands. This he set aside, nailing it to the cross" (Col 2:13-14 ESV). New life is not something we can earn for ourselves through our own best efforts or through trying hard to be good. The bones do not take the initiative to organize themselves and then, in response, receive life from God. As Ezekiel indicates, making us alive is the work of God from beginning to end. The Lord commissions and sends the prophet, he empowers his words to bring the bones together as a body, and then he fills that body with life through the power of his Spirit. So too today, anyone with faith in Christ is spiritually alive because God chose to give them life from the dead through a miraculous work of his grace.

More specifically, the Spirit brings us to new life as Christians by uniting us to Christ, the one in whom this new life is to be found. Just as the prophet Ezekiel was himself a personal model of the restorative power of God in the lives of ancient Israelites (compare Ezek 37:1-11 with Ezek 2:1-2), so too Jesus Christ is both the paradigm and pattern for our new resurrection life. What God does for us as Christians, he first did for Jesus. What he has done for Jesus, he will also do for all those who are united to him by faith, giving us life through the prophetic word preached to us (Rom 10:17) and promising to bring us safely to our heavenly homeland, the Jerusalem that is above (Gal 4:26).

Such a gospel-centered interpretive strategy allows the preacher to feed their people solid spiritual food that teaches, rebukes, corrects, and trains in righteousness (2 Tim 3:16), without moralism or allegory. It shows how the Scripture is an integrated whole from Genesis to

Revelation that finds its center in Christ and the gospel, in whom alone hope is to be found for Jews and Gentiles alike. The message about the God who raises the spiritually dead to new life in Christ through his powerful, prophetic word is thus relevant for God's people in all times and places.[38]

---

[38] For further outworking of this approach, see Iain M. Duguid, "Ezekiel," in *Isaiah–Ezekiel*, ESV Expository Commentary (Wheaton, IL: Crossway, 2022).

15

PREACHING EZEKIEL AS CHRISTIAN SCRIPTURE WITH FOCUS ON EZEKIEL 37:1-14

Daniel I. Block

Preaching Ezekiel is a challenge for many reasons.

1. The book's length: With its 18,731 words, the book of Ezekiel is the fourth longest book in the First Testament—after Psalms (19,532), Genesis (20,611), and Jeremiah (21,819)—and 10 percent longer than Isaiah (16,930).[1]

2. The book's rhetoric: Not only does the book contain oracles that represent a dozen diverse genres, but its style is often bizarre,

---

[1] Hebrew word-count statistics derived from "Statistical Appendix," in *Theologisches Handwörterbuch zum Alten Testament*, ed. E. Jenni and C. Westermann (Munich: Kaiser, 1979), 2:538-39.

bewildering, risqué, and bordering on the obscene. No wonder early rabbis prohibited Jews under thirty from reading the book.

3. The book's content: There are twenty-four chapters of invectives against Judah, YHWH's[2] own covenant people, and in Ezekiel 25–32 we encounter the same tone in more than a dozen oracles of judgment against the nations.

Interpreters find little consolation in observing that Ezekiel is the most logically ordered of the First Testament prophetic books, and the boundaries marking separate oracles are the most clearly demarked. If in the past Christians *would not* read or preach the book of Ezekiel because they were perplexed by the prophet's visions or the forms of his oracles, today some *cannot* preach it because they deem the book and the God portrayed in it as irredeemably problematic and devoid of any grace at all. How can pastors today declare its message with authority, vitality, and clarity?

In the past I had preached occasional sermons from Ezekiel but never had the opportunity to devote a protracted series of sermons to the book. However, on September 9, 2018, in faith we launched a sermon series under the broad rubric "When God Abandons His People," opening with a look at the Ezekiel 1:1-3, under the title "Where Is God When You Need Him?" On September 27, 2021, I delivered sermon seventy-one on Ezekiel 45:1-8 and 48:8-22, 30-35, under the title "YHWH Is There! The Mother Lode of Sanctity in the Holy Land." I may now speak from experience.

---

[2]While often using Yahweh in oral presentation, in print I consistently render the personal name of the God of Israel as YHWH, rather than Jehovah or Yahweh, because of the uncertainty of its original vocalization and deference to Jewish sensibilities. The consistent rendering of this Tetragrammaton ("four letters") in the Old Greek First Testament as κύριος, which means "lord, master," is misleadingly carried over into English translations as LORD. It is misleading because the notion of "lord" is represented by the Hebrew title אֲדֹנָי (*'ădōnāy*) and bears no relation to God's name. It is also unfortunate because the connotations and implications of referring to someone by name or title differ significantly—especially when that Person invited his covenant people to address him by name, YHWH. For further discussion, see Daniel I. Block, *Covenant: The Foundation of God's Grand Plan of Redemption* (Grand Rapids, MI: Baker, 2021), xv.

I will not rehearse here the details of my discussion on preaching Ezekiel presented to the Tyndale Fellowship in July 2009, available in print form in two publications.[3] However, it may be helpful to set out for the present audience the seven propositions I presented there that I thought might yield a strategy for thinking about preaching Ezekiel (albeit in a different order). In order to preach from Ezekiel with authority and clarity for the church:

> Proposition 1: We need to understand the prophet—his character (ethos), passion (pathos), and argumentation (logos).
>
> Proposition 2: We need to understand his audience.
>
> Proposition 3: We need to understand the nature and structure of the book.
>
> Proposition 4: We need to plan carefully.
>
> Proposition 5: We need to understand Ezekiel's rhetorical and homiletical strategy.
>
> Proposition 6: We need to understand the message Ezekiel proclaims.
>
> Proposition 7: We need to link his message with that of the New Testament responsibly.

With this as background, and with the assigned focus on Ezekiel 37:1-14 in mind, I have organized my reflections around the last four propositions listed above.

Proposition Four: In Order to Preach from Ezekiel with Authority and Clarity for the Church, We Need to Plan Carefully

In my view the primary goal of biblical preaching is to help people comprehend the mind of God and to facilitate God's intended message to the people—appealing to John's ambivalent use of *katalambanō* in

---

[3]Daniel I. Block, "Preaching Ezekiel," in *Reclaiming the Old Testament for Christian Preaching*, ed. G. J. R. Kent, P. J. Kissling, and L. A. Turner (Downers Grove, IL: IVP Academic, 2010), 157-78.

John 1:5. Hopefully, through the regular hearing of expositional preaching people will both become better interpreters of Scripture and be transformed by the Spirit of God through the message of Scripture. Pastor Kent Hughes encouraged me to work serially through the entire book, helping readers of the printed versions learn to harvest from every text the author's intended meaning and then showing how that meaning translates into enduring theology for Christians. After all, Jesus included the book of Ezekiel in his sweeping declaration that he came "not to abolish the Torah and the prophets, but to fulfill them" (Mt 5:17-19, my translation). Ezekiel was also in Paul's purview when he affirmed to Timothy, "All Scripture is breathed out by God and profitable for teaching, for reproof, for correction, and for training in righteousness, that the man of God may be complete, equipped for every good work" (2 Tim 3:16-17). Accepting Kent's counsel, I divided the entire book of Ezekiel into seventy-one presentations.

Once the series began, I prepared weekly notes, which we sent out two days in advance to all on the email list. I began the lesson each week reading the entire text as expositorily as I could, reminding the hearers often that what God actually says in/through his word is always more important than my fallible and often inadequate comments on his word.

The book of Ezekiel includes some literary units that are very long and some that are very difficult conceptually in our twenty-first-century Western context. Because Ezekiel 16 is problematic on both counts, I devoted four weeks to this chapter. If anything, Ezekiel 23 is even more troubling. Before I read the text orally, I retreated behind the black curtain that was always behind me and read from back there. I did not want the people to see my face; I wanted them only to hear my voice.

When we arrived at the final vision (Ezek 40–48), I began by reading the entire account of Ezekiel's tour of the temple (Ezek 40–42). I spent the rest of the time available that morning giving the people a bird's-eye view and trying to make sense of the overall design of the temple complex and the way the image guards sacred/profane distinctions. The next week we moved right into Ezekiel 43:1-9.

Figure 15.1. The pillars of Israel's security

Proposition Five: In Order to Preach from Ezekiel with Authority and Clarity for the Church, We Need to Understand Ezekiel's Rhetorical and Homiletical Strategy

Considering proposition four within the broader context of the entire book of Ezekiel, in my discussion of propositions five through seven I will focus on the text assigned to all of us, Ezekiel 37:1-14. The first step in preparing for preaching the message of any biblical text should be to go directly to the text itself. The aim of this phase of sermon preparation is to grasp the text's intent and its theology but also to have the text and its intended message grasp us. To achieve this goal, there is no substitute for close inductive reading. For the past fifty years, I have subjected every text I have intensely studied to what I learned decades later was a form of discourse analysis. The roots of my method were inspired by Walt Kaiser, my adviser as a seminary student, but I have adapted it to a form that works for me. My method assumes fundamentally that since I am not a native speaker of Hebrew and the voice of God comes to me only in congealed Hebrew textual form, in order to *hear* its message I need to *see*, that is, visualize how the text works. The rhetorical strategy of the biblical author is reflected in the syntactical and discourse grammar, to which I gain best access by diagramming the text, as in the attached synopsis.

The boundaries of Ezekiel 37:1-14 are clearly marked by the concluding recognition formula in Ezekiel 36:38 ("Then they will know that I am YHWH," my translation) followed by the initializing construction, "The hand of YHWH was on me," in Ezekiel 37:1. This clause introduces a narrative preamble for the speeches and actions that follow. The unit concludes in Ezekiel 37:14 with the recognition formula, a divine declaration of YHWH's commitment to his word, and the signatory formula, "The declaration of YHWH."[4]

This does not mean the text between these frames flows seamlessly. On the contrary, "and he said to me" in Ezekiel 37:11 introduces a new speech whose content seems to contradict Ezekiel 37:1-10. An image of innumerable very dry bones, obviously the remains of an unburied host of corpses, dominate Ezekiel 37:1-10, which links directly to people's response in Ezekiel 37:11: "Our bones are dried up and our hope is gone; we are extinguished" (my translation; see fig. 15.1). But surprisingly, YHWH responds with images of proper burials in graves and speaks of the resurrection of those whose remains have been out of sight for a long time. The shift in prophetic genre from a private visionary experience involving only YHWH and his prophet (Ezek 37:1-10)

---

[4]This abbreviated form of the signatory formula occurs elsewhere in Ezekiel only in Ezek 13:6, 7; 16:58, in contrast to the longer form, *nəʾum ʾădōnāy yəhwāh*, which occurs more than eighty times.

to a typical disputation speech in which YHWH responds to a statement reflecting popular disposition that is circulating among the exiles (Ezek 37:11) reinforces the distinction/tension.[5] To the people's quoted thesis, YHWH responds with a counterthesis answering the thesis directly and intends to turn despair into hope.

However, YHWH's reference to putting his spirit (*rûaḥ*) in "you" [Israel] and predicting their coming to life ties in with the theme question, "Can these bones live?" (Ezek 37:3) and a refrain heard five times (Ezek 37:5, 6, 9, 10). The declaration, "I will put my Spirit [*rûaḥ*] in you" obviously recalls his earlier statement in Ezekiel 36:27, but it also links this statement with Ezekiel 37:6 above, though so long as the text is talking about bones and sinews and flesh and skin, I translate *rûaḥ* as "breath."

Indeed, the lexeme *rûaḥ* is probably the key to the entire text. Some interpreters and translators argue that within a given context repeated words must be translated consistently so that English hearers grasp the lexemic coherence. However, Ezekiel was a master at using lexemes with more than one sense in his oracles; indeed, shifts in meaning are often the keys to a text's rhetorical intent. This text provides a supreme example of this strategy. In these fourteen verses (indeed, in Ezek 37:1-10 alone) YHWH and his prophet use the word in four different senses: (1) of the divine Spirit (Ezek 37:1, 14), though in the first instance the *rûaḥ* could be (2) a wind that YHWH sent to pick up the prophet and whisk him away (as in Ezek 8:3, which also refers to the divine hand grabbing him by a lock of his hair); (3) of breath that is vital for creatures made of bones and flesh to live (Ezek 37:5, 6, 8, 9, 10); and (4) of the points of a compass, that is "the four winds" (*'arba' rûḥôt*, Ezek 37:9).

---

[5]On disputation speeches, with reference to Ezek 11:1-13, see Daniel Block, *Ezekiel 1–24* (Grand Rapids, MI: Eerdmans, 1997), 330-40. On disputation speeches more fully, see Adrian Graffy, *A Prophet Confronts His People: The Disputation Speech in the Prophets*, Analecta Biblica 104 (Rome: Pontifical Biblical Institute, 1984).

With hindsight it is evident that in Ezekiel 37:1-10 YHWH already addressed the cynical quotation in Ezekiel 37:11 and provides Ezekiel with the counterthesis. But by prefacing the oracle with the vision YHWH gives the prophet the answer in advance. Here we encounter a picture of death in all its horror, intensity, and finality. Obviously, this is no Arlington National Cemetery in Washington or Flanders Fields in Belgium, where human remains are properly interred, with the crosses all in perfect rows.

The present scene is nothing like that. No heroes are remembered here. On the contrary, the scene is as hopeless and depressing as can be. Whoever these bones represented, they had been dead for a long time. But YHWH has cast the answer to the people's comments in Ezekiel 37:11 in the form of a riddle. We could have guessed this not only from the question, "Can these bones live?" (Ezek 37:3) but also from all the unanswered questions in the opening vision of the dry bones: (1) Where is this valley? (2) What sort of bones are these? (3) How did they get there? (4) Whom do they represent?

Though often overlooked, it is striking that until the very last phrase of this opening section we do not even know that they are human bones. The expression "these slain" (Ezek 37:9) offers a clue, but for all we know they could have been the bones of cattle or sheep at some grand sacrificial site, or horses slaughtered in battle, or wild animals hunted down for their meat, as used to happen with buffalo on the Canadian prairies. For those who have watched the Hobbit and Lord of the Rings movies, this last phrase could even represent animals in military combat.[6] By the time the first and longest phase of this oracle ends, we are still scratching our heads concerning its meaning, and if Ezekiel recounted this vision to his exiled compatriots independently, they too could only have speculated about its significance.

---

[6]See the reference to locusts marching in rank like an army in Prov 31:28.

If these are human bones, then we must ask why they are lying out there in the open. We may answer in part by noting that throughout the ancient Near East leaving dead bodies out in the open to be devoured by animals was the worst kind of curse one could experience. One of the curses in Esarhaddon's Succession Treaty reads: "May Ninurta, foremost of the gods, fell you with his ferocious arrow. May he fill the steppe with your blood! May he feed your flesh to the eagle and the vultures!"[7] This reminds us of Moses' warning for the Israelites in the previous millennium, which they had long since forgotten (Deut 28:25-26; see Jer 34:17-20).

In this literary unit, Ezekiel 37:11-14 functions as the anchor. The two parts, vision and disputation speech, work together like Ezekiel's signacts and their interpretation (e.g., Ezek 12:1-9, 10-16; 37:15-18, 19-28; 24:15-20, 21-27) or his extended metaphors (*məšālîm*) and their interpretation (Ezek 17:1-7, 22-24; 17:7-10, 11-21; 31:1-17, 18), except that here YHWH reverses the order of image and interpretation. The rhetoric is impressive and the message powerful.

Proposition Six: In Order to Preach from Ezekiel with Authority and Clarity for the Church, We Need to Understand the Message Ezekiel Proclaims

With the preceding discussion we may have gained access to the message of this text for Ezekiel and his BC audience. Given the exiles' hardened (Ezek 2:3-8; 3:4-11) and rebellious spiritual state, that they despaired of life returning to normal is not surprising.[8] At least six years—perhaps a decade—earlier, Ezekiel offered hope to the exiles, as described in Ezekiel 11:17-20.

---

[7]"Esarhaddon's Succession Treaty," in *The Context of Scripture*, ed. William W. Hallo (Leiden: Brill, 1997–2002), 4:36, §41, trans. Jacob Lauinger.

[8]The characterizing expression *bêt mərî*, "house of rebellion," applies to the exiles in Ezek 2:2-6; 3:9, 26-27; 12:2-3; 44:6, modified: *'el-merî 'el-bêt yiśrā'ēl*, which LXX renders *pros ton oikon ton parapikrinonta pros ton oikon tou Israel*, "to the house of rebellion the house of Israel."

However, access to this promise was neither automatic nor guaranteed, as YHWH declares in an epilogue, "'But as for those whose heart is committed to their detestable and abominable things—I will bring their conduct down upon their own heads.' The declaration of the Lord YHWH" (Ezek 11:21, my translation). Later prophecies show that Ezekiel's exiled compatriots dismissed him as "a prattler of parables" (*məmaššēl məšālîm*, Ezek 21:5 [ET Ezek 20:49]) and entertainer—a "Judean idol" among the exiles (Ezek 33:31-32). YHWH had assured Ezekiel that when his prediction of Jerusalem's fall was fulfilled, they would recognize that a (true) prophet was in their midst (Ezek 2:5; 33:33). However, despite Ezekiel's appeals to repent (Ezek 18:1-32), even as the fateful moment approaches, their cynicism and faithlessness persist. On the one hand they claim, "Certainly our crimes and our sins are upon us, and because of them we are wasting away. How then shall we survive?" (Ezek 33:10-11, my translation), and on the other hand they charge YHWH with bring unscrupulous: "The action of YHWH is without principle" (Ezek 33:20, my translation). However, in Ezekiel 33:30-33 YHWH paints the clearest word picture of their state:

> So my people come to you in droves [lit. "like the coming of people"] and they sit before you. They hear your words, but they refuse to act on them, because they act only with lust in their mouths, and their hearts pursue nothing but ill-gotten wealth. Look, to them you are like a singer of sensual songs, with a beautiful voice and a fine musical touch. They hear your words, but they refuse to put them into practice. But when it comes—and come it certainly will—then they will know that a prophet has been among them. (my translation)

With the vision and oracle of Ezekiel 37:1-14 YHWH addresses the people's despair, declaring that for the nation to be resuscitated will take a miraculous divine act. The covenant triangle has been obliterated—YHWH has left, the people have been wiped from the land (see Lev 26:23-33; Deut 28:49-57; 2 Kings 21:13), and what remains of Israel is wasting away (*nimqaq*, Ezek 33:10; see Ezek 4:17; 23:23) in a foreign land precisely as predicted (Lev 26:36-39; Deut 28:62-67). In their physical and spiritual exile Ezekiel's compatriots in Babylon continue to experience the curses that YHWH predicted he would impose on the nation within the covenant at the time of the nation's founding.

Whereas back in Jerusalem Jeremiah had at least a few supporters (Baruch, Ahikam ben Shaphan, Seraiah, Ebed-melech), Ezekiel has no one—apart from his wife, "the delight of your eyes" (*mahmad ʿêneykā*, Ezek 24:16), whom he suddenly loses overnight as an element of his rhetoric/message. Nor do we find a shred of evidence in the book of any sympathetic response to his pastoral work among the exiles. Although this vision creates tension with anticipations of Israel's restoration in Leviticus 26:40-48 and Deuteronomy 30:1-10, in Ezekiel 33:1-10 YHWH suggests that he will not wait for the Israelite community as a whole to repent and get themselves a new heart (see Ezek 18:30-32; Deut 10:16) but will unilaterally blow over them with his breath and put his animating spirit within them.

Herein lies the only hope for the remnant of the once-great nation of Israel. As YHWH emphasizes in oracles on both sides of our text (Ezek 34; 36; 37:15-28), the judgment of the nation cannot be the last chapter of Israel's history. YHWH's oath and covenant have obligated him to reconstitute fully his special relationship with the descendants of Abraham and with the land he chose for them. This will not be accomplished by self-help programs—the nation has proved itself totally incapable of that project. However, we need to recognize that Ezekiel's agenda was totally parochial; YHWH's commission for him is not to create a vision of cosmic renewal, like we find in the latter chapters of Isaiah. His concern is to put back together the Humpty Dumpty that was Israel.

How do we preach Ezekiel 37:1-14 as Christian Scripture? With this question, we have opened the door to proposition seven.

PROPOSITION SEVEN: IN ORDER TO PREACH FROM EZEKIEL WITH AUTHORITY AND CLARITY FOR THE CHURCH, WE NEED TO LINK HIS MESSAGE WITH THAT OF THE NEW TESTAMENT RESPONSIBLY

What does this mean? First, in identifying the problem it means keeping the main thing the main thing. Ezekiel's primary point was not to teach the Israelites the doctrine of individual eschatological resurrection, let alone the resurrection of Jesus the Messiah. His goal was to reassure his people that YHWH's ancient, eternal, and irrevocable promises to the descendants of Abraham had survived the holocaust of 586 BC. YHWH ends his interpretation of the vision with the recognition formula, followed by commentary, followed by his signature formula: "Then you will know that I am YHWH. I have spoken, and I will act. The declaration of YHWH." Almost by definition, the God who goes by the name YHWH keeps his word. Whether the word he performs is a threat of punishment (Ezek 22:14) or a promise of restoration after the judgment (Ezek 17:24; 36:36; 37:14), in Ezekiel when YHWH says, "I have spoken, and I will act," the reference is not primarily to the present oracle (though it is that) but to the ancient promises. The promissory and covenantal pillars on which the people of Ezekiel's day had grounded their security were indeed eternal; while subjectively access to the covenantal benefactions is always conditional on the people's response, objectively their response would not jeopardize the status of the covenant itself. The present oracle affirms that YHWH is always true to his word, including the eternality of his covenant with Israel.

In preaching Ezekiel's primary point in Ezekiel 33:1-14, we must avoid two extremes. First, we must stay clear of supersessionism (which sadly often morphs into antisemitism). Proponents of supersessionism argue that in the light of Christ's work God's covenant promises to Abraham and his physical descendants have morphed into a platonic or spiritual ideal, that these physical promises evaporate and that New Covenant believers in Christ, the spiritual seed of Abraham, replace the physical seed. This means that Ezekiel's promise of the physical resurrection of Israel also evaporates, as do all the covenant promises relating to them. However, this runs counter to Paul's forthright declarations at the beginning of his soliloquy on the status of his own "brothers," that is, his physical kinsmen (*tōn adelphōn mou tōn syngenōn mou kata sarka*, Rom 9:3):

> For I could wish that I myself were accursed and cut off from Christ for the sake of my brothers, my kinsmen according to the flesh. They are Israelites, and to them belong the adoption, the glory, the covenants, the giving of the law, the worship, and the promises. To them belong the patriarchs, and from their race, according to the flesh, is the Christ, who is God over all, blessed forever. Amen.
>
> But it is not as though the word of God has failed. For not all who are descended from Israel belong to Israel. (Rom 9:3-6)

Notice that he does not say, "and to them *was* the adoption, the glory, the covenants, the giving of the law, the worship, and the promises." But supersessionism also contradicts Paul's concluding comments regarding the future of his brothers, his physical kinsmen, in Romans 11:25-29:

> Lest you be wise in your own sight, I do not want you to be unaware of this mystery, brothers: a partial hardening has come upon Israel, until the fullness of the Gentiles has come in. And in this way all Israel will be saved, as it is written,
>
> "The Deliverer will come from Zion,
>   he will banish ungodliness from Jacob";
> "and this will be my covenant with them
>   when I take away their sins."

As regards the gospel, they are enemies for your sake. But as regards election, they are beloved for the sake of their forefathers. For the gifts and the calling of God are irrevocable. (Rom 11:25-29)[9]

A second extreme to avoid is using Ezekiel 37:1-14 to proclaim Christian Zionism, which is often tied to dispensationalism and has been widely popularized through the fictional Left Behind series by Jerry Jenkins and Tim LaHaye and published by Tyndale House.[10] In the current struggle between Israel and its neighbors, this movement advocates unqualified support for Israel, arguing that the Jewish people have eternal title to all the Promised Land and that 1948 marked a significant step as history lunges forward to the coming of the Messiah. However, contemporary Zionism is a largely secular movement, and the current state of Israel bears no resemblance to the eschatological prophetic vision of a restored nation of Israel, whose population consists of persons who are both the physical and spiritual seed of Abraham.[11]

While we grant that 1948 and the resultant state remind us that YHWH has not forgotten, let alone discarded, the descendants of Abraham, and while we grant that YHWH's covenant with Israel is eternal and irrevocable, the precondition to entitlement to the benefactions that attend this covenant relationship has always been circumcised hearts that yield love for YHWH demonstrated in grateful service to him and compliance with his revealed will (fig. 15.2). As Paul declares in Romans 10:13, in the wake of the incarnation there is no true

---

[9] For discussion of this matter, including the totally parochial nature of the renewed covenant text in Jer 31–40, a fragment of which Paul cites in Rom 11:27, see Daniel I. Block, *Covenant: The Framework of God's Grand Plan of Redemption* (Grand Rapids, MI: Baker, 2021), 280-87, 512-15, 524.

[10] Christian Zionism is represented by persons such as John Hagee and Jack Van Impe. To date more than eighty million copies of these books have been sold, as noted in Tim LaHaye's obituary: Ann Byle, "LaHaye, Co-author of Left Behind Series, Leaves a Lasting Impact," Publishers Weekly, July 27, 2016, www.publishersweekly.com/pw/by-topic/industry-news/religion/article/71026-lahaye-co-author-of-left-behind-series-leaves-a-lasting-impact.html. The book review editors at *Time* comment that these are "the best-selling fiction books of our time—right up there with Tom Clancy and Stephen King."

[11] In the 2021 parliamentary elections, the far-right National Union-Tkuma party ran under the name Religious Zionist Party for the first time. The party opposes any territorial concessions to the Arab population of greater Palestine.

devotion apart from acceptance of the grace offered in Jesus Christ, who is YHWH embodied in human flesh.

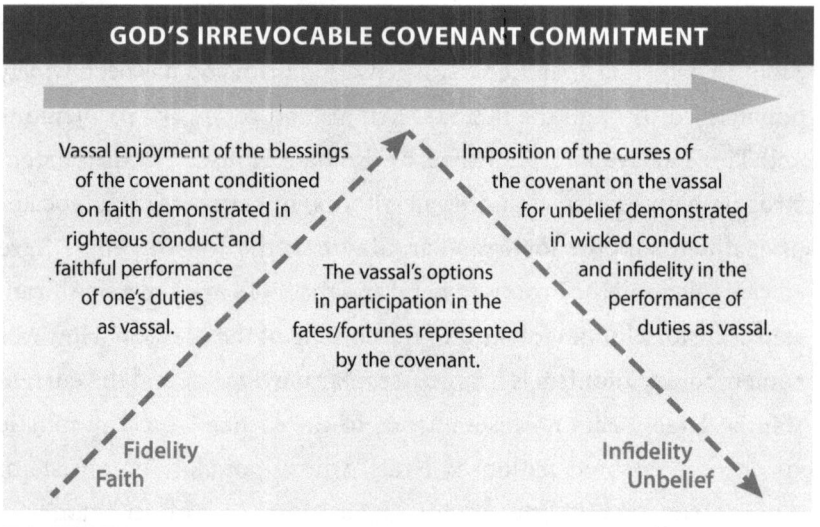

Figure 15.2. God's irrevocable covenant commitment

Having called for a responsible and disciplined application of the message to the current crises in the eastern Mediterranean region does not mean we restrict its significance for us to the current Israeli-Arab conflict. YHWH did not call Israel for Israel's sake but to be the bearers of the commission to Abraham to bring blessing to a world that languishes under the curse of sin (Gen 12:1-3). At Sinai YHWH confirmed/established (*hēqîm*) with the descendants of Abraham the covenant that he first made (*kārat*) with him in seed form (Gen 15; 17). The commission of blessing all the nations borne by the ancestors was transferred to the newly constituted nation of Israel (Ex 19:4-6). Through the covenant rituals described in Exodus 19–24, Israel both became the bride and adopted son of YHWH and was ordained to priestly ministry to mediate the revelation and grace of God to the nations languishing under the curse.

When Moses supervised the renewal of this covenant with the desert generation, he cast YHWH's vision of their role as setting them high above the nations for praise, fame, and glory (*lithillâ ûləšēm ûlətip'āret*, Deut 26:19), on which he expands in Deuteronomy 28:1-14. Through the triangular covenant involving YHWH, Israel, and the land of Canaan, YHWH aimed to create an Edenic environment that functioned as a microcosm of his vision for the whole world, declaring to all what divine grace can accomplish in a cursed context. Ezekiel hints at this role for the nation in Ezekiel 5:5 (my translation): "This is what YHWH has declared: 'This is Jerusalem; I have set her in in the center of the nations with countries all around her.'" However, instead of accepting her role as a city on a hill (see Mt 5:14), she had rebelled against her Redeemer, and her abominations exceeded those of her pagan neighbors, which had precipitated the judgment represented by the valley of dry bones and the exile's current remnant living in Babylon (Ezek 5:6-17). We need to pray that the Spirit of God would blow over that land today and transform all its inhabitants to be faithful followers of YHWH, incarnate in Jesus Christ.

With this picture of Israel's role in the divine plan of redemption, we may begin to grasp additional dimensions of significance for this text.

1. *Israel's past judgment and future restoration are paradigmatic for the human race and the world they occupy.* The bones in Ezekiel's vision present a picture of all humanity, which languishes under the curse of death. According to Paul, the wages of sin is death (Rom 6:23), and in another epistle he writes, "You were dead in the trespasses and sins, . . . [which made us] by nature children of wrath," that is, objects of God's fury (Eph 2:1, 3). So the question that God asks of Ezekiel he also asks of us, with regard to the state of humanity: "Can these bones live?" The answer is, "Indeed!" and one of these days, when the cosmos is transformed and renewed, this will indeed happen. We await the redemption of humankind, for that will mean the redemption of the cosmos (Rom 8:18-25).[12]

---

[12] According to common Christian interpretation, Ezekiel's images of the dry bones coming to life and the tombs opened depict the general resurrection at the last judgment. Indeed in Orthodox Christian tradition the text of the valley of dry bones (Ezek 37) is often read annually in churches

2. We may also legitimately associate these bones with what remains of the Western church, which historically has claimed to be the people of God and which once was the base of God's work in the world and the source of his missionary force. However, like Israel, the Western church has increasingly taken on the characteristics of the world around it. When I look at the state of the church in this land, I smell the aroma of death. Some bones are very dry. It is most obvious in the mainline churches, which have long since abandoned the revealed will of God in the Scriptures as their life-giving authority and whose congregations have shrunk almost to the point of oblivion. But what concerns me is the smell and the sight of death in the so-called evangelical church. The discrediting of the label itself reflects the problem. Many who claim this epithet treat the Scriptures and the traditional teachings of the church like an Old Country Buffet restaurant spread—claiming the privileges of admission but taking only what satisfies their palates (most of it unhealthy) and ignoring the covenantal ethic that comes with bearing the name of Jesus. Being born again is often treated as a ticket to health, happiness, and success—a modern version of ancient fertility religion—but it would have been unrecognizable in the circle to whom Jesus called to take up their cross and follow him (Mt 10:38; 16:24; Mk 8:34; Lk 9:23, which adds "daily").

This is a church that does not challenge its people to a higher morality than is common out there, and though it is passionate about political agendas it seems heartless toward people in real need. This is a church that has domesticated God rather than gratefully, joyfully, and self-sacrificially serving its Redeemer. The bones are very dry. Why is it that if you want to see the living church you need to visit South America, or Romania, or the back corners of China? Our churches have become cemeteries where people die rather than where they come to life. Can

---

during the early hours after midnight on Pascha (Easter) morning. However, these interpreters often take its predictive significance too far by treating this as a prophecy of Christ's decent to Hades to free Adam (humankind) from the prison of death.

these bones live? In my weaker moments, I become pessimistic, especially when I realize I am part of the problem. I too am one of these living corpses. Can these bones live? Lord, you know, but I sure hope so. I pray that I will.

Second, preaching this text responsibly also means recognizing in its message the solution to the problem. To answer that question we return to the text. What does YHWH say it will take to bring these bones to life? Our text offers several clues.

1. *This transition from death to life requires a new animating and transforming work of the Spirit of God.* This is what it took in the first place to create the human species as living creatures (Gen 2:7). In Ezekiel 36:27 the Lord promises that he will put his spirit into his people, and they will be restored to full and vital relationship with him. As a whole Ezekiel 37:1-14 functions as an exposition of this single idea. So what will it take to restore Israel to its status as the people of God? Nothing more nor less than a new moving and infusion of the Spirit of God. This is Moses' hope in Deuteronomy 30:1-10, where he looks forward to the time in the distant future, after Israel's judgment, when in their exile the people of Israel will turn from their wicked ways and experience divine circumcision of their hearts. This is Jeremiah's hope when, in the face of his people's judgment, he looks forward to the day when not just a small remnant, as had been the case throughout most of Israel's history, but all Israel will be the covenant people of God, having the Torah written on their hearts, truly claiming the covenant formula, knowing YHWH, and experiencing the joy of sins forgiven (Jer 31:31-34). This is Paul's hope in Romans 9–11, that one day "all Israel will be saved" (Rom 11:26). This remains our hope. Until the breath of God moves over the land of Israel and the descendants of Abraham everywhere, the nation will remain in exile, unable to realize the fullness of all of God's promises.

But what will it take to restore a *human race* under the curse? The answer is the same—a mighty moving of the Spirit of God. This is the only way. Jesus talks about this to Nicodemus, a teacher of the Jews who comes to Jesus at night with one simple question on his mind, "How can one be a part of the kingdom of God?" However, before he puts words to the question in his mind Jesus answers him, "You must be born again." Not grasping what Jesus meant, the rabbi asks him, "Do you expect me to reenter my mother's belly now, so I can be born once more?" Jesus responds with a lecture on the working of the Spirit, which he should have known, if only he had paid attention when he was reading Ezekiel. Since the kingdom of God is spiritual, one must be animated by God's Spirit.

What will it take to restore *a church* that bears the smell of death? The answer is not found rewriting the constitutions of our congregations, or getting a new pastor, or forging new alliances with one or more political parties, or even planning new and exciting programs geared to producing revival. The old adage of the psalmist is true even in the service of the house of God: "Unless the Lord builds the house, those who build it labor in vain" (Ps 127:1). The revival of the church depends on nothing more nor less than a mighty movement of God's Spirit. We need to pray that the Spirit would begin to move among us again, not necessarily in dramatic utterances of tongues or mighty healings but in convicting us of sin and driving us to repentance; in infusing us with the life breath of God; in transforming us from the self-indulgent, arrogant, compromising persons we are to humble servants of God, willing to abandon the cares of this world and to pour out our lives for the Lord. Perhaps then the world will stop ridiculing us for our excesses, stridency, and belligerence but will finally recognize us for our Christlike kindness and our devotion to Christ.

2. *This transition from death to life requires a lifting of the curse.* Before the blessings come to Israel, the curse on them has to be lifted. But only God can do this. When he does so they will begin to experience anew the

riches of his grace (Ezek 36:33-36) and Eden will become reality again. In our own day the whole world seems under a curse. If it is not nations ruthlessly competing with each other for hegemony that we fear, it is the power of nature, in the forms of earthquakes and tsunamis, of hurricanes and tidal waves, and of cancer and Covid-19 in all its variations. These are reminders to us all that we are under the curse. Until the Lord breathes life on this planet, we are all threatened. But we are also under the curse of violence and rage. The TV talk shows become ever more outrageous, the register of political speech more degraded, the media entertain us with ever more brutal and obscene behavior. In a sense it seems the church itself is under a curse. Every week we learn of another leader fallen, another church split, another denomination in trouble, another Christian home broken. We begin to scream, "Lord, lift this curse!"

Conclusion

Can these bones live? Prophecy conferences used to be devoted to trying to figure out whether and when the bones of Israel would come together and be brought to life in fulfillment of Ezekiel's prophecy. But we need to ask the question of ourselves. Can *these* bones live? Can I enjoy the life abundant that the Lord offers? Can our young people live? Can we who are engaged in the ministry live? As in Ezekiel's day, the question can only be answered by God. With Ezekiel we say, "Lord, you know! Lord, I believe that you can do it!"

This text is a glorious testimony to the power of God to triumph over death. "God, being rich in mercy, because of the great love with which he loved us, even when we were dead in our trespasses, made us alive together with Christ—by grace you have been saved" (Eph 2:4-5). From the human-response perspective, the recipe for revival remains the same as it has ever been: "If my people who are called by my name humble themselves, and pray and seek my face and turn from their wicked ways, then I will hear from heaven and will forgive their sin and heal their land" (2 Chron 7:14).

From the perspective of divine initiative, the source of that revival also remains the same. Through the death and resurrection of Jesus, the one who saves us from our sin and its cursed effects (Mt 1:21), we have hope. In the face of Lazarus's death and Martha's grief, "an intense anger was ignited within him" (*enebrimēsato tō pneumati*), "he was extremely agitated" (*kai etaraxen heauton*, Jn 11:33, my translation), and "he wept" (*edakrysen*, Jn 11:35, my translation). However, in the miracle that followed, the climactic sign-act of his life, Jesus proved that he was indeed YHWH incarnate, the source of life for a moribund world. Moments before calling Lazarus from the tomb, he had tried to comfort Martha with those amazing words: "I am the resurrection and the life. Anyone who believes in me will live, even after dying. Everyone who lives in me and believes in me will never ever die. Do you believe this, Martha?" (Jn 11:25-26, my translation). In this amazing event, he demonstrated that what YHWH had told Ezekiel of himself was also true of Jesus, for he is YHWH incarnate: "I will put my spirit within you, and you will come to life. . . . Then you will know that I am YHWH. I have spoken and I will act. The declaration of YHWH" (Ezek 37:13-14, my translation).

Let us begin to pray for the winds of the Spirit God and of his Christ to blow on us, on our churches, and on our world. Let us pray that it begins here with us. May this happen for the glory of God and the triumph of his grace.

CONCLUSION

William R. Osborne

A FEW YEARS AGO, my family and I had the chance to finish up a sabbatical by retreating to the Cairngorm Mountains in the highlands of Scotland. My wife and I had always wanted to explore this region, but truthfully, we would have probably changed the timing if we could have. It was mid-December, and it was *dark*. For nearly seventeen hours of the day, the cold darkness covered our house and the surrounding landscape. Walking out to the woodshed every afternoon/evening, I was deeply reliant on my phone light to see where I was going. When everything else was shrouded in darkness, I could walk in my small circle of light, trusting I was headed in the right direction.

The apostle Peter draws on a similar image in describing the surety and value of the prophetic word for the church: "And we have the abiding prophetic word, which you will do well to pay attention to like a lamp shining in a dark place, until the day dawns and the morning star rises in your hearts" (2 Pet 1:19, my translation). Peter's exhortation captures the spirit of this book. The prophetic word is an abiding, firm, and reliable foundation for the Christian faith. The apostolic witness was not to be viewed as manmade myth because of the eyewitness testimony of the disciples (2 Pet 1:16) and the enduring and relevant words of the prophets of old, which will guide the church until the coming of Christ, when all will be made light.

Every contributor to this volume is deeply committed to the Petrine conviction of the relevance and endurance of the prophetic word. The careful reader of these essays will quickly realize the shared commitments and immense overlap in perspective held by the contributors—this is not coincidental. Living in our current cultural moment, where fragmentation seems to dominate, it is important to hear the chorus of voices singing in unison: *The prophets proclaim the words of God! The prophets are speaking to God's people throughout the ages! The prophets declare the coming Messiah!* Such refrains remind us that, while there are differences in our interpretation of the Major Prophets, there is much more that we as contributors hold in common about these books. I am thankful for the work produced by John Oswalt, Philip Ryken, and Daniel Block reminding us that we are still a proclaiming people. The church is not merely a historical society, seeking to uncover and describe the world of the Major Prophets, but we are witnesses called to gospelize a world with the enduring message of the kingdom they announced.

But there are differences of opinion. Readers will discern that there is no singular, comprehensive interpretive schema that has guided Christians in reading Isaiah, Jeremiah, and Ezekiel through the centuries. The chapters by Mark Gignilliat, Andrew Shead, and Iain Duguid ably demonstrate some of these fascinating differences. Alien to the pressures of modernity, these chapters reveal an approach to the Major Prophets that often differs considerably from the way modern commentators write. Hearing voices from the faithful dead wrestling with these challenging books reminds us that (1) we are walking well-trod paths, despite the challenges we may encounter; (2) this is no fool's errand—theological riches await the diligent student; and (3) no community or era can claim mastery over the biblical text. Listening to divergent opinions and recognizing variations of interpretation does not equal an abdication of the search for meaning and truth. In fact, if we believe the Word of God has been given to the people of God, communal reading and interpretation is foundational to the humble pursuit of truth.[1] As in life, God often uses the voices of others to expose the errors in our thinking, reading, and living.

Perhaps it is not too hard for us to hear the words of Cyril of Alexandria or Origen and politely receive their interpretations, and then move on with little irritation about whatever differences we encounter (history tends to help us diffuse the vitriol that can so often cloud the contemporary and controversial). It is often harder for us to deal graciously with differences living down the street than those who lived a thousand years ago. Here we come to think about the varied opinions communicated in this book as to how contemporary Christians read the text in light of the Christ event. Are we to simply recite Augustine, Theodoret, Calvin, or some other hero of the faith, the validity of our interpretation being found in a footnote? Is there a certain *method* that best guides us in recognizing the Christian nature of the Major Prophets? Can we follow six steps and arrive at the enduring character of the Word of God? These questions are not meant to mock any particular view, for these are the very issues with which anyone reading and teaching the Major Prophets must wrestle. The desire of this project is to help readers hear differing Christian approaches to the Major Prophets, and we conclude by highlighting some of the central themes that emerge as a result.

Responsible Hermeneutics

While focused on the Major Prophets, this is ultimately a book about hermeneutics—or, as Anthony Thiselton defines it, the exploration of

---

[1] This principle certainly applies to geographical and cultural diversity as well as chronological.

"the conditions and criteria that operate to try to ensure responsible, valid, fruitful, or appropriate interpretation."[2] In this context, the contributors are seeking to explore—and at some level demonstrate—what "responsible, valid, fruitful, or appropriate" interpretation of the Major Prophets looks like. If we were to gather all the minds that went into this volume and sit them around a table, Thiselton's descriptors would likely emerge as some of the key vocabulary shaping what would no doubt be a lively discussion. Is our reading responsible? Are our textual conclusions valid? To what end are they beneficial or appropriate for the people of God?

Some answer these questions by appealing to the intended meaning of the original author. So, any interpretation that deviates from the intended meaning of Isaiah or Jeremiah is irresponsible or invalid. This issue is highly significant when Paul Wegner argues that an interpretation of Isaiah that views the New Testament context as an extended reference for the prophetic word is employing a reader-response approach to the text. That is, reading back into the text what was not originally there (*anachronistic* is Gary Yates's term in his chapter). The key issue here is what we mean by "deviate from the intended meaning of the original author."

Perhaps an illustration will help. In discussing paradigm shifts and scientific revolutions, science historian and philosopher Thomas Kuhn notes that Einsteinian science could have never arisen from merely amassing information through a Newtonian paradigm of science. Something new had to happen (Kuhn's anomaly).[3] But, once Einsteinian dynamics were established, they did not disprove or contradict older Newtonian dynamical equations but instead demonstrated how they were correct in their own rights. The paradigm shift of relative physics was profoundly different from what went on before, even redefining it,

---

[2] Anthony Thiselton, *Hermeneutics: An Introduction* (Grand Rapids, MI: Eerdmans, 2009), 4.
[3] Thomas S. Kuhn, *The Structure of Scientific Revolutions*, 2nd ed. (Chicago: University of Chicago Press, 1986), 92-110.

but not ultimately refuting or negating the previous system. When applied to the Old Testament–New Testament relationship, this is perhaps what John Hilber is implying when he presents his helpful axiom: the text can mean more than what the original author intended but never less.

Coming back to the hermeneutical task, the challenge is the nuance of the dialogical relationship between old and new. Does the dawning of the New Testament era provide a new interpretive horizon whereby the apostles can authoritatively declare, "This is actually what Jeremiah meant when he said . . ."? I believe the answer is yes. A tension emerges, however, in our interpretations where some see the redemptive flow of revelation moving unidirectionally from Old Testament to New Testament (what some might call *Christotelic*). Others maintain a necessary looking back from the cross-centered New Testament perspective in order to understand the true meaning of the Old Testament text. The New Testament paradigm shift transformed key concepts such as law, Israel, and kingdom, but it does not refute or negate these concepts. It is too simplistic to navigate this shift with categories such as literal and figurative.[4] Gary Yates demonstrates that typological readings do not necessarily refute an eschatological future for the nation of Israel. There is nuance here, and careful exegetes must let the Old Testament text be their guide. However, discussions of the New Covenant must necessarily consider the apostolic witness of how this covenant has been fulfilled in Christ and how that affects our definitions of the people of God. There will likely continue to be debate as to how this fulfillment affects Old Testament promises about Israel and the Promised Land, but a Christian reading of the Major Prophets must be willing to look back over the words of Major Prophets allowing the christological

---

[4]See D. Brent Sandy's now-classic work on navigating some of challenges of figural language, metaphor, and fulfillment in the prophets: *Plowshares and Pruning Hooks: Rethinking the Language of Biblical Prophecy* (Downers Grove, IL: IVP Academic, 2002).

paradigm shift of the New Testament to explain and even redefine the words of the prophets.

Inspired Prophets

Such interpretive questions would be much easier if we were simply studying ancient documents penned by any number of human authors. The deeper challenge for meaning flows from the fact that these are *divinely inspired* prophetic books. The apostle Peter once again highlights the prophetic word, saying,

> Concerning this salvation, the prophets who prophesied about the grace that was to be yours searched and inquired carefully, inquiring what person or time the Spirit of Christ in them was indicating when he predicted the sufferings of Christ and the subsequent glories. It was revealed to them that they were serving not themselves but you, in the things that have now been announced to you through those who preached the good news to you by the Holy Spirit sent from heaven, things into which angels long to look. (1 Pet 1:10-12 ESV)

The same Spirit at work in the apostles is speaking through the prophets of Israel, and Peter writes that Isaiah, Jeremiah, and Ezekiel were made aware of their service to the first-century church. It is not as though the Holy Spirit is peripheral to the prophetic ministry of the Old Testament—the Spirit is fundamental to their very identity as prophets! It is *by* the Spirit of God that these men declared the end from the beginning and proclaimed what would be. So, can we echo the words of C. S. Lewis (as cited by Paul Wegner) in saying that the connection between the words spoken by Ezekiel and the New Testament are "as we should say, accidental"?

There are no accidental words in the Major Prophets, and they are all intentionally pointing forward to what God will ultimately accomplish through his Son Jesus. Every intertextual link and echo is rooted in the divine will established from eternity past. The divine nature of the text justifies our looking back to the Major Prophets in light of the cross and empty tomb to arrive at a full canonical meaning of the prophet. This is not a reader-response method because this christological search for meaning and looking back is not a *creation* of meaning but a recognition of it from the canonical perspective of the redemptive work of Jesus. This is what has been referred to in this volume as *sensus plenior*, or a fuller sense. Instead of posing the reader-oriented question, "What does Jeremiah mean to me and my community?" the redemptive-canonical question asks, "What does Jeremiah mean now that Jesus was crucified and resurrected and has ascended to Father?" The canonical revelation of God requires all Christian communities to reflect on the words of the prophet with respect to the New Testament gospel before living those words out in their respective locations. This is the apostolic interpretive question, and it continues to be the church's interpretive question. The church will always engage in interested readings of the prophets, and it should not apologize for doing so (no more than John should apologize for writing a historical Gospel that seeks to bring people to salvation!). Interest, or identification with apostolic tradition, does not necessarily invalidate our interpretation. But neither does it validate it.

Responsible, valid, and fruitful Christian readings of the Major Prophets recognize the ongoing nature of the prophetic word and see its continued perspective and relevance throughout the biblical canon. Such readings also take seriously the historical and literary context of the words given to us in the biblical books, striving to hear how these words were first received. The process, however, continues as we observe the organic connections that arise between the words of the prophets and the revelation of God through the apostles—even when they are not explicitly quoted. There are deep theological currents running across the canon, and the careful and faithful reader can observe such connections without flippant or shallow appeals to paronomasia, numerology, and thin allegories.

Some throughout history have referred to these theological and canonical currents as the rule of faith (*regula fidei*).[5] The rule of faith is not ancillary to the Scriptures but runs throughout them and indeed emerges from them—the theological patterns that give rise to the typological framework of the apostolic witness. We continue to ride the interpretive currents of *regula fidei* in our own interpretations of the Major Prophets. Some of the contributors of this volume are more comfortable attributing the canonically Christ-shaped message of the Major Prophets to the *meaning* of the prophetic passage, while others view it as a reframed theological significance. Regardless of one's comfort level with the term *meaning*, a Christian reading of the Major Prophets refuses to stop short of finding the christological nature of the text.

Reading Like Disciples

Given the scope of books and material on Christian discipleship over the past fifty years, this final category might catch some readers by surprise. What does discipleship have to do with reading the Major Prophets? The Old Testament Scriptures were foundational to Jesus' model of discipleship, and the first postresurrection hermeneutics class took place with two of his disciples on the road to Emmaus (Lk 24:13-27). Being a disciple of Jesus requires reading the Old Testament like Jesus—authoritative, relevant, and about him. Confessing that Jesus of Nazareth is the Son of God affects everything, even our interpretations. Dana Harris describes this reality, as it is witnessed among the New Testament writers, as a "hermeneutical worldview." She writes, "These writers were concerned with showing how the birth, life, death, resurrection, and ascension of Jesus of Nazareth clarified, developed, and extended God's former revelation through prophets." What dominated the apostolic vision of the Old Testament prophets was not so much a

---

[5]For more on the rule of faith and its relationship to hermeneutics, see Adriani Milli Rodrigues, "The Rule of Faith in Biblical Interpretation in Evangelical Theological Interpretation of Scripture," *Themelios* 43, no. 2 (2018): 257-70.

particular *method* but a particular *man*. Or, more accurately, a particular *God-man*. They did not so much read the Old Testament prophets through a revised system as through a transformed reality.

Interestingly, Kuhn's work on paradigms and revolutions also dovetails into our discussion here. The anomaly that gives rise to the paradigm shift creates a new way of seeing, so that old methods will never suffice. The new paradigm demands and creates new methods, not vice versa. Only by accepting the New Testament witness do we see that Jesus is the suffering servant of Isaiah, the reigning Davidide of Jeremiah, and the resurrection and the life of Ezekiel. Kuhn describes how paradigm changes affect the way we see the world and how the student is instructed in this new paradigm: "Looking at a contour map, the student sees lines on paper, the cartographer a picture of a terrain. Looking at a bubble-chamber photograph, the student sees confused and broken lines, the physicist a record of subnuclear events. Only after a number of such transformations of vision does the student become an inhabitant of the scientist's world."[6] Hopefully, the illustration is clear enough. Paradigm changes require instruction. What is at first indiscernible takes on new and fresh meaning as the student begins to inhabit the world of the teacher. This takes effort.

Reading the Major Prophets as Christian Scripture certainly requires learning information about the history, context, and literary facets of the text. However, it also requires spiritual formation that shapes us into the kind of people who rightly understand how the prophets speak of Christ. David I. Starling writes, "Good interpretation requires not just sweat but skill, and not just skill but character. Interpretation of the Scriptures is like a craft or a trade that must be learned if we are to draw the right connections, make the right intuitive leaps, and bring to bear on the task the right dispositions, affections, and virtues."[7] From Jesus'

---

[6]Kuhn, *Structure of Scientific Revolutions*, 111.
[7]David I. Starling, *Hermeneutics as Apprenticeship: How the Bible Shapes Our Interpretive Habits and Practices* (Grand Rapids, MI: Baker, 2016), 17.

conversation on the Emmaus road, reading the prophets has always been about discipleship. We learn from Christ, We learn from the apostolic witness of the New Testament. We learn from the lives and pens of faithful saints past and present. All that we might become more astute, more sensitive, more virtuous, and more careful readers of the prophetic word, "until the day dawns and the Morning Star rises in [our] hearts."

SELECT BIBLIOGRAPHY

General Resources on Prophecy and Preaching
Brueggemann, Walter. *The Prophetic Imagination*. 2nd ed. Minneapolis: Fortress, 2001.
Carroll R., M. Daniel. *The Lord Roars: Recovering the Prophetic Voice for Today*. Grand Rapids, MI: Baker, 2022.
Chalmers, Aaron. *Interpreting the Prophets: Reading, Understanding and Preaching from the Worlds of the Prophets*. Downers Grove, IL: IVP Academic, 2015.
Goldsworthy, Graeme. *Preaching the Whole Bible as Christian Scripture: The Application of Biblical Theology to Expository Preaching*. Grand Rapids, MI: Eerdmans, 2000.
Gridanus, Sidney. *Preaching Christ from the Old Testament: A Contemporary Hermeneutical Method*. Grand Rapids, MI: Eerdmans, 1999.
Heschel, Abraham J. *The Prophets*. Perennial Classics. New York: HarperCollins, 2001.
Kaiser, Walter C. *The Messiah in the Old Testament*. Grand Rapids, MI: Zondervan, 1995.
McCurley, Foster. *Wrestling with the Word: Christian Preaching of the Old Testament*. Valley Forge, PA: Trinity Press International, 1996.
Sandy, D. Brent. *Plowshares & Pruning Hooks: Rethinking the Language of Biblical Prophecy and Apocalyptic*. Downers Grove, IL: IVP Academic, 2002.
Tully, Eric. *Reading the Prophets as Christian Scripture*. Grand Rapids, MI: Baker, 2021.
VanGemeren, Willem. *Interpreting the Prophetic Word*. Grand Rapids, MI: Zondervan, 1996.
Wright, Christopher J. H. *How to Preach and Teach the Old Testament for All Its Worth*. Grand Rapids, MI: Zondervan, 2016.

Isaiah: A Select Bibliography

Ancient Commentaries
Calvin, John. *Commentary on the Book of the Book of the Prophet Isaiah*. Translated by William Pringle. 4 vols. Grand Rapids, MI: Eerdmans, 1948.

Eusebius of Caesarea. *Commentary on Isaiah*. Edited by J. C. Elowsky. Translated by Jonathan J. Armstrong. Ancient Christian Texts. Downers Grove, IL: IVP Academic, 2013.

Jerome. *Commentary on Isaiah: Including St. Jerome's Translation of Origen's Homilies 1–9 on Isaiah*. Translated by Thomas P. Scheck. Ancient Christian Writers 68. New York: Newman, 2015.

Wilken, Robert L. *Isaiah Interpreted by Early Christian and Medieval Commentators*. The Church's Bible. Grand Rapids, MI: Eerdmans, 2007.

Modern Commentaries: Single Volume

Childs, Brevard S. *Isaiah*. OTL. Louisville, KY: Westminster John Knox, 2001.

Goldingay, John. *Isaiah*. New International Biblical Commentary. Peabody, MA: Hendrickson, 2001.

Motyer, J. Alex. *The Prophecy of Isaiah: An Introduction and Commentary*. TOTC. Downers Grove, IL: IVP Academic, 1999.

Oswalt, John N. *Isaiah*. NIVAC. Grand Rapids, MI: Zondervan, 2003.

Wegner, Paul D. *Isaiah. An Introduction and Commentary*. TOTC 20. Downers Grove, IL: IVP Academic, 2021.

Modern Commentaries: Multivolume

Blenkinsopp, Joseph. *Isaiah 1–39*. AB 19. New York: Doubleday, 2000.

———. *Isaiah 40–55*. AB 20. New York: Doubleday, 2002.

———. *Isaiah 56–66*. AB 21. New York: Doubleday, 2003.

Goldingay, John. *Isaiah 40–55: A Critical and Exegetical Commentary*. London: T&T Clark, 2005.

Oswalt, John N. *The Book of Isaiah Chapters 1–39*. NICOT. Grand Rapids, MI: Eerdmans, 1986.

———. *The Book of Isaiah Chapters 40–66*. NICOT. Grand Rapids, MI: Eerdmans, 1998.

Roberts, J. J. M. *First Isaiah: A Commentary*. Hermeneia. Minneapolis: Fortress, 2015.

Seitz, Christopher R. *Isaiah 1–39*. Interpretation. Louisville, KY: Westminster John Knox, 1993.

Smith, Gary V. *Isaiah 1–39*. NAC 15a. Nashville: Broadman & Holman, 2007.

———. *Isaiah 40–66*. NAC 15b. Nashville: Broadman & Holman, 2009.

Tull, Patricia K. *Isaiah 1–39*. Macon, GA: Smyth & Helwys, 2010.

Wildberger, Hans. *Isaiah 1–12: A Commentary*. CC. Translated by T. H. Trapp. Minneapolis: Fortress, 1991.

———. *Isaiah 13–27: A Commentary*. CC. Translated by T. H. Trapp. Minneapolis: Fortress, 1997.

———. *Isaiah 28–39: A Commentary*. CC. Translated by T. H. Trapp. Minneapolis: Fortress, 2002.

Williamson, Hugh G. M. *Isaiah 1–5*. ICC. London: T&T Clark, 2006.

———. *Isaiah 6–12*. ICC. London: T&T Clark, 2018.

Young, E. J. *The Book of Isaiah*. 3 vols. Grand Rapids, MI: Eerdmans, 1965–1972.

Other Relevant Works

Abernethy, Andrew T. *The Book of Isaiah and God's Kingdom: A Thematic-Theological Approach*. NSBT 40. Downers Grove, IL: IVP Academic, 2016.

———. *Discovering Isaiah: Content, Interpretation, Reception*. Discovering Biblical Texts. Grand Rapids, MI: Eerdmans, 2021.

Achtemeier, Elizabeth. *Preaching from the Old Testament*. Louisville, KY: Westminster John Knox, 1980.

Bos, Rein. *We Have Heard That God Is with You: Preaching the Old Testament*. Grand Rapids, MI: Eerdmans, 2008.

Childs, Brevard S. *The Struggle to Understand Isaiah as Christian Scripture*. Grand Rapids, MI: Eerdmans, 2004.

Ellis, R. R. "The Remarkable Suffering Servant of Isaiah 40–55." *Southwestern Journal of Theology* 34 (1991): 20-30.

Thompson, Bill. *Preaching Isaiah's Message Today*. Joplin, MO: College Press, 2020.

Williamson, Hugh G. M. "Preaching from Isaiah." In *Reclaiming the Old Testament for Christian Preaching*, edited by Greenville J. R. Kent, Paul J. Kissling, and Laurence A. Turner, 141-56. Downers Grove, IL: IVP Academic, 2010.

Witherington, Ben, III. *Isaiah Old and New: Exegesis, Intertextuality, and Hermeneutics*. Minneapolis: Fortress, 2017.

JEREMIAH: A SELECT BIBLIOGRAPHY

Ancient Commentaries

Calvin, John. *Commentaries on the Prophet Jeremiah and the Lamentations*. Translated by John Owen. Calvin's Commentaries 10. Grand Rapids, MI: Baker, 2009.

Jerome. *Commentary on Jeremiah*. Translated by Michael Graves. Ancient Christian Texts. Downers Grove, IL: IVP Academic, 2011.

Theodoret of Cyrus. *Commentary on the Prophet Jeremiah*. Translated by Robert Charles Hill. Brookline, MA: Holy Cross Orthodox, 2006.

Modern Commentaries: Single Volume

Allen, Leslie C. *Jeremiah*. OTL. Louisville, KY: Westminster John Knox, 2008.

Brueggemann, Walter. *A Commentary on Jeremiah: Exile and Homecoming*. Grand Rapids, MI: Eerdmans, 1998.

Carvalho, Corrine. *Reading Jeremiah: A Literary and Theological Commentary*. Macon, GA: Smyth & Helwys, 2016.

Dearman, J. Andrew. *Jeremiah and Lamentations*. NIVAC. Grand Rapids, MI: Zondervan, 2002.

Fretheim, Terence E. *Jeremiah*. Smyth & Helwys Bible Commentary. Macon, GA: Smyth & Helwys, 2002.

Goldingay, John. *The Book of Jeremiah*. NICOT. Grand Rapids, MI: Eerdmans, 2021.

Lalleman, Hetty. *Jeremiah and Lamentations*. TOTC. Downers Grove, IL: IVP Academic, 2013.

Ryken, Philip Graham. *Jeremiah and Lamentations: From Sorrow to Hope*. Preaching the Word. Wheaton, IL: Crossway, 2001.

Stulman, Louis. *Jeremiah*. Apollos Old Testament Commentary. Nashville: Abingdon, 2005.

Thompson, John A. *The Book of Jeremiah*. NICOT. Grand Rapids, MI: Eerdmans, 1980.

Wright, Christopher J. H. *The Message of Jeremiah: Against Wind and Tide*. BST. Downers Grove, IL: IVP Academic, 2014.

Modern Commentaries: Multivolume

Craigie, Peter C., Page H. Kelley, and Joel F. Drinkard Jr. *Jeremiah 1–25*. WBC 26. Grand Rapids, MI: Zondervan Academic, 2018.

Holladay, William L. *Jeremiah 1: A Commentary on the Book of the Prophet Jeremiah 1–25*. Hermeneia. Philadelphia: Fortress, 1986.

———. *Jeremiah 2: A Commentary on the Book of the Prophet Jeremiah 26–52*. Hermeneia. Philadelphia: Fortress, 1989.

Keown, Gerald, Pamala Scalise, and Thomas A. Smothers. *Jeremiah 26–52*. WBC 27. Grand Rapids, MI: Zondervan Academic, 2016.

Lundbom, Jack R. *Jeremiah 1–20: A New Translation with Introduction and Commentary*. AB 21.1. New York: Doubleday, 1999.

———. *Jeremiah 21–36: A New Translation with Introduction and Commentary*. AB 21.2. New York: Doubleday, 2004.

———. *Jeremiah 37–52: A New Translation with Introduction and Commentary*. AB 21.3. New York: Doubleday, 2008.

McKane, William. *A Critical and Exegetical Commentary on Jeremiah 1–25*. ICC. New York: T&T Clark, 2000.

———. *A Critical and Exegetical Commentary on Jeremiah 26–52*. ICC. New York: T&T Clark, 2000.

Other Relevant Works

Abernethy, Andrew T. "Theological Patterning in Jeremiah: A Vital Word Through an Ancient Book." *BBR* 24, no. 2 (2014): 149–61.

Adeyemi, Femi. *The New Covenant Torah in Jeremiah and the Law of Christ in Paul*. Studies in Biblical Literature 94. New York: Peter Lang, 2006.

Brueggemann, Walter. *The Theology of the Book of Jeremiah*. Old Testament Theology. Cambridge: Cambridge University Press, 2007.

Dempsey, Carol. *Jeremiah: Preacher of Grace, Poet of Truth*. Collegeville, MN: Liturgical Press, 2007.

Goldingay, John. *The Theology of Jeremiah: The Book, the Man, the Message*. Downers Grove, IL: IVP Academic, 2021.
Kessler, Martin, ed. *Reading the Book of Jeremiah: A Search for Coherence*. Winona Lake, IN: Eisenbrauns, 2004.
Knowles, Michael. *Jeremiah in Matthew's Gospel: The Rejected Prophet Motif in Matthean Redaction*. JSNTSup 68. Sheffield, UK: JSOT Press, 1993.
Lundbom, Jack R., Craig A. Evans, and Bradford A. Anderson, eds. *The Book of Jeremiah: Composition, Reception, and Interpretation*. VTSup 178. Boston: Brill, 2018.
McConville, J. G. *Judgment and Promise: An Interpretation of the Book of Jeremiah*. Leicester, UK: Apollos, 1993.
Moon, Joshua N. *Jeremiah's New Covenant: An Augustinian Reading*. Journal for Theological Interpretation, Supplements 3. Winona Lake, IN: Eisenbrauns, 2011.
Shead, Andrew G. *A Mouth Full of Fire: The Word of God in the Words of Jeremiah*. NSBT 29. Downers Grove, IL: IVP Academic, 2012.

Ezekiel: A Select Bibliography

Ancient Commentaries

Calvin, John. *Ezekiel I*. Translated by D. Foxgrover and D. Martin. Grand Rapids, MI: Eerdmans, 1994.
———. *Ezekiel II*. Translated by T. Myers. Grand Rapids, MI: Baker, 1996.
Gregory the Great. *Homilies on the Book of the Prophet Ezekiel*. 2nd ed. Translated by Theodosia Tomkinson. Etna, CA: Center for Traditionalist Orthodox Studies, 2008.
Jerome. *Commentary on Ezekiel*. Translated by Thomas P. Scheck. Ancient Christian Writers 71. New York: Newman, 2017.
Origen of Alexandria. *Exegetical Works on Ezekiel. The Fourteen Homilies and the Greek Fragments of the Homilies, Commentaries and Scholia. Text and Translation*. Edited by Roger Pearse. Translated by Mischa Hooker. Ancient Texts in Translation 2. Ipswich, UK: Chieftain, 2014.
Theodoret of Cyrus. *Commentaries on the Prophets*. Vol. 2, *Commentary on the Prophet Ezekiel*. Translated by Robert Charles Hill. Brookline, MA: Holy Cross Orthodox, 2006.

Modern Commentaries: Single Volume

Blenkinsopp, Joseph. *Ezekiel*. Interpretation. Louisville, KY: John Knox, 1990.
Clements, Ronald. E. *Ezekiel*. Westminster Bible Companion. Louisville, KY: Westminster John Knox, 1996.
Duguid, Iain. *Ezekiel*. NIVAC. Grand Rapids, MI: Zondervan, 1999.
Eichrodt, Walther. *Ezekiel: A Commentary*. Translated by C. Quin. OTL. Philadelphia: Westminster, 1970.
Jenson, Robert W. *Ezekiel*. Brazos Theological Commentary on the Bible. Grand Rapids, MI: Brazos, 2009.

Joyce, Paul M. *Ezekiel: A Commentary*. LHBOTS 482. New York: T&T Clark, 2009.
Odell, Margaret S. *Ezekiel*. Smyth & Helwys Commentary. Macon, GA: Smyth & Helwys, 2005.
Sweeney, Marvin A. *Reading Ezekiel: A Literary and Theological Commentary*. Macon, GA: Smyth & Helwys, 2013.
Taylor, John B. *Ezekiel: An Introduction and Commentary*. TOTC 22. Downers Grove, IL: IVP Academic, 1969.
Tuell, Steven. *Ezekiel*. Understanding the Bible Commentary. Grand Rapids, MI: Baker, 2008.
Wright, Christopher J. H. *The Message of Ezekiel: A New Heart and a New Spirit*. BST. Downers Grove, IL: InterVarsity Press, 2001.

Modern Commentaries: Multivolume

Allen, Leslie C. *Ezekiel 1–19*. WBC 28. Dallas: Word, 1994.
———. *Ezekiel 20–48*. WBC 29. Dallas: Word, 1990.
Block, Daniel I. *Ezekiel 1–24*. NICOT. Grand Rapids, MI: Eerdmans, 1997.
———. *Ezekiel 25–48*. NICOT. Grand Rapids, MI: Eerdmans, 1998.
Cook, Stephen L. *Ezekiel 38–48*. AB 22b. New Haven, CT: Yale University Press, 2018.
Greenberg, Moshe. *Ezekiel 1–20*. AB 22. New York: Doubleday, 1983.
———. *Ezekiel 21–37*. AB 22a. New York: Doubleday, 1987.
Mackay, John L. *Ezekiel*. 2 vols. Mentor. Ross-shire, UK: Christian Focus, 2018.
Zimmerli, Walther. *Ezekiel 1*. Translated by R. E. Clements. Hermeneia. Philadelphia: Fortress, 1979.
———. *Ezekiel 2*. Translated by J. D. Martin. Hermeneia. Philadelphia: Fortress, 1983.

Other Relevant Works

Block, Daniel I. *By the River Chebar: Historical, Literary, and Theological Studies in the Book of Ezekiel*. Eugene, OR: Cascade, 2013.
Bullock, C. Hassell. "Ezekiel, Bridge Between the Testaments." *JETS* 25, no. 1 (1982): 23–31.
Christman, Angela Russell. *"What Did Ezekiel See?": Christian Exegesis of Ezekiel's Vision of the Chariot from Irenaeus to Gregory the Great*. Bible in Ancient Christianity 4. Leiden: Brill, 2005.
Duguid, Iain. *Ezekiel and the Leaders of Israel*. VTSup 56. Leiden: Brill, 1994.
Lyons, Michael A. *An Introduction to the Study of Ezekiel*. New York: Bloomsbury, 2015.
Mein, Andrew. *Ezekiel and the Ethics of Exile*. Oxford: Oxford University Press, 2001.
Newsom, Carol A. "A Maker of Metaphors—Ezekiel's Oracles Against Tyre." *Interpretation* 38 (1984): 151–64.
Odell, Margaret S., and John T. Strong. *The Book of Ezekiel: Theological and Anthropological Perspectives*. Symposium Series 9. Atlanta: Society of Biblical Literature, 2000.
Olley, John. *Ezekiel: A Commentary Based on Iezekiēl in Codex Vaticanus*. Leiden: Brill, 2009.

Renz, Thomas. *The Rhetorical Function of the Book of Ezekiel*. VTSup 76. Leiden: Brill, 2002.
Tooman, William A., and Penelope Barter, ed. *Ezekiel: Current Debates and Future Directions*. Forschungen zum Alten Testament 112. Tübingen: Mohr Siebeck, 2017.
Tooman, William A., and Michael A. Lyons, eds. *Transforming Visions: Transformations of Text, Tradition, and Theology in Ezekiel*. Princeton Theological Monograph Series 127. Eugene, OR: Pickwick, 2010.
Wu, Daniel Y. *Honor, Shame, and Guilt: Social-Scientific Approaches to the Book of Ezekiel*. Bulletin for Biblical Research, Supplements 14. Winona Lake, IN: Eisenbrauns, 2016.
Zimmerli, Walther. *The Fiery Throne: The Prophets and Old Testament Theology*. Edited by K. C. Hanson. Philadelphia: Fortress, 2003.

CONTRIBUTORS

Andrew T. Abernethy (PhD, Trinity Evangelical Divinity School) is professor of Old Testament at Wheaton College. He has written several books, including *Eating in Isaiah* (Brill, 2014), *The Book of Isaiah and God's Kingdom* (IVP Academic, 2016), *God's Messiah in the Old Testament*, with Greg Goswell (Baker, 2020), *Discovering Isaiah* (Eerdmans, 2021), and *Savoring Scripture* (IVP Academic, 2022).

Daniel I. Block (DPhil, Liverpool University) is Gunther H. Knoedler Professor Emeritus of Old Testament at Wheaton College. He has authored *The Book of Ezekiel* (2 vols.; Eerdmans, 1997, 1998); *Ezekiel: When God Abandons His People* (Crossway, forthcoming 2024); *Covenant: The Foundation of God's Grand Plan of Redemption* (Baker, 2021); and *For the Glory of God: Recovering a Biblical Theology of Worship* (Baker, 2014).

Iain M. Duguid is professor of Old Testament at Westminster Theological Seminary, Philadelphia. His PhD thesis from Cambridge was published by E. J. Brill as *Ezekiel and the Leaders of Israel*, and he is the author of two commentaries on Ezekiel (NIV Application and ESV Expository Commentary), as well as commentaries on numerous other biblical books.

Mark S. Gignilliat (PhD, The University of St Andrews) is professor of divinity at Beeson Divinity School, Samford University. He is the author of *A Brief History of Old Testament Criticism* (Zondervan, 2012); *Reading Scripture Canonically: Theological Instincts for Old Testament*

Interpretation (Baker Academic, 2019); and *Micah* (International Theological Commentary, T&T Clark, 2020).

Dana M. Harris (PhD, Trinity Evangelical Divinity School) is professor of New Testament and department chair at Trinity Evangelical Divinity School. She is the author of *Hebrews* (Exegetical Guide to the Greek New Testament, B&H, 2019) and *An Introduction to Biblical Greek Grammar: Elementary Syntax and Linguistics* (Zondervan, 2020).

John W. Hilber (PhD, University of Cambridge) is professor of Old Testament at McMaster Divinity College. He is author of four books, including *Ezekiel: A Focused Commentary for Preaching and Teaching* (Cascade, 2019), and has contributed numerous academic articles dealing with ancient Near Eastern background to the Old Testament.

Alicia R. Jackson (PhD, The University of Birmingham, UK) is assistant professor of Old Testament at Vanguard University. She is the author of *Ezekiel's Two Sticks and Eschatological Violence in the Pentecostal Tradition* (Brill 2023), and her research interests include prophetic literature, eschatology, and hermeneutics. Alicia is an ordained minister with the Assemblies of God, and she lives in San Clemente, California, with her husband, Paul, and her son, Gabriel.

William R. Osborne (PhD, Midwestern Baptist Theological Seminary) is associate professor of biblical and theological studies at College of the Ozarks in Point Lookout, Missouri. He is the author of *Trees and Kings* (Eisenbrauns/PSU, 2018), *Divine Blessing and the Fullness of Life in the Presence of God* (Crossway, 2020), and coedited with Mark Boda and Russell Meek *Riddles and Revelations* (T&T Clark, 2018).

John N. Oswalt (PhD, Brandeis University) is visiting distinguished professor of Old Testament at Asbury Theological Seminary. He is the author of *The Book of Isaiah, Chapters 1-39* (Eerdmans, 1986), *The Book* *of Isaiah, Chapters 40-66* (Eerdmans, 1998), *Called to Be Holy* (Warner, 1999), *The NIV Application Commentary Isaiah* (Zondervan, 2003), *The Bible Among the Myths* (Zondervan, 2009), and *The Books of Kings, A Commentary* (Lexham, forthcoming).

Nicholas G. Piotrowski (PhD, Wheaton College) is the president and associate professor of New Testament theology at Indianapolis Theological Seminary. He is the author of *Matthew's New David at the End of Exile* (Brill, 2016) and *In All the Scriptures* (IVP Academic, 2021).

Philip Graham Ryken (DPhil, University of Oxford) is the eighth president of Wheaton College. He is the author of more than 50 Bible commentaries and other books, including *Exodus*, *Ecclesiastes*, and *Jeremiah & Lamentations* in Crossway's Preaching the Word series, and *1 & 2 Kings* in the Reformed Expository Commentary (P&R).

Andrew G. Shead (PhD, Cambridge) is head of Old Testament at Moore Theological College, Sydney. He is the author of *The Open Book and the Sealed Book: Jeremiah 32 in Its Hebrew and Greek Recensions* (Sheffield Academic Press, 2002), *A Mouth Full of Fire: The Word of God in the Words of Jeremiah* (Apollos, 2012), and *Walk His Way: Following Christ through the Book of Psalms* (IVP, 2023).

Paul D. Wegner is distinguished professor of Old Testament at Gateway Seminary, Ontario, California, with a specialty in the study of Isaiah. Previously he taught at Phoenix Seminary and Moody Bible Institute. His books include *A Student's Guide to Textual Criticism of the Bible* and the Tyndale Old Testament Commentary on Isaiah.

Lissa M. Wray Beal (PhD, University of St. Michael's College) is professor of Old Testament at Wycliffe College, Toronto. She is the author of *The Deuteronomist's Prophet* (T&T Clark, 2007), commentaries on 1-2 Kings (Apollos, 2014), Joshua (Zondervan, 2019), and Jeremiah (Baker; forthcoming), and numerous articles on Joshua, Kings, Jeremiah, and Psalms.

Gary E. Yates (PhD, Dallas Theological Seminary) is professor of Old Testament at Liberty University and teaching pastor at Living Word Baptist Church in Forest, Virginia. He is the coauthor of *The Essence of the Old Testament* with Ed Hindson (B&H, 2012), *The Message of the Twelve* with Richard Fuhr (B&H, 2016), and *Urban Legends of the Old Testament* with David Croteau (B&H, 2019).

NAME INDEX

Abernethy, Andrew, 38, 40-42, 45
Ambrose of Milan, 80, 284
Aquinas, Thomas, 72-73, 76, 80, 176, 178, 276-77
Archer, Melissa, 213
Aristotle, 176
Athanasius, 83
Augustine, 72, 80, 83, 167, 175-76, 183, 313
Barnabas, 165-66
Barth, Karl, 76
Basdeo Hill, Rebecca, 211, 226
Bauckham, Richard, 37
Beale, Greg, 265
Becking, Bob, 116
Beuken, Willem, 71
Blaising, Craig, 131
Block, Daniel, 127, 130, 134, 142, 256
Blomberg, Craig, 30, 41
Brown, Raymond, 192
Boda, Mark, 125
Boekhoven, Henry J., 115
Bronner, Leilah, 258
Brueggemann, Walter, 127, 133
Calvin, John, 72-73, 78-82, 84, 178, 201, 275, 277-78, 313
Carson, D. A., 253
Childs, Brevard, 4, 70-74, 84
Chrysostom, John, 71-72, 198
Ciampa, Roy, 16
Clement of Alexandria, 196
Clements, Ronald, 83
Clowney, Edmund, 193-95
Currid, John, 195
Cyril of Alexandria, 76, 78, 80, 84, 313
Dahlberg, Bruce, 111
de Lubac, Henri, 163
Driver, S. R., 279
Emser, 177
Erskine, Ebenezer, 285
Eusebius of Caesarea, 80
Evans, Craig, 154
Fairbairn, Patrick, 195
Fee, Gordon, 39
Fishbane, Michael, 57
Florovsky, Georges, 83, 84
Fosdick, Harry Emerson, 86
France, R. T., 14
Frei, Hans, 73
Fretheim, Terence, 127
Gaffin, Richard, 189
Garscha, Jörg, 280
Goldingay, John, 125
Goldsworthy, Graeme, 195
Gordon, Bruce, 81
Greenhill, William, 278, 283
Greenspoon, Leonard, 259
Gregory the Great, 80, 273-75, 282, 284
Gregory of Nyssa, 80
Greidanus, Sidney, 195
Grey, Jacqueline, 225
Grice, Paul, 231
Grisanti, Michael, 133
Haimo of Auxerre, 275
Hananiah ben Hezekiah, 272, 284
Harris, Dana, 43
Hays, Richard, 27, 204-6
Hess, Richard, 139
Hilber, John, 51, 69
Hirsch, E. D., 32, 34
Holland, Tom, 23
Hölscher, Gustav, 280
Hubbard, Robert, 30, 41
Hughes, Kent, 293
Irenaeus, 73, 80, 166-67, 175, 265, 273
Jenson, Robert, 84, 256, 259
Jerome, 80, 164, 167, 171-77, 179, 200, 249, 271, 273-75
Joyce, Paul, 268
Justin Martyr, 73, 165-67

Kaiser, Walter, 41, 127, 132, 295
Keller, Kathy, 202
Keller, Tim, 202
Kidner, Derek, 203
Klein, William, 30, 41
Knowles, Michael, 111, 112
Koole, Jan, 71
Kuhn, Thomas, 314, 319
Lalleman, Hetty, 114, 115
Lee, Peter, 128
Lewis, C. S., 34, 42, 316
Lindsay, Hal, 281, 284
Longenecker, Richard, 39, 53, 54
Lundbom, Jack, 126, 130
Luther, Martin, 72-73, 77-78, 80, 84, 177, 276-78, 281, 284
Mather, Cotton, 279
McConville, Gordon, 147
Mede, Joseph, 278, 284
Menken, M. J. J., 111
Meyer, F. B., 187
Nelson, Tommy, 284
Nicholas of Lyra, 176, 275
Origen, 73, 80, 167-74, 183, 313
Osborne, Grant, 50
Oswalt, John, 70
Packer, J. I., 199
Pao, David, 17
Pelagius, 174-75
Peterson, David, 124
Philo, 168
Piotrowski, Nicholas, 29, 33, 52, 110
Rabanus Maurus, 275
Radbertus, 276
Radner, Ephraim, 83
Rashi, 275
Ratramnus, 276
Richard of Saint Victor, 275
Roberts, J. J., 75

Robinson, Marilynne, 81
Rosner, Brian, 16
Rosner, Jennifer, 219
Schafroth, Verena, 226
Seitz, Christopher, 56
Shead, Andrew, 129
Sperber, Paul, 231-33, 241
Starling, David I., 319
Stewart, Alex, 261
Stovell, Beth, 213, 223
Stuart, Douglas, 39
Stulman, Louis, 123-24
Tertullian, 274
Theodoret of Cyrus, 167, 170-71, 176, 313
Thiselton, Anthony, 313-14
Torrey, C. C., 280
Treier, Daniel, 253
Vanhoozer, Kevin, 55, 253
Vischer, Wilhelm, 179, 181, 183
Vlach, Michael, 139
von Rad, Gerhard, 178-83
Walton, John, 86
Ward, Lisa, 224
Watts, John, 71
Wegner, Paul, 51, 69
Wellhausen, Julius, 279
Westbrook, April, 222
Whitters, Mark, 111
Wildberger, Hans, 70, 75
Wilken, Robert, 79
Williamson, Hugh, 71
Williamson, Paul, 128
Willitts, Joel, 140
Wilson, Deirdre, 231-33, 240
Wittgenstein, Ludwig, 73
Wright, Christopher, 122, 197, 256, 266
Yates, Gary, 51, 69
Zimmerli, Walther, 258
Zwingli, Huldrych, 277

SCRIPTURE INDEX

OLD TESTAMENT

Genesis
1, *208*
2, *166, 256*
2:7, *224, 307*
2:9, *214*
2:21-23, *202*
2:24, *31*
3, *234*
6, *234*
8:20–9:17, *234*
11, *234*
12:1-3, *132, 234, 304*
14:17-20, *117*
15, *234, 304*
17, *166, 304*
17:1, *247*
17:6, *235*
17:7, *199*
26:4-5, *132*
26:5, *134*
28:13-14, *132*
32:30, *265*
34:3, *35*
35:19-20, *108*
48:7, *108*

Exodus
1:15-16, *107*
1:22, *107*
2, *109*
3:14, *171*
6:6, *22*
6:6-7, *150*
6:7, *267*
9:14, *22*
14:24, *22*
15:4-5, *22*
17, *252*
19–24, *235, 304*
19:1–24:8, *149*
19:4-6, *304*
19:5-6, *199, 235*
23:20, *22*
24:1-8, *154*
24:4, *22*
24:8, *22, 154*
24:16-17, *264*
31:18, *126, 200*
32:13, *135*
32:15-16, *200*
32:19, *126, 135*
33:20, *265*
34:6-9, *135*
36:23, *126*

Leviticus
4:20, *134*
4:26, *134*
4:31, *134*
4:35, *134*
5:10, *134*
5:13, *134*
5:16, *134*
5:18, *134*
16:21-22, *126*
19:8, *126*
20:9-16, *219*
23, *272*
25, *23*
25:10, *23*
26:12, *134, 236*
26:12-13, *150*
26:23-33, *299*
26:36-39, *300*
26:40-48, *300*

Numbers
14:24, *134*
18:1, *126*
21:8, *37*

Deuteronomy
5:24, *265*
6:5, *133*
6:6, *134*
9:6, *135*
9:13, *135*
10:12-13, *133*
10:16, *133, 135, 181, 224, 300*
11:13-32, *268*
16, *177*
17:14-20, *235*
26:7, *60*
26:19, *305*
28, *255*
28:1-14, *305*
28:25-26, *298*
28:49-57, *299*
28:62-67, *300*
29:2-4, *134*
29:12-13, *150*
30:1-6, *236*
30:1-10, *300, 307*
30:5-6, *200*
30:14, *150*
31:27, *135*

Judges
2:10, *134*
5:19, *179*
6:22-23, *265*
13:22, *265*
18:7, *93*

1 Samuel
2:6, *257*
2:10, *113*
3:13-14, *126*
8:7, *223*
8:10-18, *222*
10:2, *108*
16:1, *12*
28:8-14, *237*

2 Samuel
7, *235*
7:8, *12*
7:16, *223*
12:1-25, *222*
12:9, *223*

1 Kings
6, *272*
6:38, *93*
8, *12*
17:17-24, *237, 257*
22:17, *220, 221*

2 Kings
4:18-37, *237*
4:31-37, *257*
13:20-21, *237, 257*
17:14, *135*
17:26-27, *93*
21:13, *299*
22:8, *126*
23–25, *179*
23:26-27, *12*
25:8-17, *12*

2 Chronicles
7:1-3, *212*
7:14, *310*
18:16, *220, 221*

Nehemiah
8:1–10:39, *153*
9:29, *135*
13:15-22, *184*

Psalms
2, *89*
2:6, *35*
2:7, *34, 35, 38, 49*
22:1, *109*
37:31, *134*
40, *120*
40:8, *134*
49:14-15, *237*
69:25, *105*
77:1, *60*
95, *52, 106*
95:8, *135*
104:3, *264*
109:8, *105*
110:4, *117*
115, *157*
119, *134*
119:11, *134*
119:29, *134*
119:73, *134*
119:80, *134*
119:97, *134*
119:102, *134*
119:108, *134*
119:113, *134*
119:117, *134*
119:127, *134*
119:163, *134*
119:165, *134*
127:1, *308*
135, *157*

Proverbs
14:12, *95*
31:28, *297*

Isaiah
1:9, *15*
2, *67*
2:2-4, *131*
5, *15*
6, *14, 53, 265*
6:5, *265*
6:9, *14*
6:9-10, *14, 15, 265*
6:9-13, *14*
7, *22*
7–8, *12*
7–9, *18*
7:2, *12*
7:13, *12*
7:14, *11, 12, 13, 14, 18, 22, 30, 35, 53*
8:3, *12*
8:8, *18*
8:10, *18*
9:1, *22*
9:1-2, *18, 33, 64*
9:1-7, *63, 64, 65*
9:3-5, *64*
9:3-7, *64*
9:6-7, *59, 64*
9:7, *64*
10:22, *15*
11, *96, 100*
11:1, *18, 22, 64, 214*
11:1-5, *63, 65*
11:1-10, *59*
11:2, *22, 59*
11:3-5, *59*
11:9, *97*
11:10, *22, 26, 214*
11:16, *57*
12, *74, 75, 76, 77, 78, 79, 84*
12:1, *78*
12:1-2, *77*
13–14, *67*
13:2, *60*
14, *67*
14:12-14, *264*
14:13-15, *67*
15:4, *60*
16:5, *63, 65*
19:24, *132*
23, *67*
24–27, *85*
25, *24*
25–26, *68*
25:6, *15*
25:8, *15, 24*
26, *16, 67*
26:19, *237*
28, *67*
28:16, *20*
28:22, *20*
28:26, *93*
29:14, *16*
30:1, *135*
32:1, *63, 65*
39:7, *58*
40, *89, 91*
40–48, *43, 44, 45, 60, 89*
40–55, *17, 18, 20, 22, 23, 89*
40:3, *18, 19, 22, 38, 53, 66*
40:3-5, *17*
40:3-11, *18*
40:6-8, *16, 20, 24*
40:9, *65, 66*
40:9-10, *19*

Scripture Index

40:10, *89*
40:12-31, *20*
40:13, *20, 37*
40:18-20, *44*
40:18-31, *157*
40:27, *58, 97*
41, *59, 88*
41–42, *58*
41–48, *89, 91, 96*
41–55, *91*
41:2, *46*
41:2-4, *44*
41:4, *19, 95*
41:5-7, *44*
41:7, *157*
41:8, *59*
41:8-9, *45, 59*
41:10, *59*
41:15, *97*
41:21-24, *44*
41:21-29, *88*
41:25, *46*
41:25-26, *44*
41:27-28, *46*
41:27-29, *47*
41:28, *45*
41:29, *44, 89*
42, *11, 25, 49, 61, 74, 75, 79, 80, 81, 84*
42:1, *17, 45, 59, 89, 92, 96*
42:1-3, *25*
42:1-4, *3, 25, 43, 45, 46, 47, 48, 49, 58, 59, 60, 61, 62, 63, 79, 81, 82, 88, 89, 97*
42:1-9, *43, 44, 45, 86, 88, 90, 91, 95*
42:2, *60*
42:2-3, *46*
42:2-4, *92*
42:3, *60, 80, 97*
42:3-4, *45, 59, 92*
42:4, *46, 48, 60, 82, 98*
42:5, *92, 96*
42:5-9, *89*
42:6, *46, 92, 95, 96, 98*
42:6-7, *19, 60, 61, 92*
42:7, *17, 24, 45, 60, 62*
42:8, *95, 99*
42:8-9, *92*
42:9, *46, 89, 99*
42:10, *88, 89*
42:17, *44*

42:18-19, *60*
42:18-25, *60, 96*
43:9-12, *17*
43:10, *95*
43:10-11, *19*
43:13, *95*
43:14, *58*
43:16, *19*
43:18-19, *23*
43:20-21, *20*
43:25, *19, 95*
44:3, *17*
44:6, *37*
44:6-20, *157*
44:8-9, *17*
44:9-20, *44*
44:22, *19*
44:24–45:7, *44*
44:28, *45*
44:28–45:2, *45*
44:28–45:7, *44*
45:1, *45*
45:1-3, *46*
45:5-6, *44*
45:13, *44, 46*
45:16, *44*
45:20-21, *44*
45:22, *17*
45:22-24, *18*
45:23, *20, 37*
46, *88*
46:1-2, *44*
46:4, *95*
46:5-7, *44*
46:5-13, *157*
46:11, *44*
46:11-13, *18*
47:12-15, *44*
48, *89*
48:5, *44*
48:12, *37, 95*
48:14-15, *44*
48:20, *17, 58*
48:22, *44*
49–53, *60*
49–55, *89, 90, 91*
49:1, *95*
49:1-7, *60*
49:1-12, *90*
49:3, *23, 90*
49:3-6, *139*
49:4, *97*

49:5-6, *23*
49:6, *17, 23, 62, 90*
49:8, *16*
49:8-10, *19*
49:14, *97*
49:18, *20*
49:24-25, *19*
50:2, *45*
50:4-6, *19*
50:4-9, *90*
50:7-8, *97*
51:3, *89*
51:5, *89*
51:17, *19*
51:18, *45*
51:22, *19*
52–53, *20*
52:1-2, *18*
52:1–53:12, *85*
52:7, *16, 17, 19, 65, 66*
52:8, *65*
52:11, *24*
52:13, *19*
52:13–53:12, *60, 90*
52:14, *19*
52:15, *16, 19*
52:15–53:12, *33*
53, *18, 20*
53:2, *214*
53:4, *20, 62*
53:6-7, *20, 62*
53:7, *19, 159, 160*
53:7-8, *17, 160*
53:7-12, *18*
53:9, *20, 62*
53:11-12, *19*
53:12, *19*
54:17, *61, 91*
55:3, *17, 136*
55:10-11, *18*
56:1-8, *61*
57:15, *66*
57:16-18, *67*
58:6, *17*
59:20-21, *136*
60–62, *85, 136*
61, *100*
61:1, *59*
61:1-2, *17, 23, 99*
61:8, *136*
61:8-9, *136*
63:10, *13*

63:15, *13*
63:18, *13*
65–66, *61*
65:1-2, *16*
65:2, *135*
65:17, *23, 55*
65:17-25, *57*
66:1, *13*
66:20-21, *13*

Jeremiah
1, *115*
1–20, *167*
1–25, *124*
1:1, *115*
1:4-19, *110, 111*
1:5, *115*
1:7, *115*
1:8, *115*
1:10, *146*
1:15, *147*
2, *148*
2–3, *202*
2–10, *147, 157*
2:2, *202*
2:5, *157*
2:6, *174*
2:8, *133, 199*
2:20, *202*
2:21, *204, 214*
3:14-18, *131, 146*
3:17, *134, 151, 199*
3:18, *129*
4:1-2, *132*
4:4, *112, 151*
4:5-6, *147*
4:19-21, *147*
4:22, *199*
4:31, *147*
5, *206*
5:4-5, *196*
5:9, *153*
5:11, *129*
5:23, *134, 151*
5:29, *153*
6:1-6, *147*
6:14, *112*
6:16, *203*
6:19, *133*
6:28, *135*
7, *203*
7:6-9, *133*

7:11, *112, 139, 203*
7:16, *206*
7:22-23, *197*
7:22-26, *133*
7:24, *134, 151*
7:26, *135*
7:32, *148*
8–10, *158*
8:8, *133*
8:13, *204*
8:22, *206*
9:3, *199*
9:9, *153*
9:10, *60*
9:13, *133*
9:14, *151, 199*
9:23, *126*
9:23-24, *37, 112, 113, 204*
9:24, *113, 114*
9:25, *148*
9:26, *134, 151*
10, *157*
10:1-16, *144, 157*
10:2, *165*
10:3, *157*
10:6-7, *157*
10:8, *157*
10:10, *157*
10:12-13, *157*
10:14, *112*
10:16, *157*
10:17-22, *147*
10:21, *220*
11, *151*
11–20, *147, 159*
11:1-13, *135*
11:4, *197*
11:8, *134*
11:10, *129, 151*
11:14, *206*
11:16, *178, 204*
11:17, *129*
11:18, *199*
11:18-19, *144, 158, 159*
11:20, *160*
12:3, *160*
12:14-17, *131*
12:16, *131*
13:1-11, *158*
13:10, *134, 199*
13:11, *129*
14:10, *152*

14:11-12, *206*
15:10, *173*
15:15, *160*
15:18, *160*
16:1-9, *158*
16:11, *133*
16:11-12, *199*
16:12, *134, 151*
16:14, *148*
16:14-15, *146, 149, 174*
16:14-18, *205*
16:15, *141*
17:1, *126, 134, 151, 200*
17:5, *134, 151*
17:9, *134*
17:17, *160*
17:19-27, *133, 184*
17:23, *135*
18–19, *204*
18:1-4, *169*
18:1-16, *169*
18:4, *169*
18:5-10, *169*
18:6, *112*
18:7-10, *131*
18:12, *199*
18:18, *133*
18:20-23, *160*
19:1, *140, 182*
19:1-13, *107, 158*
19:4, *140*
19:7, *183*
19:11, *140*
19:15, *135*
20, *159*
20:7, *160*
20:12, *160*
21–24, *147*
21:4-10, *182*
22:10, *179*
22:13-17, *173*
22:16, *126*
22:20, *60*
22:24, *112, 173*
23:1-2, *220*
23:1-4, *172, 205*
23:3-8, *146*
23:5, *148, 205, 214*
23:7-8, *148, 149*
23:18, *112*
24, *204*
24:1-2, *173*

Scripture Index

24:1-10, *173, 174*
24:2, *173*
24:3-10, *173*
24:5-6, *226*
24:6, *112, 114, 141*
24:6-7, *146*
24:7, *134, 200*
25, *147*
25:15, *204*
25:15-17, *174*
26–29, *147*
26–52, *124*
26:4, *133*
27:1-7, *158*
27:2-4, *174*
27:9-11, *174*
30–31, *108, 109, 116, 146, 147, 148*
30–32, *172*
30–33, *110, 124, 129, 131, 146*
30:1, *129*
30:1-3, *146*
30:3, *129, 146, 148, 155*
30:4, *155*
30:7, *155*
30:8, *155*
30:8-11, *129*
30:9, *146*
30:10, *129, 146, 155*
30:12-15, *199*
30:17, *155*
30:18, *146, 155*
30:20, *146*
30:21, *146*
30:22, *129, 146, 150, 200*
31, *107, 108, 110, 116, 117, 118, 119, 120, 121, 127, 128, 129, 131, 146, 149, 177, 187, 196, 197, 200, 201, 203, 235*
31–40, *303*
31:1, *129, 146, 148, 150*
31:2, *129*
31:2-22, *148*
31:4, *155, 202*
31:5, *146*
31:6, *146, 148*
31:7, *129, 155*
31:8-9, *146*
31:9, *155*
31:10-14, *146*
31:11, *155*
31:12, *148, 156*

31:12-13, *146*
31:12-14, *15*
31:14, *129*
31:15, *30, 42, 107, 108, 109, 110, 156, 204*
31:16-17, *109, 146*
31:17, *156*
31:18, *156*
31:20, *146, 155*
31:21, *155*
31:21-23, *146*
31:22, *125, 149, 156, 170*
31:23-24, *146, 149*
31:23-26, *125*
31:27, *125, 128, 146, 148, 155, 196*
31:27-28, *149*
31:28, *130*
31:29, *125*
31:31, *125, 128, 129, 130, 136, 148, 154, 155, 172, 196, 201*
31:31-34, *3, 103, 112, 116, 118, 119, 122, 123, 124, 130, 136, 137, 143, 144, 163, 167, 170, 171, 177, 183, 196, 197, 198, 201, 202, 307*
31:31-37, *221*
31:31-40, *142*
31:32, *116, 118, 125, 135, 136, 149, 151, 156, 197, 201*
31:33, *124, 129, 138, 148, 149, 150, 152, 155, 177, 188, 199, 224*
31:33-34, *119, 172*
31:34, *124, 125, 126, 127, 133, 134, 135, 136, 142, 153, 172, 176, 188, 197, 198, 201*
31:35-37, *116, 128, 200*
31:35-38, *125*
31:36, *129, 155*
31:36-37, *129, 146*
31:37, *155*
31:38, *125, 148, 196*
31:38-40, *130*
31:40, *125*
32, *130, 138, 140*
32–33, *146*
32:5, *128*
32:6-15, *158*
32:15, *146*
32:21, *129*
32:23, *133*

32:26-35, *129*
32:36-44, *130*
32:37, *146*
32:38, *129, 200*
32:38-40, *126*
32:39, *134*
32:39-40, *130*
32:40, *149, 200*
32:41, *130*
32:42, *129*
32:43-44, *130*
33:6-7, *146*
33:8, *135*
33:9-11, *146*
33:12-13, *146, 205*
33:14, *129, 148*
33:15, *140, 205*
33:16-17, *146*
33:18-22, *146*
33:20-21, *151*
33:21-22, *146*
33:22, *129*
33:24, *129*
33:25-26, *128*
33:26, *129*
34:17-20, *298*
37–39, *147*
39, *138, 147*
39:1-10, *182*
39:10-11, *138*
39:14, *138*
43–44, *112*
44:10, *133*
44:23, *133*
46:19, *131*
46:26, *131*
48:7, *131*
48:11, *131*
48:46, *131*
48:47, *131*
49:3, *131*
49:6, *131*
49:39, *131*
50–51, *167*
50:2, *158*
50:5, *128, 149, 200*
50:6-7, *205*
50:20, *128*
51:44, *158*
51:63, *126*
52, *184*

Ezekiel
1, *215, 264, 265, 266, 274*
1–2, *265*
1–24, *235*
1–32, *209*
1:1-3, *291*
1:5-10, *212*
1:10, *273*
1:13, *212*
1:15-18, *264*
1:22, *264*
1:24, *212*
1:26, *264, 266*
1:26-27, *212*
1:26-28, *212*
1:27, *271*
1:27-28, *264, 269*
1:28, *212, 264*
2–4, *254*
2:1, *257*
2:1-2, *288*
2:2, *211*
2:2-6, *298*
2:3-8, *298*
2:5, *299*
2:9-10, *211*
3, *236*
3:1-3, *212*
3:4-11, *298*
3:7, *135*
3:9, *298*
3:12, *211*
3:14, *211, 212*
3:17, *219*
3:24, *211, 257*
3:26-27, *298*
4, *259*
4:17, *300*
5:5, *305*
5:6-17, *305*
6:5, *254*
8:3, *211, 296*
9:4, *217*
9:6, *217*
10, *212*
10:1, *212*
11:1, *211*
11:1-13, *296*
11:16, *272*
11:17-20, *298*
11:19, *136, 226*
11:19-20, *223*
11:21, *299*
11:24, *211*
12:1-9, *298*
12:2, *218, 245*
12:2-3, *298*
12:10-16, *298*
12:27, *271, 284*
13:1-16, *220*
13:6, *295*
13:7, *295*
14:21, *217*
15:2-7, *214*
16, *293*
16:58, *295*
16:59, *136*
16:59-63, *136*
16:60, *136*
16:60-63, *223*
16:62, *136*
16:63, *136*
17:1-7, *298*
17:5-10, *214*
17:7-10, *298*
17:11-21, *298*
17:22-24, *223, 298*
17:24, *301*
18, *280*
18:1-32, *299*
18:30-32, *300*
20, *278*
20:49, *299*
21–37, *273*
21:5, *299*
22, *261*
22:14, *301*
23, *271, 293*
23:11, *270*
23:23, *300*
24:15-20, *298*
24:16, *300*
24:21-27, *298*
25–32, *235, 291*
26–28, *215, 218*
26:13, *216*
26:16-17, *216*
27:22, *216*
27:27-29, *216*
27:30-36, *216*
28:1-2, *216*
28:13, *215*
28:25-26, *226*
31:1-17, *298*
31:6, *223*
31:8-9, *215*
31:18, *298*
32:7-8, *216*
33, *236*
33–48, *209*
33:1-6, *219*
33:1-10, *300*
33:1-14, *301*
33:5, *219*
33:10, *300*
33:10-11, *299*
33:20, *299*
33:21, *236*
33:30-33, *299*
33:31-32, *299*
33:32, *270*
33:33, *236, 299*
34, *26, 222, 236, 245, 300*
34–48, *284*
34:1-11, *220, 222*
34:2-4, *26*
34:5, *220, 221*
34:9-22, *221*
34:11, *245*
34:11-22, *221*
34:15, *245*
34:20, *245*
34:22-25, *26*
34:23-24, *209*
34:23-25, *221*
34:24, *221, 245*
34:24-25, *223*
34:25, *221, 222, 223*
34:31, *245*
35, *236*
35–36, *236*
36, *226, 235, 236, 237, 239, 248, 300*
36–37, *246*
36:16-38, *242*
36:22, *257, 267*
36:22-23, *236, 247*
36:22-32, *266, 267, 269*
36:23, *247, 267*
36:25-27, *136, 223, 224, 246*
36:26, *136, 149, 226*
36:26-27, *223*
36:26-28, *221*
36:27, *136, 223, 226, 239, 268, 296, 307*
36:28, *267*

36:31, *269*
36:31-32, *247*
36:32, *236, 267*
36:33-36, *309*
36:35, *248*
36:36, *247, 301*
36:38, *295*
37, *225, 226, 231, 232, 233, 234, 235, 236, 240, 242, 243, 244, 247, 250, 255, 258, 260, 280, 281, 305*
37–48, *244*
37:1, *211, 295, 296*
37:1-10, *237, 254, 295, 296, 297*
37:1-11, *288*
37:1-14, *3, 208, 209, 221, 224, 225, 230, 235, 236, 237, 239, 242, 249, 250, 254, 255, 258, 260, 261, 262, 263, 268, 269, 272, 274, 275, 278, 281, 282, 285, 287, 291, 292, 293, 294, 295, 297, 299, 300, 301, 303, 305, 307, 309*
37:3, *247, 296, 297*
37:4, *208*
37:5, *296*
37:6, *296*
37:8, *296*
37:9, *296, 297*
37:9-10, *245, 246, 247*
37:10, *296*
37:11, *247, 254, 259, 273, 281, 285, 295, 296, 297*
37:11-14, *237, 298*
37:12, *261*
37:12-14, *257, 258, 259*
37:13, *236*
37:13-14, *310*
37:14, *136, 208, 226, 246, 295, 296, 301*
37:15-18, *298*
37:15-28, *225, 237, 300*
37:19, *221, 222*
37:19-28, *298*
37:21-25, *226*
37:24-25, *209, 221, 245, 247*
37:24-26, *221, 223*
37:25, *222, 223*
37:26, *136, 221, 247*
37:26-28, *223*
37:27, *222, 236, 246*

37:28, *236, 248*
38–39, *216, 236, 276, 277, 281, 284*
38–48, *275*
38:2, *281*
39:4, *216*
39:17-20, *216*
39:28, *226*
39:29, *136, 226*
40, *273, 283*
40–42, *272, 293*
40–48, *212, 213, 236, 272, 277, 278, 284, 293*
40:2, *213*
40:2-4, *239*
40:6-8, *274*
40:16, *283*
43:1-9, *294*
43:4-5, *212*
43:5, *211*
43:10-11, *285*
44, *276*
44:1-3, *276, 277*
44:6, *298*
44:6-8, *279*
45:1-8, *291*
45:15, *284*
45:17, *284*
45:18-25, *272*
45:20, *284*
47, *213, 226, 248, 279*
47:1, *213*
47:12, *214*
48:8-22, *291*
48:30-35, *291*
48:35, *248*

Daniel
7, *266*
7:9-27, *141*
7:13, *265*

Hosea
4:16, *135*
6:1-3, *237*
9:10, *173, 214*
9:15, *135*
11:1, *29, 109, 110*
11:11, *141*
14:7, *15*

Joel
2:2, *216*
2:10, *216*
2:28-29, *226*
2:30-31, *216*
2:32, *37*
3:18, *15*

Amos
9:11-15, *15*
9:14-15, *226*

Micah
4:6-7, *226*
5:1-3, *12*
5:2, *35, 38, 49*
5:2-5, *33*
5:4, *221*

Habakkuk
2:18-20, *157*

Zephaniah
3:19-20, *226*

Zechariah
2:1-2, *239*
7–8, *239*
7:11, *135*
7:12, *135*
8:13, *132*
9:11, *154*
10:2, *220, 221*
11:12-13, *107, 140*
14:15-19, *131*

Malachi
3:1, *22*

APOCRYPHA

Sirach
17:12, *118*

NEW TESTAMENT

Matthew
1, *11, 12, 18, 22*
1–4, *110*
1:1, *11, 22, 107*
1:1–4:16, *107*
1:6, *223*

1:17, *11, 22*
1:20, *12, 22*
1:21, *107, 310*
1:21-23, *48*
1:22, *12, 13*
1:23, *11, 18, 22, 35*
2, *107, 108, 109, 110*
2:1-6, *12, 158*
2:2, *223, 247*
2:3, *111*
2:5, *35, 37*
2:6, *22, 107*
2:7-8, *107*
2:9-12, *107*
2:10-11, *107*
2:13-15, *62*
2:15, *29, 107, 109, 112, 156*
2:17-18, *41, 107, 204*
2:18, *30, 42, 107, 109, 156*
2:23, *18, 22*
3:2, *234*
3:3, *37, 53*
3:8-9, *107*
3:15, *35*
3:16, *22*
3:17, *107*
4, *18, 64*
4:1-11, *62*
4:3, *107*
4:6, *107*
4:13-17, *22*
4:15-16, *18, 64*
4:16, *22, 107*
4:17, *234*
5, *101*
5–7, *98*
5:14, *305*
5:17-19, *293*
6:9-10, *223*
8:11, *140*
8:11-12, *140*
8:17, *18, 160*
9:14-15, *202*
9:18-26, *224*
9:27, *26*
9:36, *221*
10:5-6, *205*
10:6, *139*
10:38, *306*
11:10, *37*
11:21-22, *218*
11:28-30, *203*

12, *61, 62*
12:1-32, *47*
12:14, *47*
12:15, *61*
12:15-21, *26, 61*
12:17, *43*
12:17-21, *25, 49*
12:18, *48*
12:18-21, *46*
12:19-20, *47*
12:20, *48*
12:21, *22, 26, 48*
12:23, *26*
13:32, *223*
13:48, *35*
14, *111*
15–16, *18*
15:21-28, *61*
15:22, *26*
15:24, *205*
16, *107, 111*
16:13-20, *110*
16:13-23, *110*
16:14, *107, 110, 111*
16:24, *306*
19:28, *140*
20:28, *18*
20:30-31, *26*
21:1-11, *212*
21:13, *139*
21:14-15, *26*
21:18-22, *214*
21:23, *112*
21:43, *140*
22:7, *140*
23, *18*
23:23, *65*
23:27-28, *220*
23:32-36, *140*
23:37-39, *139*
24:29, *216*
26:28, *18, 112, 140, 154, 197*
27:3-8, *140*
27:9-10, *107, 112, 140*
27:11, *223*
27:12, *18*
27:24, *219*
27:25, *140, 219*
27:29-30, *223*
27:46, *160*
27:51-53, *18, 272*
27:52-53, *225*

27:57, *18*
28:18-20, *62*

Mark
1:1, *19*
1:2, *22*
1:3, *18, 22, 53, 66*
1:14-15, *19*
1:15, *234*
1:16-20, *205*
1:22, *19*
1:31, *19*
2:5-7, *19*
2:10-12, *22*
2:12, *19*
3:13-14, *22*
3:27, *19*
4:11, *19*
4:32, *223*
5:13, *22*
5:21-43, *224*
5:42, *19*
6:32-44, *19*
6:34, *245*
6:48, *22*
6:48-49, *19*
6:50, *19*
6:51, *19*
8:18, *218, 245*
8:22-23, *19*
8:27, *19*
8:27-30, *110*
8:34, *306*
9:1, *154*
9:33-34, *19*
10:32, *19*
10:38, *19*
10:43, *19*
10:45, *19, 22*
10:46, *19*
10:52, *19*
11–16, *22*
11:1-11, *212*
11:12-14, *204*
11:12-25, *214*
11:17, *139, 203*
12, *15*
12:1-11, *15*
13, *203*
13:10, *19*
13:34, *216*
14:24, *19, 22, 154*

Scripture Index

14:62, *265*
15:2, *223*
15:4-5, *19*
15:5, *19*
15:17-19, *223*
15:34, *160*
16:8, *19*
16:394, *154*

Luke
1:79, *24*
2:8, *205*
2:25, *139*
2:32, *23*
2:38, *139*
3:4-6, *17, 53*
3:31, *223*
4:16-21, *99*
4:17-19, *17*
4:18-19, *23*
7:11-17, *224*
8:9-10, *14*
8:18, *14*
8:40-56, *224*
9:18-21, *110*
9:23, *306*
10:13-14, *218*
10:15, *67*
11:43, *101*
13:6-9, *214*
13:19, *223*
13:34, *139*
15:1-7, *205*
16:29, *191*
19:28-44, *212*
19:41-44, *139*
20:9-18, *204*
21:24, *141*
21:25, *216*
22:20, *116, 138, 143, 154, 197*
22:29-30, *140*
22:37, *160*
22:42, *204*
23:3, *223*
23:34, *160, 219*
24:13-27, *318*
24:25, *41*
24:25-27, *144, 190*
24:26, *41*
24:27, *40, 41, 58, 207, 239*
24:44-46, *144*

24:44-47, *40, 41, 58, 190, 285*
24:47, *17*

John
1–11, *224*
1:14, *214, 215*
1:23, *53*
2:10, *15*
2:19, *214*
2:20-21, *15*
3, *225*
3:5, *223, 246*
3:5-8, *225*
3:6-8, *225, 246*
3:14, *37*
4:14, *214*
5:39, *190*
5:46, *190*
7, *78*
7:38, *78*
8:56, *190*
10:1-18, *245*
10:14-15, *221*
11:1-44, *224*
11:24, *262, 282*
11:25, *209, 225, 262*
11:25-26, *310*
11:33, *310*
11:35, *310*
12:12-19, *212*
12:36-43, *20*
12:38, *160*
12:38-41, *53*
12:41, *190, 265*
15, *214, 286*
15:12-13, *221*
16:8, *269*
17:5, *99*
17:22, *99*
18:33, *223*
19:2, *223*
19:12, *223*
19:19-20, *223*
20:22, *225*

Acts
1:1-8, *210*
1:6, *209, 225, 234*
1:6-7, *240*
1:6-8, *141*
1:7, *225*
1:7-8, *141*

1:8, *17, 23, 226*
2:1-21, *226*
3:6, *158*
3:16, *158*
3:19-21, *141, 225, 240*
3:22-23, *10, 141*
3:24, *10, 141*
4:23-26, *158*
6:12, *13*
7, *12*
7:1-53, *242*
7:2, *12*
7:4, *12*
7:9, *12*
7:29-30, *12*
7:34, *12*
7:36, *12*
7:43-44, *12*
7:44-47, *13*
7:47, *12*
7:49, *13*
7:51, *13*
8:28-33, *17*
8:32-33, *160*
8:32-35, *33*
9:2, *18, 24*
10:43, *191*
13:34, *17*
13:46, *172*
13:46-4727, *17*
13:47, *23, 62*
15, *210*
18:9, *115*
19:9, *24*
19:23, *18, 24*
22:4, *24*
23:3, *220*
24:14, *18, 24*
24:22, *24*
26:16-18, *115*
26:18, *24*
28:17, *14*
28:23, *14*
28:24, *15*
28:31, *234*

Romans
1:22, *112*
2:15, *116, 224*
2:24, *20*
2:29, *112, 224*
3:10, *206*

4:11-12, *287*
5:5, *201*
5:6-8, *219*
5:14, *36*
5:17, *36*
6:23, *305*
8:1, *245*
8:2-4, *247*
8:11, *209*
8:18-25, *305*
8:20-21, *155*
9–11, *132, 139, 141, 210, 307*
9:3, *302*
9:3-6, *302*
9:4, *141*
9:6, *15, 16*
9:8, *241*
9:19-23, *204*
9:21, *112*
9:27-29, *16*
9:28, *20*
9:33, *20*
10, *66*
10–12, *148*
10:13, *37, 303*
10:15, *20, 66*
10:15-17, *16*
10:16, *20, 160*
10:17, *288*
10:20-21, *16*
11, *141, 154*
11:1-6, *142*
11:5-6, *142*
11:7-10, *142*
11:13, *115*
11:13-24, *226*
11:17, *205*
11:17-36, *287*
11:25-26, *174*
11:25-27, *138, 226*
11:25-29, *302, 303*
11:26, *15, 142, 307*
11:26-27, *139*
11:27, *198, 303*
11:29, *141*
11:34, *20, 112*
11:34-35, *11*
14:11, *20, 112*
15:4, *58, 191*
15:8-9, *214*
15:12, *214*
15:14-21, *16*

15:21, *20*
16:25, *40*

1 Corinthians
1, *113*
1:2, *10*
1:18-19, *16*
1:18-30, *113*
1:18-31, *204*
1:31, *37, 112, 113, 114*
2:16, *37, 112*
10:4, *191, 252*
10:6, *191*
10:11, *9, 10*
11:25, *116, 138, 143, 154*
11:29-30, *246*
15:3, *219*
15:50-54, *263*
15:51-57, *24*
15:54, *24*

2 Corinthians
1–7, *138*
1:21-22, *130*
1:22, *138*
3, *138, 200*
3:2-11, *130*
3:3, *172, 200*
3:5-14, *143*
3:6, *116, 138, 200, 247*
4:6-7, *138*
4:7, *130*
4:11, *263*
5:11–6:2, *16*
5:17, *23*
5:17-20, *16*
6:2, *16*
6:16, *199, 246*
6:17, *24*
10–13, *114*
10:4-5, *115*
10:8, *112, 114, 115*
10:17, *112, 113*
13:10, *115*

Galatians
1, *115*
1:15-16, *115*
2:19, *177*
3:16, *286*
3:28, *287*
4:6, *224*

4:26, *174, 288*
6:16, *241*

Ephesians
1:13-14, *209*
2, *287*
2:1, *305*
2:3, *305*
2:4-5, *309*
2:11-13, *155*
2:15, *247*
2:20, *192*
4:30, *246*
5:14, *20*

Philippians
2:6, *37, 81*
2:6-11, *37*
2:9-11, *158*
2:10, *37*

Colossians
1:13, *156, 234*
1:15-19, *158*
1:17, *84*
1:26, *31*
1:26-27, *40*
2:11, *224*
2:13-14, *288*

1 Thessalonians
4:8, *246*
5:3, *112, 220*

2 Thessalonians
2:4, *216*

2 Timothy
3:15, *56, 191*
3:15-16, *58*
3:16, *188, 283, 288*
3:16-17, *293*

Titus
2:14, *246*

Hebrews
1:1-2, *105, 144, 254*
1:2, *118*
1:3, *266*
1:5, *34, 35, 38, 49*
3–4, *118*

3:7-19, *106*
3:7–4:11, *118*
5:1, *116*
5:1-10, *117*
5:5, *34, 35, 38, 49*
6:13-20, *116, 117*
7, *117*
7:1-3, *106*
7:1-28, *117*
7:11, *118*
7:19, *117*
7:22, *117*
7:25, *206*
7:26-28, *117*
8, *116, 117, 119, 120*
8–9, *171*
8:1-6, *117*
8:1-8, *221*
8:1-13, *117*
8:1–10:18, *117*
8:3–10:18, *137*
8:6, *117, 118*
8:7, *118*
8:7-8, *197*
8:7-13, *117*
8:8, *118*
8:8-12, *103, 137, 143*
8:8-13, *286*
8:9, *118*
8:10, *119, 224*
8:11, *119*
8:12, *119*
8:13, *118, 154*
9:1-22, *117*
9:1-28, *117*
9:1–10:18, *119*
9:23–10:18, *117*
9:26, *198*
9:27-28, *284*
10, *119, 120*
10:5-7, *120*
10:11, *119*
10:12-13, *119*

10:15-18, *119, 120*
10:16, *188*
10:16-17, *116, 137, 143*
10:17, *188*
10:18, *116*
10:29, *168*
10:37, *16*
11, *154*
12:7-11, *246*
13:17, *219*

1 Peter
1, *54, 92*
1:10-11, *41, 190, 286*
1:10-12, *27, 43, 92, 144, 316*
1:12, *54*
1:19-20, *189*
1:23-25, *16, 20, 24*
2:4, *252*
2:9, *20, 241, 286*
2:20-23, *20, 62*
2:22-25, *160*
4:17, *218*

2 Peter
1:16, *312*
1:19, *311*
3:16, *104*

1 John
2:1, *206*

Jude
14–15, *104*

Revelation
1, *260*
1:6, *234*
1:10, *211*
1:13-15, *212*
1:17, *37, 212*
2:7-10, *216*
4, *265, 266*

4–5, *244*
4:2, *211*
4:2-3, *212*
4:5, *212*
4:6-7, *212*
5:1, *211*
6:8, *217*
6:12-13, *216*
7:3, *217*
8:12, *216*
9:4, *217*
10:9-10, *212*
11:11, *245*
11:15, *234*
13:8, *189, 219*
14:1, *217*
14:2, *212*
16:6, *179*
17–18, *215*
17:3, *211*
17:4, *215*
18:9, *216*
18:11-13, *216*
18:15-19, *216*
18:22, *216*
19:6, *212*
19:6-9, *202*
19:11, *65*
19:11-16, *221*
19:11-21, *216*
19:15, *221, 222*
19:17-21, *216*
20–22, *244*
20:7-10, *216*
20:12, *65*
21–22, *213, 244*
21:2, *202*
21:3, *199, 213*
21:10, *211, 213*
21:22, *213*
22:1, *213*
22:1-5, *248*
22:2, *214*